MODERN
WAREHOUSE
MANAGEMENT

Complete Guide to

MODERN WAREHOUSE MANAGEMENT

CREED H. JENKINS

PRENTICE HALL
Englewood Cliffs, New Jersey 07632

Prentice-Hall International (UK) Limited, *London*
Prentice-Hall of Australia Pty. Limited, *Sydney*
Prentice-Hall Canada, Inc., *Toronto*
Prentice-Hall Hispanoamericana, S.A., *Mexico*
Prentice-Hall of India Private Limited, *New Delhi*
Prentice-Hall of Japan, Inc., *Tokyo*
Simon & Schuster Asia Pte. Ltd., *Singapore*
Editora Prentice-Hall do Brasil, Ltda., *Rio de Janeiro*

© 1990 *by*
PRENTICE-HALL, Inc.
Englewood Cliffs, NJ

10 9 8 7 6 5 4

Library of Congress Cataloging-in-Publication Data

Jenkins, Creed H.
   Complete guide to modern warehouse management / by Creed H.
Jenkins.
      p.   cm.
   ISBN 0-13-155409-3
   1. Warehouses—Management. I. Title.
HF5485.J39   1990
658.7′85—dc20

                89-29493
                CIP

ISBN 0-13-155409-3

PRENTICE HALL
BUSINESS & PROFESSIONAL DIVISION
A division of Simon & Schuster
Englewood Cliffs, New Jersey 07632

Printed in the United States of America

Dedication

To old pros and new aspirants in the fascinating field of warehousing and its kindred fields:

Accounting
Inventory Management
Logistics and Physical Distribution
Production
Purchasing
Sales and Marketing
Traffic and Transportation

About the Author

CREED H. JENKINS is a pioneer in warehouse operations. Formally, he was national Warehouse Operations Manager of Kaiser Aluminum as well as Chief Industrial Engineer. He is now an independent warehouse and small-business consultant with a diverse background of academic and practical experience. With a MS from USC, Mr. Jenkins taught warehousing and company organization at the university level. His practical experience includes production superintendent, administrative procedures manager, chief industrial engineer, and national manager of warehousing and trucking for companies in the top 500. He has been CEO of five small-to-medium size companies and founder of three of these.

This is Mr. Jenkins second text book on private and public warehouse operations, describing how warehousing contributes to the broader fields of logistics and physical distribution in product-oriented companies. His first was *Modern Warehouse Management,* published by McGraw Hill in three languages, French, Spanish, and English. He contributed sections to two other textbooks, *Handbook of Modern Manufacturing Management* (McGraw Hill) and *Handbook of Industrial Engineering and Management* (Prentice-Hall, Inc.).

As if to round out an already diverse background, Mr. Jenkins gained insight into governmental warehousing as warehousing representative from the private business sector to the Cost Reduction Task Force for the State of California, working directly for the then governor and since two-term president of the United States, Ronald Reagan. Further, at the personal request of two different chiefs of state of Latin American countries, he served gratis as warehousing and physical distribution consultant. Speaking engagements include a national speaking tour of major U.S. cities, company conventions and seminars, and talks at universities and professional organizations. Past or present fraternal memberships include National Council of Physical Distribution (NCPDM, now Council of Logistics Management), Warehousing Education and Research Council (WERC), and Institute of Industrial Engineers (IIE).

When asked, "In the context of such a diverse background, what do you consider the three major considerations of good warehousing?", his answer is, "In terms of importance: (1) People, (2) People, and (3) People; in terms of responsibilities: (1) Accountability, (2) Responsiveness to customer requirements, and (3) Overall productivity."

What this Guide Will Do for You

This practical how-to-do-it *Guide* provides all the help you'll need—for everything from making a case for the feasibility and cost justification for a warehouse to design and operation of a modern facility.

For the warehouse manager, it is designed to be a ready guide and reference covering problems and their solutions for increasing the effectiveness and efficiency of all operations. For employees in other related departments of the company who use and depend on its services—accounting, customer service, production, purchasing, traffic, sales, and top management—it provides immediate solutions on how to coordinate efforts to achieve a better, more harmonious total effort. For top management it provides insights on how to maximize warehousing's total effectiveness in relation to the company's overall objectives. And for the public warehouser, its coverage of operations and equipment is equally applicable but it has the added constructive advantage of providing a valuable window into the functioning of its major competitor, private warehousing.

You'll find this book to be the most current and authoritative guide on the subject, providing detailed steps on how to manage and plan overall warehouse operations. You'll find that it shows you

- How to deal effectively with the priority pressures brought by production, purchasing, and sales, which depend so much on warehousing to achieve their objectives.
- Where to locate the warehouse to achieve the best services and greatest economic advantage, taking into consideration the many influencing factors such as labor market, transportation, taxes, telephone, communications, and others.
- How to assure that warehousing's inventory accounting responsibilities are fulfilled.
- How to stay current with the latest warehousing equipment and systems technologies.
- How to evaluate the physical facilities for factors that will affect overall costs.
- How to plan and lay out the warehouse to maximize operational, storage, and service effectiveness.
- How to take physical inventory, and principles and techniques of cycle counting.
- What materials handling equipment is available and how to use it effectively.
- What you need to automate on a low budget, including the big breakthroughs of high-rise facilities, automated storage and retrieval systems (ASRS), and electronic data processing; and when to reautomate.

○ How to design, organize, and implement a warehouse quality program.

○ How to measure warehouse performance, including how to increase productivity, provide the tools for analysis and planning, and control performance through use of labor and space utilization standards.

○ How to prepare written economic justifications for purchasing or modifying equipment and facilities including those related to safety and work environment.

○ What step-by-step procedures to follow to perform efficiently and effectively the three basic functions of warehousing: receiving, storing, and shipping.

○ Ways to get major cost savings without large expenditures for equipment.

○ Inventory management and physical distribution techniques.

The presentation of this information is emphasized and reinforced by a liberal number of checklists, charts, graphs, forms, drawings, and case studies.

The *Complete Guide to Modern Warehouse Management* is a down-to-earth, comprehensive guide to operating a warehouse and gives you an unusually authoritative insight into the influence of many outside factors.

Creed H. Jenkins

Contents

Chapter 1

Trends in Modern Warehouse Management

CHAPTER HIGHLIGHTS

Welcome to the fascinating world of warehousing, where dramatic changes in business and technology create a frontier of opportunity to discover ways in which business can be conducted to prohibit further encroachment by foreign competitors and to regain some of that which has already been taken away.

This chapter presents an overview of modern warehousing and the aspects that are receiving top priority today and why. Emphasized are the science of warehousing as well as opportunities created by the changes in attitude toward inventories and warehousing and the possibilities manifest by the technological advances in bar coding, computerization, and equipment automation.

"Warehousing" is a common term and most people have an image of what it is, but the field is far more complex than most observers would think. Moreover, it is rapidly becoming more complex as industry takes a harder look at how best to conduct business. Paralleling its growth in complexity is its growth in importance. This has resulted in a host of new opportunities to be grasped and problems to be solved. The art and science of warehousing is becoming a more vital part of commerce with a vitality and future greater than almost any other segments of modern industry. Why? Because much of modern business technology focuses on inventories, distribution, and customer service. These are all components of modern warehousing.

NEW TECHNOLOGY

Many people still think of warehousing as simply storing materials, that is, "Warehousing is inventories at rest and transportation is inventories in motion." Flowthrough warehouses where some inventories are there for only a few hours are rapidly replacing the "at-rest" concept. Modern warehousing concerns speed and efficiency; it concerns automation, computerization, and exotic new means of communication.

LESS INVENTORY

Warehousing (which probably got its name from housing wares) is still, to many, the time-honored function of issuing a receipt for wares that it will store and be accountable for until relieved of responsibility. These are still the basics of warehousing, but in modern business they constitute only a part of the total. The storing function in particular is becoming a lesser part of the total.

The radically new thought at the frontier of business technology is that large inventories are really not only not necessary, but to some of the more forward thinkers, they are *evil*. They are "evil" because they tie up capital, and they serve to cover up poor management practices. The application of this concept reduces the quantity of wares to be housed and shifts the emphasis of warehousing to flowthrough rather than storage. While the principle that the best inventory level is the lowest viable level is gaining increasingly wide acceptance, only a few companies in this country have developed the disciplines and systems necessary to put this philosophy into practice effectively. The future appears obvious: those who don't do what is necessary to incorporate the principle into their companies are going to find the competitive pressures from those who do increasingly hard to withstand. More companies will go the bankruptcy route. Others will be saved for awhile by mergers with companies who can profitably use losers for tax shelters. However, mergers often do not remedy the ills of the losers that are absorbed. When their value as tax shelters are milked dry, they simply go out of business or are passed onto other profitable companies to further exploit their tax shelter feature. When they are of no further use, the business stops.

The *(JIT) just-in-time inventory* concept (also called *Kanban*), first developed by Toyota in Japan, asserts that just enough inventory arriving just in time to replace that which was just used is all the inventory that is necessary. Any more unnecessarily ties up money, adds warehousing costs, increases damage, risks obsolescence, and possibly the worst of it all, obscures opportunities for operational improvements. This concept, as simple as it is, is a major breakthrough. Its application and other dramatic technological advancements (such as computerization, computer-to-computer communication, electronic mail, bar-coding systems, computer modeling, etc.) have brought about major changes in what warehousing does, or should do, or will be called on to do in the future.

HIGH-VELOCITY INVENTORIES

Modern warehousing is in the process of evolutionary change from an emphasis on storage to an emphasis on flowthrough, from inventories at rest to inventories in motion. These changes will entail lower inventories per account but considerably more activity per inventory amount. JIT calls for high-velocity inventories, specifically, just the right amount in the pipeline to do the job. It necessitates eliminating the problems in the pipeline rather than covering them over with excess inventories.

A harsh but realistic approach to solving the inventory-related problems is to reduce inventories continually and as one problem after another is exposed, they are solved until the system is problem-free. The objective is to determine the minimum inventory required to operate in a problem-free system; this is the right amount of inventory.

The drive to operate a warehouse with JIT inventories, lowest-cost operations, and high-quality service brings with it four important changes:

1. Smaller, More Frequent Orders. Rather than process orders that cover customer inventory requirements for as long as a week, or more, the orders may cover only a few hours' requirements. This new emphasis on activity as opposed to storage causes a new orientation. Rather than pull all orders from storage, more will be filled by diverting the inbound material directly from receiving to the staging area to ship. This change necessitates different warehouse layout, procedures, and attitudes.

2. Higher Freight Costs. To avoid unbearable freight costs as a consequence of shipping small amounts, it is necessary to consolidate more orders to achieve economical shipping quantities. Full truck, container, or car load quantities are preferable.

3. More Pool Distribution. When it is not possible to achieve economical shipping quantities to one particular destination, orders for different destinations are brought together and loaded in the carrier in sequence of unloading. The carrier is given a preplanned routing to drop off the proper orders to customers along the way. If access to cargo in the middle or front of the trailer is commonly needed before the back is unloaded, doors installed along the sides of the trailer will provide access to any material at any time with minimal rehandling. Trailers with side doors are used with the same advantage when pool pickups are made for consolidation.

The main point of both pool distribution and consolidation is to get the economies of traveling the long hauls with large economic loads and to make the delivery of the comparatively more expensive individual small orders as short as possible. The same principle applies to air, ocean, and rail freight. It is employed by private warehouses as well as public warehouses.

4. Greater Accuracy. In the past a certain tolerance for error was acceptable. In modern warehousing, there is no allowance for error. Errors are bad. Errors are costly and cause ill will.

Occasionally the function which encompasses the error can be eliminated altogether. Madam Gilbreth (wife and successor of Frank B. Gilbreth, founder of motion study and leader of industrial engineering in its early days) said about procedures analysis: "Many procedures are improved that should be eliminated." Major cost reductions, often accompanied by better quality can be achieved by the application of Madam Gilbreth's sage observation.

HIGHER QUALITY

The more sophisticated consumers of products and services now expect and even demand absolute quality, zero errors, and zero defects. The term "quality" has emerged as the single most important stipulation of doing business. Until about the last quarter of this century, foreign-made merchandise was considered inferior to that made in the United States. This was particularly the case with Japanese-made products. However, Japan has accomplished a nearly complete turnabout. It, along with other foreign countries that have heeded the importance of quality, has taken the business away from those who didn't change or didn't change enough.

This dire need for quality improvement applies to warehousing as well as to production and sales. It applies to communications, paperwork, packaging materials, handling, and storing as well. In modern warehousing, it is not enough to think and to perform efficiently. Quality, as an inseparable feature of doing business, must be accepted as a prerequisite to efficiency. It is gratifying, however, that quality improvement results in efficiency improvement. "Do it right the first time," is a basic principle of high quality and results in a giant step toward high efficiency. The concept that is expressed in: "We cannot afford better quality" is obsolete. Quality improvement has become the primary means for the United States to regain its status as a major product producing nation. Otherwise, it will move more and more to a service nation bringing with it a host of economic problems never faced before.

MORE RESPONSIVE SERVICE

Facing modern warehousing is the challenge of providing more responsive service with substantially less inventory. This has brought a new dimension to the planning of warehouse inventories. Some enlightened warehouses have already accepted this and have incorporated it as a way of staying in business. More have not, but to survive they must.

The investment in inventories has the attention of investors and management as it never had before. Demanded is the better use of inventories to achieve better return on investment. This translates to operating with less inventory per sales dollar. For example, if $2.00 worth of inventory generates $10.00 worth of sales, they want it to generate $20.00 or more sales, and then more and then more. The same concept applies to raw material and in-process inventories.

What a change this is! Don't say IMPOSSIBLE. Some are making it work and reaping bountiful harvests.

Making the most out of what inventory is available requires many things. One of the most important of which is giving customer service maximum support by providing the most responsive service. For warehousing, responsive service includes the following:

1. Establishing with sales, transportation, and the customer how and when deliveries will be made; then do as agreed. This requires reaching back to the warehouse suppliers to include them in the agreement. It also includes having sufficient penalties built into the delivery cycle that error or failure are severely penalized. Whatever is agreed upon "must" be attainable. Top management "must" provide the means to make it attainable. Then warehousing "must" do the job.

   The service goal of warehousing can be nothing less than absolute quality. If the total service level is less (due to inventory outages, other's errors, etc.) top management "must" recognize where the problems are and solve them or live with them—as long as competition permits.

2. Offering courteous, businesslike performance. Delivery of the proper products at the proper time goes a long way to providing the necessary responsive service, but it is not enough. All activities of the warehouse must be performed in a courteous and businesslike manner. All warehousing's customers (including suppliers, other company personnel, and the public) must receive courteous, businesslike attention.

Modern warehousing entails a whole new attitude toward service. Investors cannot tolerate the mediocre return on investment that results from mediocre performance; domestic and world competition will not let them. There are just too many other suppliers throughout the world that can clearly demonstrate they are not tied to poor performance levels of the past. They can and do demonstrate that investors can expect better returns on investment than that which results from mediocrity. Even when products are produced with less than the best physical features, the best quality service may be enough to create and sustain a thriving business.

3. "Treating others as you wish to be treated": the warehousing motto. This sentiment should be a commandment.

BETTER EQUIPMENT AND FACILITIES

Modern warehousing has access to many new sophisticated tools to operate more accurately and efficiently. Briefly discussed here and in greater detail in later chapters are some of the technologically advanced facilities and equipment available to warehousing.

1. Computerization. While computerization has had a tremendous impact on business, medicine, science, and our personal lives, warehousing has been thus far only minimally affected compared to what the future holds. Generally warehousing has always lagged behind in the most advanced computer systems and technology. The main reason for this is that it was believed warehousing had to remain responsive to the needs of production and sales, and to do this it had to remain flexible. Flexibility was believed to be foreign to the environment of standardization, which was considered a prerequisite to computerization and automation.

Advancements in computer technology and its potential for drastic cost reduction, along with the realization that warehouses were holding so much of the company's money in inventories, has brought a new prominence to this long-neglected area of business. Too, warehousing has always been labor intensive, and the fierce global competition dictates reducing labor costs wherever found.

While the pursuit of reducing costs will result in fewer people in warehousing, there is an effort to increase the amount of work done there. It is to move work into warehousing from production and sales, where labor and salary rates are generally much higher. This transfer often results in opportunities for integration, consolidation, and elimination of work, which yields further savings and systems improvement.

2. Automatic Storage and Retrieval Systems, ASRS. The lift truck has been the "work horse" of warehousing. Probably it always will be. But now the ASRS (automatic storage and retrieval system) not only does better work but much more. ASRS is a system for more efficient materials storing as well as more efficient handling. Also, it provides the capabilities of being automated more effectively than lift trucks. Where appropriate, such a system has the potential for dramatically reducing costs and improving service. For certain warehousing it is a panacea for many things: less labor, greater storage density, increased reliability, improved safety, less damage, tighter security, and a better housekeeping. Its initial cost is generally more, but its long-term benefits can be substantial and can outweigh its high initial cost. Installation of ASRS can be the giant step that takes a warehouse from mediocrity to the cutting edge of technology.

Briefly, the material handling mechanics are that of a crane moving along prescribed paths permitting movement of the load in two directions at once—up or down, forward or backward. It travels within minimum width aisles, 1 or 2 inches wider than the load. It will go as high as it is designed to go. There are many such systems in the range of 60 to 80 feet high and some over 100 feet high.

The companion storage system of an ASRS can be designed for ultrahigh density. Also, stock locator systems work particularly well because of the permanence of each and every storage position. The traveling crane can be manually controlled or semiautomatic or completely automatic. It can be designed to achieve exceptionally high productivity by causing it to deliver the storage loads on its way to picking merchandise for shipping; the crane can use computer logic to determine the most efficient routing. It can be programmed to assure first-in, first-out (FIFO) inventory rotation. Furthermore, it can be programmed to place inventory in storage in relation to activity so that minimum overall travel time is required. More is said about ASRS in Chapter 11.

3. High-Rise Facilities. Before the advent of the lift truck, warehouses were built with low ceiling clearances. These were commonly as low as a person could lift plus the load height, about 7 to 10 feet. With the lift truck, it became common for warehouses to be constructed with height clearances up to 28 feet. With the stacker cranes and with ASRS, warehouse operations can be conducted safely and efficiently over 100 feet high. Several factors contribute to lower costs as height increases and crane-type material handling equipment is used:

- ○ *Lower Initial Construction Cost.* The construction cost of cubic storage space is less going up than out.
- ○ *Lower Land Cost.* A building that can accommodate 60 high-storage feet would have to cover four times the ground area if it could accommodate only 15 high-storage feet. This permits major cost avoidance in land and site preparation.
- ○ *Lower Material Handling Cost.* In high-rise space, crane-type material handlers are used to move materials into and out of storage versus the conventional lift truck. Cranes are designed to move in two directions at

the same time while a lift truck is prohibited by safety considerations to lift or lower while the vehicle is moving forward or back. The combination two-directional movement of the crane can result in considerably lower handling time and correspondingly lower costs.

○ *Lower Maintenance and Longer Life.* High-rise buildings will have less roof and floor to maintain. In addition, the costs of maintenance and depreciation are much less for crane mechanisms compared to conventional lift trucks. The useful life of cranes is from 15 to 50 years. For lift trucks it is from 5 to 10 years. This constitutes a major advantage of cranes over lift trucks when both are evaluated as long-term investments.

○ *Safer Materials Handling.* During stacker crane or ASRS operations, the operator is never under the load. During lift truck operation, the operator is commonly under the load. Cranes operate in fixed routes in space away from human traffic while lift trucks operate all over the warehouse, making ASRS high-rise systems inherently safer.

○ *Greater Adaptability to Automation and Computerization.* The crane mechanism used in the high-rise storage system is more easily automated and computerized than the lift truck. ASRS equipment moves only in rigidly fixed paths within rigidly fixed storage systems. Standardization is at its zenith. Automation and computerization are far more effective in this type environment.

○ *More Effective Security and Sanitation.* Storage at these heights greatly reduces the ability to steal inventory. It also reduces the likelihood of infestation by insects, mice, and rats, which are real problems particularly in some commodity-type warehouses.

○ *Greater Use of Automated Material Transfer Equipment.* A variety of guidance systems make it possible for material transfer carts and trains to travel unattended making the transfer of material at the least possible cost. The search for cost savings makes any repetitive human-attended transfer of inventories a candidate for automatic transfer.

PHENOMENAL BAR CODING

Bar coding is becoming an indispensable tool for warehouse automation and computerization. Much of warehousing's cost is related to the clerical functions of the vast amounts of inventory and labor distribution data. Bar coding is the special ingredient that has made it possible to streamline this and many other time-consuming paperwork chores. Not only has the cost of data input been slashed, the information is input faster and with greater accuracy. Valuable information about inventories and work scheduling can now be made available on a timely basis for effective decision making that without bar coding or its equivalent would not be possible. With bar-coded packaging, the taking of physical inventories is much less tedious. Stock locator systems, staging-conveyor systems, labor distribution, and cost control systems have all benefited by the inclusion of this new technology. Bar coding as a tool of warehousing and inventory control would rank highly as a contribution to the technological advancement of warehousing. In brief bar-code system advantages compared to manual systems are:

Greater accuracy
Faster input and transmission

Less clerical and operating labor

Less work interference

Less worker stress and frustration

Compatibility with automation and computer systems

IMPROVED COMMUNICATIONS

Modern warehousing will remain handicapped as it has been in the past unless major changes are made in communications. It will continue to have to fight for information that directly influences its effectiveness, efficiency, and quality of operations and services.

Modern warehousing is not alone with the problem of poor communications. It permeates throughout U.S. business. As a division of a company, warehousing probably suffers more than other divisions because it is often in the uncomfortable position of being subject to the real or not so real requirements of supply and demand—production or purchasing being supply and sales or customers being demand.

This is not to imply that information is maliciously doctored or withheld, although the results are the same. The reason for the bad information that warehousing so often is forced to use in its planning and scheduling is a basic fault in U.S. business.

There are too many organizational compartments in what is basically a continuum of making and marketing. The continuum is divided horizontally into too many divisions and then into too many layers of supervision. The result is an overwhelming communications problem.

The country's large companies have hundreds of departments with 15 or more levels of supervision not uncommon, while in Japan for comparably-sized companies the job gets done with no more than 5 levels. Our medium-sized companies characteristically have 5 to 8 levels; Japan functions with 2 to 3.

Making matters worse, U.S. business supervisors tend to strengthen the barriers of each compartment to identify separation. The barriers are reinforced with job descriptions and organization charts until the companies are composed of great fortresses and—"Woe be unto they who encroach on another's turf." (See Figure 1.1.)

The situation worsens with strong unions. Organized labor pulls in one direction and management in another. This polarization is superimposed on too many divisions and too many layers.

Large corporations in this country have been likened to a log with thousands of ants scurrying about, floating downstream; each ant believes it is steering the log.

Modern warehousing is caught up in this strangling labyrinth of communications and to escape is difficult. Change will have to come through top management.

FIGURE 1.1   Ivory Towers Inside Companies

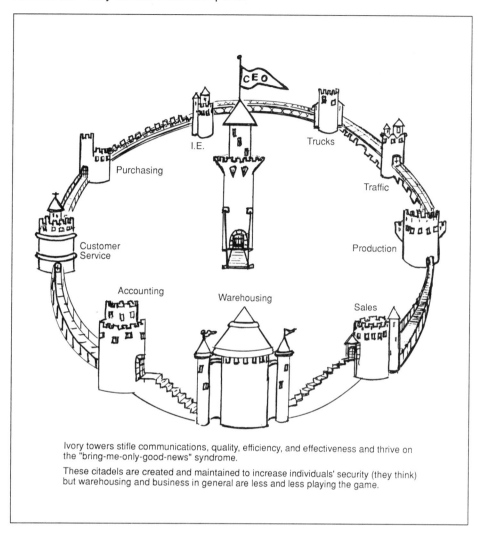

Ivory towers stifle communications, quality, efficiency, and effectiveness and thrive on the "bring-me-only-good-news" syndrome.

These citadels are created and maintained to increase individuals' security (they think) but warehousing and business in general are less and less playing the game.

Chapter 2

Types and Characteristics of Warehouses

CHAPTER HIGHLIGHTS

This chapter describes the types and characteristics of warehouses along with such basic similarities as receiving, storing, shipping, accountability, and customer orientation and such profound differences as environment, equipment, and procedural and legal concerns. A common thread of professionalism should tie together all warehousing.

Determining the right type of warehousing for your needs is certainly more difficult than is buying a new blouse or shirt, and the consequences of making a mistake are far worse. This statement is meant only as an introduction to what often seems to the novice a simple purchase. To those fully acquainted with the concerns involved, it is a complex process that should be handled by professionals. But all too often a sales manager selects a public warehouse based on how well he or she is treated by the warehouse salesperson.

Just as a warehouse manager should not adopt the role of salesperson, so a sales manager should not select a company warehouse. A production manager, a chief accountant, or a purchasing agent also should not make the selection, unless he or she has the education and training and possesses the objectivity to do it. This is highly unlikely if the person is practicing another trade or profession. The process of determining what type of warehouse facilities to use is the job of a warehouse professional who will enlist the help of other professionals in fields that will be affected, such as accounting, industrial engineering, production, sales, and traffic. The alternative to proficient warehouse people selecting the facility is to engage an expert in physical distribution who is oriented to warehousing or who is sufficiently wise to enlist expert warehousing help.

Considerations of warehouse location are dealt with in Chapter 4. Discussed here are the different types and characteristics of warehouses.

1. Cold storage
2. Temperature controlled
3. Bonded
4. Records
5. Household goods
6. General merchandise
7. Commodity
8. Foreign trade zone
9. Mini
10. Private and public
11. Government

COLD STORAGE WAREHOUSING

Except for the tremendous buildup of supplies to support major military campaigns, there has probably never been as great an impact on warehousing as that of cold storage. This is most evident in grocery stores. Shelf space devoted to merchandise requiring cool or cold temperatures is increasing at an average rate of over 10 percent compounded annually. This means that over a ten-year period refrigerated space has increased about three times. This is due to the technological improvement in refrigeration processes, the scientific breakthrough in freezing foods, and the changes in eating preferences. Cool and frozen foods have taken a major share of grocery store space and the need for cold storage warehousing has followed.

Characteristically cold storage warehouses offer temperature ranges from −40°F to +50°F. They are equipped to quick freeze or to slowly bring incoming materials to their proper storage temperatures. The prices charged vary with

1. The services required.
2. The energy used relative to the storage temperature required.
3. The energy used to bring incoming merchandise to the storage temperature.

While the material handling and storing are similar to dry-storage warehousing (noncold storage warehousing), the costs of creating, maintaining, and operating in the cold environment are substantially more. Following is a list of factors that contribute to the high cost of cold storage.

1. The building must be highly insulated.
2. The doors must be specially designed to lose minimal cold.
3. The refrigeration units are massive.
4. The air must circulate, proper humidity must be maintained, and the temperature must be reliably controlled.
5. The equipment used must be designed to operate reliably in sub-zero temperature.
6. A separate dock area isolated from the storage area is needed.
7. The energy source for the refrigeration units is a major element of operating costs and is approximately the same cost of the space being used. (Roughly if the lease cost of space is $40,000 a month, the cost of energy used for refrigeration will be about the same.)
8. The warehouse workers must dress with warm gear according to the environment they work in. Sometimes premium pay is expected and justified.
9. Inventory insurance costs are at a premium.
10. The transportation carriers must be kept refrigerated, in a few instances ice or dry ice may be sufficient.

An unusual feature of cold storage warehousing is the necessary extra care and effort taken in receiving merchandise into the warehouse. Surface and inside temperatures of inbound materials must meet specified acceptable levels. If the commodities require additional energy to lower their total temperature, additional costs will be incurred.

Too low or too high temperatures may cause damage or spoilage. Cheese becomes brittle when frozen. Ice cream should be kept about $-15°F$. Fruit and vegetables cannot be frozen.

Each product type and its ingredients dictate the temperature and humidity environments. Deviations can be costly and are a source of concern not present in other types of warehousing. It should be no surprise that costs and prices reflect these concerns and greater risks.

Cold storage warehouses commonly provide freezing service where fresh commodities will be brought in at outside temperatures, using special processes, their temperatures will be lowered to proper storage levels. Some cold storage warehouses also produce block and particle ice as by-products of their main warehousing function. Further, some cold storage warehouses will lease space to other companies that, with their own equipment and employees, will operate their own segregated space of the facility. Cold or cool (above-freezing-level) storage is becoming a much larger share of total warehousing.

TEMPERATURE-CONTROLLED WAREHOUSING

There is a segment of warehousing called temperature controlled, that is in between cold or cool storage and "dry" or ambient outside temperature. Normally its temperature range is from 50° to 68°F, and it usually includes humidity control similar to that of cold or cool storage. While the number of commodities that require this environment are not as great as those for cold or cool storage and certainly not as many as dry storage, there are enough to justify warehouses that specialize in it totally or as a segregated part of either the cold or cool warehouses.

Usually these facilities employ air conditioners, heater units, and humidity control fixtures to keep the environment within the range required. Because the temperature range is not as severe and risks of product damage are not as dear, the costs of operation are not as great as cold and cool storage warehousing. These costs are, however, more than the cost of dry storage where temperature and humidity are of minor or no concern.

Some warehouse facilities can achieve adequate temperature control without freezer or refrigeration equipment. There are certain localities, usually in temperature zones near large bodies of water with consistently warm currents, that keep the stored products within the prescribed temperature-controlled limits. Usually these facilities require exceptionally good insulation, mechanical means of controlling the amount of hot air escaping through the roof, and tight control over air coming through the doors. Merchandise stored in these warehouses should be of the nature that slow changes of temperature are less harmful than the extremes. For example a change from 48° to 70° over a two-day period will not harm the product to the extent that the same change over a few hours would.

BONDED WAREHOUSING

The term "bonded" when referring to warehousing can mean many things. The warehouse may be bonded to comply with regulation by the Public Utilities Commission, the Alcohol and Beverage Control Commission, or the Customs Services and for many other reasons.

An example of a bonded warehouse is one that handles and stores wine "in bond." In this case the warehouse is bonded to assure that the taxes on wine will be paid when it is shipped "out of bond." Wine is kept in bond during its production, transfer, and storage and can be kept indefinitely in private or public warehouses that are bonded without paying the wine taxes until it is transferred out of bond. The same type of bonding applies to warehouses in federal trade zones to assure that duties and taxes are paid. Warehouses may be referred to as bonded for many other such reasons as well.

Occasionally warehouses will include the term "bonded" in their names such as "XYZ Bonded Warehouse" with the intention of implying a high degree of security. Actually they may not be any different than warehouses that do not have "bonded" as a part of their names. The term is occasionally employed loosely, and a buyer of warehouse services should not let the term influence decision making unless it is clearly stated what the bond means and that feature is a requirement of your inventory. If it is intended to mean that a bond is maintained to ensure that merchandise will be protected or to ensure that taxes or duties will be paid, these are important and could be legal requirements of the particular warehousing provided. Often more important is what is covered in the warehouse contract which states the services, charges, and liabilities. Normally public warehouses do not insure their customers' inventories while in their custody regardless of whether or not they use the term "bonded." The owner of the inventories at a public warehouse should insure the inventories as though they were in the owner's warehouse.

RECORDS WAREHOUSING

The warehousing of records is becoming a larger and more important part of warehousing in general. Office space commonly costs many times that of warehousing space, and if there is need to maintain numerous records, warehousing could provide the lowest-cost alternative. If a company has its own warehouse, it could isolate a part of it for records retention and provide the functions of filing, storing, retrieving, and pickup and delivery. If the warehouse area where the records are stored is "sublet" to a division of the same company or an outside company where their office personnel maintain the files, the records area should be physically segregated from the rest of the warehouse. It should be made clear that only warehouse personnel are permitted in the regular warehouse area. If the security feature is not enough to accomplish this, publicity covering the safety hazard to people unfamiliar with the dangers of moving equipment and high storage should provide sufficient ammunition to support and enforce this policy.

Some public warehouses that specialize in records storage provide prompt pickup and delivery service for their customers. Even medical doctors are finding that they can effectively use outside records warehousing. Since most patients' visits are by appointment, it is possible to have the patients' records delivered in plenty of time before needed. Cost savings can be substantial: the space cost savings is obvious, but there can also be a handling cost savings. A filing and retrieval system can be developed in which the handling of many requests in a programmed, least travel sequence is far more sufficient than a medical clerk handling the files of one patient at a time.

Records warehousing should be conducted in an environment which is appropriate to storing sheets of paper and confidentiality. Humidity, dust, and grime are not friendly to records storage. Access to the records should be restricted even to the extent that the carrier pouches used to pickup and deliver to any office involving confidential information should be sealed during transit. While confidentiality is a serious concern, it is possible to devise ways to assure that this is maintained.

The future of records warehousing is one of growth. The margin of savings is often great enough to overcome the minor problems of not having the records in or adjacent to the office. Because the cost difference is substantial, records warehouses should be able to justify the necessary expenditures to assure full compliance with the reliability of and security requirements. Consideration should be given to complete automation such as a devoted automatic storage and retrieval system. A further refinement could be to have terminals at the clients' offices to access specific information on a real-time, instantaneous, basis.

Microfilming records reduces the space required to store records and the need for records warehousing provided an office can economically justify the equipment. However, microfilming is appropriate for only a portion of the records that are kept in business. The need for hard copies is still so vast there seems justification for records warehousing to expand considerably and to provide a service for the foreseeable future. Also, warehouses can be equipped to handle computer storage disks and microfilm and to transmit the data from the warehouse to the office via telephone, FAX or other means. The original hard copies need not leave the warehouse.

HOUSEHOLD GOODS WAREHOUSING

Warehousing household goods is considered a distinctly different type of warehousing from the other classifications discussed here. There are many reasons why this is so. Often the customers are individuals and families that rarely use the other types of warehousing—although many companies employ household goods warehouses for the convenience of their employees. The modes of transportation, usually extremely high-cube vans, are different—yet industry has high-cube trucks also and in some circumstances their trucks would be more efficient if they were designed like moving vans. It can be argued that household goods require a different environment, yet here too the environment is not different from a large share of other warehousing. Even the multistory buildings common to household storage have certain advantages over the high single-story warehouse used for other types of warehousing.

Some general merchandise warehouses also successfully handle and store household goods. Even makers of delicate medical and electronic equipment may use household warehouses because they believe their merchandise will receive better care. Household warehouses are equipped with special packing materials, and much of their loading and unloading is done manually with care that is often unusual in other types of warehousing. But these characteristics are not so special that they cannot be learned, equipped for, and adopted by other warehouses that have equivalent environments.

On the other hand, different types of warehousing should be merged only when there are distinct and compelling advantages. Never should a warehouse willingly take on different functions unless it is equipped to do so. This includes the proper space, equipment, systems, organization, training, and the philosophy to maintain high-quality performance.

GENERAL MERCHANDISE WAREHOUSING

By far the largest share of warehousing is that referred to as general merchandise warehousing. It is perhaps best defined as that which is left when specialty and commodity warehousing are removed, though it will include some merchandise usually found in a specialized or commodity warehouse. General merchandise warehousing can be private or public, bonded or unbonded, and may or may not have customs and free trade zone rights. In general it is a catch-all classification. However, general merchandise warehouses do not include everything. They tend to specialize to an extent because of particular peculiarities of certain merchandise. For example, grocery warehouses have facilities and methods oriented to handling and storing groceries. The trucking they employ, whether their own or public, is equipped and oriented to delivery to grocery stores or grocery warehouses. It is all too common for trucks to be lined up waiting to be unloaded at the receiving grocery facilities. It is a must with many grocery houses to make appointments for delivery, and the relationship between trucker and grocery warehouses is particularly important. To an extent, these same features are found in apparel warehouses and other store merchandise. Truckers that handle general merchandise with only occasional deliveries to stores will find difficulties not experienced by those truckers that make regular deliveries.

Most users of public warehousing services will investigate general merchandise facilities because they are capable of handling such a wide range of products. The search should, however, continue to find the warehouse that can do the best job for the particular merchandise involved. If a warehouse is found that successfully handles a large volume of the same merchandise, this one deserves closer scrutiny.

There are many other things to be considered, but the fact that a public warehouse already handles like products offers some assurance that it will be proficient in handling similar business. A real obstacle may be, however, that if the warehouse handles competitors' merchandise, it may not be able to take your account. The company that already has the contract may have specified that the warehouse must not handle competing accounts. Even if it is not in the contract, the public warehouse knows it would run the chance of losing a customer they already have. The company looking for a warehouse may also not want its products in the same facility with those of competitors. Regardless, it is important to learn from a public warehouse who already utilizes it.

COMMODITY WAREHOUSING

This type of facility specializes in handling and storing commodities such as cotton, potatoes, tobacco, wool, and so on. Such warehouses deliberately restrict their services to a particular type of commodity and can be either private or public. Their specialization starts with location, which should be convenient to the origin or destination of the particular commodity. Often this is adjacent to the source or consumer and is connected by conveyers or other convenient means of transferring from the producer to the storer or from the storer to the user. When public warehouses commit to such facilities, there must be good relations between the two, terms that are mutually advantageous, and a carefully worded contract which protects both from the other's performance problems.

Inherently these warehouses have the opportunity to be highly efficient because of their specialization. Facilities can be custom engineered to handle and store the specific commodity. Personnel training relates directly to the one commodity so there is the opportunity for exceptionally high proficiency. This in no way negates the need for good policies and procedures. It simply aids in effecting high-quality warehousing.

On the other hand, many commodity-type warehouses are subject to extreme work load fluctuations due to seasonal or other factors. As a result, many of the workers may be employed only a part of the year. This results in using temporary unskilled employees to a far greater degree than does a warehouse that has a relatively steady work load. A particular concern of commodity warehouses is to find a way to level out the work to be done throughout the year so that they can attain a more constant work load. This same problem to a lesser degree faces most all warehousing regardless of type, but normally not to the extent it does commodity warehousing.

FOREIGN "FREE" TRADE ZONE WAREHOUSING

This is warehousing under the unusual circumstances of the facilities being legally outside U.S. Customs territory and is done to attract and promote international trade. The foreign trade zones usually are located in designated areas in or near customs ports of entry. Within these zones and under the regulation of the Foreign Trade Board, companies can have light industry manufacturing, warehousing, merchandise displays, and office facilities along with loading and unloading facilities for container, ship, rail, trucking, and air freight. All zones do not include air freight, and inland zones, of course, do not include port facilities.

The Foreign Trade Zone Board approves applications to establish foreign trade zones and may approve any zone or subzone that it deems necessary to serve adequately "the convenience of commerce." The board also regulates the administration of these areas and the rates charged by companies operating within them.

The following is an example of the charge rate structure. The rates shown in the example are for comparison between the different functions and are not meant to be realistic in magnitude.

Comparable Charge Rates for Warehousing in
A Foreign Trade Zone

General: Handling in and out is a one-time charge assessed when merchandise is received.

Storing charges are based by cube or weight, whichever is greater.

Merchandise received by the fifteenth of the month will be assessed a full month's storage charge. Merchandise received after the fifteenth will be assessed one-half month's charge. Merchandise in storage at the first of each month will be assessed a month's charge.

	Handling	**Storing**
Per cubic foot	$ .20	$ .25
Per 100 pounds	.35	.45
Minimum handling charge	$17	
Minimum monthly charge	$80	
Outbound order charge	$15	
Miscellaneous labor charge	$29 per hour (minimum 1/4 hour)	
Miscellaneous labor charge	$36 per hour (with lift truck)	

The Foreign Trade Zone Board regulates the rates charged by zone "grantees."

USES AND ADVANTAGES OF FOREIGN TRADE ZONES AND SUBZONES

1. Reduce customs duty by disassembly or otherwise change merchandise to quality for lower duty rate. Commonly disassembled merchandise qualifies for a lower duty.

2. Borrow on your merchandise stored in the zone by use of negotiable warehouse receipts. Your goods are protected under U.S. Customs security control, which provides additional security for the lender.

3. Hold merchandise in excess of the country-of-origins quota until next quota period, paying import duty only when taken out of the "free zone."

4. Sort through goods and discard substandard items before paying duty on them.

5. Reduce charges by having duty determined on the raw materials received from abroad before assembly and manufacture in the "free zone."

6. If reexport from the "free zone" occurs, no U.S. Customs duty is owed.

7. Stockpile items for sale to the U.S. embassies, ships, and aircraft at places free of duty and internal revenue tax when for use in "U.S. territories" and aboard U.S. vessels.

8. Save insurance costs by covering the cost of the merchandise only, avoiding insurance on duty and taxes while the merchandise is in the zone.

The federal trade zone and subzones provide an alternative to establishing production and warehousing operations abroad. Many of the benefits can be realized without the uncertainties of investing in foreign operations.

In summary, the savings resulting from utilizing the federal trade zone can result in (1) either reducing costs of the merchandise by true avoidance of duty and taxes or (2) improving cash flow by delaying payment of these costs until the merchandise is sold and shipped. True avoidance of cost is accomplished by paying duty and taxes on a lower value of raw material or modified goods and by shipping abroad again without bringing the materials out of the free zone. This can also be done by shipping from the free zone to U.S. consumers in international commerce or to duty and tax-free areas.

The feature of improving cash flow by postponing payment is as real a savings as cost avoidance because money costs money, that is, interest. If the money tied up in duties and taxes can be avoided until the merchandise is sold, this time interval and the rate of return placed on invested capital will provide the amount saved. For instance, if a company expects a rate of return on its investments of 1 percent per month, for every month $100,000 in duty and taxes that can be postponed, a savings of $1,000 is realized.

Foreign trade zone warehouses can be public or private warehouses. If your company's management believes that it can save money utilizing the zone privileges but you do not want to use public warehouses, apply to the Federal Trade Zone Board to become a "grantee." If it is physically unrealistic to locate within the zone, apply for a subzone location. It is the purpose of the board to stimulate commerce with foreign markets and vendors.

MINIWAREHOUSES

Miniwarehouses serve as other types of warehouses in that they are a secure place to store but have few other similarities. They are not staffed with employees, and they are not concerned with interaction with other functions. They are simply intended as extra storage space—from 20 to 200 square feet—dedicated to those who pay the rent and abide by the regulations of the complex. Normally a large number of separate storage spaces make up the total facility.

A caretaker generally resides at the complex and provides full-time custodian services, and material handling equipment can be rented by the hour or is made available as a part of the rent. Lift trucks or elevators serve multistory facilities.

Miniwarehouses have proven to be in many instances exceptional investments. Construction costs are lower than those for apartments or houses or other comparable segregated space in industrial or warehouse facilities, yet the rent income can be comparatively much greater. Land costs are usually high because they should be located convenient to populated areas, but the lower construction and lower utilities costs combine to make favorable total costs, which translates into attractive rent compared to the alternatives for millions of people and thousands of companies.

Another important feature of miniwarehouses is their convenient accessibility for renters. After contracting for the space, there is little or no paperwork involved, mostly just mailing a check each pay period and perhaps signing in and out of the secured premises. There are however hazards of break-ins by thieves coming through the walls of adjacent units. The walls separating the units generally are no deterrent to the determined invader. The locks are not much of an obstacle either. Strong biceps and bolt cutters cut the door locks but leave overt evidence of the break-in, which is somewhat of a deterrent. Cutting through walls is not evident from the outside and is a preferred method by most thieves. Regardless of these hazards, many new miniwarehouses are coming on the market. For each action there is a reaction. Ways to reduce the theft hazard are being found and implemented with sufficient success to keep this a growing part of warehousing.

PRIVATE AND PUBLIC WAREHOUSING

This is an important consideration that is involved in all warehousing. Should we do it ourselves or have someone else do it for us? The consideration whether to operate your own warehouse or use a public warehouse is one of those big ones that a company has to make. To complicate matters further, the right decision now may not stay right for long, and rarely does so indefinitely. See Chapter 15, *Contract and Public Warehousing Opportunities* for in-depth coverage on how to decide between these types of warehouses.

PUBLIC OR PRIVATE WAREHOUSE CONSIDERATIONS

1. A company determines that a warehouse inventory is definitely justified. It has only one production plant, and this has extra space available for a warehouse. The market served is within the same-day or next-day delivery. In the past, customers have had to wait for their orders to be produced, receiving their merchandise some time within 1 to 30 days. Other suppliers' services are as bad or worse. Little overhead need be added at the plant because the warehouse work is a line operation similar to that of the production facility. Should the company use a public warehouse or set up its own?

   You are right. The correct answer is to operate its own warehouse.

2. A company determines that it should expand its market from the West Coast across the nation. This will require establishing warehouses strategically located to provide no more than three-day service to customers. The expected orders will be mostly within the range of 1,000 to 5,000 pounds. The projected space requirements for the inventories range from 2,000 to 10,000 square feet per location (assuming storage height to be 20 feet). The traffic department, from an analysis of the expected shipments, finds that ten warehouses properly located will permit serving 95 percent of the potential customers within sales prescribed time limits. The company has been able to handle its West Coast business from its own warehouses at its production plants in Los Angeles and Portland. The operation of these warehouses has been adequate. However, sales claims being located at the plants and reporting to the plant managers have caused the warehouses to be managed more for productions benefit than for sales.

   There are several considerations other than whether to have the new warehouses operated by the company or to use public warehouses, but this is the question that concerns us here.

You are right again! The correct answer from the information given is to use carefully selected public warehouses at least until the dust has settled on the expansion program and the best physical distribution configuration becomes obvious.

GOVERNMENT WAREHOUSING

Government warehousing is a technological paradox. It has some of the most advanced systems and equipment, at the cutting edge of technology, and some quite the opposite. It operates with fat budgets for some and lean for others. Parts of it are operated by government workers, other parts by nongovernment workers. Warehousing is practiced in all branches and levels of government: federal, state, and local. The sum of the military branches constitutes the largest type of warehousing as it should because the largest share of the tax dollar is spent in this area.

The Internal Functions of Warehouse Management

CHAPTER HIGHLIGHTS

A great concern is determining where warehousing fits in a company's organizational plan when there is and when there is not a formal physical distribution division in a company. Warehousing is an organizational maverick that does not neatly fit in any organization because it is comprised of both line and staff functions. Many of the things it does as staff are not unlike those of accounting, purchasing, and engineering, while many others are operational, such as production with its hourly paid, often union, workers. As a result, the warehousing activity should probably report to physical distribution, which should report to the chief executive officer. We also consider why and how warehousings objectives fit into the company's objectives and what happens when they do not. Finally, there is the question of what top management wants—efficiency or service—which at times seem at odds with each other.

HOW COMPANY FUNCTIONS RELATE TO WAREHOUSING

The list of functions warehousing can do or must do out of necessity is a long one. Of primary importance is the type of company involved. If the company's business is public warehousing, the list will include all the business functions characteristic of any product-oriented company—sales, accounting, and staff support groups—as well as its main function of material handling and storing for others. Those who are thinking about starting or buying and operating a public warehouse should be knowledgeable about far more than warehousing. They will be engaged in a company operation with all that entails. Their management experience and knowledge will be as important or possibly more important than their material handling skills.

Distributors are similar to public warehousing because the main part of their business is warehousing, except that they actually buy and own the products warehoused. Generally they buy in large quantities and sell and ship in smaller quantities at a price that should provide for sufficient margin to cover costs and provide a profit. The terms "distributor" and "broker" are occasionally used interchangeably, but they should not be. Brokers differ in that they never buy or take possession of the products they sell. They only sell other companies' merchandise. Shipments are made directly from the producers or distributors to the customers who placed their orders with the brokers. Brokers are justified in the marketplace because they normally offer several related products and provide the companies they represent with sales representation at a lower cost than having their own sales personnel.

This section is oriented to warehousing as a division of a company whose main function is to manufacture or purchase and rehandle general merchandise. Warehousing in this context may or may not be the dominant function of the company.

Which functions a warehouse should have within its formal responsibility depends largely on the type of business, the extent of their business logistics sophistication, and the size of the company. The size of the company is important because in a small company, everyone is expected to do more than one function. For example, clustering together the following functions under one responsibility is not only necessary, it is highly efficient for very small companies:

- Warehousing
- Purchasing
- Traffic and transportation
- Customer service
- Inventory management

As the company grows, it is common to set up each of these functions as a separate responsibility. Too frequently, ivory towers are erected for each division and communication breaks down as the towers grow stronger (see Figure 1.1). As this occurs, overall efficiency and quality of service deteriorates and results in a major problem for the company. Because of this problem the concept of physical distributor or logistics management was invented.

In very small companies complete coordination of these functions is natural when all are performed by one person. This is not possible when more than one person is involved due to the inherent difficulties of communication between people. The problem of communication should be given a high priority in all organizations, not just when warehousing is involved. However, communications between warehousing and other company divisions takes on an added importance because warehousing has the capability of making many very costly errors.

Consider the cost of sending a critically needed car load order to a customer in Newark, California, when it is needed in Newark, New Jersey, or of a daydreaming lift truck operator who tips a stack of unit loads of premium wine.

There are many functions that warehousing is capable of handling because of its dual status of being partly line and partly staff. Its line operations include labor that physically handles the product. Its staff functions may include customer service, inventory planning, purchasing, and traffic responsibilities.

The accompanying list of business functions that are directly or indirectly related to warehousing contains brief notes indicating the nature of the relationship. Following the list, each function is discussed in some detail. This review of functions is designed to assist in analyzing and evaluating what should be included as warehousing responsibility and just how the other groups should relate. Keep in mind that the more separate divisions there are in a company, the more potential there is for creating ivory towers that thwart communication. The list can also be used to analyze and evaluate which functions to join to comprise a physical distribution or business logistics division for the company.

FUNCTIONS DIRECTLY OR INDIRECTLY RELATED TO WAREHOUSING

1.	Receiving, Storing, and Shipping	Basic responsibilities of warehousing.
2.	Inventory Records	Warehousing control by store keeping unit, or SKU. Fiscal control by accounting.
3.	Inventory Levels	Input from all affected divisions, including warehousing, within guidelines set by the CEO.
4.	Inventory Acquisition	Responsibility of purchasing or warehousing depending on several factors.
5.	Inventory Accountability	Basic responsibility of warehousing.
6.	Transportation by Common Carriers	Basic responsibility of warehousing assisted and audited by traffic group.
7.	Company Trucking	Best oriented to warehousing or separate department within logistics division.
8.	Traffic	Assisting and auditing both production and warehousing transportation functions.
9.	Product Finishing Operations	Normally responsibility of production but some best done by warehousing.
10.	Customer Service	Part of warehousing or separate department within logistics division.
11.	Logistics or Physical Distribution	Comprising all factors influencing movement and storing of merchandise with warehousing being a major consideration.
12.	Production	Warehousing should be an active participant in production planning.
13.	Purchasing	Warehousing should be actively involved with purchasing for any purchased merchandise it will handle including supplies as well as inventoried merchandise.

14. Production's Store Keeping and Ware-housing Functions	Best oriented to warehousing because of similar work and accountability responsibility.
15. Office Store Keeping	Best oriented to warehousing because of similar work and accountability responsibility.
16. Accounting	Compliance with accounting's fiscal and record responsibilities but with the right to challenge any excessive work caused by accounting.
17. Sales	Basic responsibility of providing responsive service to customers and aiding sales efforts.
18. Hazards of Combining Certain Functions	

1. Receiving, Storing, and Shipping   Obviously the physical handling and storing of inventories are warehousing's responsibility. But with these primary functions comes the responsibility to perform in an exemplary manner. This means having a goal of absolute quality. Look sharp, be sharp. Take a clue from the U.S. Marines: "Don't walk, strut!" Be outstanding and proud of it.

Total familiarity with the best systems and equipment technology is necessary. Warehouse staff and management should become recognized experts in material handling and storing. They should also be able to offer consulting service to production for its handling and storing functions, including store keeping for both accounting and production.

2. Inventory Records   Warehousing must have inventory records that are current and accurately reflect the complete status of the inventories, including

- Salable and nonsalable
- On order
- On hand
- Committed to customers
- Available for sale
- Aging (length of time inventories have been in the warehouse)

These records must be reconciled with any other records of warehouse inventories in the company, particularly those of accounting. In this age of computerization, having current and accurate information is not the horrendous chore it use to be. Warehousing should have a reputation of being on top of the true inventory situation at all times.

3. Inventory Levels   Establishing the desired level of inventories is not the responsibility of warehousing per se. This is the job of the head of the company (the CEO) because inventories are a major part of the company's assets. Determining how much to carry is a strategic top-level decision. Input is needed from sales, production, purchasing, traffic, accounting, warehousing, and the owners of the company. Warehousing's input can be extremely valuable because it probably has the best records of what happened in the past. Warehousing should also be able to design the system to maintain the desired levels, but the specific levels should be specified by the user or users of the inventory (such as sales or production). To establish overall levels without guidelines from the CEO and the company owners would be remiss, because a large part of the company's assets are often tied up in inventories and inventory levels influence customer service.

4. Inventory Acquisition   Warehousing must be tied into or actually issue the orders for acquisition of its inventories whether they are produced by the company or purchased from outside. The justification for an inventory and its levels should be others' responsibility for reasons cited in the paragraph before. But warehousing at a minimum must know what has been ordered and when it will be delivered to plan personnel, space, and equipment requirements. Inexcusably, in some companies warehousing still does not have this information and is left to take care of whatever comes. This mode of operation is costly, inefficient, and ill-mannered.

5. Inventory Accountability   Accountability for inventories in its charge is an inalienable responsibility of warehousing. Any error should be loudly investigated and noticeably corrected. This responsibility is one of the main reasons warehousing must have its own inventory records, and these records must be reconciled with the accounting department's records. Logically, warehousing cannot be held responsible for inventory accountability and have it measured against others' records. Warehousing's accountability for its inventories should be the same as a bank for its money.

6. Transportation by Common Carriers   Warehousing should arrange for the transportation of the merchandise it ships. If there is a separate traffic department, warehousing should cooperate with it and give strong consideration to its guidance and monitoring functions, but warehousing should have the final control over the carriers it uses. Warehousing's relationship with carriers should be that of a buyer of transportation services. The common carriers should feel obligated to the warehouse for the freight they handle, certainly not to another department whose function is to guide and monitor. Of course, warehousing should not have completely free rein. There are many reasons other than warehousing concerns to favor certain carriers. These include legitimate reciprocity between companies. Accounting and auditing should maintain their vigils to ensure the liberty warehousing has in this area is not abused.

7. Company Trucking   The warehouse operation is a line organization, like production and trucking. It physically handles the company's products, and it initiates much or all of the company's freight. It therefore follows that company trucking reasonably should be or could be a warehouse responsibility. If it is, there must be a good cost control and accountability systems that help warehousing manage, and others monitor, its performance. Since common carriers' services are usually available, a company should have its own trucking only when it saves money or provides services that common carriers cannot provide (such as better delivery service or better customer relations) or provide an advertising value for the company. Many companies can justify their own trucking for one or more of these reasons. Rarely should company trucking be justified by the type of rationalization expressed as: "It's only company money," as though company money were less dear than other money.

8. Traffic   Traffic is a staff function that assists and monitors the company's transportation services. If it has the added responsibility for arranging transportation services (scheduling carriers), it should report to the operating division it serves with a "dotted line" relationship on the organization chart to the manager of physical distribution.

Occasionally warehousing reports to traffic, an unwise organization relationship. One of traffic's most valuable services is to monitor those who have the cost and service responsibilities for transportation, and it is unrealistic to have traffic monitor itself as it would if it has warehousing reporting to it. Furthermore, traffic is a staff function that requires staff skills. Warehousing is largely a line operating function that requires appropriate line operating skills. There is little logic in having a line operation reporting to a staff organization.

9. Product Finishing Operations   Warehousing should not take over too many production operations; however, there are certain production-type operations that are best performed by warehousing. For production to perform these would be awkward and probably less efficient. A few examples are listed here.

1. Shearing small customer order sizes from large metal, paper, or plastic sheets.
2. Filling small custom containers from large vats of granular or liquid material.
3. Labeling bare containers with the customer's labels.
4. Cutting short lengths of wire or rope from large coils to fill specific customer order requirements.
5. Paralleling several different strands of electrical wire together on a single spool to facilitate threading the combination through conduit.

Production-type operations have been performed in warehousing all along. There is, however, a new and strong impetus to examine more closely the possibilities of moving more functions of production into warehousing. The reason for this is simple—cost reduction. Customarily warehouse labor is paid less than production labor. The reasoning is that by moving work from production to warehousing, costs will be reduced even though the same equipment is used and the same rates of production are maintained.

The influence of strong labor unions in certain areas of industry have attained higher labor rates for certain types of work. Sometimes the degree of skills accounts for the differences, sometimes not. Owners and managers of businesses look to this discrepancy to reduce costs. Philosophically it can be argued that such transfers of work are unethical. The same work performed in production or warehousing should receive the same pay. On the other hand, competition from abroad is so fierce that ways must be found to reduce costs, or the companies affected must shut their doors and go out of business. Certainly not too much of production should be moved into warehousing, or it will fail in one of its basic functions—responsive service.

10. Customer Service   The process of communication with customers about their orders is commonly referred to as customer service. A company's customer service should handle both orders to be shipped directly from production and orders to be shipped from warehouse inventory. If the company does not have warehousing, customer service would only deal with production orders, and if the company has only warehousing, customer service would handle only warehouse orders.

Customer service is a staff function that combines the interests of sales and production and/or warehousing. Its primary purpose is to give the customer what he or she wants courteously, but to stay within the capability of what production and warehousing can do. To accomplish this, customer service must be tied closely to the organization that will ship the merchandise. What is to be shipped must be available, and time must be allowed to prepare for shipment and transportation to the customer. About the worst that can happen is for delivery to not be made as promised. This at minimum will disappoint the customer, but could be as bad as to cause the customer to shut down a production line with loss of its customers. The satisfactory performance of customer service depends very much on how well it is supported by production and/or warehousing. Alternatives as to whom customer service could report organizationally are

- ○ Sales.
- ○ Production.
- ○ Warehousing.
- ○ Physical distribution.
- ○ Chief executive officer.

Whichever one is best depends on many factors, but whichever one is chosen, a strong tie must be maintained between the shipper, production and/or warehousing, and customer service. When customer service loses credibility with the customers, everyone loses.

11. Logistics or Physical Distribution This group, like customer service, has to know not only the requirements and capabilities of sales, production, and warehousing, but also has to take into consideration many other factors such as cash flow and return on investment. Logistics planning entails analysis of all pertinent data to arrive at the best solution for the company. In a real sense, it determines the course of action that the chief executive officer would choose if he or she had the time and resources at hand to make the decision.

The single most effective consideration employed by physical distribution or logistics management is "trade-offs." Because of the complex interrelationship of the many elements and functions that are involved, clear-cut quick decisions are often not the best. Commonly, the elements of money, quality, and time, and the functions of customer service, production, purchasing, sales, transportation, and warehousing are carefully weighed to determine the best course of action. Trade-offs are made with some factors of the equation being losers and some being gainers, with the sum of the negative and positive being what is perceived as best for the company. Warehousing is commonly an important factor in these sophisticated equations. Consider, for example, the difficulty of determining what is best for the company if a certain proposed action will reduce costs in production, warehousing, and sales but will entail a risk of losing customers.

12. Production Warehouse operations is closely tied to production for basically three reasons:

1. Production is the source of inbound merchandise to warehousing.
2. Warehousing makes possible longer, more economical production runs.
3. An effort is underway to move more and more production operations into warehousing to reduce labor costs and to improve service.

Warehousing should be kept advised of what is being produced for its inventories and it should keep production advised of its priorities. The scheduling of production when all or part of what is produced goes into warehouse inventory should be a cooperative process with warehousing. Physical distribution should be involved as well to evaluate the various other vested interests.

By producing more merchandise than is needed at the time production can amortize its expensive equipment set ups over more items. This can be illustrated by changing the quantity of production run as shown:

Quantity per Production Run (units)	Setup Cost	Run Cost per Unit	Total Run Cost	Total Unit Cost
1	$200	$2	$202	$202
10	200	2	220	22
100	200	2	400	4

The cost per unit for equipment set-up dramatically reduces as the number of units run increases. Of course the extra units produced over what can be sold immediately must be warehoused until needed. To determine how many to warehouse consideration has to be given to the cost of carrying inventory, the probability of the rate at which the inventory will be sold, how important it is to sales to have stock availability, and the rate of return needed on the investment in inventory. All this constitutes a complex problem for the physical distribution or logistics planners.

In the search for further cost reduction and better service, there is a concerted effort to move more and more of productions' finishing operations into warehousing. This is because the wage rates in warehousing are often lower than in production, and warehousing is more responsive to customer service requirements. It is important, however, to keep in mind that warehousing cannot be all things. Granted, it is in good position, being both line operations and staff service, to expand its responsibilities, but too many other functions could cause warehousing's normal work to become subordinate.

With too much of production in warehousing, it will have to assign priorities like production does. This will cause it to compromise one of its primary purposes of being responsive to customer requirements. With too many service functions, it takes on the character of physical distribution, which it should not. Physical distribution has to be able to weigh objectively trade-offs of different functions of the company to find the best solutions. One of the main trade-off functions is warehousing, and it is unreasonable for warehousing to objectively weight the trade-off of itself.

13. Purchasing   Purchasing's relationship to warehousing is similar to that of production's (as discussed in the preceding section). Both supply warehousing's inventories. Purchasing acquires from outside suppliers while production produces within the company.

Purchasing buys for more than warehousing. It purchases production's input materials, and supplies and services for all the divisions of the company. Yet all physical things purchased for the company's consumption or inventories should be received by or at least coordinated with warehousing. Why so? Because of the loss of accountability and the confusion that often results from having more than one receiving function—and because of the inefficient use of receiving employees, equipment, and facilities that results from separate receiving operations. However, if the handling of these non-warehouse items cannot be within warehousing's responsibility (for some valid reason), they should be at least covered by the same accountability and operating procedures.

At the very minimum, purchasing should keep warehousing advised of what is ordered and when it is scheduled to arrive for warehousing's inventories.

However, if this is all purchasing does by way of coordination, much will be lost by warehousing not playing a more important role in the process.

Warehousing's input can be valuable concerning

1. How inbound materials should be packaged, unitized, or palletized.
2. The type of delivery vehicles that will be compatible with its receiving facilities.
3. Where and when to make deliveries.
4. What is special about the inbound materials to assist in doing a better job of receiving, such as unusual quantities inside the packages, subtle indications of concealed damage, and so on.

Often errors made by purchasing and suppliers can be detected during the receiving operation when the receiving personnel know what to look for. This is much better than finding the errors when the materials are about to be used.

Purchasing should provide warehousing with a copy of purchase orders for warehouse inventories. This can be accomplished either by a hard copy of the completed form or by access to this information through a computer system with a CRT (cathode ray tube) viewer and terminal in the receiving area. The more complete the information about things to be received, the more effectively and efficiently warehousing can receive them.

14. *Production Store Keeping and Warehousing* Production's dominance in many manufacturing companies results in the commonly accepted idea that warehousing should deal only with finished goods, leaving to production its store keeping, its warehousing of raw materials, and its shipping of its finished goods to its customer—as productions's turf. A pioneering consideration is that perhaps this is not how it should be.

Often companies start as job shops where materials are produced only to customers' firm orders. As the companies grow, there is a point where they realize that, instead of everything being produced in a job shop environment, producing to warehouse inventory would result in lower cost and better customer service for many products. Therefore, a warehouse for finished goods is established. Later sales initiates the action that results in the warehouse carrying some products made by other companies. These additional vender-supplied products round out the company's own offerings, thereby increasing the sale of the company's products as well as increasing total sales and profit. The warehouse grows as a finished goods facility. Production continues its raw material warehousing and store keeping. These grow with production and stay under its responsibility because there are no pressures for them to be moved to warehouse operations. They do not offer the advantages that warehousing does of providing means for longer production runs or giving sales more responsive service. However, raw material warehousing and store keeping require the same professional material handling and storing that warehousing provides for finished goods. The controls and accountability responsibilities should be the same for these inventories as they are for warehousing-controlled inventories.

Consideration should be given to having raw materials handling and storing (as well as store keeping) within the warehousing division's responsibility. Money spent in these areas is the same as money spent in warehousing. Accountability and responsive service are applicable in all three functions. Commonly, however, less attention is given to effective cost controls, accountability, and service of raw materials and stores when these come under production. This is because these operations are dwarfed in comparison to production. Of course there are times when it will be found that production's handling of raw material and store keeping are performed better than that of the warehouse. This only adds support to the suggested merger. If production has a better manager of stores or raw materials or shipping, he or she should head up all warehousing.

Of course there are exceptions to this merger concept, but when they exist, they should be recognized as exceptions. Extra care should be taken by top management to see that there is a sharing of material-handling knowledge and that the responsive service and inventory accountability features are applied equally to all departments responsible for inventories.

15. Office Store Keeping The same considerations that are applicable to production's store keeping apply to office store keeping. The only difference is that one deals with supplies used in production, the other applies to supplies used in the office. Good procedures, controls, and accountability apply equally to stores as well as to warehousing. There may be different pay scales for justifiable reasons, but these can be accommodated by additional job classifications such as adding a store keeping classification to warehousing's wage-rate structure. Also, there may be personality and union problems that have to be overcome or accepted. Procedures, equipment, and accountability should apply equally to all. This can be achieved more effectively and efficiently if all come under one responsibility regardless of what the commodities are or what the functions are called. There are companies whose stores operations are larger than their warehouse operations; however, comparative size is not as important as that the best apply consistently to all.

16. Accounting Webster's *New World Dictionary* (second college edition) defines accounting as "the principles or practices of systematically recording, presenting, and interpreting financial accounts." Even more pertinent is that the Internal Revenue Service requires, as a matter of law, that proper records be maintained. Therefore, the accounting department's inherent rights and responsibilities reach into every segment and function of the company, because all company actions require records and affect finances. Accounting has the right to challenge and cause correction of any procedures and forms that influence records and finances. Warehousing is commonly a big part of their concern because here is found considerable record keeping and a large share of the company's financial resources tied up in inventories. Accounting should be convinced that the records, reports, and security measures are proper and provide the necessary results to satisfy their financial and record responsibilities. Neither warehousing nor any other department should go about doing things that influence these responsibilities without coordinating with accounting and making certain they meet its requirements.

This does not mean that accounting should maintain warehousing's inventory records. And it does not mean that accounting should be checking warehousing's every move. It does mean that it should make certain that proper but efficient records and controls are being maintained to comply with the company's accountability requirements. It should ensure that physical inventories are taken, audited, and reconciled, often enough to assure the effectiveness of these controls.

The degree of accuracy of the ongoing inventory records should have an inverse relationship to the frequency of physical inventories. Unless there are extenuating circumstances, one annual complete physical inventory should be enough, thoroughly reconciled with warehousing's and accounting's inventory records.

Acknowledgment is made here of accounting's responsibilities and authority as it relates to warehousing. There is a need in any business for accounting and where large inventories are involved, these rights should be amplified. With rights go responsibilities. Accounting should be extremely careful that no more work is put onto warehousing than is necessary to accomplish their fiscal and record responsibilities. For example, if accounting requires frequent physical inventories, something is basically wrong.

There are three main causes that contribute to the need for frequent physical inventories. All are bad, having negative consequences for the company. They are

1. Warehousing is not doing its job. Errors in its inventory records are too common, receiving and shipping are not in tight control, or there is recurring theft.
2. Accounting's inventory records are incorrect or their reconciliation is faulty.
3. Accounting has the mistaken idea that frequent physical inventories achieve something worthwhile. (Mostly they waste labor and interrupt service.)

In summary, if frequent physical inventories are truly necessary, there is something wrong with the record and/or material accountability systems. It is far better to correct the systems than it is to take physical inventories. Warehousing should first make certain its house is in order; if this does not eliminate the discrepancies, it should constructively challenge and help accounting put their house in order. When proper systems are operating effectively, once a year should be often enough to take physical inventory.

17. Sales   Generally, warehousing's relationship to sales should be separate yet very close. In fact, one of the main reasons for warehousing is to support sales efforts. A frequently heard phrase from salespeople is: "You can't sell from an empty cupboard." This means, of course, that you cannot sell when the merchandise you are trying to sell is not available. This is where warehousing enters the picture. It can make merchandise available so that salespeople can offer both the merchandise and the delivery times that together generate customers' orders.

In companies that are extremely sales oriented, there is ample justification for having warehousing report organizationally to sales. If the dominant costs of the company are spent in sales effort, it may be penny wise and pound foolish to set up warehousing independently. For companies not so disposed, much of warehousing's potential to contribute to profits can be compromised if warehousing reports directly to sales and must thereby respond to its demands without equal regard for other functions of the company.

More and more companies are recognizing the importance of a physical distribution or logistics division of the company that serves as a balancing agent between sales, production, warehousing, and the rest of the company. In most companies there are trade-offs between the many functions involved in supply and distribution. When warehousing can be freely considered in analyzing these trade-offs, the company benefits. When warehousing reports independently to or through logistics to the CEO, it can be objectively weighed in the trade-off formulas discussed before. But if it reports to sales (or production for that matter), there is the strong possibility that objectivity will be compromised. This is quite natural and should be expected. If the sales manager is rewarded in direct relationship to how much the sales division sells, and if warehousing reports to the sales manager, warehousing will be used to further the interest of sales. If warehousing reports to production, the same line of reasoning and conclusion apply. It is up to the CEO to see that warehousing reports to where the most good will be done for the company in total.

18. *Hazards of Combining Certain Functions* There is a subtle danger inherent in putting the acquisition and disposition of materials under the same command. This action embodies, like Pandora's box, a host of potential evils. Consider this:

A warehouse manager is given the responsibility for purchasing inventories, approving payment to suppliers, as well as warehousing inventories, and shipping to customers. In this situation the manager has an opportunity to commit several criminal acts. Add to this an accounting that is not as sharp as it should be and these temptations follow:

1. Materials can be ordered from suppliers, paid for, and never received.
2. A continuing minor shortage can be arranged with certain large suppliers. If detected by persons outside of the warehouse organization, the loss would be just a fraction of a percentage point and could be excused in many ways even as innocent record-keeping errors.
3. When public carriers that haul the warehouse shipments are contracted for by the warehouse and have their freight invoices approved for payment by the warehouse. Overcharges are difficult to detect by anyone other than those trained for this purpose and even then a concerted and objective effort must be made to find them.
4. Excessive gratuities from outside suppliers, common carriers, or anyone providing equipment, supplies, and services can obligate warehouse personnel to favor them with business.
5. Loans can be made to the warehouse manager by suppliers who postpone calling for payment for as long as they receive preferential treatment. This means of payoff is difficult to detect and even more difficult to prosecute.

A common way to avoid such unlawful acts is to separate the functions of buying, approving for payment, and the actual payments organizationally. However, because creating additional departments to avoid collusion is inefficient and expensive, it is better to do it with effective systems and procedures.

PHYSICAL DISTRIBUTION AND WAREHOUSING'S ROLE WITHIN IT

Physical distribution is a broad concept, one that covers many functions, including warehousing. In the attempt to clarify just what it does mean, physical distribution has often been described as one leg of a three-legged stool, the other two legs being production and sales, with the stool representing the company. This gives as good an insight to the term as can be expressed in simple terms, provided that the term production includes mining and agriculture as well as manufacturing.

Even the National Council of Physical Distribution, a fraternal organization with thousands of members, had difficulty with the term so it changed its name in 1985 to the Council of Logistics Management. The consensus of the organization's leaders was that physical distribution really did not describe adequately what was meant. The military term "logistics" was adopted which they believed was a better description. The problem with the word logistics,

approach would be to equate the two considerations and decide what was the best thing to do. In this example the obvious thing seems to be for warehousing to work overtime and get the order out. However, this may not be the case. There may be extenuating circumstances. Suppose that the warehouse was involved in a critical issue of union negotiations, there was not sufficient time to give the proper lead time to ask employees to work overtime, and overtime was the critical issue of the union-management dispute. Add to this the fact that the production union had stated it would go on strike in support of the warehouse union if it went on strike. Physical distribution's role would be to weigh all the influencing factors and decide what was best. Good solutions to such problems as these need the wisdom of Solomon as well as an effective physical distribution team.

TRAIN CAR LOAD FREIGHT SAVINGS VERSUS INVENTORY BUILDUP

The traffic department seeking to minimize freight costs insists that trains be used for shipments between production plants within the company. Parts fabricated at one plant are shipped to other plants for future work and final assembly. Included in traffic's plan is a provision to hold up enough less-than-carload orders to make up full carloads. This was the phase of the plan that yielded most of the calculated savings. Because traffic had been given the authority to designate carriers, the plan went into effect. The result was that regularly traffic reported to top management the large sums of money it was saving the company. The traffic manager got a nice salary increase and was heralded for the smart move.

Later the company set up a physical distribution department and hired a highly qualified manager. One of the first situations investigated was the rule that traffic had set about interplant shipments being made only by rail. The reason this was investigated first was because the warehouse manager told the physical distribution vice president that one of the main reasons warehousing's costs had increased was because of the big shift to rail cars. He was told that it took twice as long to load and brace a rail car as it did a comparable amount sent by truck.

The investigation confirmed the warehouse manager's contention, but it revealed another effect of the plan that was far worse. The company's inventory of unfinished parts had increased significantly. In fact, each plant that received parts had increased its inventory to protect against outages due to holding back orders to make full rail car shipments—outages that would shut down expensive production lines and cause poor plant shipping performance and therefore cause loss of customers.

Before the rail shipment rule the plants could rely on replacement inventories being delivered within a week's lead time. Now with the rule in force, plants would get what they ordered anytime from a week to a month. They had to set their buffer stocks at a month's supply plus a cushion. The result was these inventories had to be increased almost in direct ratio about five times.

It was found that the cost of the additional investment in inventories had caused the company to borrow more money. And the interest paid on the like amount borrowed was greater than the amount traffic was saving by rail shipments. An additional cost was an increase in inventory obsolescence. It was not uncommon in this industry for new technology to be introduced that made products that had been used for years obsolete. The result of such obsolescence was far more expensive to the company now that its in-process inventories had significantly increased. Before when a product was declared obsolete, the cost of salvage or scrapping was minor compared to what it was now with inflated inventories.

Physical distribution found that what had initially looked like a great idea, when taking all into consideration, was just short of disastrous. What was eventually worked out was a plan where more rail shipments were made than before the carload rule but that truck and even air freight were used to give nearly 100 percent reliable deliveries within seven days. With the emphasis on reliability, the plants' inventories were reduced below that which existed before the rule was put into effect. The traffic manager was transferred to a sales position where his talents could be used more effectively.

WAREHOUSE INVENTORY TURNOVER VERSUS FREIGHT COSTS

A distribution system existed where large orders were shipped directly from the production plants to customers and small orders were filled by the nearest field warehouse of a national network of warehouses.

At one point the company president was advised by accounting of the high cost of warehousing inventories and that if inventories could be turned over six times a year (instead of the present three times) the costs of carrying these inventories would be reduced by a substantial amount. So the president demanded that sales get six turns a year on warehouse inventories. (In this case the warehousing department reported to sales.)

The sales and warehousing management tried to plan their inventories more carefully, but the effect was only a minor step toward meeting the president's edict of six turns a year. The sales manager began to worry about the problem more and more; his ulcer started to act up. What could he do? One restless night the answer came to him like a revelation. All he had to do was to increase the size of the orders placed on field warehouses, as opposed to shipping all the large orders directly from the production plants. With this high volume going through the warehouses, there would be no problem meeting the president's goal.

Soon thereafter the target of six turns a year was met and exceeded. The cost per unit came down at the warehouses. Even production's shipping labor costs and their outbound freight per unit came down. Everyone was happy. What was not realized was that the total freight cost for the company climbed higher but this was hardly noticed on the financial statements. "The increase was probably due to freight rate increases," the president thought.

What had happened was that an extra leg of transportation was added to a lot of merchandise. Instead of going directly to the customer from the production plants, it was going to warehouses, rehandled and then shipped to the customer.

If the company had a good physical distribution department, it would have understood the fallacy of using inventory turnovers alone as a criterion for evaluating the performance of inventory management. It would have showed legitimate ways to reduce inventory and keep average unit costs down. In the process of making all these improvements, it may have caused less use of warehouses, more direct shipments to customers from the plants and increase unit cost of warehouse inventories—with the net result a less costly total physical distribution system. The warehouses would be used, as they should be in this situation, as an emergency supply only when the plants could not meet the customers' delivery requirements. They would also be correctly used when it would cost more in freight to ship LTL (less than truckload) from the plant than the sum of the costs to ship CL (carload) or TL (truckload) to the warehouse plus the warehousing operating cost plus the freight from the warehouse to the customer.

The mistake of using turnover as a sole criterion of inventory management is all too common. However, qualified physical distribution management never should make this mistake, but if it does, it should make it only once.

JUST-IN-TIME (JIT) INVENTORIES VERSUS SETUP COSTS

In the attempt to reduce inventory levels, inventory management decided to place smaller, more frequent orders on production and through purchasing. Inventories came down just as planned. Inventories were a big step closer to the inventory concept of "just in time." The new technology that Japan had introduced to the world seemed to really work. All that was needed was smaller orders placed more frequently. But while inventories came down the total costs went up. Production costs increased because their expensive equipment setups were amortized over fewer units. Purchasing costs went up because purchases were made without the ability to take advantage of quantity discounts. The suppliers had the same problem that production had within the company. Freight costs went up because more inbound shipments came in smaller, high-unit-cost LTL deliveries.

Good physical distribution people should realize that the application of JIT involves far more than ordering in less quantity more frequently. A successful JIT program will include finding ways to reduce both setup costs and small shipment freight costs. If equipment setup costs can be reduced, the quantity of production runs can be reduced in direct proportion. If LTL orders can be consolidated, the unit costs of freight will be lowered. Freight will cost more than in TL quantities but the costs will be held down and what extra freight costs do occur can be evaluated as a trade-off to gain the greater savings of operating with lower inventories.

HOW TO MAKE WAREHOUSE OBJECTIVES COMPATIBLE WITH COMPANY OBJECTIVES

Warehousing objectives cannot be set independently from either objectives for other divisions or for the objectives of the company as a whole. Divisions of a company are not islands unto themselves. They are inseparable parts of the whole. Such abstract goals as "we will do better," "we will incur less down time," "we will reduce costs," and any number of other vague notions are virtually useless, perhaps even worse than none at all. How can a warehouse improve unless its objectives are made within a framework of expectations of it, the tools and facilities available to it, the outside influences affecting it, and a valid means of evaluating its performance in relation to just what it is going to do better?

If any of these factors change without having a valid means of bridging the change, relating the old to the new, it is really not possible to know whether performance is better or worse.

Suppose a warehouse set a goal to reduce total labor costs the coming year. Then the company suddenly discontinues a major product line that had been handled by the warehouse. The warehouse then could easily meet its goal because it would have less work to do and could reduce overtime premium and lay off a number of employees. Actually, its costs for handling the remaining products might well increase. They certainly would if warehousing's overhead (often referred to as "burden") and its space were not reduced accordingly. At budget review time the warehouse manager might well receive undeserved laurels for meeting and exceeding goals. However, without the ability to bridge the change with reliable standards, it would be impossible to tell whether a better or worse job had been done.

Where Warehousing Fits into the Organization

Warehousing as part of a company could be at the division level or lower depending on the nature of the business and what part warehousing plays in the total company effort. If large amounts of inventory or considerable inventory activity are entailed, the head of warehousing should report directly to the CEO or to the CEO through a physical distribution or logistics organization unit. The additional problems incurred by warehousing's reporting to production, sales, or any other division should be avoided if possible. There are situations when personalities are such that proper organizational principles can be violated and still maintain effectiveness, but this is the exception rather than the rule. If good organization is warped to accommodate strong or weak employee personalities, what happens when that person leaves?

Specific Warehousing Objectives and Performance Measurement

The "how to" of establishing and measuring objectives is dealt with in Chapter 12. Here treated is the concept of objectives and performance measurement as effective and distinct means of management by objectives. A brief but very important consideration is that the more the system of management by objectives is used, the more reliable and valid the system will be; conversely the less it is used, the less reliable and valid it will be.

The point of this discussion of management by objectives is to delve into what type of warehousing objectives for the different kinds of performance measurements should be considered and how to establish them.

Start with Input from Others   Warehousing objectives must be created within the parameters established by others, including the CEO's general directives and the specific input from the other divisions: sales, production, traffic, accounting, and so on. Parameters are established by getting answers to these questions:

- What services will be provided?
- What facilities, including buildings and equipment, will be available?
- What product mix and quantities will be stored and handled?
- What new equipment and space will be made available?
- What new facilities will be made available and how can their need be justified if necessary?
- What seasonal patterns and other activity and inventory fluctuations should be anticipated?
- What will constitute the incentive program?
- What freedom will be given to deal with internal personnel opportunities and problems? How should external problems that influence warehousing be handled?

○ What type of help will warehousing receive for correcting faults of and filling voids in the objectives and performance measurement system?

All these elements of the system seem at first consideration a bit overwhelming, but they are not when viewed in the perspective of the availability of superefficient computers, bar-code technology, quality systems, real-time in-line communications, and so on. Before these advance technologies existed, this type of management was indeed overwhelming for most companies. Changes and adjustments required such considerable effort and time that the backlog of systems repair and maintenance projects caused many erroneous results. As a consequence, credibility was commonly in doubt. Even when good output was provided, management could well have been reluctant to take action based on it because there was a cloud of apprehension over the entire management-by-objectives system. Now businesswise systems can provide the same high degree of quality that is achievable in the products the company must produce to keep competitive.

Compatibility Is Essential While the details of how objectives and standards are established and how performance is measured are covered in later chapters, the concepts just discussed should be made more meaningful with the following examples of how warehouse objectives must be compatible with the other company objectives to produce an integrated whole.

EXAMPLE OF THE COMPATIBILITY OF WAREHOUSING'S OBJECTIVES

After receiving the CEO's company objectives and what was expected from his division, the sales vice president provided a detailed plan of sales for the coming year. After considerable rework, the CEO accepted it. The sales forecast, which was prepared in monthly intervals, was passed on to warehousing to plan its part of the program. After reviewing the sales plan, the manager of warehousing just could not believe what was presented. It was much too conservative. During the past years before the system of management-by-objectives was implemented, the sales division had commonly exceeded its forecasts. Warehouse management expected it would do the same this coming year. There was a lingering suspicion that sales provided ultraconservative forecasts so that it could look good when it exceeded them.

The warehousing manager hedged the sales forecast by building more into the warehousing plan than was justified by the sales forecast. This was done by using a factor to scale down warehousing's forecast of performance to below that which was currently being experienced and which could reasonably be expected.

When the industrial engineers with accounting's help checked forecasted profits from the data base provided by all the divisions, it was found that the projection of profits was less than expected. A more detailed analysis revealed that not only warehousing but other divisions were hedging against the sales forecast. As instructed, the industrial engineers passed this on to the CEO with facts to support the contention that certain divisions had loaded their forecasts. The CEO called a general meeting of division heads and went over again the rules of the system, in particular that each must use the information he or she is furnished. Any exceptions must be treated as "minority reports" which would be considered but only as secondary, intuitive feelings. Furthermore, without naming divisions, the CEO pointed out that game playing by individual divisions was a thing of the past, before the new management-by-objectives system was adopted. The division heads were sent back with instructions to recheck their plans and objectives.

EXAMPLE OF AN HONORABLE TURNABOUT

The company's warehouse manager had a proud reputation for an uncanny memory and an intuitive knowledge of what, how, and when things could and should be done. He had over 30 years of experience in warehousing at this same company. Some suspected that he might even make things he foretold happen. Until the recent pressure from foreign competition and the need for new improved concepts such as just in time, lower inventories, absolute quality, computerization, bar-coding, and so on, he was considered a real asset to the company. He enjoyed the status of "guru" of warehousing and other areas closely related.

But things are changing rapidly in warehousing. This company's top management found that the way things were done in the old days was just not good enough now. Their best analysis revealed that foreign competition produced a better quality product at one-third less cost than this company could with the best performance it had ever had. The future looked dismal. What could be done? Their "best" fell far short of "good enough." As a last resort, a top-quality efficiency consultant was brought in (at an "astronomical" price it seemed)—about five times the pay per hour that the company's CEO was being paid. After a comparatively short time, in relation to the magnitude of the company's problem, the outside expert turned in his preliminary survey.

As is the case with many highly paid consultants that offer the opportunity to "save" American corporations, he blasted at the heart of the basic tenets by which the company had been operating. He stopped just short of spelling out that this company's management was composed of idiots or at least were mentally retarded.

Such a crude approach, at this level, is not uncommon in the consultant arena in which the very future of companies is at stake. It is intended to see if company management can come down from their pedestal and be open minded about such radical concepts as zero inventories, absolute quality, paperless offices, robotonics, and the like. The consultant assumes that how management deals with being labeled stupid quickly tells how big a project he or she is facing. People who have been managing are obviously not truly stupid. They certainly are not if they are smart enough to call in outside experts to get answers on how to keep the company alive. It is only insecure and devious management that truly takes offense to outside help. What the consultant is testing is their ability to relinquish both the old ways and their pride of authorship. Management's willingness to accept that doing business as usual, in the face of proof of the company's total inability to remain competitive really is stupid.

The consultant used the warehousing division as an example of what was wrong with the company. For the CEO he laid out graphically, with facts and figures, what it was costing and what it should cost and offered a comparison of warehousing's performance with that of other domestic competitors and those foreign competitors who were beating the socks off all domestic competition.

The consultant summarized his findings thus:

Elements Considered	This Company's Warehouse	Average Domestic Competition	Average Foreign Competition
Handling performance	65%	68%	98%
Storage space utilization	70%	65%	99%
Handling costs	$0.11/lb	$0.10/lb	$0.07/lb
Storage costs	0.09/cwt	0.10/cwt	0.06/lb
Order processing time	5 days	6 days	2 days

"How could this be?" asked the perplexed CEO. "Our reports show our handling performance to be in the high nineties and the same for space utilization. As for costs, you are probably right, but I am dismayed at how low costs are for foreign competition. It must be their lower labor rates. About order processing time, I knew we were better than domestic competition, but I thought it was a lot more than you indicate. As for foreign-operated warehouses here, I don't see how they can do it."

"Believe me, they do it," replied the consultant. "The reason why your performance is so low is that you have lousy standards. I have used the published "fair day's work" standards accepted by the Society of Industrial Engineers. Yours are the result of using historical average-times developed from not-too-good records and your warehouse manager's estimates. They represent pretty well what is happening but not what should happen. As for excusing higher costs by blaming differences in labor rates, that just won't wash in this case. Warehouse workers in the foreign base I used have as good, or better, standard of living as those in the good ol' U.S. of A."

"It is time for you to pull your head out of the sand. You told me that your foreign competition makes the same products that your company does at one-third less cost. I know this to be true. I have just showed you why in one area of your operations. The same holds true, I suspect, in the rest of the operations. What are you going to do about it, get with it or go out of business?"

A meeting was set up with the CEO's initiation with the warehouse manager, the consultant and himself to go over the same material. The CEO wanted to see how one of his key managers would accept the dramatic findings of the consultant. The consultant made the presentation as before. The reaction of the warehouse manager was interesting. He asked for a five minute recess to collect his thoughts.

When the meeting resumed, the warehouse manager said he accepted what the consultant had revealed to them. He knew the faults of what the warehouse was doing and could see that under the proper conditions it could attain the results their foreign competition was achieving. He had just three requisites:

1. That the CEO firmly and clearly give his support to the new program.

2. That he, the warehouse manager, receive help with establishing the engineered standards based on a fair day's work.

3. That he install the necessary computerized and bar coding systems that would permit immediate access to what was going on with performance measurement on an in-line real-time basis to keep him and his staff abreast of progress and enable them to quickly detect where help was needed.

The CEO was stunned, but pleased, with the warehouse manager's response. He asked: "If you believe what has been presented here, and you feel you can meet the challenge, why have you not done something about it before?" The manager responded: "I learned a long time ago to play the hand that was dealt me—a matter of pleasing the boss. Now I can see a new deck is about to be introduced, and a new hand is about to be dealt. I am confident that my people are as good as any warehouse people in the world. Given the tools and top management support, I see no reason why we can't do as well and possibly better. Two things about these new approaches that I particularly like are that I'll be equipped to do the best possible job, which I've always wanted. The other is I know that workers respect management in direct relationship to how well they perceive it knows what it is doing.

Many times in the past I've been depressed with knowing there were much better ways of warehousing our products, but the company was not ready to accept the big changes necessary." The chief executive officer had always known the warehouse manager was exceptional. This had proved him right. With the valuable insight he had acquired by this meeting, the CEO knew to go ahead with the consultant. At worst, they would improve some (enough to survive), and the possibility existed for a quantum leap putting his company way head of domestic competition and in a position to give foreign competition a real fight for the markets.

WHAT DOES TOP MANAGEMENT WANT—EFFICIENCY OR SERVICE?

This question has been around since commerce first found use for warehousing—a long time. Warehousing is unique in that it is neither all line nor all staff; this makes the answer to the question more difficult. Warehousing is like a "mugwump," a label for those who straddle political parties, one whose "mug" is on one side of a fence and whose "wump" on the other.

One part of warehousing includes line operations, like production and trucking, with emphasis on efficiency. The other part includes staff operations like traffic and customer service with an emphasis on responsive service to sales and to customers. The effect of these opposing forces is to keep many warehouse organizations off balance and in a quandary.

Whether efficiency or service are to be emphasized never really gets settled. Worse, warehouse managers may play a game with the question: "Which do you want, efficiency or service?" This always puts the person asking something of warehousing in an insecure position. The requestor usually does not have the right to choose one over the other. He or she is put in an untenable position. If the answer is "service," the pressure is relieved on efficiency. If the answer is efficiency, the pressure is relieved on service.

If warehousing organizationally reports to sales, and sales makes the request, warehousing would be inclined to say: "service!" If warehousing reports to production, and production makes the request, warehousing would be inclined to say: "efficiency!" If warehousing reports to, or through physical distribution or logistics to the CEO, the answer should be: "both!" The game of "diluting responsibility" by the warehouse manager should never get started, and if it is already ongoing, it should cease.

Yes, warehousing should and can be both efficient and provide top-quality service. The way this is accomplished is to have

1. Clear understanding of what is authorized (the charter to do business) and to stay within authorized guidelines established by top management.
2. Valid standards and performance measurement for all the warehouse work.
3. Valid space utilization standards and performance measurement for all the merchandise it stores.
4. Top-notch service standards and performance measurement for all the warehouse services.

The following is a brief discussion of each of these warehouse management tools:

What Should Be Included in a Warehousing Charter

Unfortunately, too often warehouse management is expected to know what, when, and how without clear signals from the top echelon. Often as not, top management really does not know what it wants from warehousing. This is because warehousing is the variable in the make-and-sell equation. It varies to balance production and sales needs. It is intended to twist, turn, and jump up and down to level out production and to meet sales' promises. Top management is often reluctant to establish specified objectives and limits of warehousing's authority because there are many extraordinary things it is asked to do and often should do for the benefit of the company. However, it is wise warehouse management that constructively seeks a charter for warehousing, and it is a happier warehouse management that gets it. It is a frustrated warehouse management that takes upon itself to please everyone and to act like it knows what is best for the company. Even successful CEO's know what is best for the company only a little over 50 percent of the time, according to their own honest admissions.

The warehousing charter should answer at least the following questions:

1. To whom does the warehouse manager report? It is hoped, to only one person—the CEO—or answers to the CEO through someone who has the total physical distribution responsibility.
2. What is the manager's authority to hire and fire, discipline, and promote warehouse employees? It is hoped, these rights are clearly spelled out with commensurate responsibility to make him or her accountable for the actions taken.
3. What are the limits on incurring expenses? These should be equal in measure to the delegated authorities and responsibilities.
4. What is the authority to acquire capital equipment? (Capital equipment is usually more costly than expense items and is accounted for and depreciated through the company's official asset ledger.) The company should have a reasonable capital equipment acquisition procedure. The warehouse should not be expected to do things that it is not equipped to do.
5. How is warehouse management's performance measured? It is hoped, it is measured against clearly established goals and standards, and these correspond with the company's overall objectives.

Nothing is so frustrating as trying to answer questions about warehousing efficiency and service without objective information on which to base the answers. There is just no substitute for quick, objective, and reliable data on which to base answers and thereby maintain credibility. Credibility is an essential feature of effective warehousing.

Following are characteristics of good work and space utilization standards and performance measurement.

Characteristics of Good Work Standards

1. Standards should be developed and maintained by professionals such as industrial engineers or others that have the appropriate training and objectivity.

2. Standards should provide written and diagrammed descriptions of the best (standard) way to perform the functions as well as the times allowed to accomplish them. To achieve standards of this high quality requires methods analysis to determine the "best" way, and the application of appropriate time allowances based on the rate of a "fair day's work" (example: walking at the rate of three miles per hour on a level surface).

3. Standards should be maintained to currently reflect the specific equipment and other conditions on which the standard ways and times are based.

4. Actual times to perform the standard functions should be accurately reported and in increments that correspond to how the standards are developed.

5. Performance measurement (actual time compared to standard time) preferably should be accessible on a real-time (instantaneous) basis particularly for high-volume, large warehouses. For smaller operations daily, weekly, or even monthly may be adequate.

6. The development, maintenance, and performance measurements should not be burdensome. They do not have to be. With effective use of computer, bar-coding, and predetermined standard time elements, the effort and time required can be minimal. Possibly the other benefits of increased accuracy and better control of inventories will more than pay for the added costs of the necessary equipment, systems records, and reports. If this is the case, the extremely valuable performance measurement can be considered free.

Characteristics of Good Space Utilization Standards

1. Developed and maintained by professionals the same as work standards.

2. The standards should provide written and diagrammed descriptions of the best (standard) way to store each type of inventory.

3. The standards should be based on cubic feet allowances under specified conditions—racks, bulk, palletized, etcetera.

4. Performance measurement (actual space used compared to standard space available) should be accessible as needed, probably not as current as performance measurement for warehouse work.

5. The development, maintenance, and performance measurement for space utilization should not be burdensome provided that the processing of data and reporting are done in conjunction with that used for the work standards.

Characteristics of Good Service Standards

Good warehousing service can only be defined by first establishing the parameters of the company's service policy. These will differ from one type of industry to another and from one company to another. Warehousing service can only be measured after top management has advised what it wants from warehousing. There is little need to give next-day delivery, for example, if the company only asks for delivery within seven days. The extra cost of providing next-day delivery in this would be unnecessary—a waste.

Therefore warehousing must be given goals or at least direction for what type of service is expected. Then performance measurement is a relatively simple matter, provided the tools with which warehousing has to work are commensurate with the service it is to provide.

Assuming that top management is customer oriented and that nothing is too good for its customers, there are many ways warehousing can make such a policy materialize. There are also many overt and covert ways it can sabotage such a policy. Even when you think you are making decisions for "what is best for the company," those decisions can inadvertently be contrary to what the CEO and board of directors want. Poor communications in many companies foster different divisions to march to different drum beats. It causes different people to pick up different meanings to the same message. The old adage—"we see things not as they are but as we are"—is truly applicable.

Service standards, performance measurement, and means and authority to accomplish the extraordinary are needed to create and maintain top-quality customer service. Following are warehousing service functions that can be measured objectively:

1. *Order processing time.* This is the interval between receiving an order and shipping it. Unlike premium wine, orders do not improve with age. This performance measurement is a little more complicated than it appears on first consideration. To be effective, order processing time must be divided into categories such as

   ○ Those orders that are to be held for later shipping—as requested by the customer, and those that are to be shipped within the normal shipping schedule.

   ○ Those orders that should be shipped immediately, those that can wait for a time, etcetera. Perhaps orders should be classified by priority: "A" class, "B" class, and so on.

2. *Order delivery time.* This measurement should be separate but related to the order processing just described. It should be treated separately because it is a measure of carriers' (truck, rail, air, and sea) performance. The results of this should be used to reward and discipline their service.

3. *Telephone etiquette.* This includes how the phone is answered, how many times the customer is requested to hold while another call is answered or because something else takes priority—and for how long the customer is kept waiting. The local telephone company can probably help in designing your telephone etiquette system and provide a convenient means to collect data by category. Watch out that the system is not overused resulting in destroying employee morale.

4. *Customer rating of performance.* Customer rating of warehouse services using questions and calling for answers that can be objectively scored.

Such a plan should be incorporated into a companywide system, but if this is not possible at least warehousing should apply it.

Customer relations for warehousing should include employee relations. Treat other employees as you would outside customers. Good customer relations starts with good employee relations and cannot be truly effective without both. It seems obvious that disgruntled employees cannot avoid passing on to those they deal with their ill-humor and moroseness. They mirror to customers how the company treats them.

Typical Inquiries and What You Need to Know to Answer Them

With real-time information provided by in-line computers and engineered standards, warehousing knows where it stands at all times. Armed with noncontroversial, objective facts and figures, the person answering for warehousing can speak with conviction about what is involved. The following are typical inquiries made of warehousing. With clear limits of authorization, good standards, and performance measurement, the warehouse can constructively analyze the situation and give constructive, objective answers.

1. Inquiry—Can a new product line be warehoused? Known will be
   - Whether the warehouse has authorization (its charter).
   - Amount and type of storage space available.
   - Amount of personnel that will be required and a fix on that which is available now.
   - Type of equipment needed and whether it is available or must be acquired.
   - Availability of the skills necessary to handle the new merchandise properly.

2. Inquiry—Can a new, large customer order be given top priority to ship ahead of other orders? Known will be
   - Status of orders that have already been committed, their promised ship dates, and what orders will have to be set back if any.
   - Backlog of work and capacity of equipment and manpower to handle the increased load in the time available.
   - Just how much extra cost will be incurred to give top priority to the order.

3. Inquiry—What will be the effect of carrying out a 20 percent reduction of personnel with no reduction in work load requested of all departments of the company? Known will be
   - Whether an increase in efficiency by those remaining can realistically absorb the work of those laid off.
   - If overtime work will have to be employed to make up the difference and how much and what it will cost.
   - If service will suffer, to what extent.

The point is that warehousing should be so much in control that inquiries about efficiency and service should be decided and answered from strength and conviction. Whether this or that should be or can be done is decided objectively based on facts.

Facts are really quite easy to obtain provided that the following basics are established:

1. What is the warehousing charter?
2. How much space is required to provide proper storage based on the type of space and storage equipment involved?
3. How effectively is the space being used considering the constraints involved?
4. How long should it take to do each type of work involved?
5. How effectively is the labor being utilized considering the present constraints involved?
6. Based on the foregoing, what shipping dates can be realistically promised?
7. How effectively are the promised shipping dates being met?
8. What is the status of customer relations?

The Proper and Improper Use of Standards

The standards and performance against these standards should be computerized. Minimal time should be consumed to make inquiries of the computer to provide data on which to base decisions or to provide others with the data for them to make decisions. However, care should be taken to avoid using the basic standards per se for decision making. When it comes to determining answers to inquiries about scheduling and actually what will happen, basic standards must be modified by performance to reflect actual experience.

For example, the unloading of certain merchandise from a certain type of rail car should take one hour according to the standard. Actual experience is that it has taken an average of one and a half hours. Performance measurement shows that this particular work is at 67 percent of standard (1.0 hour ÷ 1.5 hours). When estimating how long it will take in the future to do this work, the 67 percent performance (1.5 hours in this car) should be used.

To those who are not fully acquainted with the use of work standards for scheduling the example given may initiate valid questions such as

1. Is the standard correct?
2. If the standard is correct, why doesn't supervision make the employees unload within the standard time?
3. If the standard is so inaccurate (1.0 hour standard versus 1.5 hours actual), why use standards?

Probably the standard is correct. There are many reasons why the workers are not meeting standard. Maybe they are using wrong methods, and supervision has not gotten around to teaching the correct (standard) way to perform the function.

Standards should be based on the best methods. These may or may not be what the employees are using. Perhaps the standard is wrong, and it should be corrected.

There may be a backlog of standards which requires investigation and correction or instruction on how to perform the work to conform to the standards. In any case, the process of using standards need not wait until all standards are perfect. The use of performance measurement is a valid means to factor standards to actual performance. The fact that in this case performance was only 67 percent tells supervision there is a problem, and it should be investigated as soon as priorities permit.

Space Utilization Standards

Commonly, the effective utilization of warehouse space receives less attention than does that of personnel and customer service, yet the best utilization of space is nearly as important as the best utilization of employees, except that the well-being of employees should always take precedence over buildings and equipment. Both cost money, and usually one or the other rank first or second in the magnitude of warehouse operations costs. As a general rule (but one that has many exceptions), the lease cost of 10,000 square feet of 20 feet clear storage space costs about the same as one warehouse operator.

Space utilization standards and the performance measurement system require the same engineering analysis as do work standards. While space utilization standards are expressed in decimal parts of a cubic foot per unit for a particular stock keeping unit (SKU), the work standards are expressed in decimal parts of an hour per unit for a particular SKU and specific function (such as staging or putting into storage).

Performance measurement for space utilization tells management something quite different than it does for work standards. It tells how much unused storage space there is if all inventories were stored according to their standards. This is important to know. For example, if the space utilization performance is 70 percent for a 1,000,000-cubic-foot storage area, a bit of quick arithmetic will reveal there is 300,000 cubic feet not being used, available for more products. It also says that the warehouse cannot take an additional 500,000 cubic feet of storage, and if imposed on it, the aisles will be filled with inventory, work efficiency will drop off drastically, and warehouse activity may even come to a screeching halt.

The answer to the age-old question of whether efficiency or service should be emphasized is *both*. The way to do this is to base answers to questions about performance on valid data that the standards and performance measurement provide. The old adage that everything has a price is appropriate. Valid standards and performance measurement provide objective answers to what the effects of warehouse demands will cost in personnel, equipment, and space.

Chapter 4

How to Evaluate and Select the Warehouse Site and Location

CHAPTER HIGHLIGHTS

This chapter focuses on the many things that should be considered in the evaluation and then the selection of, first, the general location of a warehouse and, then, the specific site. A pioneering effort is taken to segregate clearly those factors that relate to location and those that relate to the site and then to interface them to arrive at the optimum place for the warehouse. Included is a discussion of how a computerized model can help. There are many factors that affect the twofold location-site concern that too commonly do not receive the attention deserved; for location alone, a dozen factors are discussed. Then because the facility represents a major investment, innovative ways to finance the venture are offered with the cognition that how it is financed is as real a cost as the bricks and mortar. Finally, insights are provided about the interesting question: What about mineral rights?

Before determining the right location and best site for your warehouse, you need to be certain that warehousing is truly justified. Considerable time and effort can be wasted in determining the right place for a warehouse and then to learn that the facility will not materialize because it has not been adequately justified and authorized.

Whether a warehouse is needed or not is really not within the warehouse manager's scope of authority and responsibility. You should be deeply involved in both design and operational concerns, but the justification should come from the broader view of physical distribution or business logistics. The final decision making should then come from top management (either the head of the profit center or the CEO).

Establishing a new warehouse generally constitutes a major investment in people, inventories, and capital expenditure or lease commitment. Of course, if the warehouse is only a small operation with a nominal investment in inventory, the expense and commitment are considerably less. This chapter is oriented more to substantial warehousing, though it relates to smaller warehousing as well.

WAYS IN WHICH INVENTORY IS INFLUENCED BY ADDING WAREHOUSES

An aspect of warehousing receiving more and more concern, as the United States strives to retain its producer status is the amount invested in inventories. Before a new warehouse location is added, all that is possible should be done to determine whether it is necessary, and if so, to what extent.

The application of the JIT (just-in-time) concept is supposed to reduce inventories. Substantive warehouse inventories should not be necessary if your company is practicing or is committed to practicing JIT in the near future. On the other hand, if your company is in the position of supplying materials to another company that is committed to JIT, the client company probably is pushing a good part of its inventory support back, thereby causing you to carry more inventory than before business ever heard of JIT. Additional warehouse locations tend to increase inventories (which are being scrutinized more closely than ever before). The following section addresses this thorny subject.

The question that must be answered before the search for and evaluation of locations can be pursued is: What will be the effects on inventories by adding warehouses? If the location study is to replace an existing warehouse, the effects will be minimal. If, however, it is to add one or more facilities, the effects could be substantial.

It should be recognized that the more warehouse locations a company has, the more total inventory will be required to serve the same customer shipments—even though there is no change in the market served and no change in the number of SKUs (Store Keeping Units) warehoused. Therefore, the sum of the benefits of having additional locations must be more than the extra inventory-carrying costs that will be incurred.

Inventory increases with the number of locations because of the quantity of reserve stock carried at each location. This extra inventory is intended to prevent outages caused by unexpected delays in receipts and unexpected increases in shipments. The quantity of inventory which is established to improve delivery time to customers is composed of two parts. First is that quantity which the company is expected to ship during the time it takes to order and receive a replacement from the supplier. The other part is that inventory held in reserve to use in case there are unexpected delays in supply and/or higher than expected customer demand.

For example, if the quantity of outbound shipments of a specific SKU is 100 during a 28-day period, and the lead time to receive the replenishment supply is two weeks, maintaining an inventory would require a stock replenishment order of 50 units to be placed as the previous order of 50 is received every two weeks. If, however, supply and demand are not constant, a "reserve" stock (also referred to as "safety," "buffer," "cushion," or "minimum" stock) would have to be carried to cover these fluctuations. The reserve amount depends on how drastic the fluctuations are, and to what degree customer shipping delays are acceptable. What is acceptable should be expressed as a company objective or degree of quality that is approved by top management. Many warehouse managers think this is within their realm of authority, but it is not so unless he or she is also the CEO.

Figure 4.1(a) illustrates the effect on inventory when demand (customer orders) and supply (replenishment from production or outside suppliers) are constant. Figure 4.1(b) shows only demand fluctuations, and 4.1(c) shows both demand and supply fluctuations. The dashed diagonal lines show how inventory is depleted over time by outbound shipments to customers. The vertical lines show inventory replenishment with the arrival of stock from the supplier, the company's own production facility, in this case.

The constraints of the graphically illustrated inventory processes are that production can accept from the warehouse only one order every two weeks. It is supposed to produce all asked of it at that time, but it cannot deviate from the every-two-week schedule. This is because the equipment setup time to produce these units is prohibitively expensive if done more frequently.

How much is ordered depends on how heavy warehouse-to-customer shipments have been for the previous two weeks. The warehouse orders from production the amount to bring the inventory level to what it expects to be a two-week supply, 50 units.

Figure 4.1(a) shows the orderly effect on inventory when supply and demand rates are constant. A quantity of 50 units is ordered from production every two weeks and delivered to the warehouse two weeks later—just as the last of the previously received stock is depleted (a classical example of JIT). This has all the niceties of inventory management. An average of only 25 units (maximum of 50 units and minimum of "0") inventory supports sales of 100 units every 28 days. This is ideal, but it is not reality. It just does not happen this way.

Figure 4.1(b) shows the amount of reserve inventory necessary to make good the commitment of 100 percent on-time customer shipments when demand fluctuates from the normal 50 units to 100 units during a two-week interval. The sole purpose of this extra reserve is to take care of sales fluctuations which can be twice normal (100 units) over a two-week period. Now the inventory to support sales varies from 100 units to 50 units and occasionally (when demand doubles) to "0."

Figure 4.1(c) shows the effect on inventory by having both a reserve stock of 50 to cover when demand doubles and an additional reserve of 50 units to cover delays by production of up to two weeks in supplying the warehouse. Now the 100 units reserve stock permits satisfying the quality level of 100 percent on-time shipments even when demand doubles and production is two weeks late shipping the replenishment stock. This increases the average inventory again. How much depends on the probability of demand increases occurring at the same times as supply delays.

Even Figure 4.1(c) does not truly represent the real world; it is still too orderly. If the real world were really like this, other steps could be taken other

FIGURE 4.1 How Warehouse Inventory is Influenced by Fluctuations in Supply and Demand (effects upon reserve inventories)

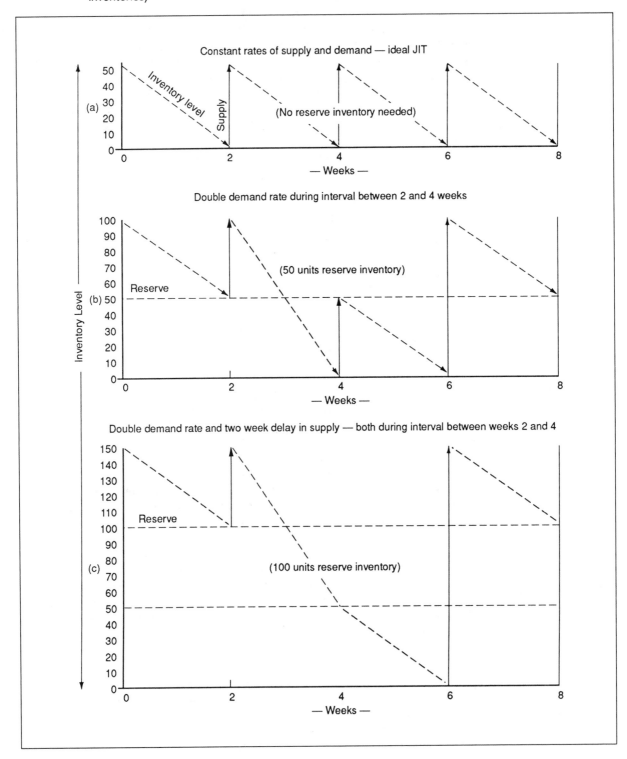

than increasing inventory, for example, finding ways to reduce the high production costs for setups, having a depot inventory at the factory to permit quick shipments to cover the unexpected, decreasing the number of field warehouses carrying this product, and so on. This last reason relates directly to the subject of adding and therefore locating warehouses. You are not confronted with the task of selecting a location if there is no need for the warehouse.

A precise formula could be devised to show how much inventory increases in total by adding warehouses. Such a formula, however, would be extremely complex and unwieldy if all influencing factors are included. If they are not, the validity is reduced correspondingly. In most cases, it is enough to recognize that as inventory is duplicated, the total inventory increases to maintain the same level of delivery service. This statistical phenomenon is illustrated in throwing dice. Your chance of throwing "snake eyes" or "box cars" or any other doubles is 1 in 36 throws (6×6). The greater number of times you throw, the greater the likelihood the law of averages will prevail. The same applies to inventory: the more orders shipped from an inventory, the more accurately you can predict averages; conversely, the fewer orders placed on an inventory (which occurs when you add warehouses), the less predictable are occurrences. Simply, there are fewer chances for increases and decreases offsetting each other.

Using the analogy of throwing dice again, if you throw only one die, your chance of any specific number coming up is 1 in 6. When you throw two dice, the chance of a specific double coming up is 1 in 36. Translating this to warehouse inventories, with the same customer orders, you have a better chance of predicting what will happen with one warehouse than you do when the same orders are split between two warehouses.

All this discussion of effect on inventories assumes an inventory situation consisting of many different customers ordering varying amounts at random or nearly at random. Of course, the farther from random the situation is, the less need for making decisions based on chance. For example, if all customer ordering is 100 percent predictable, adding warehouses need not increase inventories at all, provided of course that supply is also 100 percent reliable. Here there is no need for reserve inventories.

If everything that affects inventories can be predicted and planned perfectly, there is no cause to increase inventory regardless of how many warehouses are added. There is, however, a bit of a problem matching a perfect inventory situation with perfect planning.

TWELVE FACTORS THAT AFFECT THE GENERAL LOCATION

Once it has been determined that a warehouse of a certain size will be used in the physical distribution plan, the next step is to choose its location. Proper selection of warehouse locations is essential to an effective distribution system. The difference between carefully selected locations and random selections could well mean the difference between a successful warehouse system and one that is doomed to failure.

Inappropriate locations could result in many serious problems such as poor service to customers, high operating costs, excessive loss due to theft, and inordinate freight costs. The selection of warehouse locations is occasionally based on either the warehouse or sales manager's desire to live in a certain place. Sometimes it is based on another, nearly as bad, reason—an exceptionally good buy in real estate. Such personal and incidental reasons should remain secondary to those that have a direct bearing on the success of the warehouse operation—at least from the view point of high-quality warehousing.

Note: Computer programs are available to assist in determining the optimum location for warehouses in a physical distribution system. The term "optimum" is used here because it is truly an unusual situation where all the factors influencing location are clearly positive or negative. Usually some factors are positive, others negative, and still others are neutral. Consultants as well as computer programs can be employed to help determine the optimal warehouse locations. In many situations either or both can be appropriately used and are well worth their price tag.

Of critical importance is that the factors that influence location are understood by someone in the company. Presumably this will be a warehouse staff analyst, the warehouse manager or someone within the physical distribution department.

Computers are only as good as their programs and input data. The same program and resultant data are not equally applicable to all companies. This is so even with companies that produce the same products such as canned foods. Many things affect warehouse location other than product type, for example, the size of company, its marketing objectives, and the location of its supply source(s).

The process of determining the factors to be considered is not a function for the computer. Nor is the process of assigning values to components. These are value judgments that reside with the corporate decision makers. However, after the parameters of the study have been defined and all parts weighted as to their relative importance a computer assessment can be afforded.

In the paragraphs that follow, 12 factors that influence warehouse location, including a discussion of important considerations for each, are considered. A valuation chart is provided that illustrates how to organize the study of these factors; it is designed to be used with or without computer assistance. Perhaps the chart's most valuable contribution is in motivating those who make the location study to become aware of the many pertinent considerations—and to recognize that these factors should be weighted differently with reference to their contribution to the main objectives of the facility.

Determine the Main Objective(s) of the Warehouse

The overall objective of the warehouse is the single most important consideration. As in the case of not seeing the forest for the trees, so it is possible to become so captivated with one or two advantages of a certain location that the overall purpose of the warehouse is severely compromised. This could be as simple as the dominant person involved pressing for a given location because he or she would like to live there. Another example is having transportation costs weighted out of proportion to their true value because the traffic manager is the dominant person in the evaluation or simply because transportation costs are most obvious and can be more easily measured.

For instance, if the main purpose of the warehouse is to support the sales effort by providing more responsive service, this should be established and remain foremost in the study and evaluation. The elements that contribute most to support this should be valued higher than those that are not directly related.

If, however, the sole purpose of warehousing is to improve delivery time (which is only one part of customer service), this indicates the solution to be a location near the customers or simply a more rapid means to reach customers from the existing inventory location. If rapid transit is too expensive (such as air freight) or is just not practical for other reasons, close proximity to the customers is probably the answer. On the other hand, if the main purpose is to absorb the oversupply of inventory that results from economical production runs, the location may be altogether different. The location should probably be at or near the production facility with secondary importance being assigned to customer delivery time.

If the purpose of warehousing is mainly to serve an isolated community or region, obviously the warehouse should be located in that limited area, and priority given to those things that will contribute most to its success. After satisfying this basic requirement, attention should be directed to the secondary (yet possibly very important objectives), such as potential for real estate appreciation and avoiding a certain labor union or organized labor altogether.

Determining the optimum warehouse location can be rather complicated and can include many different factors. The company's objectives for the warehouse should be kept in focus throughout the process of research, evaluation, and decision making. So important is this, the search for location should not begin until these objectives have been clearly and authoritatively established.

Evaluate Transportation Costs and Service Issues

Transportation is for many warehouse location studies the most important consideration. It is common, however, to give it too much importance because it is so obvious, and it seems relatively easy to measure. Also it is all too common to treat transportation costs as being ordained rather than costs that require thorough engineering to assure validity within context of the warehouse objectives. Transportation has a great deal of potential for logistics trade-offs which should be competently explored, evaluated, and determined before reliable transportation costs can be nailed down.

Total transportation-related costs include the cost effects of other warehouse functions not normally considered transportation—such as vehicle loading and unloading. It also affects inventories as related to transit times, the likelihood of damage, and service reliability. Further, transportation is inextricably involved with the often sensitive areas of reciprocity, the issue of private versus common carriers, gratuities, and rate negotiations. The costs of transportation are not valid until the best means have been objectively determined and then other related factors optimized in relation to trade-offs and the overall objective of the facility.

Trucking Costs and Services   Nearly all warehouses use some form of truck service. The following questions should be asked about trucking costs and services.

1. What truck lines serve the location and will they meet the warehouse's requirements? What are their reputations for costs and services?

This evaluation should start with becoming well acquainted with the prospective trucking firms and their charges, procedures, policies, equipment, and terminals. Then check their references with operations similar to your own that use their services.

2. When will pickups and deliveries be made—early morning or late afternoon? Do the truck schedules and routings satisfy the warehouse requirements?

A warehouse can be located adjacent to a truck terminal but be unable to use its services or receive worse service than if the terminal were many miles away. This could be because the trucking is for another purpose altogether or the service is poor because the nearby warehouse falls victim to the trucking company's most efficient routing. The trucks are routed to make deliveries on their way out and pick up shipments on their return to the terminal for consolidation to other places. The time of pickup and availability of space to pick up at an adjacent warehouse is commonly dependent on the time taken and space consumed in delivery to and picking up for the more distant customers. The result is that the nearby customers often receive the worst service.

3. To what extent should proprietary trucking be used?

If employed with prudence, a warehouse or a system of warehouses can often operate its own trucks with better service and at lower costs for at least a part (if not all) of the freight. The warehouse can select that freight which is best for its trucks (contributes most to savings) and give the remainder to public carriers. Yet, caution should be exercised in carrying this practice to an extreme which would result in giving only the poor freight to common carriers. If this happens, it is to be expected that the common carriers will give poor service in return or find reasons to avoid the warehouse account entirely. However, nonprofitable freight for a proprietary trucking operation does not necessarily mean nonprofitable freight for common carriers. It could fit in nicely with their equipment and routings but not those of the warehouse.

4. What are the costs and services for handling piggybacks and containers?

If there is extensive use of these means, costs should be lower and service better by locating near a piggyback terminal and container loading dock. Charges and service for pickup and delivery of piggyback and containers should be investigated before the warehouse location is selected. The charges should be compared to the warehouse costs for performing the service with leased or owned equipment. If the savings are substantial, the proprietary service costs should be used in the location study. If marginal, the common carrier charges should be used. A location should not be based on the marginal savings of a warehouse operating its own trucks.

5. To what extent will small-shipment services such as Parcel Post (federal government) or United Parcel Services (private company) be used? If considerable, these costs and services should influence where the warehouse is located. Certain delivery times are guaranteed routinely by these organizations such as next day or second day. These could play a significant part in the customer service capabilities of the warehouse provided small shipments are a substantial part of its shipping.

Water Transportation Concerns   If water transportation is commonly used serious consideration should be given to locating at a port. Occasionally situations arise where locating with access to water transportation will make possible substantial land transportation savings. Having the alternative of using water transportation can be used as leverage to negotiate lower truck or rail charges. There are circumstances where the following statement effects wonders. "If you want our freight you'll have to haul for the water rate."

Another consideration is that of locating within a free port zone. This may permit substantial savings in duties, taxes, insurance, and interest on money tied up in inventories. (The many advantages of locating within a free zone are discussed in Chapter 2.) There are also inland free zones that should be considered if water transportation is not an integral part of the warehouse's transportation. This would permit the warehouse to realize the free zone privileges without locating near the docks. In some cases locating near the water entails higher land cost, more traffic congestion, and higher wages than for inland warehouses.

Extent That Rail Transportation Would Be Used If railroad transportation is commonly used, the warehouse must have its own rail siding connected with the right main line.

Railroads provide different services and utilize alternate trackage to various parts of the country. Some are only trunk lines over short distances; others can service large sections of the country with their own tracks. Most often distant shipments involve changing from one railroad to another, possibly many times. Time delays and varying costs will result—depending on the routing and the many authorities involved.

The initial value of rail service in the United States has diminished in favor of truck service. In comparison to other technologically advanced countries, railroads here have been sorely neglected. The reasons for this are many. Primarily claimed is that the railroads must install and maintain their own railways while trucking contributes considerably less than their share for truck ways (highways). Although truck companies vigorously deny this allegation, the results (claim the proponents) speak for themselves.

Another important reason for the subordination of railroad transportation is that of political influence on government. The combination of suppliers of truck (and bus) related transportation has far more lobbying power than that of the railroads. On the side of trucking are those companies that supply the vehicles, tires, diesel, or gas and the powerful Teamsters' Union. The economical and political clout of this consortium is awesome. True, the makers of rail engines and cars, and the suppliers of railroad diesel fuel, could form an alliance to thwart the trucking influence, but they constitute far less power in comparison. In fact the suppliers of trucks and fuel are mostly the same as the suppliers for rail. Their reasons to give more support to the trucking industry is that much, much more equipment and supplies are used per ton mile of trucking than that of rail. Indicative of this difference is the comparison of trucking costs and those of rail to move materials. The fuel utilization difference alone is quoted as high as 40 to 1, meaning it costs 40 times as much for fuel per ton mile to move freight by truck as it does by rail. The main reason is the relationship of friction and resistance imposed by rubber tires on the roadway compared to steel wheels on steel rails. Further, the useful life of railroad equipment is correspondingly advantageous. Even the "ancient" Pullman cars, so popular in this country during the late nineteenth and early twentieth centuries are still in active use in "less developed" countries.

How all this relates to location studies is that in general having a rail siding is not as important a requirement as it used to be. This is evidenced by the far greater share of warehouse buildings being constructed by speculators without rail sidings. This does not necessarily translate into a premium charge for sites with rail service as the scarcity would indicate because the market for such buildings is correspondingly less.

Of course, if your operations require rail service, obviously you have to concern yourself with rail-served locations. You could pay more for the land because of this feature; on the other hand, you may pay less for the same reason—if the land is owned by a railroad company, you will be looked on with favor if you use rail. Railroad companies would prefer all its land purchasers use rail services.

Cautions About Transportation Cost Studies   The warehouse should be located to permit the lowest total inbound and outbound freight costs—within the constraints of the facility's objectives. You should not go about achieving the lowest transportation on its own, irrespective of its objectives and its charter to do business. It is not difficult to attain the lowest freight costs, but it is something else to achieve the lowest freight costs within the framework of meeting the warehouse's total objectives.

Transportation costs are relatively easy to measure and highly visible. This is both good and bad. Not too many costs in business can be so clearly identified. This characteristic, however, can easily lead to erroneous conclusions. For instance, transportation costs may be weighted more than they truly should be and dominate the results of the location study, when other elements that are not so easily determined should be given greater consideration.

Students of transportation costs assume that under a given set of circumstances there exists a specific rate for a certain type of freight of a definite quantity going to a particular destination via a specific mode of transportation. The problem with this reasoning is that the set of circumstances that serves as the foundation for the rest of the line of reasoning is not specific. It is a variable that entails many alternatives. These alternatives (which are each composed of several factors) can drastically alter the conclusion of the study.

Taking all eventualities into consideration would be too costly and too unwieldy to manage for many warehouses, especially those that have a wide variety of product types, shipment sizes, and carrier options. It is important, though, that at least the significant factors are given consideration to the extent that the results of the study are valid in the real world of warehousing.

A common error is to attribute unwarranted validity to hypothetical transportation studies that are based on "nonengineered" freight situations. An example of this is to use quoted rates without research and negotiations to determine the lowest freight rates within the warehouse service objectives. As warehouse operating time standards should be based on the most efficient methods and procedures, so freight costs used in transportation studies should be based on the most efficient means within the constraints of the company's objectives for customer service.

Following is a list of errors and oversights common to transportation studies:

1. Basing costs on published freight rates without research and negotiation to determine the lowest-cost modes and routings.
2. Using freight rates for modes of transportation that are not consistent with the company objectives for service, customer relations, and so on.
3. Performing insufficient study to determine load sizes—using loads too large, too small, or not representative in other ways.
4. Neglecting to include tare weights in addition to product weights (to arrive at total ship weights) or comparing freight rates in which some include tare weights but others do not.
5. Failing to compare proprietary carrier costs and service with those of common carriers.
6. Using proprietary carrier costs that are not realistic because the cost center to gather pertinent data is ill-defined and/or poorly maintained.

7. Not making appropriate assumptions about the use of consolidations and pool distributions—too much or too little.

8. Failing to include the extra costs for consolidation and pool distribution such as extra handling, stop-offs, and so on.

9. Overlooking the different warehouse costs relating to the different types of transportation.

10. Neglecting to take into account the application of just-in-time inventory control which usually means more frequent, smaller shipments, and possibly captive and specialized carriers.

11. Causing simple arithmetic errors which are common when processing large quantities of statistics for a one-time study.

All these cautions about transportation studies are not meant to put down such studies. To the contrary, it is recognized that freight cost is often the major cost element and therefore the most important consideration. Because of this, extra caution should be exercised that such studies should be conducted with the utmost care and professionalism, commensurate with their importance. A small error here may have greater effect on the conclusion than a large error in one of the other considerations.

Accessibility of the Warehouse to Employees   A different type of transportation that should be considered is that which involves moving people, particularly employees. More and more management is accepting the fact that the overriding consideration in conducting business is people. Therefore, the accessibility of the warehouse to employees and others who come to conduct business is an important consideration of location.

If the warehouse is located too far from residential areas, the commuting problem will probably reflect in employee relations. Commonly this is manifested in the need to pay higher wages and salaries to compensate for the extra travel. Another consideration is that many companies pay for employees' relocating expenses if their place of employment is moved over a certain distance. To retain valued employees, the company adopts a policy to pay moving expenses. While this is not a major factor in comparison with most other considerations, it should be given its due recognition—with greater emphasis if the warehouse is a part of a distribution center that houses sales, accounting, and other personnel of the company.

If the warehouse in consideration is one of a network of many warehouses, there will probably be visitors from other locations and the company headquarters in particular. This suggests that further consideration should be given to accessibility to a national airport so that visiting the warehouse does not become too great a chore. From the warehouse manager's point of view, it may be desirable to put obstacles in the path of visitors from headquarters, but for the "good of the company," it is probably best to keep this to a minimum.

Personnel Considerations

Whenever any change is made in business, consideration should be given to its effect upon employees. Frequently it is given too little importance, or it is biased favoring certain types of personnel, usually management. Locating a warehouse is one of those occurrences that can easily involve improper considerations of employees.

It is not uncommon to locate the warehouse where the warehouse manager or sales manager would like to live. On the other hand, top management might overreact to this bias by going overboard to avoid letting where people want to live influence the location. Both approaches in the extreme are wrong. Clear perspective is required for unbiased judgment to prevail.

Labor Supply   While labor availability is generally not as great a concern in warehousing as it is in many other aspects of industry (such as those requiring more specialized training or greater number of workers), it is still an important factor. Of particular importance is to locate in an area that is conducive to warehousing. This could be where there is other warehousing, provided the area is not known for labor problems. It could be where the surrounding industry is completely foreign to warehousing—such as farming or ranching. The labor supply for warehousing is often very good in communities which are predominantly agricultural. Jobs in warehousing here are often prized, because of their more regular hours and more regular paychecks. The workers are used to hard work on the farm or ranch and are accustomed to putting in the full hard days common in warehousing.

Caution should be exercised about surrounding industries having predominantly highly skilled and/or strongly organized employees. Your best warehouse employees are attracted to better-paying jobs, or the unions of these higher-paid workers take over the warehouse employees. It is not unusual to have machinists, longshoremen, steel workers, or other types of unions organize and take in less numerous warehouse workers. By asserting their union affiliation on warehousing, they impose work rules and wage scales characteristic of their own work, which may not be at all compatible. Another incompatibility is that of paid holidays. Observed holidays by warehousing should agree with those of the main segment of business it serves. For instance, a warehouse which serves residential construction should have holidays that coincide with this industry, not with that of grocery clerks. Normally the best labor supply for warehousing is in warehousing communities or in communities not dominated by highly organized unions that are foreign to warehousing.

Equal Opportunity Employment   While it has always been that people should be given equal employment opportunity—regardless of race, color or creed—the application of this lofty concept has been rather late in coming in U.S. history. Equal opportunity for both sexes has been recognized even later, and its application is also still in the process of being fully implemented.

What this means to locating warehouses is simply to recognize that equal opportunity is now being seriously implemented. Unless company management wants to put its facilities in the forefront to spearhead justice, it should avoid communities where this is a hotbed of contention. Obvious extremes are to locate in an all-white community and employ only black warehouse personnel, or vice versa, or to employ only males or only females. Sex, race, color, or creed have yet to be found significant in assessing the competence of warehouse personnel.

Real Estate Considerations

A warehouse constitutes a piece of real estate and a corresponding value quite independent of the functions that will be performed there. For this reason help should be enlisted from real estate specialists. The values that can be realized by taking into consideration the real estate potential can be substantial. Of course, if the real estate considerations take precedent over those of warehouse operations and transportation, it should be only with very top-level executive authority. This is not to imply it should not happen, because sometimes it should—depending on the company's goals and objectives. It does mean, however, that warehousing should not be compromised for the sake of real estate unless clearly understood and sanctioned by the appropriate company authority.

Appreciation Many companies have realized bonanzas through luck or design by locating their warehouses in areas where property values have greatly appreciated. Some public warehousing companies exist and operate with the primary objective being to service the property debt through public warehousing while the facility appreciates in value for eventual sale to realize a capital gain.

One of the largest ever (in space availability) public warehousing companies developed an impressive 80,000,000 square feet of high-cube warehouses using public warehousing as the means to buy land cheap and to service debt. Their building design was standard: multiples of 40,000 square feet, 28-foot clearance, 48-inch dock height, rail siding, many truck doors, and minimum to no office space. Later when real estate appreciated, it sold off the properties at inflated prices and quit the warehousing business. The grandiose venture was apparently very profitable. It was made even more profitable by being able to buy land cheap, cheaper than other buyers because the company bought from railroad companies with the implication that the railroad company would benefit from the considerable rail freight the warehouses would generate. This involved some legal problems, but apparently not enough to prevent making huge fortunes for the owners. While it is not expected that everyone can pull off such a venture, the concept applies in lesser measure to the location and ownership of any warehouse.

A company need not own its facilities to realize the real estate benefits in the manner here discussed. Ownership of the property is the most common means, but it is not the only way. Favorable lease arrangements provide another means to capital gain. When I headed up a public warehousing company, we purchased a sublease from a primary lessee which had 15 years to go on a constant, "flat" rate. At the time the lease rate was about 50 percent of comparable other leased space. We paid up front to the lessee which was a large oil company, the equivalent of three years' savings afforded by the lease. The result was that both the lessee and the sublessee (us), benefited—to the chagrin of the lessor, the landlord.

Flat-rate leases are not as common as they were before the high inflation rates of the late 1970s and early 1980s because landlords feel they lose money by not being able to raise their rates to keep pace with inflation. They are probably not as badly off as they claim, particularly when they use borrowed money at fixed rates to build initially. Those who develop facilities with cash and give long-term fixed-rate leases definitely lose out during inflation. They use strong money to develop the facilities and get paid back with weak money.

If money is borrowed at variable rates and the lease rates are also variable and both are tied to the same index, all should come close to equity regardless of inflationary effects. Relating this to warehouse location studies, real estate considerations are very real and can be paramount in choosing a location. Different locations have different appreciation potentials. There are occasions when paying more for property initially to get the best is the wisest investment. Of course, it is desirable to have "Lady Luck" on your side as well.

Nationally Recognized Distribution Centers When locating a warehouse or a system of warehouses, management should look first to the distribution centers of the nation. Certain cities and localities are natural centers for physical distribution. Locating in or near these will greatly reduce the risk of warehouse investment. Some cities have a much greater proportion of their business and real estate related to warehousing than do others. This is so because they are geographic centers of industry or population or because they serve as a hub or gateway for rail, truck, or water shipping.

Another reason, quite unrelated to the natural flow of goods, is that certain cities and states induce warehousing to locate within their boundaries by establishing favorable tax conditions and financial arrangements. For these reasons and others, including the promotional efforts of interested parties, a large part of the economy of certain areas depends heavily on warehousing. Other localities that may have greater population or are centers of a specific type of industry will have little or no warehousing. Some of the major marketing and warehousing centers of the nation are

> Seattle
> Portland
> San Francisco–Oakland Bay Area
> Los Angeles Basin
> Kansas City, Kansas, and Missouri
> Dallas
> Houston
> New Orleans
> Atlanta
> Miami–Jacksonville
> Nashville
> State of New Jersey
> Great Lakes Region (Chicago, in particular)

This list is by no means conclusive. The list is not static, either. New centers will emerge and be added to, or take the place of, those that are now most prominent. Also, certain localities such as Reno, Nevada, and Salt Lake City, Utah, while not tremendous population centers, have disproportionately large amounts of warehousing. This is because Nevada and Utah encourage, with tax advantages and other means, companies to locate depot warehouses to serve the West Coast industrial and population centers. Railroad companies assist in this effort by freely offering through rates from the origin of the freight to the West Coast even though the merchandise comes to rest in Nevada or Utah then later is reloaded on rail for the next destination at the West Coast. The same mix in the outbound car does not have to correspond exactly to that in the inbound car under certain conditions. The railroads do charge a stop-off charge, but this is minimal compared with the savings.

Industrial Parks   Located within the major distribution centers (and many of the lesser centers) are industrial parks or communities which are zoned and maintained to favor warehousing. These parks consist of defined areas, generally in the suburbs of a large city, that are developed and promoted to attract light industry and warehousing. The developers obtain local zoning ordinances and establish specific ordinances of their own to attract and hold the type of business they are after. Although these industrial parks are developed with the primary interest of making money for the landowners and promoters, the parks do provide many real advantages as warehouse locations. Consequently, they are located throughout the nation. It is becoming more and more unusual to build a warehouse in an area all by itself. Warehouses and light industry locate together in clusters whether the name and constraints of "industrial park" are adopted or not.

Advantages of the "industrial park" type of location are the following:

1. Carrier service

   Because an industrial park generally has many businesses that ship and receive, carriers can economically provide regular and reliable service to the area. If payloads cannot be picked up from one customer, they probably can from another. The industrial park provides a ready-made market center for common carriers' services. On the other hand, if a warehouse were to locate by itself away from other businesses that provide freight, it is quite likely that carriers would not provide such good service, because it would be uneconomical for the limited and uncertain amount of freight available. Even railroad companies are able to provide better switching service when many businesses requiring this service are located in the same area.

2. Common interests

   The purpose of industrial parks is to provide an area where the zoning and services will attract and hold certain types of business. Most industrial parks today are set up to attract warehousing and light industry. One advantage of a community that is made up of this type of business is that many interests are common to all. Although the businesses may be competitive in other ways, they have certain similar requirements that can be better served when several companies are doing similar types of business. One business establishment standing alone has only its own strength and resources to draw on, while many collectively are much stronger.

   Some of the common interests that are best satisfied in an industrial park community are

   > Police and security patrol protection
   >
   > Street cleaning and repair services
   >
   > Truck and rail services
   >
   > Low property tax assessments
   >
   > Favorable zoning controls
   >
   > Good restaurants in vicinity
   >
   > Availability of labor supply
   >
   > Increased strength in labor negotiations
   >
   > Availability of equipment and repair services

3. Protection of your investment

   Another important consideration in selecting a warehouse location is to find one that is good now and will remain good. The industrial park location offers some assurance of this. Because of the common interests discussed before, there is a greater likelihood that the community will not change into one that will be undesirable for warehousing. The united pressures that can be brought to bear to maintain favorable conditions serve to protect the individual warehouse investments. A warehouse that is located alone has much less chance of maintaining the desired environment. Other economic or residential interests may exert a stronger influence to satisfy their requirements. If these interests are in conflict with those of warehousing, the warehouse may find its operation being restricted by new zoning laws or some other form of impediment. Since the future of any location involves some hazard, it is best to locate "among friends" who have the same general interests and objectives, thereby minimizing the inherent risk.

4. Effects on financing

Some form of financing will be involved whether the warehouse is to be constructed or use made of an existing building and whether owned or leased. If the facility is to be leased, the better the location (such as in a prime industrial park in a recognized distribution area), the more difficult it is to negotiate favorable terms. This is because the lessor can be more selective about who leases the space. The favorable location will be sought by more potential lessees. If the parent company is one of *Fortune*'s top 500, the lessor will try harder to offer a better deal. If the lessee is a small, new, relatively unknown company, the chances of getting a favorable lease in a prime location are less—far less.

If the warehouse is built-to-suit or purchased outright the better the location the easier it will be to borrow money using the facility for security. Lending institutions look on favorable locations as better security. This becomes obvious if you visualize yourself as the lender. You would want the most favorable location possible to secure a loan because the potential success of the borrower in a prime location is better. If the borrower does default, the chances of getting other tenants to take over the payments or to purchase the facility are also better.

Tax Considerations

Real estate, inventory, and payroll taxes are important in selecting location. A not uncommon mistake is to assume that tax rates are the same throughout the country. They certainly are not. They can vary from none and minimal to high and prohibitive.

There are states and communities within states that deliberately avoid or minimize one or more of these taxes to attract warehousing. There are others that severely apply all these taxes and add assessments on top of them to discourage warehousing in areas that are otherwise extremely attractive to warehousing. These areas find they can extract a good part of their government revenue through these taxes and still not significantly discourage warehousing. For example, certain large cities can apply stiff tax penalties and still be attractive to special types of warehousing because of their unusually high density of people and industry.

Exercise caution about locating in growing bedroom communities, those areas which are mostly residential and people living there commute to other areas to work. The costs of local schools and government are normally high, but their industrial tax base is low. Commonly what industry is there is levied with high taxes and assessments to make up for lack of a substantial industrial tax base. Occasionally, taxes are used by the local government to discourage industry, even light industry like warehousing, from locating there. They want to keep their communities oriented to those of affluence who can afford the luxury of "high-quality" residential living without the nuisance of industry and all that goes with it. They are apparently willing to pay the high real estate taxes that result without the aid of industrial-related taxes.

It is not enough to compare real estate tax "rates." Methods of assessment must be taken into consideration as well. Unfortunately the means of assessment are not precise or even consistent. Some real estate taxes are based on market value, others on initial cost. Complicating this more is that percentages and ratios of the market value and initial cost are used. For example, the tax formula may be 40 percent, 50 percent, or any percent of the market value or initial cost. This has the advantage for the tax collector of arousing less opposition to the tax. Let us say the tax were 12 cents per $100 of 50 percent of market value of $100,000. The formula would read 12 cents per $100 on $50,000. The taxpayer, not knowing the mysteries of taxation, is fearful of complaining because he or she knows their property is worth more than $50,000. The taxpayer is afraid to call attention or "they" might raise it to $100,000.

Some inventory taxes are based on actual cost of inventory as of a specific date; others are based on average cost or standard cost and average inventory. The combinations that have been used are many. Whoever is heading up the location study should get help from appropriate tax experts or spend the time and effort required to develop his or her own expertise. It is not illegal to avoid taxes legitimately; it is intelligent business. Keep in mind that tax collection is based more on fear than logic.

Telephone and the "Three T's"

A time-honored platitude about warehouse location studies is: "Take care of the three T's, and the location will take care of itself." (The three T's are transportation, taxes, and telephone.) The expression has some validity, at least to the extent that if any one of these is overlooked you will have a big void in your study, and the location selected could result in dire consequences. Certainly if telephone communication or transportation were faulty or inadequate, the warehouse could soon become inoperative or incur intolerably high costs. High taxes do not cause operational problems like the other T's, but the excessive costs would cause such a handicap that the only way to get out of the dilemma would be to move again to a more favorable tax climate.

One of the warehouse locations I once selected involved a peculiar telephone situation. It was a build-to-suit leaseback new warehouse. While checking out the telephone aspects of the site, it was learned that the office part of the facility was right on the line separating the jurisdictions of two different telephone companies. The one company covered a relatively small area, and its services were well known to be very poor. The other, a much larger company, had a superior reputation.

Further investigation revealed that the new warehouse design could affect which company to use. The warehouse was quite large, over 100,000 square feet with about one-half of it over 40 feet high. The office and its elaborate telephone system as designed would be located within the boundary of the lesser quality telephone company, or the design could be flipped over so the office would be located within the other company's district. The goal was to have the office within the authority of the best telephone company.

Physical Proximity to Customers

Delivery time to customers directly affects where to locate the warehouse. The following factors affect delivery time.

- The required times to meet the warehouse company's service objectives.
- The availability and costs of transportation to make possible these required times.

○ The travel distance to customers.

○ The *actual travel time* to customers.

These factors will not be always the same at different locations due to the availabilities and costs of different types of transportation. Also of vital importance is the order processing time from when the customer's need is recognized to when the merchandise is delivered to the place of need within the customer's facilities (commonly referred to as "order lapse time").

A lot was said in the preceding two paragraphs. The extent to which these particular concepts are thoroughly studied, developed, and implemented depends on the validity of the transportation phase of the study, possibly the most important part of the location evaluation. Furthermore, making matters more difficult is that each element of the equation should be examined for improvement and feasible alternatives. For instance, if it requires a full day to convey the customers' orders to the warehouse, could the process be shortened by better use of the FAX, telephone, computer-to-computer tie ins?

The two main reasons to locate close to the customers served are psychological and physical. Customers generally "feel" that if a supplier is close by they are better off to deal with it rather than other suppliers that are more distant. The physical part of this is that it is normally the shortest distance between need and supply that results in the least travel time. Experienced warehouse and transportation people know, however, that there are so many exceptions to this that each location must be researched separately for its own peculiarities and uniqueness. A major factor that should not be overlooked is whether customers want to make their own pickups. This will involve taking into consideration the customer's as well as the warehouse's travel distances and times.

Proximity to Other Warehouse

If customer service were the only location consideration, there should be a warehouse in every market locality. For companies that sell nationally, this would mean warehouses in hundreds of cities. Actually, some companies do have hundreds of warehouses in their vast distribution systems. Chain lumber store warehouses are an example of this. Whenever prompt delivery or convenient custom pickups are necessary, companies may require a warehouse in every one of their market localities.

The number of warehouses and where they are located in relation to one another is dependent upon the trade-offs of customer service with the costs of freight, communications, carrying inventory, operations, and so on. The optimum balance of these values will result in the maximum return to the warehouse company.

Normally the more warehouses there are, the better the customer service that is possible because of the closer proximity to customers. Also the more distribution points there are permit the lowest outbound freight costs. This is favorable but only if there is sufficient inbound freight to assure that the savings of outbound freight are not traded away by the increase of inbound freight caused by smaller shipments. It would not be prudent to lower the outbound freight costs at the expense of higher inbound freight unless the better service is of such paramount importance that the higher total costs are more than offset by increased sales.

On the other hand, total inventory and operating costs generally increase with more locations because more locations mean smaller facilities and duplication of inventories. Larger operations generally permit lower unit operating costs because facility fixed costs are spread over more variable units. Fewer separate inventories permit lower total inventories. This is because each location must carry some reserve or buffer stock to cushion against fluctuations in supply and demand.

To the extent the JIT concept of lower inventory is implemented, the need for larger inventories with more points of physical distribution is offset by more effective inventory control. The complete application of JIT, however, is probably not possible in a large network of service-oriented warehouses. This is because the logistic problems increase in a nearly geometric progression as additional locations are added; that is, in ratios of 1, 2, 4, 8, and 16 (two locations twice 1, three are 4 times 1, and five are 16 times that of 1, etc.).

Figure 4.2 shows (in simplified form) the logistical factors of sales income, freight costs, and operations costs and how they relate in providing warehousing service for the huge and sprawling market of Southern California.

Although the figure shows that three warehouses are better than two or four, keep in mind this is only a hypothetical example. Under different circumstances, one warehouse or many strategically located warehouses could be best. The figure does illustrate, however, the nature of trade-offs when dealing with more than one warehouse serving a defined region.

FIGURE 4.2 Logistics of Serving Southern California Market (values expressed in 1000s)

Alternative Distribution Plans	Inventory Units	Sales Income	Freight Cost			Operations Cost			Other Inv. Carrying Cost	Total Costs	Gross Income
			In	Out	Total	Direct	Indirect	Total			
One Warehouse											
Los Angeles	10	$300	$20	$40	$60	$50	$20	$ 70	$40	$170	$130
Two Warehouses											
Los Angeles	8										
San Diego	5										
Total	13	390	28	32	60	72	28	100	50	210	180
Three Warehouses											
Los Angeles	6										
San Diego	5										
Santa Barbara	5										
Total	16	450	35	25	60	80	30	110	60	230	220
Four Warehouses											
Los Angeles	5										
San Diego	5										
Santa Barbara	5										
Long Beach	3										
Total	18	460	42	23	65	88	32	120	70	255	205

When the number of warehouses is increased to serve the same area, the following tends to happen:

  Total inventory increases
  Total sales income increases
  Total inbound freight costs increases
  Total outbound freight costs decreases

There is a point at which adding warehouses reduces the gross income. For this illustration the three warehouse plan is that point.

To determine net profitability, the cost of materials, sales, and other company costs must be added to those included in this exhibit.

The figure further shows that for this particular circumstance, each additional warehouse increases sales income but also increases the costs of freight operations, and inventory carrying costs. There is the point, however, that additional warehouses reduce net income. In this case the third warehouse maximizes profits. The one-, two-, and four-warehouse systems are not as profitable as the three-warehouse system. In most similar studies, the number of warehouses added should stop at the point of maximized profits—but not always. This is not a warehouse management decision. Perhaps top management wants to incur the extra costs of adding one or more warehouses beyond those providing maximum profitability. This, for example, might be a part of a grand strategy to block competitors getting a foothold in the market, or for many other reasons. It is quite enough for warehouse location analysts to show those who have the responsibility what the effects are of adding warehouses. Good decision making becomes easier in direct relation to the quality of information on which judgment is based.

Facility Cost and Value

Facility cost stands as the prime factor in warehouse site selection considerations, and the particular site cost is commonly the main component of the facility cost. A common error is to compare purchase prices of different sites as though they are absolutes. One of the very poor reasons for this is because it is such a relief to have one fixed value per site to plug into the overall cost formula. All the other components involve considerable study to derive clean, reliable figures for comparison. Facility costs seem to be one component that can be taken at face value and move on to the other factors. Unfortunately, this is not so. Like any other component of the location and site selection process, facility cost encompasses a host of variations and alternatives. This part of the study should be explored as diligently as any other.

The cost and value of a location are not absolutes; they vary with the methods used in their determination. Different sites entail different financial problems and opportunities because the owners, buyers, and financiers have their own preferences and requirements. An understanding of these differences should help in dealing with this important part of warehouse location.

The real estate cost of a warehouse facility is deceptive. To be able to compare the costs of different facilities, in fact to make any sense at all out of "cost" or "value," you must carefully define what is and is not included. The following are just some of the different things facility costs can mean.

1. The cost of constructing the facility, without including the costs of land, engineering, fees and permits, financing, and so on.
2. The total cost of constructing the facility, including land and all other costs related to bringing the facility to "turn-key" completion.
3. The cost to lease, which can be any one or combination of the following:
   - *Gross Lease.* Lessee pays a monthly amount that includes base rent, taxes, maintenance, and so on. The application of a "gross" lease is usually for relatively small space requirements which are a part of a larger facility and for a relatively short lease term. The landlord, lessor, handles most everything, similar to leasing or renting an apartment. The actual payment of utilities by agreement can be made by either the lessee or the lessor. It varies by the magnitude of these charges, which indicates whether separate meters are justified.

○ *Net Lease and Net, Net Lease.* These two terms are not precise. They are used inconsistently, but even with this limitation they are used occasionally. They generally mean that the lessee pays for some of the related costs and the lessor pays the others. For instance, a net lease could mean that the lessee pays the base rent plus utilities and the lessor pays all other space-related costs. A net, net lease may mean the lessee pays the base lease plus utilities and maintenance of walls and floors and the lessor is responsible for taxes, roof maintenance, insurance, and all else. Net and net, net leases must clearly specify responsibility for each cost because these terms in actual practice are ambiguous.

○ *Triple Net Lease.* This is the most common type of lease for warehouse facilities. It has a far more precise meaning than does net or net, net lease. It is intended to convey the idea that the burden of using the facility is entirely on the back of the lessee. This includes the base lease rate, utilities, taxes, insurance, maintenance, and so on. Everything falls on the lessee, except normal wear and tear, and there should not be too much of that. For example, if the roof leaks, the lessee pays for the repair. The lessor is intended to be free of all concerns except collecting the monthly lease payments. To reduce even this concern, included in the contract are stiff penalties for late payments.

4. The cost to replace the facility, commonly referred to as "replacement cost." This is intended to include all costs starting from scratch to reproduce the same facility as it exists now. If you had a movie film of the total process of creating the present facility and ran the film backward to the virgin site just before purchase, this would include all the components that make up "replacement costs." Probably the cost of mistakes and bungling that seem to some extent common to most large-scale construction projects would be disallowed but little else.

Normally the replacement costs are greater than the initial costs to produce turn-key facilities. This is due to

○ Inflationary influence (land and building materials are now more expensive).

○ Building code and environmental concerns that may have not existed before are now requirements.

5. Total cost to bring the facility to operation—the ready state. This includes the total facility costs plus equipment. This may appear to be extending facility costs a bit too far. Not really. Material handling and storing equipment are becoming more and more an inseparable part of facilities costs. Automatic storage and retrieval systems (ASRS) are commonly constructed right into the building. Some actually utilize the storage racks to support the roof and occasionally the roof and walls. (See Chapter 11.)

6. Value resulting from capitalizing the net income stream. This is a common way to determine the value of leased facilities. It comprises determining what amount of money would have to be invested to yield, at an acceptable interest rate, the triple net income resulting from a facility lease. This sounds more complex than it is. An example may help to clarify. A facility that is leased at a fixed rate (a flat lease) for $120,000 annually ($10,000 monthly) triple net is equivalent to the yield of $1,200,000 invested at 10 percent per year. Therefore, $1,200,000 is the capitalized value of the facility at 10 percent yield.

Affecting this value are the term of the lease (or the remaining term of the lease if it is process) and the financial strength of the lessee. These considerations complicate the valuation process somewhat, but it helps that they follow what can be logically expected. An extension of the foregoing example should smooth this added wrinkle. Assume the lease is for a term of 20 years, and now there are only 10 years to go with an income stream of $120,000 annually. This converts to a value for the facility of $1,200,000, but the replacement cost in this instance is determined to be $2,500,000. The initial cost to put in the facility 10 years ago was perhaps $1,000,000, but it has now appreciated 2.5 times to $2,500,000. In summary the income stream translates to a value of $1,200,000, but the replacement cost translates to a value of $2,400,000. Consequently, what is the present value of the facility—$1,200,000 or $2,400,000?

The reason its value based on capitalizing the income stream is less than half the replacement cost is due to the "fixed" rate of the lease. The resulting income of $120,000 annually is all that can be expected regardless of what the facility is worth in relation to replacement costs or any other measure of value for the next 10 years anyway. Although this may seem unfair to the owner, this is just too bad. The real value is $1,200,000, not $2,500,000. The courts have a history of upholding this type of lease to the chagrin of owners.

For this particular example, the financial strength of the lessee has no effect on the capitalized value of the lease. The value would remain the same even though the lessee had fallen on hard times and developed a bad credit rating even gone into the first phase of bankruptcy, Chapter 11. The lease from the lessee's point of view would retain its extra value (the difference between the capitalized value of the lease and replacement value—as one measure of worth) because even though the lessee cannot, for instance, stay in business to reap the benefits of low monthly payments, the lease still has this intrinsic value. The lease with its 10 more years at relatively low payments is an asset that could be realized by sublease to another company for these remaining "golden" years. Of course, the lease contract must include the right to sublease, which it probably would due to it being a long, 20-year lease.

From the owner's viewpoint you might question: does not the fact that the lease only has 10 years to go at the low rate count for something? Is there not the likelihood that the lease rate can be brought to market value then, which could be three or four times what it is now?

Actually in the world of warehouse finance 10 years into the future is a long, long time. The fact that the lease rate can be increased at that time has little effect on today's valuation. If lucky you might get 10 percent more than the capitalized income stream, but do not count heavily on it.

7. Combination of land lease and construction cost. This results from structuring the finance to benefit two types of investors: one most concerned about an income stream in which income tax is not a concern, such as religious and nonprofit organizations, which are by law exempt from income taxes, the other is definitely concerned about income tax shelters, such as the affluent who will benefit most from them. To accommodate each, the total is divided. The land is leased usually for 30 to 50 years. Since land cannot be depreciated and as such provide tax shelter, this arrangement is best for religious and nonprofit organizations. This has the

added advantage of having the land and improvements revert to the lessor (or the descendents) at the end of the lease period.

The money funded for the improvements is depreciable and thereby provides a tax shelter for the other investor. The tax shelter is particularly attractive because all the costs of the facility, except the land, can be written off. This arrangement has the further advantage that the lessee can declare the lease payments as tax write-off. Handling the facility financing in this manner gets the government to "subsidize" the entire venture.

This is the concept, but exercise caution in trying to apply it without current expertise on what is and what is not allowable by the Internal Revenue Service. Income tax rules have a way of changing from one year to the next. Purportedly they change each time for the better, but what happens is often quite the opposite. The only safe bet about IRS changes seems to be that the forms and rules become more ambiguous.

The value of the facility when the land is leased and the improvements owned is generally decided by capitalizing the income from the land lease separately and then adding replacement value or capitalizing the net income from lease of the improvements. The sum of the two elements equals the total value.

Operating Costs

Operating costs, like facility costs just discussed, can be treated as location-related costs, as site-related costs, or as both. To the extent that operating costs are different from one city to another, the costs should be related to location. Suppose that by comparing different locations, the labor costs are substantially different. These differences should be reflected in the location study. Labor rates vary from one location to another because warehousing can be organized by almost any union with their unique rates or have no union at all. Labor rates can be forecast with a relatively high degree of confidence. The details of determining operation costs are covered in Chapter 5.

Company Image—High or Low Profile

The impression the warehouse facilities make on customers and the public at large can be very important to a company and should be given careful consideration when selecting a location. Image contributes negatively or positively to goodwill and reputation in total. These can have a substantial negative or positive value in marketing company products and in valuing the facility.

The site selection discussed later in this chapter can usually influence image more than in which city or region the warehouse is located. Occasionally, however, there are situations where certain cities have better connotations than others. An example is some of the unusual names of Amish towns in Pennsylvania. Another example is the effects of locating in small hamlets off the traveled highways when company exposure is important. Much better would be to locate on a well-traveled highway or near a hub of highways, or in or close to a well-known city. Of course, the opposite is true if it is in the company's best interests to avoid recognition. Then the little-known or little-seen location would be the best. This is not as unusual as you might expect. A low profile is the best profile for some companies, for instance, those processing hazardous materials and waste.

Community Resources

While the location resources such as availability of transportation services, labor supply, and so on, are pressing requirements to operate efficiently, so community resources of a personal nature are also important. Often these are not recognized for their importance until an error is made in ignoring them with bad results.

Listed here are a few of the community resources that could favorably or unfavorably influence the facility operations and employees' well-being.

1. Effectiveness and responsiveness of the police force.
2. The attitude of the community toward your particular type of warehousing.
3. The adequacy of the schools and colleges for the employees' children as well as for their own educational growth.
4. Availability of repair services for the facility's equipment.
5. Avoidance of areas with pollution problems.
6. Availability and responsiveness of snow removal services if applicable.
7. Availability of housing at reasonable prices.

HOW TO PREPARE THE LOCATION EVALUATION

The factors affecting location explored here may seem to constitute an extremely complex approach to selecting warehouse location. This really is not the case. All factors are pertinent to a varying degree to most warehouse location studies. As such, they should be given due consideration. If the elements affecting location are known and objectively considered, the likelihood of a major error is remote—which by itself is of considerable value.

Big mistakes do happen. One huge production plant and warehouse combination constructed by a company in the top half of *Fortune*'s 500 was located in a very small town situated a large distance from an airport along a lonely stretch of two lane road—"in the middle of no where," according to those who had to live near or visit the facility. Of course, some bad locations are willingly accepted to benefit from otherwise unattainable government subsidies. And if that had been the case here, the governmental concession would have had to have been enormous to have made up for the bad location.

In this case, management thought that by bringing in thousands of employees, it could make over the town as it liked. But it did not happen that way. Before the company came, the high school was not accredited; ten years later it was still not accredited. About everything else that could go wrong did. Labor and management polarized at opposite extremes, as did the company and town people—whose heritage for many went back numerous generations. Not long after the facilities opened, some employees quit rather than accept transfer to the company's "Siberia."

Aside from the severe personnel and community problems that surfaced, the facility went many years without turning a profit. Other companies no doubt have made similar location mistakes. Most of these could have been avoided had even the elementary location factors been given consideration.

A form to assist in comparing different locations is presented in Figure 4.3. Its purpose is to help to organize the various constituents that relate to the warehouse locations being studied. The purposes and factors used in this figure hypothetically relate to locating a warehouse to serve the San Francisco Bay Area.

FIGURE 4.3 Sample Warehouse Location Evaluation

Date _____

Main Purpose(s):

MAIN: Drastically improve customer service to San Francisco Bay Area — 100% next-day delivery

Availability of stock to assure compliance with next-day delivery requirement

NEXT: Lowest total cost to assure compliance with above

Relevant Factors and Values By Location:	Transportation Total	Personnel Commute	Real Estate Values	Impact on Personnel	Taxes	Telephone	Proximity to Customers	Operating Costs	Facility Costs	Company Image	Community Resources			
San Francisco	200	10	70	30	20	30	40	100	50	60	50			660
Oakland	300	20	70	40	40	50	50	150	60	50	40			870
Benecia	250	10	100	10	50	50	20	170	80	30	10			780
* Comparative weights	300	20	100	40	50	50	50	200	80	60	50			1000

Reference Notes:

*Comparative weights have been assigned in relation to the total value of 1000. Values by location and relevant factor are assigned in relation to the total comparative weight of the factor — with the highest quantitative value being best.

Prepared by: Creed H. Jenkins

Instructions:

Establish company's purpose(s) then numerically value each relevant factor by location as part of a total value of 1000. Assign values in relation to their contribution to the main purpose(s).

The value system illustrated in the figure is intended only to indicate relative values. For example, after the warehouse purpose(s) and other relevant factors have been decided (which are the two most difficult parts of the study on which to reach agreement) "comparative weights" totaling 1,000 are assigned. In this example, "Transportation" is assigned a value of 300, which makes it the most important single factor. Transportation as dealt with here is a combination of costs and delivery service within the context of the purposes of the warehouse. Another way the valuation could be made is to separate transportation into three different components: freight costs, directly related operating costs, and delivery service. Still another way is to use separate forms for each of the components and then summarize these on one form.

The following are examples of subdividing factors into component units to assure that the composition of the major elements represents fair and thorough evaluation:

Major Factor	Composition	Value
Transportation	Trucking service	100
	Trucking cost	80
	Rail service	70
	Rail cost	50
	Total	300
Operating costs	Direct costs	120
	Indirect costs	80
	Total	200

The means of assigning values in this example may be less appropriate than using a two-value system that entails assigning cost values where applicable and service values where not. This involves subdividing transportation into several parts for a specific location based on a forecast (for a stated time interval) of receiving and shipping activity. Following is an example of this treatment:

Transportation	Cost $1000	Service Value*
Inbound rail	100	7
Inbound truck	40	9
Outbound rail	30	6
Outbound truck	200	10
Total	$370	32

*Best possible for each component is 10.

There are many other ways to evaluate warehouse location. Described here is a variation of one. The most important consideration is that the methodology adopted provide for assigning relative values to the various pertinent elements so that the different locations can be systematically compared. Of overriding importance is that the methodology used should be of the nature that permits top management to easily and objectively see comparisons and why one location is recommended over others.

Top management may modify the values you assign and possibly even decide upon another location. If this happens, the author of the initial analysis and evaluation should not feel discouraged. Providing the study results in a comprehensive and valid manner is the most difficult part of the project. Top management has information and insights which lower management does not. It should appreciate receiving objective input to which it can apply its more extensive background. Regardless, top management should have the final responsibility for what is such an important decision for the company. The choice of location sets into motion many costly routines that influence many different parts of the company and for a long time. The high costs in dollars and services (often not conspicuous) suggest that location and site selection are two of the most important endeavors in which warehouse management will participate.

SELECTING THE OPTIMUM SITE

The process of location then site evaluation is somewhat like focusing a high-powered telescope. After sighting in on the general part of the heavens where your target is *located,* you then switch to a more refined focus to isolate and pinpoint the *precise site* of the heavenly body.

With the need for a warehouse satisfactorily justified and the general location identified, there follows the important function of prudently selecting the specific site, that particular piece of land which the facility will occupy. Discussed here are several important questions that should be answered in choosing the site.

Environmental Impact of the Warehouse Site

Is an environmental impact study required? If so, what will it involve?

Warehousing generally has an easier time with environmental concerns than do production facilities. Listed here are some of environmental elements that warehousing may face:

1. Hazardous inventories
2. Roadways with prohibition of certain size trucks or material transfer
3. Residential homes near enough to cause concern about warehouse and truck noise and possibly exhaust fumes
4. Neighboring companies that are involved in handling chemicals which will corrode or otherwise adversely affect your warehouse inventories
5. Neighbor enterprises that are not wholly compatible with your type warehousing such as shopping malls, offices, medical centers, and so on
6. "Acid rain," ocean air, dust storms, odors, hurricanes, and so on, that will adversely affect operations and inventories
7. Earthquake and floodprone sites
8. Archeological disturbance
9. Preservation of endangered species' habitats
10. "Hot dirt" (farmland with too much residual pesticide)

Total Site Costs

What is the total cost of the land site, including any less obvious costs, such as unpaid assessments, land-leveling and clearing, removal of unusable buildings, laying roads to the property, parking areas, walkways, and so on?

Start with the asking price of the land; then add to this the costs of the many things that have to be done before it is ready to accept a building. Some of the unusual things that may be involved are listed here—all of which I have personally experienced.

1. Active springs flowing unwanted water
2. Difficult excavation requiring blasting
3. Unusually high cost for retaining walls
4. Sewer system already at capacity

5. No fire hydrants or not enough

6. Insufficient water pressure

7. Poor soil on which to build

8. Good earth covering old dump site

9. Rights-of-way on which no building is permitted

10. Land fill of wet lands

Zoning and Building Codes

Can the building as it is designed meet the local zoning and building restrictions? Does it exceed height requirements? Is it of the proper building materials? What are the fire and sanitary control laws? What are the setbacks and fencing requirements? What are the sign restrictions?

Sometimes zoning and building restrictions can be changed to accommodate your requirements, but never buy land before the restrictions are removed or buy subject to securing the variances or whatever is necessary to remove restrictions. Obtain competent legal help, preferably from an industrial real estate lawyer, to make certain that all money is returned if "subject to" or other provisions covered in the purchase contract are not satisfied.

Rail Siding

If the site is served by rail, is the switching service adequate? What is the cost of installing the rail siding turn-out and other trackage?

Probably a new rail siding will be required when constructing a new facility. This will entail a sizable investment, but in some cases it is refundable by the railroad company that owns the main line.

The rebate process functions like this. The railroad company pays you a fee, say, $20, for every rail car it spots on your siding until the initial cost of the siding has been repaid in full (without interest). The reasoning behind this is that the rail siding benefits the railroad company by providing freight it would not get if the siding were not installed. You pay the initial cost for the switch and siding, which increases the railroad's income so it compensates you in this manner.

Vehicle Accessibility

Is the site near major highways? Can trucks and automobiles get to and from the property without encountering excessive traffic? Is the regular trucking service to the site adequate to meet the warehousing requirements?

Usually warehouse land prices reflect their accessibility to main highways. If your warehouse entails a lot of truck activity, you may be better off to acquire the higher cost land. It is not difficult to compute the value of a trucking handicap. If the additional cost has a better payback than your company's other investments, it follows that you should acquire the site more favorable to trucking. It is not like you were losing the premium cost. The site's intrinsic value will be there as long as its advantages remain.

Neighborhood Compatibility

Is the neighborhood compatible with warehousing? Will the warehouse be out of place and cause hard feelings because it is in or near a residential area? Is it in an area known for high incidence of theft and vandalism?

Just as there are good and bad residential neighborhoods, so there are good and bad warehouse neighborhoods. It will be well worth time and money spent to check out the neighborhood before you locate your warehouse there. This is important to the real estate investment as well as to the operation of the warehouse.

The local police will advise about the crime rate of the area. Also they will advise what services they provide. Some include patrols of the warehouse area, which is of great value in crime prevention. Commonly, however, they will not repeatedly come out and investigate every time the warehouse security alarm system goes off. Not known is the percentage of valid intrusions to the total times that alarms are tripped, but it must be very small. Cats, dogs, mice, faulty equipment, and careless employees are no doubt the major offenders. For this reason the police may require that someone from the warehouse personally meet them at the facility to investigate together. Since the alarms seem to go off at the most inconvenient times, this constitutes one of the most disagreeable assignments in warehousing.

Advertising Value

Will exposure of the building to heavily traveled highways add to advertising value? What kind of sign will optimize the exposure? What advertising message does your company want to convey?

If advertising or company image are important, the added costs of the site with the most favorable exposure could be the best investment. Keep in mind, though, that attractive building, good landscaping, appropriate sign, and suitable maintenance are all necessary to benefit from exposure. It would not do for a company that wants exposure to have a rusty metal-clad building in disrepair with shifting tumbleweeds for landscape.

INNOVATIVE WAYS TO FINANCE THE VENTURE

Before seeking a site, the method of payment preferred by the warehouse company should be determined. Acquisitions comprising substantial investments for land and building can be structured several ways other than simply paying for them from your own money on a construction progress and completion schedule. Following are a few of the alternative ways to finance that illustrate the innovative possibilities to improve on conventional financing. Included is the conventional way to round out the treatment of the subject.

Combination Lease and Purchase

Acquire a long-term (possibly 50-year) land lease and finance only the building. This is a popular means to maximize tax shelter with the lowest initial outlay of cash. Commonly nonprofit and religious organizations like to buy land and lease to others. Since land cannot be depreciated, it does not provide tax shelter. Normally the company is better off to lease the land and own (or have some other investor who wants a tax shelter own) the building, which can be depreciated with attendant income tax avoidance. Congress often changes what can be used as tax shelters, so it would be prudent to investigate the current rules of the Internal Revenue Service before counting on this means of financing. (See the "Facility Cost and Value" section of this chapter for a more detailed discussion of this means of acquisition.)

Tailor to Fit Unique Needs of the Affluent

Find someone who is currently experiencing unusually high income such as a movie star, athlete, or top corporate executive. Have this person buy the land and pay for the construction, then lease the facility to your company. This is called a "build-to-suit leaseback." The innovative trick in this plan is for the lease rate to be structured to start low and then have a substantial increase when the owner expects his or her high earnings will peter out. An example is for a famous football player that wants tax shelter now and knows he will be through playing by a certain time in the future. This works well for the lessee as well as the lessor, particularly when accelerated depreciation can be used as tax shelter. The football player shelters his high income now and gets a higher return from the lease when he retires from the game. Again, make certain you check the current IRS rulings for applicability.

Reward Executives

A fairly common method, yet one that should be used with extreme caution, is for a company to reward its top executives by permitting them to own the facilities personally and lease them to the company. The usual developer margin is either retained by the company or passed on to the executive who owns the facility—or they split it. The company pays no more for the lease than if it were leased from a developer. The developer's margin is used as an extra reward for the executive or is taken by the company to lower lease payments. This method of rewarding company executives is not recommended because a conflict-of-interest situation may result. If it can be done openly and completely above reproach, however, it can be used advantageously. The problem is that it can be easily abused, and long after all outsiders to the agreement should have forgotten it and it is out of its initial context, it may surface as an embarrassment or, worse, a lawsuit by a disgruntled or "suit-happy" stockholder.

Employ Government Assistance

The prospects of financing partially or wholly with government assistance is commonly touted to be much better than it really is. Everything about government-backed loans in the beginning appears much simpler than what they turn out to be. Unfortunately, what appears to be good intentions (on the part of the legislature that passes financial assistance laws) gets obscured in the bureaucracy of implementing them. Perhaps worse is that much of the government-backed financing that is intended to help minorities and small business in reality ends up in the already deep pockets of large corporations. Yet it is accomplished in the guise of it helping minorities and small business. The problem is that these "needy" businesses may be owned or just controlled by very large companies. The irony is that large companies have the in-house legal help and lobbying power necessary to get this type of government assistance. The little company for whose benefit the help is intended often has neither the legal nor lobbying means required. They simply cannot afford them. In brief, it takes the clout of big business to materialize the help purported for little business. It appears to be little problem for large companies to control one way or another the many little partnerships and corporations which qualify for government help.

But, as with many seemingly difficult or impossible things in life, there are enough exceptions to the usual that getting government assistance for minority and small business is still a viable way in some circumstances, provided it can survive the bureaucratic obstacle course. Of paramount importance is to determine what government help is currently available before embarking on this pathway to finance. Government financial backing, it seems, is a political football. Whatever is available now is usually foreseen by some gurus of business to be changing soon. What they foresee, however, often does not come about. The huge bureaucracy does not change easily. There is just too much big business imbedded in the status quo for substantial changes in policy to come about quickly—even slowly. Advocates of change have to outlobby and outvote advocates of "as is." Commonly those in favor of keeping things the same stay in the background until their favored way is threatened, then they emerge in strength from the proverbial woodwork. They are the ones who got through in the past what is now. They do not give up easily.

Probably if you have read this far about government financial assistance, you will feel that most of what has been said is from the minority and small business perspective. That is true, simply because large businesses have their own financial expertise, which no doubt contributes to their staying strong and getting stronger.

If you pursue government help, your chances of success are much better with the help of specialists. Having government loans has spawned many companies whose product is the service of helping others to secure government loans. It is doubtful that this is an area for do-it-yourselfers. Those who specialize in this and have a successful track record (which should be investigated) can save you a lot of frustration. Some do not take their fee except if the loan or loans are secured—which adds to their credibility.

Ways to Secure Government Assistance

Listed here are some of the avenues that are at times open to small and/or to large businesses.

- Loans to veterans through the Veterans Administration.
- Various types of loans through the Small Business Administration.
- Bonds secured by local governments to attract certain types of business.
- Property tax forgiveness for so many years to attract desired business.
- Block grants whereby a town will get money through the government in a "block" of dollars. The town then lends the money to new business (usually at very favorable terms) that builds in the town and employs locals. When the town is paid back, it may use the money again and again for business that will strengthen the town's economy and provide jobs, or it can be used for town-owned improvements such as parks, libraries, and so on.

There are no doubt many other ways government can assist in financing your warehouse facility. The most efficient way to search for these is to let your fingers do the work in the Yellow Pages.

The advantages of this type of finance are that the interest rates are lower than commercial financing and they can be subordinated to commercial loans. An example of this type financing follows:

Total cost of the warehouse facility based on reputable cost estimate by licensed contractors and appraisers		$1,000,000
Your company's cash input	$200,000	
Commercial bank loan	400,000	
Government-backed finance	400,000	
Total		$1,000,000

Such a financial structure is still considered quite conservative even though you have only put in 20 percent, or $200,000. The debt to ownership is only 4 to 1 ($800,000 to $200,000). From the commercial lender's viewpoint, it is 2 to 3 ($400,000 to $600,000), because the government-backed finance and the owner's investment are both subordinate in security to the commercial lender's investment; that is, the commercial lender holds the first mortgage on the facility. It must be paid before other lenders and the owner get anything, or it can legally take over the ownership causing the initial owner to lose all.

Other More Common Means

Probably the most common way is conventional borrowing in which a lending institution lends 70 to 80 percent and the owner puts in the rest. Another common way (for at least the most profitable companies) is to pay all cash—no borrowing. This is favored particularly by companies that have more earnings than they can otherwise productively use. Possibly the Interstate Commerce Commission will not let them buy or buy into more companies that they would like to control. They see that investing in themselves is the best combination: (1) the least government interference and (2) the most profitable use of their money.

A common variation of a part of the financial structure is for the land owner who sells you the land to carry a note on the unpaid balance with a subordination clause. This means that the seller is providing a share of the total financing and is willing to subordinate the security for this to another loan which is secured by a first mortgage. Of particular importance when using this instrument of finance is that the subordination clause be so structured that neither the seller nor the buyer is put to unnecessary risk.

There are many other ways of financing, limited only by creativity and legality. Acquiring the site and constructing a warehouse often creates a host of lucrative opportunities, which, if not taken by the warehouse company, will be taken by others.

RETAINING MINERAL RIGHTS

You may well ask what mineral rights have to do with warehouse site selection? They do and often cost nothing. They can be simply passed on to the buyer along with the land title or can be retained separately by the seller. They may be accidentally or deliberately left out of the title transfer. It behooves the buyer to investigate. If they are not transferred automatically with ownership, an innocuous request should be made—sort of as an afterthought. If this does not get them, a more deliberate request should follow. Depending on how motivated are the buyer and seller (along with what the prospects are that these rights are of value), decide how much will have to be given to secure them.

Experience indicates how valuable these rights can become. When natural gas prices were first climbing at an alarming rate, for example, a combination paint factory and warehouse with which I was involved was prompted to make use of its rights for natural gas. The company used large quantities of the gas in its paint process. Inflationary prices for this essential commodity were raising havoc with profits.

Because there were natural gas wells in the vicinity, the company employed a geologist to determine if there was gas on the property that could be plumbed for use. The company drilled and hit a good gas supply. Thus, with a relatively small investment, the company turned adversity to advantage. It had its own dependable low-cost fuel source. This constitutes ingenuity at its best.

Whenever considerable excavation is necessary for site preparation, which is often the case in mountain country, soil and rock removal is done with fingers crossed. This is particularly the case in highly mineralized areas such as California's Gold Country. Geologists claim that no more than 10 percent of the gold was taken during the Gold Rush days back in the midnineteenth century. Mineral rights in this area are cherished, even though the chances of utilizing them are slim to none. They are next to none even when "pay dirt" is discovered if the site is in a developed residential or business area.

Paul Getty, the oil tycoon who became one of the richest men in the world, is purported to have said (in effect): "The poor and humble may inherit the earth, but the rich and powerful will retain the mineral rights."

CORRELATING SITE AND LOCATION

Many of the location factors discussed earlier apply as well to site selection. For example, the discussion of industrial parks relates both to general location as well as to specific site selection. When investigating location, an important consideration is the availability of good industrial parks. All other influences being equal, locating in a good industrial park could make an important difference.

If, however, it appears that equally attractive sites are in different industrial parks, a thorough study of each is essential. You could find big differences, particularly in property values and costs as well as other factors. There are good, poor, and bad industrial parks, just as there are most everything else.

Company image and advertising are also directly involved in both location and site selection. Image contributes to institutional advertising, which, if favorable, contributes to the company "goodwill." Marketing and sales advertising—though directed at increasing sales—also influence image. The point is that both should influence the place for your warehouse. For some this will be where there is the most favorable exposure, but for others it could be where there is the least exposure. Warehouses handling hazardous materials, for example, may best locate in the most innocuous place. Most location and site selection factors interface one way or another. The best way to not overlook pertinent considerations is take one phase at a time with an eye fixed on the influence one has on the other.

CHECKLIST OF SITE CONSIDERATIONS

The following is a checklist of factors that influence site selection. It also serves as an outline of topics covered in this chapter and other sections of the book. The best way to use the list is to find those factors that you want to explore further and refer to the index to find where else the topic is discussed as well as in this chapter.

FACTORS	RELATIVE TO
Environmental impact	Odors
	Hazardous inventory
	Hazardous environment for inventories
	Earthquake, flood, etc.
	Archaeological implication
	Endangered species habitat
Land costs and related other concerns	Asking price plus site preparation
	Active water, springs, creek, lake, etc.
	Difficult excavation
	Sewer
	Fire hydrants
	Soil suitability
	Easements, rights-of-way
	Sand storms
	Right wind direction
	Assessments
Zoning and codes	Limitations on use of land
	Building restrictions: height, construction materials, coverage of building to land, etc.
	Fire insurance rating
Rail service	Right railroad
	Rail siding (rebate)
	Services and limitations
	Connecting railroads
	Freight rates
Truck services	Maneuverability
	Access/egress
	Traffic congestion
	Access to highways
	Freight rates
	Tolls
Neighborhood	Conflicting interests
	Crime rate
	Police services
	Similarity of neighboring businesses

Advertising value	Compatibility with company objectives
	Exposure to highway traffic
	Image of facility
Commercial financing	Land lease
	Build-to-suit leaseback
	Tax shelter for the affluent
	Executive reward
	Lease-rate manipulation
	Subordination
	Conventional borrowing
Government financial assistance	Veterans Administration
	Small Business Administration
	Block grant
	Bonds
	Tax forgiveness
Mineral, gas, and oil rights	Potential value
	Acquisition with land title

NEXT STEP—FACILITY DESIGN

The next step in the process of constructing a warehouse or acquiring an existing facility is its design features. Do not put off thinking about design until the issue of where it will be has been settled. Actually, you have to have a good idea of several design factors to know where to look for the general location and the specific site. Such elements as size, height, accessibility, appearance, and so on, must be at least generally known before the search is launched. Otherwise, considerable time and expense will be incurred to no avail. Without deciding what knowledge should come first, let us dodge this issue entirely by saying everything in this book should be absorbed and understood before any major long-term action is taken. After settling this and having "where" decided, "what" to be confronted next is the facility design—the subject of the next chapter.

Chapter 5

How to Design a New Warehouse and Evaluate an Existing One

CHAPTER HIGHLIGHTS

Designing a warehouse to optimize the combination of the numerous influencing (often conflicting) factors is one of the most important projects which will ever be assigned to warehousing management. The investment is substantial. How well it is done will affect operations and real estate value for the life of the facility (about 40 years, more or less). Doing it well should be of serious concern for those who are charged with this responsibility.

Designing a warehouse facility is too important to leave to architects. Certainly there is a place in the design process for an architect or design engineer, but it is too much to expect they can design the best warehouse for your particular operation. They should be viewed as valuable, possibly essential, staff assistants, whether they are in-house employees or outside experts.

To assist in the decision-making process is a checklist of 22 "critical" components of facility design. Not considering these factors before construction could impose nonstop handling and storing impediments over the life of the facility. What should prove to be of particular interest to students as well as scholars of warehousing is the insights provided into the continuing quandary of *size versus capacity* and *the square versus the cube* phenomena as related to building configuration. For those who have not yet been initiated to the subtleties of these phenomena, some surprises are in store for you.

The most important part of the design process is covered with these three key considerations:

1. Knowing the purpose and objectives of the facility. As discussed many times throughout this book, these should be in compliance with those in the company for whom the warehousing is being performed and should be in compliance with the overall company objectives.
2. Knowing the functions necessary to attain the objectives, including
   ○ Inventory product mix, quantities, and activity.
   ○ Accountability, procedures, and audits.
   ○ Methods and equipment alternatives to perform warehousing functions efficiently and effectively.
3. Knowing and being able to relate alternative building designs and building materials to optimize the value of the facility according to its objectives.

These key requisites of the design process must come from warehouse operations. The important additional information about facility design, building materials, building codes, stresses and strains, indicative costs, and so on should come from the architect. To take the effort and time to blame the architect later for not taking into account warehousing theory and operations is simply counterproductive. Warehouse management enlists architects to design a facility to meet warehousing's needs. Warehousing cannot abdicate this responsibility and be deserving of professional warehouser status.

This is not to say that all top-level management sees it this way. It is more likely that some have not taken the time and effort required to determine which authorities and responsibilities their warehousing organization should have to do the most effective and efficient job. When lesser assignments are given to the warehousing group, its ability to rise to its capabilities of contributing most to the company's well-being is thwarted.

KEY IDEAS FOR ACQUIRING AN EXISTING FACILITY

Acquiring an existing warehouse facility is more common than is constructing a new one. Many industrial buildings come on the market either from companies having no further use for them or from developers who build with the anticipation of being able to lease or sell them. Such developers are "speculators" hoping to realize a margin of profit for their contribution of having a building ready for occupancy. This saves the buyer or lessee the effort, expertise, time, and money required to design and build a warehouse themselves. These ready-made facilities are commonly referred to as "spec" buildings (connoting that they are built not by owner-operators but by speculators).

The terms "speculator" or "spec building" in no way is intended to be deprecatory. In the realm of industrial real estate, both are as acceptable as the terms "owner," "lessor," and "lessee." Providing ready-made facilities is a needed function particularly in a fluctuating economy. Commonly companies unexpectedly arrive at the realization they need a facility to take advantage of a new opportunity or to fulfill a recent commitment. They need more space in a hurry. They cannot wait for the lengthy process of design, land acquisition, and construction. Even if companies had the time and expertise, they may not want to take on the long-term obligations entailed in ownership or build-to-suit leasebacks, preferring to devote their assets to their main line of business rather than to real estate.

Another purpose that spec buildings serve is to accommodate companies that do not have the financial strength to build on their own. These companies usually have to pay higher lease rates than do *Fortune* 500 enterprises. This is a penalty for financial weakness. It is but one of many reasons why the cost of facilities for small, new companies is comparatively high.

What to look for when shopping for an existing warehouse is essentially the same as that which you would design into a new facility. Everything expressed in this chapter about new facilities is equally appropriate to features and specifications of existing ones. The only difference is that a lot more compromising will be involved in accepting an existing facility. Some things would probably cost too much to modify to better fit your requirements. However, others should be changed if there is the intention to stay in the facility for long. Certainly anything that is hazardous must be corrected; this should be at the top of your shopping list of requirements. The salesperson showing the facility will not belabor its inadequacies or problems. His or her motivation is to highlight the good points and to maneuver for a quick close. The shopper with a comprehensive list of requirements should methodically ask about and personally check the physical evidence of each item.

Warehouse management should have the same important role in acquiring an existing facility as it has in designing a new one. Others' help should be enlisted to make certain the best possible deal is made, but from the operational point of view, that which is paramount to effective and efficient operations should prevail. When it comes to scrutinizing the lease or bill of sale, your company's real estate department (if there is one) and certainly the company's legal counsel should approve it. As for the physical features and condition of the facility, an appropriate, qualified engineer should provide a report on these. Particular concern should be paid to the floor capacity. Commonly floors of spec buildings are inadequate to take the heavy beating that some warehouse operations give them. If this is not confronted and dealt with in the negotiation stage and then made a part of the lease, the lessee could be slapped with substantial repair costs during the life of the lease and even more at its end.

In purchasing a facility, the same diligence (if not more) should be given to the physical features. Floors, walls, and roof conditions should be thoroughly investigated and their apparent "good condition" guaranteed by whomever is selling the facility. Watch out particularly with metal buildings for protective bumpers in all places where there is exposure to trucks and other material handling equipment. If damage is possible, expect it. This is an overriding concern about all industrial facilities, but particularly in warehousing. Warehousing is singled out because it characteristically involves more material handling than does any other phase of commerce. It is therefore the most prone to cause building damage because it is only material movement that causes damage and moving materials is warehousing's primary function.

HOW TO COMPILE BASIC DATA TO SUPPORT DESIGN

Certain basic data is needed to design a warehouse facility effectively. If you do not already have it when starting the design process, you have some important remedial investigation and learning to get out of the way. Listed here are the basic data requirements followed by discussion of each.

1. Reliable forecasts of everything that will influence the warehousing functions: receiving, storing, shipping, transportation, and so on.
2. The tools and equipment that will be available to carry out these warehousing functions.
3. The established objectives for warehousing (which must be in compliance with those of the organization hierarchy within the company).

Reliable Forecasts

Forecasts are simply predictions of what is expected to happen. Their reliability depends on the quality of insight the predictors have. While there are gifted people that can foretell the future with little helpers such as cards, tea leaves, runes, and crystals, businesspersons generally are not so favored. They have to rely on statistical analyses of the market and their company's place within it. Then they temper these results with their company's capabilities and objectives. Further, they must make modifications based on their company's historical performance and realistic predictions of future performance.

Warehousing has a critical need for reliable forecasts of inventory activity and quantity by store keeping units (SKUs) for it to make its own plans for the future. The required forecasts should come from every part of the company that influences warehouse operations. These definitely include those that directly influence the supply and disposition of warehouse inventory such as

○ *Production*—if warehousing receives merchandise from production or supplies it with raw materials.
○ *Purchasing*—if purchasing initiates orders for warehouse inventory.
○ *Sales*—if sales uses warehouse inventory to supply customers' requirements.
○ *Physical Distribution or Logistics department*—if involved in deciding which orders will be shipped directly from production and which from warehousing, what and how much warehouse inventory will be carried, and other considerations about physical distribution trade-offs.

To be useful for design and layout, these inputs must be expressed in terms of immediate and long range, particularly if they influence facility design considerations. The warehouse design should encompass as long a period as the company's long-range plans, perhaps longer. Then realistic alternatives should be included if and when the plans do not materialize. Always the consideration should be made to maximize real estate value in case the company discontinues operations and has to sell or lease the facilities. It is unusual that a specific location and design will best serve the company for as long as the building will last. If I had to guess how long even a well-designed facility will be optimal for the company's requirements, I would base my prediction on the usual modifier, "it depends on ＿＿＿＿ ＿＿＿＿ ＿＿＿＿." I would then give my predictions in two parts: when it will become less than optimal and when it will become essentially obsolete. The following is a list showing (by time intervals) what the chances are of a warehouse facility becoming less than optimal and essentially obsolete.

Interval (years)	Less than Optimal	Essentially Obsolete
5	25%	10%
10	60	30
20	90	60
30	99	85
40	*	99

*Not measurable.

Most warehouse facilities have an average life for some productive use of about 40 years. This simply means that business situations change (in some areas, often). Therefore it is wise to give recognition to this probability in the beginning. This means to design for the greatest long-term efficiency yet keep within the confines of general purpose at least for a significant part of the market. These two objectives may be contradictory. If this is the case, strive for a design that is a realistic composite of the two, with priority given to that which is best known, the short range.

Availability of Tools and Equipment

With what warehousing will be called upon to do (based on reasonable forecasts), what corresponding tools and equipment will be made available? Warehousing cannot be expected to perform effectively and efficiently if it is not equipped with the means for such accomplishment.

How much to invest in facility and equipment depends on what payback is needed for the company to divert investment away from alternatives to warehousing needs and how effectively these needs are championed.

What warehousing has to work with largely dictates design and layout. It would be a waste of time to design for high-rise storage if the building is not high-rise, or to plan layout for a large number of rail shipments when there is no rail siding and no practical way of installing one. If high-rise and rail shipments are desirable, these should be made part of the initial site selection and facility design processes.

Unfortunately, many buildings are acquired as warehouses by sales or production managers or by the company's real estate department without qualified warehousing input. Generally, the buyers know little about the design requirements of warehousing; it is not their business to know.

In addition to knowing that handling and storing equipment will be provided, the means of transportation also must be known before embarking on design and layout. This includes knowledge of truck and rail docks and staging areas that serve to support truck and rail shipments. For example, most warehouses need dock heights to match the heights of the floor levels of the trucks and rail cars they use. Others best perform their loading and unloading functions at ground level, as is the case for flat beds. This only justifies further knowing in advance what activities and inventories the warehouse will deal with so that the facility features are compatible with the transportation means and warehouse capabilities.

Facility Design and Layout Objectives That Are in Compliance

Does what top company management wants from warehousing conform to what warehouse management thinks it wants? As sometimes happens, warehousing gets out of step and marches to a different drum beat. It may be performing "its thing" in a commendable manner, but "its thing" may not be what top-level management wants, as discussed in detail in Chapter 3, "How to Make Warehouse Objectives Compatible with Company Objectives." The message conveyed there is the same as it is here: All objectives within a company should conform to those of the next level of management; otherwise, communication breaks down and all the warehousing evils in Pandora's box are unleashed.

Facility design and layout objectives, as with all other company objectives, must be determined within the parameters of what the company wants; otherwise, they conflict. For example, what is ideal for warehousing of bags of sugar is totally different from canned goods. A warehouse used as a showcase of company products is totally different than one whose function is to absorb demand fluctuations so that production can avoid costly machine setups.

Another less obvious contrast of layout and design factors is shown in the example of two warehouses carrying the same product mix, and serving the same market, yet one having three times the shipping volume of the other. Management of the low-volume operation may wisely give more importance to space utilization so it can get by with less building space (a dominant cost in this type of warehousing). The other may organize to attain the best handling efficiency, which, with its high activity, is where most of its costs are lodged.

To provide the basis for building design and layout, the following should be clearly established:

○ The type and priorities of customer services.
○ The type and priorities of suppliers.
○ The value assigned to the facility for serving as a showcase of company products.
○ The return on investment expected by the company to justify capital expenditures. This provides guidance in the justification and acquisition of cost-saving equipment.
○ The emphasis on efficiency and its relationship to service.

PREPARING DRAWINGS AND OTHER SPECIFICATIONS

Generally there are two different approaches to developing the drawings and other specifications for a new facility. One is do-it-yourself—"the inexpensive way." The other is to utilize architectual and/or engineering expertise which incurs greater initial expense. Probably a combination of both will provide the best results. Certainly to do it all yourself is obviously not the best. Alternatively, to put the entire project on an architect or design engineer is just as bad—unless they are also experts in your company's warehousing, which is very unlikely. They may design a beautiful warehouse facility, but there is strong likelihood it will not best satisfy your requirements.

The desirable approach is for you and others having the most knowledge of your warehousing requirements to put on paper methodically those features and specifications that best apply. Work and rework these so you are quite sure of what you want. Acquire know-how and guidance from periodicals and books on the subject. Then with your warehousing experience and knowledge of what top management wants, you should come close to the right set of specifications.

This part of the process, involving the development of your own design and specifications, is necessary regardless of what is done next. Architects and construction engineers will know more than you about building materials and processes, but they do not know what is necessary for your specific warehousing and the company constraints within which you must operate.

During the process of developing your design and specifications, you should call on different vendors to get further information about availabilities and costs. Vendors constitute the best source and lowest-cost means for developing the body of knowledge needed for quality design, even though vendors' information is biased in favor of the things they sell. It is not too difficult to sort out and discard the prejudicial data while retaining the factual information you want. If their products are the best value, you should go out of your way to buy from them in repayment for their help when you needed it.

At this point a choice must be made either to go directly to competitive bidding with the design and specifications your team developed or to enlist the help of a qualified architect or construction engineer for further refinement and more exacting drawings and specifications. Both ways have their advantages and disadvantages. If you go to direct bidding with your design and specifications, it will be without the architects' or engineers' valuable input. What you present to the contractors is a situation which encourages their own input more than when you give complete and final documentation. If your data goes to four or five qualified contractors with encouragement to improve on it as they usually can, you could wind up with better design and specifications than you would with only an architect's or engineer's input.

The limitations to having contractors bid on less than professionally prepared design and specifications are that the quotations you receive back may not be for the "same" facility; you could end up comparing "apples and oranges." This problem can be kept to a minimum if what you provide for bid has been carefully researched and presented in sufficient detail to eliminate most of the questionable areas. Another limitation is that contractors are more and more reluctant to spend a lot of time and money on the chance they "may" get the job. This obstacle can be overcome to an extent by your conscientiously giving them more complete and organized data on which to base their quotations.

It really boils down to what expertise and time the company seeking bids have and are willing to devote to the project. The design and specifications of most warehouses are not extremely complicated unless a high-rise or an automated facility is involved. The design of most warehouse buildings is not as involved as designing a motel or a shopping center, but it is not simple either. Unless quality warehousing, engineering, architectual, and financial skills are included, costly errors could be cast in concrete and bonded in steel—for a very long time.

CONSIDERATIONS FOR CHOOSING AN ARCHITECT

The first decision about an architect is whether or not to use one. Architects say that they save you more than they cost—this is probably true, assuming the one you use is highly qualified. Your primary concern is to make certain the one you enlist knows the warehousing business, has a track record of designing quality warehouses, and has a good reputation with contractors and owners.

Start by contacting companies that are in your type of business and have employed architects. Probably a sampling of three or four recommended architects is ample. Rarely should you stop with one or two.

Another good source for information about architects is through construction contractors. Contractors who have had good experience with architects should speak well of them and disparage the bad ones. Use this source with caution, though, because contractors want to maintain good relations with all architects because much of their work comes through them.

A truism about contractors' quotations is that the more precise the specifications, the lower and more reliable will be their quotations. If they have to make assumptions about what is wanted, their contingency factor will be larger. They have to build this uncertainty into their quotations whether they show it as a larger contingency factor or bury it in higher component costs. Furthermore, using nonprecise specifications reduces the value of getting competitive quotations. Each quotation received will be based on at least some different specification so you will have difficulty in making valid comparisons. A low quotation may mean it is based on lower-quality materials or simply errors and omissions.

On the other hand, your architect may not have the best ideas on the many things that go into constructing a warehouse facility. Both you and the architect should want input from the builders about what they believe is the best way to satisfy the facility objectives. While ultraprecise specifications have plenty of merit, they can shut out better alternatives. To have your cake and eat it too, provide "closed specifications" spelling out everything in detail and then request two quotations, one based on the "closed specifications" and the other based on improvements the contractor suggests. Using this technique, the door is left open. Suggestions are solicited, but the basis for valid comparisons is also provided. Then apples can be compared to apples, not to oranges, and if oranges are introduced they can be easily identified and evaluated separately.

Avoid the pitfall of using the phrase "or equal" in your specifications. This equates to having "open specifications," which again sets up the situation of apples being compared to oranges. You really do not know what you are getting. For example, you may want metal studding used in the office walls for your own reasons, but the builder likes working with wood studding, and to him both are "equal." So his quotation is based on using his preference, not yours. This slack in specifications may cause serious problems. It is far better to require quotations on what you have specified and then encourage the builders to submit their suggested alternatives as well. The contractors that offer the most valuable alternatives should be given "credit" when the final evaluation is made to decide who will be awarded the contract.

A little-known concern about using architects is that the drawings and other specifications they produce are probably their property, not yours, even though you paid the architects to prepare them. The logic behind their ownership is that you might use the drawings and written specification to build the same facility elsewhere. Then if something adverse happens, there could be a suit against you, the contractor, and the architect. The architect designed only for one location and one set of zoning requirements; his or her liability does not extend to another site.

ESTABLISHING CRITICAL COMPONENTS OF FACILITY DESIGN

This discussion of facility design constitutes a combination of industrial engineering principles and practical warehouse experience. It is neither a technical treatise comprised of starry-eyed theories nor a series of platitudes and cliches that presume blanket acceptance. Intended is a practical application of engineering theory—with concepts and principles applicable to the reality of warehousing. A further intention is to provide thought-provoking ideas.

Checklist of 22 Facility Design Components

A checklist of facility design components is provided here followed by explanation and discussion of each entry.

Permits and zoning requirements
- Intentions good, results often not so good
- Growing environmental concern and cost
- At times, bureaucratic nightmare

Building "size" versus "capacity"
- Common error to assume both are same
- As height increases capacity cost decreases
- Many warehouses over 40 feet, some over 100 feet high

Office considerations
- Where to locate office
- Total space and fixture requirements
- Provision for future contraction or expansion

The "square" phenomenon
- Footprint (floor configuration) directly affects construction and operating costs
- Magic of a square design (four equal sides)
- When the square loses its attraction

The "cube" phenomenon
- Cube (six equal sides) directly affects construction and operating costs (cube is theoretically ideal)
- Lost clearance between storage height and roof structure also favors cube design

How the cube principle is applied to high-rise ASRS
- Two-directional versus one-directional travel
- Lower construction costs with racks supporting sides and roof
- Cylinder and sphere configurations mostly not viable for general merchandise warehousing

Land and related costs
- Best site with highest cost is often wisest investment
- Total cost of land site is not known until all related costs are included
- Provision for contraction or expansion

Site preparation (including Inca legacy)
- ○ Include everything done to prepare site for facility construction
- ○ Hazards of inadequate site preparation
- ○ Inca gift to posterity

Drainage system
- ○ Topography survey
- ○ Innovativeness really pays
- ○ Substantial component of site cost

The importance of floors
- ○ Cause of extremely high load factor
- ○ Case histories of faulty floors
- ○ Factors affecting floor capacity

Comparison of wall materials
- ○ Not enough warehousing attention paid to walls
- ○ Masonry: tilt-wall, precast, continuous cast, block, brick
- ○ Metal: aluminum and steel

Roof materials and configurations
- ○ Consequences of leaky warehouse roof
- ○ Different roof configurations
- ○ Composition, aluminum, and steel

Skylight materials and configurations
- ○ Plastic bubble and sheets; pane glass
- ○ Different configurations
- ○ Benefits of natural light

Electrical concerns
- ○ Cost has increased disproportionately
- ○ Need for electrical and lighting expertise
- ○ Alternative means of lighting

Plumbing concerns
- ○ Cost has increased disproportionately
- ○ Water requirements
- ○ Waste disposal
- ○ Efficient layout is key to plumbing economies

Canopies over doors and docks
- ○ Commonly overlooked
- ○ Benefits generally outweigh costs
- ○ Materials, configurations, and dimensions

Door types
- ○ Deserves higher priority than normally given
- ○ Different types and characteristics
- ○ "The hinge enigma"

Fire sprinkler system
- ○ High initial cost versus continuing lower insurance costs

- Code requirements, including high storage racks
- Factors that influence the degree of fire hazard

Roof support columns, enemy no. 1

- Adverse effects on operations and real estate value
- Warehouse operations' input necessary
- Ways to oppose cost-savings motive for more columns

Truck and rail docks

- Whether to elevate warehouse floor or depress vehicle approach
- Dock levelers
- Formal rail siding and dock specifications

Paint and esthetics

- Value of an attractive facility as related to employees, customers, and public relations
- Applications inside the warehouse
- Need for expert advice on facility esthetics

Other design concerns not covered before

- Outside security

   High crime rate is a reality

   What to do to thwart crime

- Ramps

   Elevated warehouse floors require ramps

   Ramps to be constructed to last as long as the building

- Fueling and charging material handling equipment and in-house personnel carriers

   Gasoline and diesel pumps and LPG tanks outside

   Battery recharging inside

   Provision for continuous use of electrically powered equipment

- Truck maneuvering room

   Location of building on site is of paramount importance

   For big rigs from 100 to 120 feet

   For local delivery trucks from 50 to 60 feet

Permits and Zoning Requirements

Anywhere a warehouse can be built there are governmental restrictions. At their best they are by-products of civilization and are intended to improve or at least maintain the quality of life. At their worst they contribute to bureaucratic strangulation. The best that can be done is to determine what the requirements are and then accept or seek legal variance of them. If you do not feel you can live with them, petition in a businesslike manner for variances. If you cannot change them and cannot live with them, come to this realization as soon as possible and move on to another site that does not involve such harsh encumbrances.

While the fees levied for permits and approvals are relatively minor compared to the costs of the land, building, and operations, they can run a few percentage points of the total facility cost. The actual money paid to the government agencies for permits and approvals is generally a small part of the total costs that will be incurred in complying with them. Meeting specifications for setbacks, building-to-land ratios, insulation, plumbing, electrical, building materials, environmental requirements, fire protection, landscaping, and so on can drive up facility and operating costs beyond what is viable to remain in business. Your choice is simple. Try to get variances on those things that make it impractical or go elsewhere. Do not go down with a sinking ship out of stubbornness. Warehouses should not be built everywhere even though business may not like finding this out.

Government regulation varies from locality to locality. Try not to locate a warehouse where restrictions are onerous, but keep in mind that many of the specifications and regulations imposed on warehouse facilities are really for the warehouser's benefit or the benefit of the community. Certainly an active large warehouse should not be located in, or in close proximity to, a residential district. Nor should it be located adjacent to a school or in any environment that is foreign to its own. Zoning for light or heavy industry is usually compatible with most warehousing, unless it is a warehouse that also serves as a retail store. Then it could be in a commercial zone.

A consultant (or lobbyist) may be employed when a government agency is heavily involved in new construction. Of course this will constitute an additional expense but perhaps less than what it would cost in time and money to take on the fight by yourself. If you are like most warehouse people, your forte is in material handling and warehousing methods, procedures, and systems. It is not in dealing with government agencies.

Building "Size" versus "Capacity"

With the theory and practice of facility location and site selection covered in Chapter 4, the primary question now is how big to build the facility.

While it is common to think in terms of size when referring to design and layout, the concern really should be for how much it will hold—capacity. The two definitely are not the same. Size is expressed in relationship to dimensions, such as 100 feet wide by 200 feet long by 20 feet high. Capacity relates to usable space and what it will hold. After capacity requirements have been established, they then must be translated to size dimensions for the construction contractor or for those charged with finding an existing building.

The intention here is to highlight the common error of assuming size and capacity are the same. It is not intended to confuse with a riddle of "size versus capacity."

To illustrate the difference in size and capacity, consider the comparison of two different dimension facilities (see Figure 5.1). The square footage of buildings A and B are the same, 10,000 square feet. Building A, however, has a usable storage height of only 14 feet while building B has a 28-foot storage height. Because of the different configuration of products stored in each building, A requires aisles 12 feet wide. Building B can operate and store efficiently in narrow aisles, only 5.5 feet wide, except for one two-way traffic aisle. The dramatic capacity difference as computed under each drawing shows A to have capacity of 40,320 cubic feet, in contrast to B's 109,760 cubic feet, 2.7 times more storage space. Conversely, A has only 37 percent the capacity of building B, yet both have the same "footprint," 10,000 square feet.

As a rule, by simply doubling the height of the building, keeping the same footprint, the storage capacity is doubled. Admittedly this is a comparison of

FIGURE 5.1 The Dramatic Difference between Two 10,000 Square Foot Warehouses

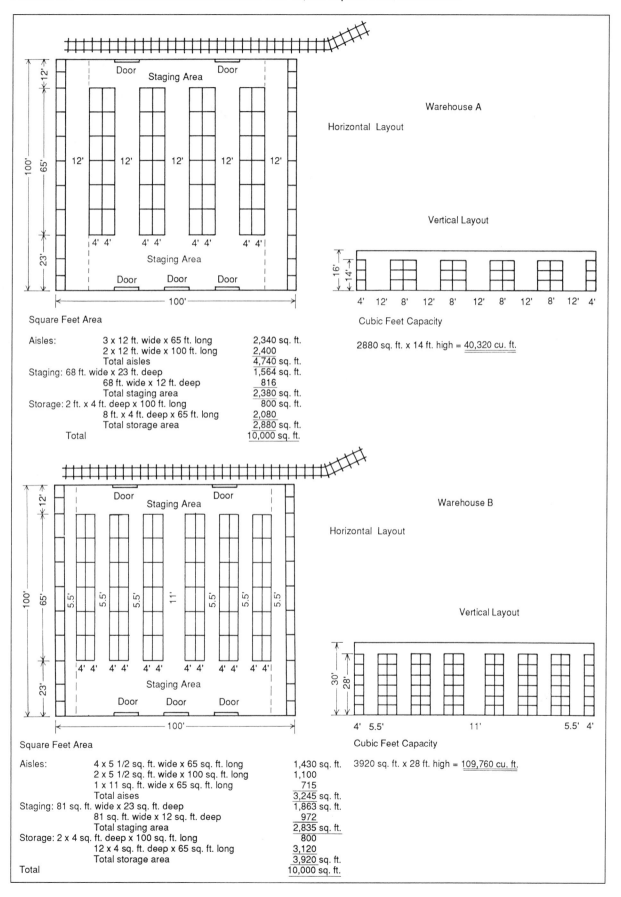

Warehouse A

Horizontal Layout

Vertical Layout

Square Feet Area

Aisles:	3 x 12 ft. wide x 65 ft. long	2,340 sq. ft.
	2 x 12 ft. wide x 100 ft. long	2,400
	Total aisles	4,740 sq. ft.
Staging:	68 ft. wide x 23 ft. deep	1,564 sq. ft.
	68 ft. wide x 12 ft. deep	816
	Total staging area	2,380 sq. ft.
Storage:	2 ft. x 4 ft. deep x 100 ft. long	800 sq. ft.
	8 ft. x 4 ft. deep x 65 ft. long	2,080
	Total storage area	2,880 sq. ft.
Total		10,000 sq. ft.

Cubic Feet Capacity

2880 sq. ft. x 14 ft. high = 40,320 cu. ft.

Warehouse B

Horizontal Layout

Vertical Layout

Square Feet Area

Aisles:	4 x 5 1/2 sq. ft. wide x 65 sq. ft. long	1,430 sq. ft.
	2 x 5 1/2 sq. ft. wide x 100 sq. ft. long	1,100
	1 x 11 sq. ft. wide x 65 sq. ft. long	715
	Total aises	3,245 sq. ft.
Staging:	81 sq. ft. wide x 23 sq. ft. deep	1,863 sq. ft.
	81 sq. ft. wide x 12 sq. ft. deep	972
	Total staging area	2,835 sq. ft.
Storage:	2 x 4 sq. ft. deep x 100 sq. ft. long	800
	12 x 4 sq. ft. deep x 65 sq. ft. long	3,120
	Total storage area	3,920 sq. ft.
Total		10,000 sq. ft.

Cubic Feet Capacity

3920 sq. ft. x 28 ft. high = 109,760 cu. ft.

extremes. In actual practice the comparison may have to be compromised to accommodate certain merchandise which prudently should not be stored high. Nevertheless the ratio of comparison is essentially a direct relationship. If storage height is increased 25 percent, storage capacity is increased 25 percent. If the height is increased 50 percent, storage capacity is increased 50 percent, and so on. While all this may seem rather elementary, the fact is that apparently it escapes many warehouse designers and top company management. Otherwise why would there be so many low-height warehouses? Probably because buyers and lessors of buildings generally do not comprehend fully the potential of high cube warehouses. Their concerns and expertise must be for and in other things, such as price and square footage, without regard to what capacity is being acquired—which really should be the primary concern.

The increased storage capacity that results from increasing the building height does not come free. There are several additional costs involved. The total building cost will be more in relation to square feet, due to the need for a stronger foundation, higher walls, and the more costly equipment necessary to utilize the higher space. An extra system of fire sprinklers may even be required inside as well as above the storage racks. It may cost more to operate, but this is doubtful. It may very well cost less. The difference depends on the type of storing and handling equipment employed (discussed in Chapters 9, 10, and 11).

Figure 5.1 confirms that square footage is an inadequate measure of capacity. Building A is laid out for the use of conventional, counterbalance lift trucks. The 14-foot storage height combined with wide aisles severely restricts the available space. Building B, while having the same square footage, is laid out for narrow-aisle equipment, except for a center passing aisle. This aisle also serves for rapid movement between the rail and truck docks. With its increased height of 28 feet and narrow aisles, building B allows for much better utilization of storage space. Both have the same staging areas; however, the utilization of this space also can be improved by using staging racks. This would make the contrast between buildings A and B even greater.

The economics generally favor increased height unless there is some peculiarity about the warehousing situation that prohibits the use of high space. High storage should be thoroughly examined in relation to the specific warehousing situation.

It is not a truism that greater storage height always equals lower costs. However, a thorough understanding of the concept and its application provides an important means for lowering warehousing costs. Increased height enables lower space costs largely because only the cost of the walls and their footings increases as the height of the building increases. The costs for land, site preparation, floor, roof, rail spur, parking, access roads, and so on all remain essentially the same, regardless of how high the walls. The actual cost for doubling the height of the warehouse described in Figure 5.1 could be as little as 20 percent of the total facility cost including land. This percentage figure is used here for discussion purposes only. It should not be adopted as a hard and fast rule. In practice the percentage will vary with different circumstances. The 20 percent is used only to highlight the dramatic savings that are possible in designing even a moderately high warehouse. Actually high-rise warehouse facilities are much higher than the 28 feet used in Figure 5.1. There are many in the 60 to 80 foot high range and some that exceed 100 feet. At these heights the economics of the facility and operational costs take on a new meaning that involves more sophisticated economics (as discussed in Chapter 11).

Office Considerations

One of the first concerns in designing a warehouse facility is how much space to allow for the office. Next is where to put it, inside or outside the warehouse building? Followed with, how actually to design the office? There are many office-related alternatives and trade-offs. Discussed here are the aspects of the office as they influence building size and configuration.

A rule-of-thumb of industrial real estate speculators is that in the absence of specific information, allow 5 percent of the total square feet of the facility for office. For example, a 20,000-square-foot building should contain 1,000 square feet of office space. A 100,000-square-foot building should have 5,000 square feet and so on. This rule-of-thumb is not foolproof, but experience shows it to be as good an indicator as there is when a warehouse facility is built on pure speculation (for a yet unknown tenant).

For a facility being constructed to the specifications provided by an existing company, the office size requirement should be calculated the same way the handling and storing areas are determined—by forecasts of the affected departments in conformance with the company approved goals and objectives. Armed with this information you will know the functions and number of employees to be housed. This, along with careful planning and allowances for equipment, should provide the dimensions of the office.

Some of the important considerations about office design in relation to total facility design follow.

○ Will other groups of the company (other than warehousing) require space? If so, how much?
○ What are warehousing's personnel requirements?
○ What are space and other requirements of the office equipment?
○ What are the requirements for

  Restroom (include handicapped access)

  Lunchroom

  Kitchen (microwave, refrigerator, sink, etc.)

  Conference rooms

  Lounges

  Lobby and receptionist

  Heating and air conditioning

  Electrical equipment and lighting

  Electronic equipment

  Noise level

With all this input, the size of office can be fairly well predicted. Consideration should then be given to how the office space can be expanded or contracted to meet future requirement changes. One provision for later expansion could be to allow for additional office space above the initial office. If this alternative is planned, the first floor office should be designed to support a second floor. It should also be free of ducts, conduits, air-conditioning and heating units, and any other permanent obstructions.

Two additional benefits of providing in the beginning for the later use of the second floor are that the top of the office can be used for storage in the meantime and the real estate value is increased correspondingly. The increased real estate value perhaps may be more than the extra cost of providing for it initially. If and when the facility is sold to another company (as most eventually are) whoever is examining the facility for purchase will no doubt "discover" the potential of better use of the space over the office. It seems only human to be unusually pleased with ourselves to find a better way to use things that others apparently have overlooked. The potential for later expansion over the office may just serve as a lure to entrap potential buyers or at least get their serious attention.

Another provision for later office expansion is to initially design the office so that it can be expanded horizontally with few problems. To do this, first you must determine which side of the office would be most favorable to expand. Make certain there is access to that side without cutting through an existing office or being blocked by permanent fixtures. You must also provide for whatever amenities will be required for the added space, such as capacity for additional heat, air conditioning, restrooms, lounges, and so on. The additional cost of these at time of construction will be a lot less than what it will be later to modify existing facilities.

Another major decision that has to be faced is where to put the office in relation to the larger area devoted to warehousing operations. The following questions should be addressed:

○ What are the costs and other values of locating the office outside but connected to the warehouse building or inside the building?

○ Will appearances be improved with the office in front of the warehouse building?

○ What is the height of the warehouse compared to that of the office? (This is needed to determine how much space over the office will be lost if it is located inside the warehouse building)

Having the office inside the warehouse building generally costs less to construct because its floor, one or two side walls, and the weather protection part of the roof are already provided. It does, however, take away space that otherwise could be used by warehouse operations. It also may take away from the favorable esthetics of the facility by reinforcing the bland impression of a big rectangular building. A good case can be made for having the office inside or outside. By aligning the pros and cons, the concern comes into focus and assists in making the best decision. It also leaves a record that the alternatives were considered which is a lot by itself.

The "Square" Phenomenon

Discussed in the preceding section is the importance of the dimension of height in determining building capacity and that capacity (expressed in cubic feet) is a more meaningful measure than size (expressed in square feet). Here discussed is the importance of the width and length dimensions. Like height, the ratios of these dimensions are more important than commonly suspected.

A curious phenomenon of the width-length ratio is that it has a direct effect on construction costs. Two buildings having the same height, floor, and roof areas can have different wall areas. Yes, this is so. No, it is not a riddle. It is an application of basic arithmetic.

How construction is affected by this little-heralded phenomenon is illustrated by the three different footprints in Figure 5.2. Each building has the same floor space, 40,000 square feet, but the cost of the long narrow building is

FIGURE 5.2 The Wall Area and Travel Time Differences Related to Different Width and Length Dimensions with the Same Square Foot Areas

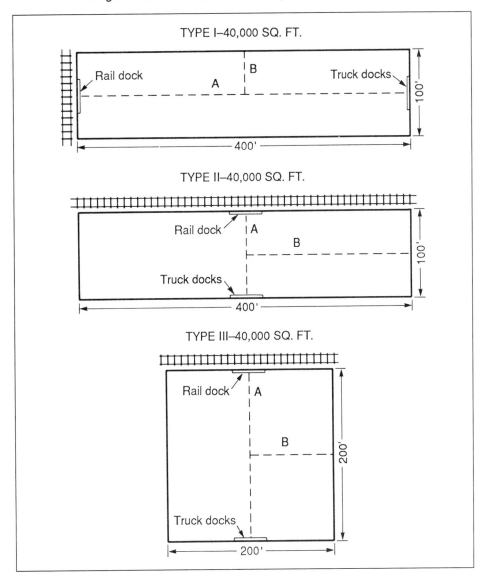

considerably more. This fact is clearly illustrated in the comparison of the amount of wall construction required for each structure, assuming the height to be the same for all three buildings.

The long narrow buildings require 200 linear feet more wall to enclose a 40,000-square-foot warehouse than is required by a square building. The roof and floor areas are the same.

This phenomenon is compounded when the height dimension is included. Suppose the walls were 20 feet high. The area of wall difference would be substantial.

These design comparisons net a difference of 4,000 square feet of wall with the same floor and roof surface, all due to the different width-length configuration. This is a 20 percent difference. A 20 percent reduction in wall material translates to a substantial cost difference.

The phenomenon becomes more dramatic as the height of the warehouse increases. Assume the height is 40 feet as opposed to the 20 feet used in the

Types I, II	Long narrow	
	Two long walls × 400 ft. each	800 ft.
	Two short walls × 100 ft. each	200 ft.
	Total linear walls	1,000 ft.
Type III	Square	
	Four walls × 200 ft. each	800 ft.
Difference in walls		200 ft.

example above. The difference in wall space for the long-narrow configuration would be an increase of 8,000 square feet. This is a quantity too large to shrug off as inconsequential.

There are many other things that are affected by the configuration of a building, such as the availability of land sites with desirable dimensions and the economics related to roof spans between support columns. The differences in width-length dimensions, however, remains a substantial factor in construction, and improved operating efficiency as discussed next.

Long narrow building, types I and II:
   20 feet high × 1,000 linear feet = 20,000 sq. ft. of wall area

Square building, type III:
   20 feet high × 8,000 linear feet = 16,000 sq. ft. of wall area

---

How Operating Efficiency Is Affected by Width and Length Dimensions
There is an inherent difference in operating efficiency for differently shaped buildings. The long narrow shape, illustrated in Figure 5.2, Type I, shows the rail and truck docks at the far ends of the building. Assuming that all incoming freight is by rail and all outgoing freight is by truck, the minimum travel distance for materials is from one dock to another (line A), 400 feet. The maximum distance is 500 feet (line A plus 2 × line B), for an average travel line of 450 feet: (400 ft. + 500 ft./2).

The Type II warehouse has the same outside dimensions, but the rail and truck docks are positioned close together. The minimum travel distance is along line A, 100 feet. The maximum travel distance is 500 feet (line A plus 2 × line B). The average travel distance is 300 feet: [(100 ft + 500 ft.)/2].

The square warehouse, illustrated by Type III, has a minimum travel line from the rail dock directly through to the truck dock (line A) of 200 feet. The maximum travel line is 400 feet (line A plus 2 × line B). The average travel distance is also 300 feet, the same as warehouse II.

This comparison (which ignores aisles for purposes of simplicity) illustrates an important principle of warehouse construction. The configurations of buildings II and III have the same area and same travel distance; however, warehouse II would cost considerably more to construct than warehouse III. It requires an extra 200 feet of wall because of its long narrow shape. The principle involved here is that, for the optimum combination of initial cost and operating efficiency, a warehouse should be as nearly as possible a perfect square and dock placements should aim for the minimum average travel distances. Different storage patterns, turnover, and the changing of dock positions will influence the operating efficiency, but the general application of this principle holds.

An example of a square building not being as efficient as a long narrow one is a truck terminal, where freight comes in LTL (less-than-truckload) quantities, is consolidated by outbound routing, and shipments are made within a short time span. Truck doors or inside docks enabled loading and unloading all along the two longest (and opposite) sides of the building. No inventory is maintained, and the shortest distance between inbound and outbound is the most efficient. The same occurs when the concept of JIT (just-in-time) is applied to a warehouse. This is commonly referred to as "flowthrough" warehousing. As in a truck terminal, inventories stay essentially in motion compared to the conventional warehouse where most inventories are at rest for at least a short but indefinite time.

The "Cube" Phenomenon

The previous section dealt with the substantial gains to be realized with a square footprint (four equal sides). This is a valuable tool in establishing warehouse design. It permits breakthroughs in constructions and operations costs that can result in substantial savings. Further, it provides a way to demonstrate the professionalism of warehousing.

The cube concept (six equal surfaces) is an extension of the square concept. The first encounter with this phenomenon is nearly as exciting as that of the square phenomenon. It would be even more so were it not that the square is an integral part of the cube. In fact the cube "rule" (and it should be elevated to the stature of a rule) encompasses the square (which by itself is deserving of being a rule). Of course, these "rules" apply to all buildings, but they are more important to warehouses because of the importance assigned to maximizing space utilization and material handling efficiency. Recognition of both rules constitutes a major technological advance in warehouse design. The phenomena has always existed but they are commonly not given due recognition.

Both have their areas of applicability. The square rule is most important to low-rise warehouse design, and the cube rule is most important to high-rise. The latter is of course, only pertinent if there is no overriding requirement which prevents constructing high-rise. The square footprint rule is equally applicable for low- and high-rise, but the cube principle simply does more for high-rise. It takes advantage of height as well as width and length. The cube principle applies to low-rise to the extent that the closer a warehouse design approaches the shape of a cube the more savings will result. This is another way of saying again that increasing the height of a warehouse is smart business. It is the least costly means of increasing capacity and, often, operating efficiency.

Figure 5.3 illustrates the relationship of capacity as height increases to a perfect cube. Buildings designated as A, B, and C (all with the same footprint of 100 feet by 100 feet) show how capacity doubles as height doubles. Some may think that this is not all that impressive since higher construction increases building and particularly equipment costs to use the higher altitude productively. The response to this is yes and no.

Yes, costs increase if the plan is to use only concrete or brick construction and the high-rise equipment is charged against the high-rise. No, it does not cost more and probably much less, if the storage racks provide the support for the walls and roof. Further support for the high-rise is provided by lower operating costs, better security, more reliability, and so on. Chapter 11 covers in detail these additional benefits.

Buildings C and D of Figure 5.3 show the comparison of a high-cube design and a low-rise design, both with a capacity of 1 million cubic feet. Building C

FIGURE 5.3 How Building Dimensions Relate to Capacity and Surface Areas

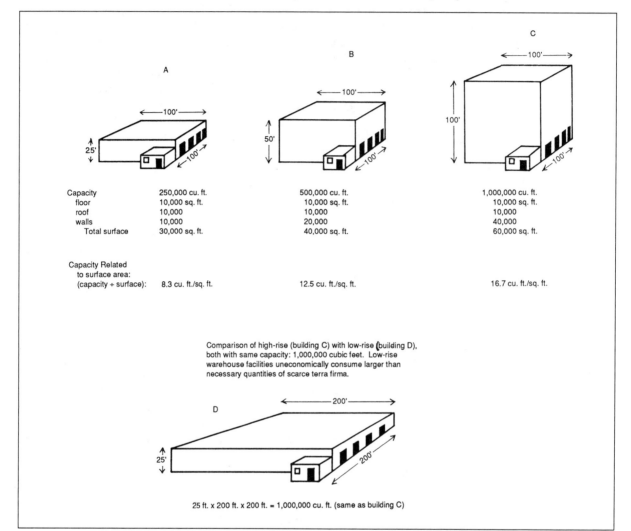

Capacity	250,000 cu. ft.	500,000 cu. ft.	1,000,000 cu. ft.
floor	10,000 sq. ft.	10,000 sq. ft.	10,000 sq. ft.
roof	10,000	10,000	10,000
walls	10,000	20,000	40,000
Total surface	30,000 sq. ft.	40,000 sq. ft.	60,000 sq. ft.

Capacity Related
to surface area:
(capacity ÷ surface): 8.3 cu. ft./sq. ft.   12.5 cu. ft./sq. ft.   16.7 cu. ft./sq. ft.

Comparison of high-rise (building C) with low-rise (building D), both with same capacity: 1,000,000 cubic feet. Low-rise warehouse facilities uneconomically consume larger than necessary quantities of scarce terra firma.

25 ft. x 200 ft. x 200 ft. = 1,000,000 cu. ft. (same as building C)

has a footprint of only 10,000 square feet, while building D has one that spreads across the landscape, 40,000 square feet, four times as much.

Note that these designs do not take into consideration the usual nearly 3-foot clearance code requirement between roof structure and the highest storage. This is omitted to keep the comparisons simple. Actually this factor is in favor of increased height. For instance, if the 3 feet of space is related to building C, the "unusable" area would be 30,000 cubic feet (3 ft. × 10,000 sq. ft.). For building D the unusable space would be 120,000 cubic feet (3 ft. × 40,000 sq. ft.) or four times that lost in building C.

How the Cube Principle is Applied to High-Rise ASRS

Figure 5.4 illustrates two different configurations of high-rise ASRSs. Dealt with here is how the shape of the buildings affects construction cost and operating efficiencies. Building A represents a rectangle edifice 50 feet wide, 200 feet deep, and 100 feet high with a storage capacity of 1,000,000 cubic feet. Building B is a design with the same storage capacity, but is a perfect cube (all six surfaces equal). Considering only the surfaces directly affected by the storage system, the following differences result:

Front, Back	Two Sides	Total
Building A		
2 × 100 ft. × 50 ft. = 10,000 sq. ft.	2 × 200 ft. × 100 ft. = 40,000 sq. ft.	50,000 sq. ft.
Building B		
2 × 100 ft. × 100 ft. = 20,000 sq. ft.	2 × 100 ft. × 100 ft. = 20,000 sq. ft.	40,000 sq. ft.
Wall-surface difference favoring the cube		10,000 sq. ft.
Percentage (50,000 sq. ft. / 40,000 sq. ft. – 1)		25%

The cube configuration incurs 10,000 square feet, twenty-five percent, less outside walls. While this is substantial, the continuing savings resulting from increased operating efficiency (which translates to cost savings) is more important. How much of an improvement there is depends on how many material handling units are employed and their versatility. Commonly there is one included for each aisle to avoid the lost time in transferring between aisles.

Assuming there is a material handling unit for each aisle, a comparison of horizontal front-to-back distance shows building A to be twice the distance of building B (200 ft. versus 100 ft.). Since the units move in two directions at a time, a comparison of the diagonal travel lines is more meaningful. The diagonal movement noted for the *width* dimensions of the two buildings is ignored because this capability is unusual for such systems. The length-height diagonal is common to all ASRSs. For building A this is 224 feet and for B, 141 feet, a difference of 83 feet (224 ft. – 141 ft.) or 166 feet per round trip—a 59 percent difference, which should highlight the importance of investigating building configurations. The means for determining the diagonal distance is covered in Chapter 11.

If the material handling units service more than one aisle, this will change the comparison by the time necessary to transfer between aisles. This offsets part of the advantage of the cube design because of the less storage area per aisle. If the units are manually operated, the time taken to transfer from one aisle to another becomes more significant. If the system is automated, this time difference becomes less important. Batch picking and storing also reduces the impact of aisle transfer because all work for an interval (say, a shift) for an aisle is completed before aisle transfer is necessary.

When the building and equipment are designed to maximize the advantages of the cube, the ideal of current technology is reached. Only levitation would be more ideal. Such a consideration may seem far-fetched, but is it really? Levitation is practiced in some eastern religions, reported by authorities with so-called impeccable reputations. Even this country's laser technology has advanced to the point that light within certain constraints can levitate physical objects.

Early in the use of air as a means of moving things in industry, I was involved in employing it to move heavy loads in a factory environment. In one case heavy stacks of metal sheet (up to 8,000 pounds) had to be moved between bays. Low ceiling prohibited installing a jib or other type crane to move the loads, and there was not enough room to use a lift truck, or even a low boy (low-platform motorized material mover). The only choice seemed to be rearrangement of the equipment, which would be expensive and would introduce a costly inefficiency. Jokingly the manager said: "Too bad we do not have a Sampson to move the loads or someone with powers of levitation to float them across."

The term "float" lingered in my mind. I remembered seeing small bumper

FIGURE 5.4 Comparison of High-Rise ASRS Storage Configurations (both systems have 1,000,000 cubic feet capacity; roofs and walls are attached to and supported by the racks)

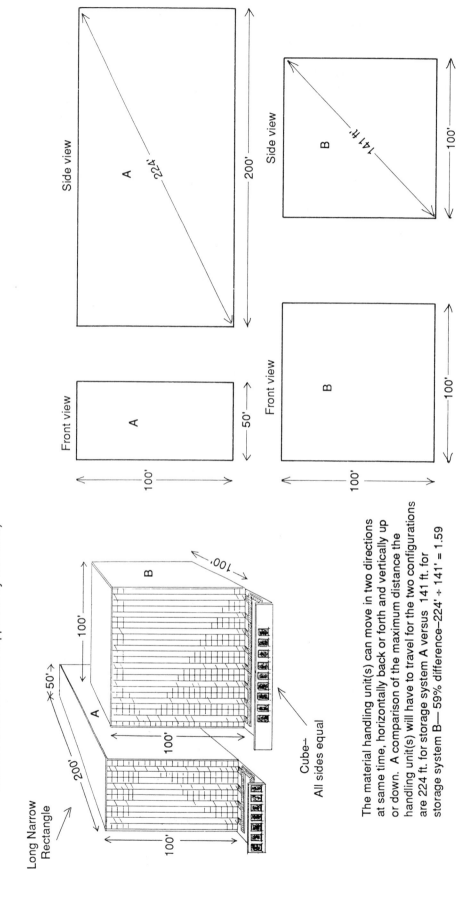

The material handling unit(s) can move in two directions at same time, horizontally back or forth and vertically up or down. A comparison of the maximum distance the handling unit(s) will have to travel for the two configurations are 224 ft. for storage system A versus 141 ft. for storage system B— 59% difference–224' ÷ 141' = 1.59

cars at an amusement park that drivers, young and old, would crash into each other. The cars floated above the floor. Starting here the search led to a major airplane manufacturer that employed the system to move around huge planes in final assembly. We reasoned if huge aircraft can be moved on air with a slight push, it would certainly work with our little 4-ton problem. It did and at a surprisingly low cost, considering it was a prototype.

If air can be used to move enormous weights by overcoming static resistance, is it so unbelievable that levitation is not far behind? Considering the very hard work of lumping (manually loading and unloading), it seems that lumpers in particular would agree that levitation to replace brawn cannot come too soon. The air float system is discussed in detail with illustrations in Chapter 9.

Words of Caution   If you are considering an ASRS, make certain you investigate the cube phenomenon discussed here. I have worked with vendors and engineers to learn about these systems and have designed three and installed two high-rise modified ASRSs. Not once have the relationships discussed here been brought to my attention. I only discovered them while playing with different warehouse dimensions out of curiosity to see "what if . . .?" All this told me is that this phase of ASRS and high-rise systems has not received the attention it justly deserves. Perhaps vendors and customers are so enamored with the major technological breakthrough these systems make (compared with low-rise lift-truck systems) that they fail to squeeze out the last bit of good. As the most successful admirals and generals know, when you have a breakthrough, that is the time to pour on the steam and maximize gains.

What About a Cylinder or Spherical Configuration?   The subject of the best configuration for warehouses design should also include mentioning the cylindrical and the spherical shapes. Granted, either of these will require less building material to achieve the same cubic space. A cylinder configuration also would be reasonable to construct using the continuous cast process discussed later in this chapter.

For general merchandise the sphere would be totally impractical. It fails due to not having a flat floor or vertical walls. If this were not enough, how do you prevent a huge ball from rolling away? The cylinder would not have this problem, being flat on top and bottom, but storing and handling in a sphere would be exceedingly difficult for most warehouse materials. There are, however, notable exceptions, for example, silos for grain and relatively small spheres for liquids and gases. The cylindrical and spherical configurations are ideal for certain types of commodities, but they are essentially out of the question for general commodities such as canned goods, TV sets, and so on. However, now after writing this, some inventive reader will consider it a challenge and design a way to prove me wrong. Let us hope he or she does. Warehousing is ready for a breakthrough in design.

Land and Related Costs

Rarely does a company waste money acquiring the very best site for a warehouse facility.

The total cost of land includes the purchase price and any additional costs to make it ready to start construction. Some of these less obvious costs follow.

- Survey fees
- Unpaid assessments

- ○ Land leveling and clearing
- ○ Removal of unusable buildings
- ○ Easements
- ○ Laying of roads to the property
- ○ Environmental impact studies
- ○ Sewer and water hook-up fees
- ○ Provision to increase water pressure
- ○ Additional fire hydrants
- ○ Costs to bring in electrical and telephone lines
- ○ Extra municipal and school support fees
- ○ Poor soil conditions such as

> Large rock formations
>
> Water table too close to surface
>
> Trash dump below surface
>
> Drainage problems
>
> Excessive trees and roots
>
> Wrong soil consistency to support building
>
> Fill of wetlands
>
> "Hot soil" (contaminated with pesticides)

The total cost of land, in addition to the purchase price, includes costs to be incurred due to any of the factors listed or any others that have been overlooked here. The sum of all these costs to ready the site to accept the building improvements yields a truer land cost and one that permits more valid comparison with other sites.

Figure 5.5 shows a 160,000-square-foot building on a 320,000-square-foot lot (7.3 acres (320,000 sq. ft./43,560 sq. ft.)). This translates to building coverage of 50 percent of the land (160,000 sq. ft./320,000 sq. ft.). The figure also illustrates three different site configurations with the same land-to-building ratio (2 to 1). Note that where the building is situated on the property directly affects what can be done with the outside space. The nature of a warehouse's functions will dictate the best configuration to meet its own particular requirements.

The building may cover a higher percentage of land than 50 percent, but more common is for zoning to restrict the building to 50 percent or even less. The trend is to increase the portion not covered by building and to devote more to landscaping and parking. These requirements constitute real concerns and additional costs that have to be considered along with the purchase price and other costs of the land. On the other hand, these requirements may have positive values, particularly when the facility is viewed as a real estate investment as well. The congestion and overbuild appearance that results from not providing for open space adversely affects real estate value.

A good-looking building with extensive attractive landscaping will go a long way toward creating and maintaining good employee, customer, and community relations. It is unusual for owners to regret creating the very best image of their facilities—within reason.

Another important consideration when buying land for a warehouse facility is whether to buy enough for later expansion. Warehousing is notorious for inventory fluctuations causing variations in space requirements. It is important to determine in the design process what can be done if there is a long-term change in space needs.

FIGURE 5.5 Comparisons of Site Configurations for 50 Percent Building Coverage of Site

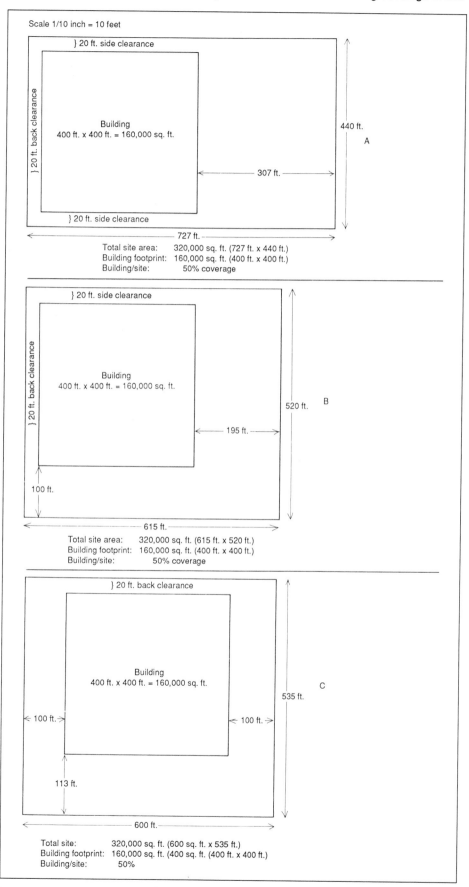

Scale 1/10 inch = 10 feet

A

} 20 ft. side clearance

} 20 ft. back clearance

Building
400 ft. x 400 ft. = 160,000 sq. ft.

307 ft.

440 ft.

} 20 ft. side clearance

727 ft.

Total site area: 320,000 sq. ft. (727 ft. x 440 ft.)
Building footprint: 160,000 sq. ft. (400 ft. x 400 ft.)
Building/site: 50% coverage

B

} 20 ft. side clearance

} 20 ft. back clearance

Building
400 ft. x 400 ft. = 160,000 sq. ft.

195 ft.

520 ft.

100 ft.

615 ft.

Total site area: 320,000 sq. ft. (615 ft. x 520 ft.)
Building footprint: 160,000 sq. ft. (400 ft. x 400 ft.)
Building/site: 50% coverage

C

} 20 ft. back clearance

Building
400 ft. x 400 ft. = 160,000 sq. ft.

100 ft.   100 ft.

535 ft.

113 ft.

600 ft.

Total site: 320,000 sq. ft. (600 sq. ft. x 535 ft.)
Building footprint: 160,000 sq. ft. (400 sq. ft. (400 ft. x 400 ft.)
Building/site: 50%

If less space is needed, the choice is whether to move or to find some profitable means of using the excess space. Moving has serious limitations. Essentially, you go back to square one to begin the process of location, site selection compliance with code and zoning requirements, design, and construction. After all this is done, you are faced with the costly move of inventories, changes of address, transfer of personnel, and disruption of service. Also the company is faced with what to do with the vacated facility. If it is leased, you are faced with the penalties of breaking the lease or subleasing to some other company (provided there is provision for this in your lease contract). If the facility is owned by your company, you are faced with selling or leasing it. This may seem profitable if the facility has appreciated since the time of its acquisition. It would have to appreciate a lot, however, to more than offset the costs of the move. Then, too, the warehouse you move to may have appreciated over this time as yours did. It is improbable that moves of warehouse operations actually reduce facility costs unless the moves are to less space, a less desirable location, or a lower-quality facility.

If there is a long-term need for more space, this can be provided by moving (with all the problems just discussed) or enacting one or both of the following alternatives. Provision for these must have been made when your warehouse was first constructed. Go "out" or "up" for the needed extra space.

1. The alternative of constructing additional contiguous space requires that extra land be acquired in the initial purchase or that additional land can be purchased "when needed." Counting on it being available for purchase when needed is risky business. The chance is slim that the extra land will wait patiently until you need it.

    The certain way to provide for more space in the future is to build extra space in the beginning and lease it to others on short-term contracts until you need it. Both buying extra land and holding it or building on it have merit. Real estate appreciation has been a pretty sure thing for many years—if for no other reason than land's diminishing availability. If the alternative selected is to buy and hold vacant land and not construct until the additional space is needed, make certain the extra land is at least minimally landscaped and maintained to avoid its becoming an eyesore.

2. Another alternative is to provide for expansion by allowing for a taller building than initially required. Then as more capacity is needed, the low-rise equipment that served in the past is sold to help buy the specialized handling equipment and storage racks needed to use the higher space productively. However, the extra cost of constructing the higher building is money that is invested in an anticipated need that may never materialize. This alternative may be the most prudent one if the extra capacity can be provided for less cost than the other ways discussed—and there is a strong probability this will be the case. For certain if there is no extra land to buy, or it is too costly, the increased height alternative will look particularly attractive. If the company's financial situation is that speculative land investment is frowned upon, the increased height hedge for future requirements may provide a good compromise.

    If the future is one of contraction rather than expansion, and the provision was made for additional space either by acquiring extra land or extra capacity, the alternatives are to sell the extra land, sell the total facility, lease the extra capacity, or find some alternative use such as taking on the warehousing for other companies as a public warehouse.

    The alternatives for profitable dispensation of extra space can be attractive as compared to needing additional space and having not provided for it. The worst you can do is to ignore the risk of needing less or more space when the facility size and dimensions are initially determined. This is flagrant procrastination, which may or may not catch up with the guilty. Whatever the reason, it is negligent management. It is the type of business decision that sacrifices long-range benefits for immediate cost avoidance, to *maximize short-term profits*.

Site Preparation

This is an extension of the preceding discussion about land costs. It includes anything that must be done to ready the site to receive facility improvements. This can be as little as removing enough top soil to get rid of soil saturated with pesticides residuals to blasting an unwanted rock formation or draining a swamp.

Those who have tried to get by with less than code specifications or prepared the site to inadequate specifications have been very lucky or have eventually paid the piper. Warehouse facilities unfortunately are not held up by levitation, yet. Inadequate site preparation covered with concrete or asphalt only hides the problems for a short time. The costs of repair later, if at all possible, are many times more than doing it right the first time.

Drainage System

The drainage system for the warehouse site should be an integral part of the site preparation plan. Because of its importance it is discussed here as a separate subject. Normally the site drainage provision can be taken care of with engineered contouring of the land. In some cases the land will already have the topography necessary to provide natural drainage; however, this is unusual. Most often considerable earth must be moved and fill brought in to develop the right elevations to permit proper drainage.

The drainage plan should begin with a topographical drawing resulting from a detailed engineering survey of elevations. This is to determine the optimum use of the existing land contour in relation to the storm sewer, drainage ditch, or other means to carry off the excess water. Of course, the local building code and engineering office must be consulted very early in the planning stage to determine what is required. The local sanitary department will have the greatest influence over what drainage system is required. Of particular concern are the controls over what industrial wastes are permitted to feed into the municipal drainage system. Rightly these have become increasingly stringent. Normally industrial wastes are not a problem in warehousing because objectionable wastes such as toxic chemicals are the result of factory operations, not warehousing.

The expense of the drainage system can be a major component of the total cost of new construction, and it should be related to the price of the land. What might look like a good land value can be actually a very poor one if it is costly to implement a proper drainage system. Ingenuity in how best to drain a property can often reduce the costs. However, a fairly close estimate of its cost should be made to determine the "total cost" of the land. Figure 5.6 illustrates alternative ways to solve a drainage problem.

The Importance of Floors

There are few other places in industry where floors are subjected to the excessive strain and abuse that they are in warehousing. The same problem exists only where floors are recipients of frequent heavy loads concentrated in very

FIGURE 5.6 Alternative Ways to Drain Property

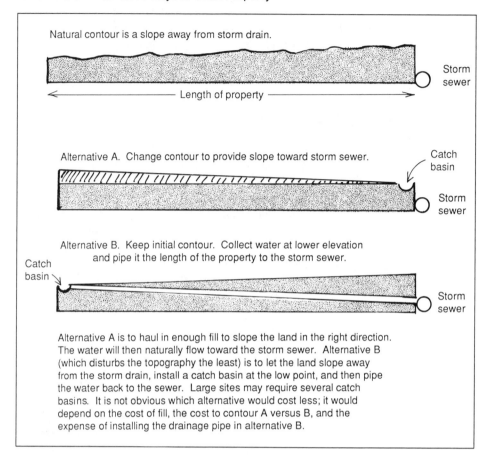

Alternative A is to haul in enough fill to slope the land in the right direction. The water will then naturally flow toward the storm sewer. Alternative B (which disturbs the topography the least) is to let the land slope away from the storm drain, install a catch basin at the low point, and then pipe the water back to the sewer. Large sites may require several catch basins. It is not obvious which alternative would cost less; it would depend on the cost of fill, the cost to contour A versus B, and the expense of installing the drainage pipe in alternative B.

small areas. The pressures are extreme at the four small surfaces where the hard rubber tires of a lift truck meet the floor and at the foot of the upright beams used in storage racking.

Even if the floors seem to be taking the pressures for a while, there is a fatiguing effect going on to break down the cohesiveness of the concrete. Cracks develop first. Next one side of the crack depresses more than the other. Then chipping on the high side starts. Bad becomes worse. The different sides develop a more pronounced difference in elevation from one side's compacted fill giving more than the other. Both sides of the crack erode more every time the handling equipment rolls over them. Nowhere do these old and worn adages apply more than to warehouse floors: "an ounce of prevention is worth a pound of cure" and "do it right the first time."

Fill and Compaction Regardless of whether the floor is to be elevated to truck-bed level or is to be at ground level, there is a need for fill and compaction. A paved floor is not poured directly onto virgin ground. The earth must be prepared. The land must be brought to the desired level. Any undesirable foreign material must be removed such as tree stumps, boulders, soft soil, "hot" dirt (high-chemical-content fertilizer), and so on. If the floor is to be elevated, enough good soil or aggregate must be hauled in to bring the floor to the proper elevation. All soil must be compacted normally between 85 and 95 pounds per square inch. There must be enough incline to provide drainage (normally about 6 inches per 100 feet). Provision must be made for disposal of the runoff water—into a storm drain or other approved system. All this can be minimal, or it can be prohibitive. Most of the time it is somewhere in between.

An important factor in the cost of fill and compaction is the availability of good earth or aggregate for the purpose. In some areas there is an abundance of good fill, and the cost is mainly for hauling and compacting it. In other areas fill can be exceedingly scarce and thereby expensive. A common sight on vacant lots is a sign saying "clean fill wanted." An owner or developer is trying to acquire free fill or to find a source where at least a good price can be negotiated. It is fortunate where the proceeds from a site excavation can be used as fill for the same site.

Compaction of the fill is essential. Lack of compaction can be disastrous to the building: foundations will sink and floors will buckle, crack, or sink. To illustrate this consider the example of covering a desk top with a glass plate which is commonly done to provide a smooth writing surface. Assume a pencil is placed under the right and left edges of the glass, between the desk top and the glass. With a very light blow in the center of the glass, it will break. The support beneath the glass is not uniform. Now visualize placing a glass plate directly on top of a hard desk top without the pencils. Strike the glass in this case and nothing happens. The glass is uniformly supported with a surface that will not give. The same situation exists with fill beneath a cement slab. With poor compaction the slab will break the same as the glass plate that was supported by only two pencils.

The compaction of the fill is just as important, probably more important than the thickness of the concrete slab. Adding thickness to the slab will not make up for inadequate compaction.

Fill and compaction requirements also relate to the truck maneuvering areas, truck landing pads in front of the docks, parking spaces, and driveways. These areas are just as important as the warehouse floor. They are, however, much easier to repair. The rule should be that all places where asphalt and concrete are used should have appropriate specifications with a healthy safety margin. Then make certain the specifications are followed to the letter during construction.

Whether asphalt or concrete is used depends on the battering and abuse the paving will take. Asphalt is normally less expensive than concrete, but because it relates to the price of oil, this cost comparison could change at any time.

Asphalt paving can be made exceedingly strong, and it can be sealed in a manner that competes with concrete flooring in warehouse situations where balloon-tire material handling equipment in particular is used. When hard rubber tires are used, concrete is best and most commonly used.

The outside areas to be paved do not require the same paving specifications. The best paving is required where there is trailer or container parking. Concrete of lasting durability is definitely needed in front of the truck docks. The cement pad that supports the landing gear at the front of the van and container takes the heaviest beating and should require the best fill, compaction, and concrete. Warehouses that have a lot of this type of parking should embed metal plates in concrete where the landing gear rests. It is sad to see a heavily loaded trailer sink its landing gear through the paving. Bringing in an expensive heavy-duty crane to right the trailer may be the only remedy. Such cranes are hard to get and very costly to engage.

The automobile driveways and parking areas, if separate from the truck parking and driveways, require only automobile-use paving specifications. Truck driveways and maneuvering areas should have the same rigid specifications used by the state or federal highway departments, whichever is the more stringent.

It is not necessary and should be considered wasteful to have highway specifications for automobile areas. It is exceedingly important, however, that with different specifications for different areas there is no violation of these prescribed zones. Trucks must stay out of automobile parking areas and driveways. If this is not possible, the automobile areas must meet the more rigid highway specifications. Otherwise the heavy trucks will tear up the paving in short order.

Concrete Specification The composition and application of concrete and asphalt are not specified here because determining them is an evolving science, and requirements can be different from one locality to another. Also the fill and compaction specifications are interdependent on the paving material specifications. If everything else is correct, warehouse floors are usually poured concrete 4 to 8 inches thick with appropriate reinforcement, at least 6×6 inches, number 10 wire mesh.

Provision for expansion is made by dividing the concrete into rectangle sections. There is special concrete which does not require expansion joints. This should be investigated for applicability.

Three Case Histories About Faulty Floors It is not uncommon to hear that the warehouse floor is the single most important part of a warehouse facility. Those in rainy areas with roof problems may debate this. However, there is no denying that a bad floor can be disastrous to both warehouse operations and real estate values.

I have had several experiences with bad floors. On one occasion, the floor started to drop away along the entire length of a 200-foot wall. Operations restricted the inventories stored in the area to only the lightest merchandise, but the floor continued to drop. After it had sunk about 8 inches, we broke the lease and found another warehouse facility.

Another experience involved a build-to-suit leaseback warehouse that developed unusual floor problems. Before the warehouse was five years old the rectangular sections of concrete that were separate for expansion purposes began heaving up and down. As a lift truck crossed the floor, each slab would dip at the leading edge and raise at the far edge. The slabs took on a teeter-totter effect. It was almost comical to watch. The problem was not the concrete—that was strong enough to hold together except where the rectangular slabs met. As lift-truck tires left a depressed slab to meet the higher edge of next slab, edge chipping occurred. The teeter-totter effect worsened and the erosion continued with wider and deeper voids, until the lift trucks jolted as they crossed each chasm. The cause of the problem was inadequate fill and compaction.

The landlord tried to correct the problem by pumping concrete under the slabs, which proved only a temporary relief. This caused cracking due to the uneven support of the pumped in concrete. Operations had to stick it out until the end of the first five-year increment of the lease; then the option to extend the lease was not exercised. Operations moved on to another facility that had an adequate floor.

The third experience relates to the finish and age of a concrete floor. The building had been a factory for over 70 years. It was acquired in a complex transaction engineered by the director of real estate and the president of the company. They thought the facility could be converted to a warehouse, and by doing so, their total scheme would be made highly profitable. I was advised after the fact of the nice thing they had done for warehousing.

After removing all the low beams we dared, inventories were received and full operations began. Before a year was out the most traveled floor areas started to break down. First the surface gave up the sand and lime in its finish. Then small pebble aggregate broke loose followed by larger aggregate. Not only did it constitute a hazard for the lift trucks with heavy loads, but the fine powdery material (which was a by-product of the sand, lime and aggregate coming loose) floated through the air settling on the inventories and, worse, breathed by the employees. Filter masks were made a requirement along with hard hats. Eventually the property was sold for the land value which had appreciated enough to provide proof of the initial wisdom in buying it. The warehousing part of the transaction suffered, but service was maintained and clean merchandise shipped by extra effort and plain old fashion "grit."

Cause of Extreme Load Factor   It takes a thorough engineering analysis to determine in advance the extreme abuses a floor will take over the years. Consider, for example, the load concentration at the small area that tires of a lift truck make contact with the floor. (See Figure 5.7.)

The weight of the lift truck is probably in the range of 2,000 to 8,000 pounds plus the pallet load. There is a tremendous pressure transmitted though the very small floor areas covered by the four hard-rubber tires. Assuming a lift truck weighing 8,000 pounds is carrying a load that weighs 6,000 pounds. A pressure of 14,000 pounds is being transmitted to the floor through the four wheels. Now assume the contact area is a generous 3 square inches per tire. Through a surface area of 12 square inches—4 wheels × 3 square inches/wheel—an average pressure of 1,000 pounds per square inch is being transmitted (12,000 pounds/12 sq. in.). This is the minimum pressure on the floor. Consider the greater pressure created when the load is being lowered and comes to an abrupt halt, or when a traveling lift truck runs over a bump in the floor. Even when the loaded lift truck is stopped or at normal uninterrupted travel, the front wheels near the load transmit far greater pressure than the back wheels. The front wheels act as a fulcrum. This is glaringly demonstrated when an operator tries to lift something that exceeds the capacity of the lift truck. The back end of the lift truck rises off the floor. Occasionally you will see a fellow operator climb up and sit on the back end to give that extra leverage needed. This is frowned on for safety's sake, but it does happen when the concerned employees "do what is necessary to get the job done."

FIGURE 5.7   Extreme Load Factor Where Small Area of Lift Trucks Hard Tires Contact Floor

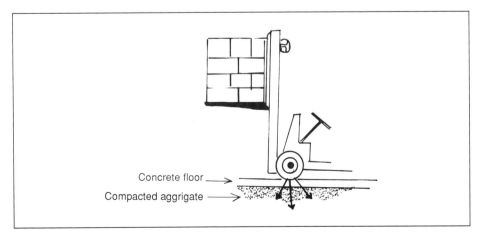

Nine Factors Affecting Capacity and Life of Warehouse Floors The capacity and life of a floor is mainly determined by the following factors:

1. Quality of the fill
2. Compaction of the fill
3. Quality of the concrete
4. Quality and quantity of reinforcing steel and the positioning of it within the concrete
5. How the concrete is poured and worked
6. Thickness of the concrete
7. Provision for contraction and expansion
8. Curing period
9. Finish

Another important consideration in developing specifications for the floor is that the life of the building is probably 40 years or more. During this time it could be put to many different uses. An extra investment in a good floor during its initial construction is well justified. Positively the floor is a poor place to economize. There are other areas that would be far better, many of which are discussed throughout this book.

Comparison of Wall Materials

Generally the walls of a warehouse are given little design consideration by anyone other than the architect and builder. This should not be the case. There are many important alternatives to consider. Examples are what material should be used, esthetics, insulation qualities, and wall height. Warehouse height is discussed extensively elsewhere in this book, and its importance as a consideration is fully emphasized. It is enough to reiterate here that in general the cost of cubic space decreases as the height of the building increases. Mainly discussed here are the materials used and the alternative designs of walls.

The common building materials used are concrete, metal, brick, and cinder block. Brick and block are less common probably because the technology and economies of erecting concrete and metal buildings are rapidly outpacing them. The increasing cost of labor makes the use of materials that require a lot of labor to be less and less attractive.

Tilt-Wall Concrete This process involves pouring the walls horizontally in sections on the completed floor. The sections are then picked up and positioned vertically with a crane. They are braced into position; then columns of steel reinforced concrete are poured where sections meet to provide a sturdy continuous wall. This process provides nearly ideal walls for a warehouse. They are sturdy, will take considerable abuse, an insulation material can be sandwiched within, and minimal space is lost by wall/roof support columns. Furthermore, the cost of construction is generally very competitive, particularly when constructing larger facilities.

There are also limitations to tilt-concrete construction. The technology in some areas of the country is not as common as it is for other building materials. Where this wall system is not common, it is expensive and difficult to find builders that are equipped to provide it. Further, unless the walls are well designed and well constructed, cracks will develop, and they can lead to a maintenance problem. Another consideration is that it is commonly believed that bare concrete is esthetically unattractive, that the concrete should be painted. On the other hand, there are some that believe concrete in its natural state is attractive. If the walls are painted, the maintenance problem as with any painted surface must be faced. The use of high-quality paints with proper application will minimize this problem to perhaps a new coat once every ten years.

An important consideration in the use of tilt-concrete construction is that it requires the use of large cranes to lift the wall segments into place (see Figure 5.8).

Building contractors who specialize in tilt-wall construction require use of these heavy-duty cranes. Without access to such a crane, a builder is shut out from the tilt-wall business. In certain parts of the country you cannot get competitive quotations. You cannot even get tilt-wall quotations unless you accept the substantial extra costs to transfer the crane a long distance and deal with out-of-the-area contractors who know this business. The requirement of a large crane dictates certain rather interesting economics about tilt-wall buildings. Normally this type construction is more expensive compared to using metal when erecting small buildings, perhaps up to 50,000 square feet, yet it is competitive and sometimes less expensive for larger buildings. The main reason for this is that setup costs for tilt-wall construction are relatively high compared to those of other types of construction. The setup costs include bringing in and returning the powerful crane to maneuver the wall panels and

FIGURE 5.8 Concrete Tilt Wall Construction

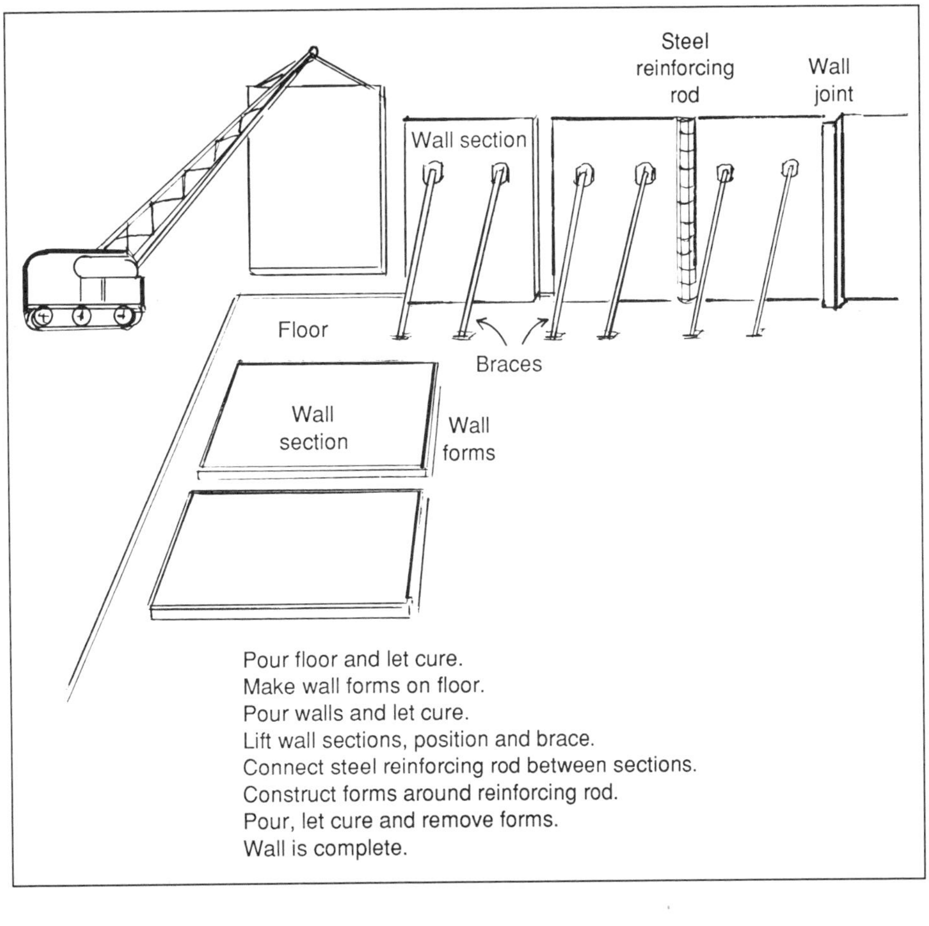
Steel
reinforcing
rod
Wall
joint
Wall section
Floor
Braces
Wall
section
Wall
forms
Pour floor and let cure.
Make wall forms on floor.
Pour walls and let cure.
Lift wall sections, position and brace.
Connect steel reinforcing rod between sections.
Construct forms around reinforcing rod.
Pour, let cure and remove forms.
Wall is complete.

the cost of making the wall-panel forms for casting the concrete walls. The total of these two costs plus any other one-time costs directly related to tilt-wall construction must be amortized over the total cost of the building. The larger the building, the less these setup costs are a factor.

Precast Concrete   A building method that is in many ways similar to tilt-wall construction is that of precast concrete. This method is similar because the wall sections are poured in a horizontal position and later lifted and attached vertically. However, this method is also different because the precast panels are produced in a factory environment and then hauled to the job site (rather than being produced at the site). The advantages of the precast method are that weather conditions have less effect and production takes place in the more efficient factory conditions at the generally lower wages of factory workers. The disadvantages are that factory production requires extra handling and more difficult transportation problems including the hazard of handling and in-transit damage.

Precast is not as common as tilt-wall construction. In certain areas of the country, however, it is more common. Whether this is due to economics, the state of the technology, or custom is not clear, and perhaps not important. Under certain conditions either one can be the best. Therefore, consideration should be given to both.

Continuous Cast Concrete   Another means to build walls with concrete is the continuous-cast process. A structure of reinforcing rods from 3 to 6 feet high is positioned in the wall foundations. Wooden or steel forms are secured to both sides of the future walls. Then the concrete is poured progressively around the building. As one layer becomes sufficiently set, the next level of reinforcing rods are inserted and the forms are moved up to take another pour. This routine is followed until the desired wall height is reached. The system is similar to that of compacted earth walls, one of the oldest means of building walls and one that from time to time over the years is revived as a return to nature away from synthetics and plastics. The big advantage of the compacted earth walls is the low cost of material. Often soil from the same site can be used.

Metal: Aluminum and Steel   Metal walls deserve serious consideration in warehouse construction. Under certain conditions they are the best; under other conditions they are less desirable and quite often are simply prohibited. The student of warehousing should be aware of the various building materials so that a valid comparison can be made and the appropriate one can be specified.

Both rolled sheets of aluminum and steel are common as warehouse building materials—with steel being the most common and aluminum slowly gaining in popularity. Aluminum is generally more expensive but is lighter and easier to handle. While both have a salvage value after the functional use of the building, aluminum's value will probably be greater. Both can be factory-painted under controlled conditions. This normally provides superior paint qualities compared to paint applied at the job site to concrete and masonry materials.

An important characteristic of metal buildings is their appearance. This can be both favorable and unfavorable. There are in some localities shoddy-looking old metal buildings that have given an unfavorable reputation to this type of construction. Rusty deteriorated steel buildings in particular have contributed most to this. However, with today's painting technology and proper architectural design, there is no reason why metal buildings cannot equal or exceed any other building materials' esthetic qualities.

A note of caution: There are many warehousing and industrial localities where the building codes and zoning prohibit metal buildings. Perhaps these restrictions are not warranted, but they are a fact and must be so acknowledged.

Because metal buildings are generally less acceptable, there is often greater difficulty in acquiring favorable outside financing for them. Lenders commonly prefer to finance buildings made of tilt-wall, precast, brick, and building block over metal (either aluminum or steel). As a result it may be necessary to provide a higher return for the investor, and if this is the case, the total cost of the building is increased. If it is necessary to pay just one percentage point more interest, when the going rate is 10 percent, this is equivalent to a 10 percent total cost increase in the amount borrowed. For example, a loan of $1,000,000 amortized over 20 years at 10 percent interest costs about $160,000 more than does a loan at 9 percent—or about $660 additional each month.

Comparing the cost of a building constructed of metal to one of tilt-wall or precast concrete is a worthwhile exercise (provided metal sheathing is not prohibited). You will probably find that metal is less expensive up to approximately 50,000 square feet. Concrete is favored for larger warehouses, provided all costs are considered, including interest on finance, maintenance, and resale value. There are exceptions, of course, but the 50,000-square-foot size can serve as a general rule-of-thumb until you develop your own based on your company's special requirements and competitive cost quotations.

A particular problem related to metal buildings is the shape of the roof-support columns that also serve as wall columns. Although this problem is more common to metal-wall construction, it can be found in buildings constructed of other materials. Due to the increased strength-to-weight ratio that can be developed, the design engineers and architects specify columns that are much wider at the top than at the bottom. While this may be good architecturally and cost-wise, it is bad for warehousing as it uses valuable cubic storage space. When the columns are not vertically straight, space next to the column is lost or poorly utilized.

Buildings used for manufacturing can be designed with the tapered columns and the loss in space is often not noticed or is of little importance. In warehousing, space utilization is of prime importance, and any negative influence such as inside tapered columns should be avoided. Obviously, vertical, straight columns should be favored over inside tapered columns. If tapered columns are used, they should result in sufficient construction cost savings to overcome the cost of lost space over the entire life of the building—about 40 years. A viable compromise would be to have the expanded column width take place outside the perimeter of the building.

Brick Masonry Brick plays a lesser but still important role in warehouse construction. Next to wood, brick is the oldest building material. Today wood is rarely used except for outside cosmetic touches. Brick, however, continues to have at least a minor role as a material for walls as well as being commonly used in place of wood for outside adornment features.

Except for the higher labor costs, brick has a lot to recommend it. Commonly brick buildings look good and retain their real estate value possibly longer than does any other material. Brick and mortar are generally more expensive as a construction material than are concrete and metal walls, but this is not always true. If the building is in an area with low labor rates and the large cranes have to be transported for long distances, usually more is done with brick than with concrete and metal.

While brick is touted for its superior esthetic qualities, very attractive walls can be achieved with sculptured designs and exposed aggregate using concrete walls. Metal sheathing can also be designed to be very attractive. Much depends on the ingenuity and artistic talents of the designer. This is an area where artistic talent can be far more valuable than its cost.

Walls need not be all one type of building material. Two large, high-cube warehouses that I designed used precast concrete for the first 20 feet of wall then metal sheathing for the next 24 feet, providing a wall 44 feet high. The office was constructed of brick and was placed in front, connecting to the warehouse building. The combination proved economical and very attractive. Combined were the best features of brick, concrete, and metal. While this was best for that particular time and place, it will not hold true in all geographic areas and all warehouse configurations. If you want to consider different alternatives, get competitive quotations on each to sort out the best materials and combination for your company in the locality where your warehouse facility is to be constructed. In the case cited, we were permitted to use metal sheathing in a locality that otherwise prohibited its use by using it only above the 20-feet-high concrete walls and combining the two materials to create an attractive total facility.

Cinder Block Masonry   This is a building block made of concrete and fine cinders. It comes in a variety of shapes, sizes, and finishes. It has the important advantage over brick in that it requires less labor per area because it is several times as large. A completed wall can be constructed just one block deep using reinforcing steel rod and poured concrete through the hollow spaces. Brick must be laid two deep, or a cement wall must be built to which the brick is attached.

Recent attempts to make building blocks more attractive have been successful. Not infrequently they will be used in place of brick or wood to improve the esthetics of otherwise drab buildings.

Like brick, however, cinder block construction normally requires more labor than the concrete and metal types discussed earlier.

Roof Materials and Configurations

The warehouse roof is one of those things that is taken for granted—until it rains or snows. Then if it is faulty it promptly moves to top priority. Roofs are important everywhere, but there are few places they are of such importance as in warehousing. Suppose, for example, that rain comes through on an area of stacked pallet loads of premium wine. What can happen is scary. First, the cases become soggy, losing strength. This continues through several layers of cases. Then a column of pallet loads tips against another column starting others to tip in a domino effect, resulting in a huge and extensive jumbled pile of wet cases. In the process, many of the bottles of wine are broken, mixing their delicate bouquets with rain water to cause further inventory destruction. Bottles not broken get their labels soaked off or stained badly enough to require relabeling. Other roof-related disasters have involved high-tech instruments, museum artifacts, and expensive books.

Insurance money may be difficult to collect when the damage is due to a leaky roof. This is because a "prudent man" (so described in most legal documents) would not put inventories under a leaky roof. CEOs and owners may, in their desire to maximize quick profits, cause warehousing to inhabit quarters whose roofs have not been properly maintained, but this excuse "does not hold water" with insurance companies either.

Different Roof Configurations   Warehousing is performed under many differently shaped roofs—from geodesic to prismatic and everything in between.

Why there are so many is because a lot of them were initially designed for purposes other than warehousing (such as factory operations). When these other operations stopped for one reason or another (outgrowing the building, bankruptcy, etc.), the facilities were used for warehousing. This is due to the nearly archaic concept that any dry space is all right for warehousing. Although such contentions drive professional warehousers "up a wall," there is a modicum of truth to this type of thinking. Warehousing can fit almost any building configuration—if there is little concern about being cost effective and service responsive.

Figure 5.9 shows various roof configurations. Probably each is best suited for a specific circumstance. For example, the "sawtooth" design was commonly used for factories a generation ago as it permits the entrance of natural light and promotes ventilation. The vertical part of each saw tooth is comprised of glass panes with sections that louver out for ventilation. This type roof is not utilized in modern warehouses, but since so many were built in the past, warehousing has inherited them "to do with as best it can."

A detailed knowledge of roof designs is not a major requirement of warehouse management; this is more the province of architects, design engineers, and building contractors. The brief discussion here is meant mostly to remind

FIGURE 5.9 Alternative Roof Configurations

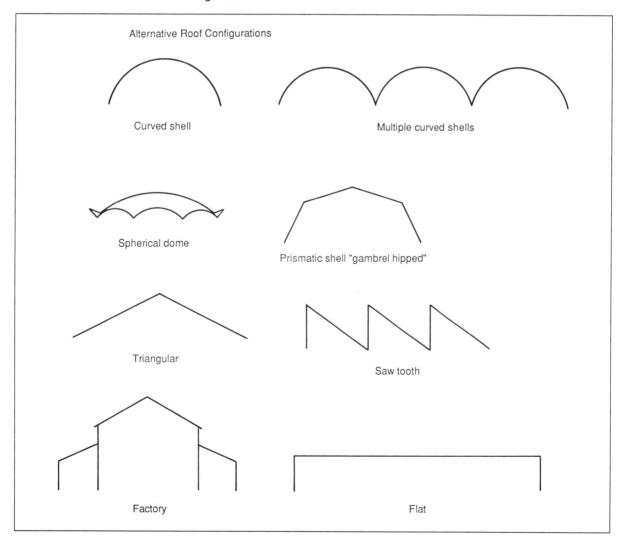

management that there are many different designs. Armed with this knowledge, you will be equipped at least to ask the experts why a certain kind of roof is being planned. The experts may not have as good reasons as their manner would imply. But your questions may just cause the "experts" to rethink their proposal and provide a better design than they would otherwise have done.

Three Basic Roofing Materials Types of material used for roofing warehouses are two: composition and metal. Both have advantages and disadvantages. Normally composition roofs are used with concrete and masonry buildings and metal roofs with metal-wall buildings, but composition roofs can be used with metal-wall buildings and metal roofs with concrete and masonry-wall buildings.

Asphalt composition roofs are made up of a series of layers of asphalt and felt fiber binders (glass fiber is also used) on a supporting ceiling structure of wood, metal, or even concrete in some cases. The top surface is often coated or loosely covered with a layer of fine silicon particles, small pieces of dolomite, or gravel to provide a tougher surface and to diffuse the sun rays. The quality of roof is determined by the combination of the quality of materials used, the workmanship in laying the materials, the thickness or number of layers applied, and the appropriateness of the specifications. Because the roof is so critical in providing a dry building, because the quality of the roof is not clearly evident until it has been thoroughly tested, and because roofs are expected to last many years with minimum maintenance, it is common practice to have roofs bonded, guaranteed, or warranteed. The roofing contractor may provide the bond or provide guarantees to assure a bondable roof, and a third party such as an insurance agency actually provides the bond. The term "bondable roof" used to be a common way to express the quality of roofs. A good roof for a warehouse was expressed as a 20-year bondable roof. This said the roof was guaranteed under specified conditions to last 20 years—or that it qualified for such a bond even though not actually bonded. Roof suppliers now more commonly give assurances with guarantees and warranties rather than bonding. Regardless what the assurance is, study it carefully because what it assures has a pretty good chance of being eventually put to test. Roof problems are all too common in warehousing.

The metal roof when designed and laid properly can provide very secure and permanent shelter. Aluminum used for this purpose can be left bare or can be painted. The painting adds little to the permanence of an aluminum roof. It is applied mainly for purposes of appearance either to reduce the natural glare of bare aluminum or to add color. Using bare aluminum is a way of reducing the cost of the building without affecting its functionality. This is particularly appropriate for the top side of the roof, since most modern warehouse buildings are so tall that the roof is usually not visible from ground level anyway.

Steel roofing is applied similarly to aluminum roofing, taking into account the different design characteristics due to the natural difference in the metals. Because aluminum is a lighter and more malleable metal, the design configuration of the rolled sheet and the structural design for strength requirements are different. To outward appearance the two look the same, particularly when both are painted (which is commonly the case). Steel roofing as a material generally costs less than does aluminum; however, because of aluminum's light weight, it is often easier and quicker to apply. The cost of metal and the cost of application tend to offset one another to some extent giving steel less of a cost advantage. Taking into consideration the long term, aluminum becomes more competitive because it is less corrosive—resulting in lower maintenance. It also has a greater salvage value when the building is eventually torn down.

As a note of interest, aluminum actually corrodes faster initially than does steel (if both are nonpainted). Very soon aluminum forms a thin, dull white oxide film that seals the surface and prevents or severely slows the corrosive process. On the other hand, the corrosion of steel continues until all is turned to rust. With today's improved steel coating, this may take a very long time, but it would behoove the owner to get a written guarantee of just how long.

Both aluminum and steel are adversely affected by high salinity or acidic atmosphere. This suggests caution in using either near the ocean or downwind from acid-causing pollutants belching forth from factories. Painted surfaces help particularly for steel, but are not a guarantee by a long shot.

A strong impetus was given to both aluminum and steel buildings when the modern systems for factory painting were developed. Exceptionally good water-base paints can be now applied at the rate of several hundred feet a minute and be bake-dried in the same continuous process. The process makes possible a better paint finish at a lower cost than is possible when applied at the job site. For steel it provides a rust-resistant coat that takes the place of the galvanizing (tin and zinc) that has been in use for many years. For aluminum the painting process is not as important as a corrosive retardant since corrosion resistance is the prime feature of aluminum. The paint, however, adds some more corrosive resistance and provides color which is characteristic of modern warehousing architecture.

Mentioned earlier was the consideration to install bare aluminum on the roof instead of painted aluminum, particularly if the roof is not visible from ground level. This was suggested as a means for reducing costs while not affecting the functionality of the building. A similar cost saving is available for painted steel. Since galvanized steel is cheaper than painted steel, consideration should be given to its use wherever a painted surface is not important for appearance purposes.

While unpainted roofing material is suggested as a cost-saving alternative, there is an esthetic difference. Perhaps more important, white-painted ceilings have definite lumination and psychological advantages. White-painted ceilings are particularly attractive, and because less artificial lighting is necessary, lighting fixture costs are reduced. After the warehouse is in operation, moreover, electrical costs are lower. Finally, the sterile appearance that it provides contributes to good housekeeping practices.

Skylight Materials and Configurations

Skylights permit natural light to enter the enclosed building through the roof. They are made in various sizes, shapes, and materials (see Figure 5.10). When corrugated metal roofing is planned, clear or slightly colored corrugated plastic sheets formed in the same configuration can be used in place of the metal sheets, and installed at the same time, to provide economical and effective skylights.

Plastic-bubble skylights are a more recent development. Compared to plate glass skylights the plastic bubbles are easier and quicker to install since they are one piece. They are also less difficult to make weather-secure. They are factory preformed to standard shapes and sizes and are installed by simply securing the edge lips.

Glass-plate skylights are still common, but are used more often in factory-type industrial buildings where there is a high concentration of workers and lighting requirements are greater. Various frame designs are employed to hold the glass including the pyramid, double pitch, and flat panel, as shown in Figure 5.10. These frames also can be hinged to open for ventilation. Glass-panel skylights are more easily broken (in case of falling or thrown objects) and involve

FIGURE 5.10 Alternative Skylight Configurations

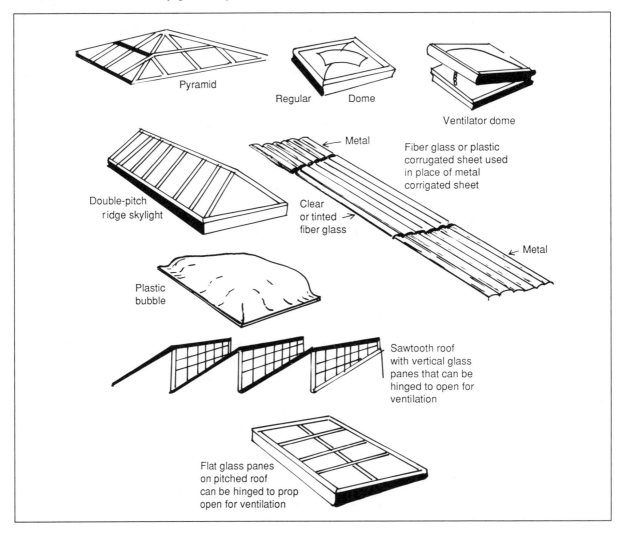

extra maintenance to keep seals water tight since the skylights are exposed to the maximum weather conditions of the area. The putty or plastic used for seals may have to be replaced several times over the life of the building. There are, however, technological improvements in the seals that will reduce the size of this problem.

Although there is always an extra initial construction cost, and there is some maintenance over the lifetime of the building, skylights do offer important advantages. Probably the most important is the reduction of lighting costs. (There is less need for artificial light.) Some feel there is also a favorable effect on employee morale apparently because of their preference for natural daylight over artificial light. For the relatively low additional construction costs and the definite advantages gained, skylights should be given favorable consideration in planning a new warehouse. Of course if natural light causes color fading, and this is a concern, other lighting alternatives should be employed.

Electrical Concerns

The two major costs of building a warehouse that seem to have climbed disproportionately over the years are electrical and plumbing costs. The main reason for this is that both involve a high labor-to-material ratio. Although material prices have increased, labor costs particularly related to electrical and plumbing systems have increased even more. Unfortunately electrical and plumbing construction work have not had breakthroughs in greater productivity in warehouse construction that some other phases of construction have had. There is still about as much effort expended to install electrical and plumbing systems now as it took decades ago. Another cost-influencing factor is that the trade unions that represent electricians and plumbers have been unusually strong and have won higher wages and better fringe benefits than most other workers. These elements combine to make electrical and plumbing work expensive factors of warehouse construction. Fortunately they are not the dominant costs.

Although warehouses generally use less electrical power than do most other industrial-type facilities, there are several important things that you should consider in designing a warehouse facility:

- What voltage outlets—100V, 220V, 440V—are needed?
- Where should the outlets be installed?
- What type of artificial lighting—incandescent, florescent, mercury vapor—is best?
- What level of lighting (foot candles) in the various inside areas—office, staging, aisles, storage—is needed?
- What perimeter lighting to provide for safety and security in the various outside areas—door entrances, walks, docks, driveways, landscape, steps, parking lot, storage yard—is needed?

The engineering involved in the electrical system for a warehouse is specialized, fairly technical and is outside the scope of this book. The basic electrical requirements of a warehouse, however, are far more the concern of the operating manager than of the architect, as the operating manager knows far better what is needed to operate efficiently and safely.

The type and amount of lighting required depends on the operations involved. The first consideration should be for safety. Next should be operating efficiency. Both considerations may indicate the same lighting level, but if not, give priority to safety requirements.

The ideal lighting system would provide lighting that can be easily moved to correspond with different warehouse layouts and can be varied with different visual requirements. To determine an economical system for providing variable lighting levels for large spaces that are characteristic of warehousing would be a great project for an innovative lighting engineer or a warehousing expert.

Electrical costs are a substantial and increasing part of both construction and operating costs, and with more attention given to employee safety, the lighting system plays a far more important role in warehouse design. Obtaining expert advice on the lighting system is probably the wisest approach to this area of design. Light bulbs are being made to last longer and use less wattage. Means are available to change the lighting automatically to conform to changes in natural light and provide consistent lighting levels. Use of spotlights on material handling equipment to supplement other lighting provides additional means for getting light where and when needed, and avoiding electrical costs when light is not needed. What must be avoided is big changes in the level of lighting from one area to the next. As all have experienced loss of ability to see when moving from a lighted area to a dark area, so a lift truck operator will do the same with hazardous consequences.

The intensity of light is measured in footcandles and expressed as candle-power. The range of candlepower for most warehousing ranges from 10 to 60 candles. However, there are many facilities where owners impose, and operations tries to get by with, light as low as 5 candles. This is generally insufficient and may be hazardous. When close work is a requirement, the level of lighting should be nearer that required for office work—from 60 to 100 candlepower.

To review, there is a need for lighting experts to evaluate which type is best on a current basis for a particular situation. It could be the latest type to come on the market, or it could be an old type that has been improved. It could even be a combination of different types in different areas of the warehouse. Lighting is just too important a concern to leave up to amateurs.

Plumbing Concerns

As noted, plumbing and electrical costs have followed the same cost trend—upward. Fortunately in warehousing there are fewer requirements for either, and particularly for plumbing, than there are in most other types of industrial build-ings. Normally the plumbing requirements are only those required for drinking, fire sprinklers, landscaping, kitchen use, restrooms, showers, and safety con-cerns such as eye washing. Even though not a major factor, there are important considerations to be made. Listed here are a few of the principal ones.

○ Meet applicable OSHA requirements for number of drinking fountains and their proper accessibility to work areas.

○ Provide both male and female restrooms. Make provision for the handi-capped.

○ Consider drains for efficient cleaning of restrooms.

○ Provide adequate wash facilities for janitorial use.

○ Have a sink with hot and cold water in lunch room.

○ Provide means for showers and eye wash if hazardous materials are han-dled and probably even if they are not. Even if not "required," these conve-niences may pay off in better employee relations.

○ Install outlets for watering landscape.

○ Provide adequate pressure for fire sprinkler system.

○ Consider separate restrooms for office and warehouse workers. Take care that prejudice is avoided. All restrooms should be of equivalent quality.

Significant savings can be realized in designing the most efficient physical relationship of facilities that use water and require ventilation and drainage. Generally these should be consolidated into one area. When this is not possible, they should be located along the same water and drainage lines. It is possible to have a major difference in costs for plumbing under different layouts of the same plumbing fixtures. Figure 5.11 shows a highly centralized plumbing system.

Canopies over Doors and Docks

During the process of designing a warehouse, it is all too common to not provide for shelters over the doorways and docks. This omission is an easy-to-make oversight. Even when the need is recognized, this is a convenient way of reduc-ing construction costs. Often the operating personnel will not recognize, or at least not feel, the impact of not having canopy shelters until the onset of first

FIGURE 5.11 An Efficient Design for Rest Rooms

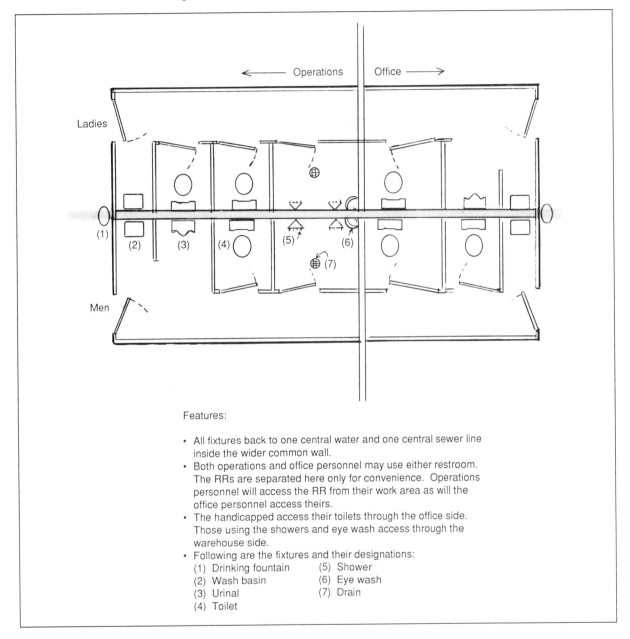

Features:

- All fixtures back to one central water and one central sewer line inside the wider common wall.
- Both operations and office personnel may use either restroom. The RRs are separated here only for convenience. Operations personnel will access the RR from their work area as will the office personnel access theirs.
- The handicapped access their toilets through the office side. Those using the showers and eye wash access through the warehouse side.
- Following are the fixtures and their designations:
  (1) Drinking fountain   (5) Shower
  (2) Wash basin   (6) Eye wash
  (3) Urinal   (7) Drain
  (4) Toilet

inclement weather. And by then it is probably too late to tie into the initial construction authorization and finances. Construction costs will have been avoided, but the costs of not having these shelters will be incurred whenever an employee has to work in the rain, snow, or hot sun. Operating management should recognize the importance of protecting these areas from the weather and insist that the shelters are installed during initial construction. The justification for canopies should be obvious when attention is brought to their need. If not, use the most poignant reason for them which is *employee safety*. Help whoever must approve visualize a lift truck skidding off the dock with a load and hapless operator because of a wet surface. That should bring immediate approval. While canopies can be installed anytime, installation is more costly later when finished walls must be broken through and extra bracing provided.

Another common error made in providing canopies is their size. Too often a short, inadequate shelter is provided when if extended a short distance it would be far more functional for a minor increase in cost. This applies to the width of canopies as well as to their length. The purpose of the shelter is to protect from rain, snow, and sun, all of which can beat in the sides as well as the front. The wider and longer the canopies are in relation to the doorway or dock, the more protection will be provided. A further consideration is that the canopies should be no higher than necessary to permit adequate clearance. Increasing the height has the same effect as reducing the width and length.

Another reason for canopies is esthetics. Properly designed and situated, they can improve the appearance of the building.

Canopies can be constructed of many different materials. Metal, plastic, and wood are commonly used because they are functional and cost comparatively little. Cement-slab canopies are quite common with tilt-wall concrete buildings because they compliment the esthetics of this structure. Metal or wood shingles are used to add decorative value which often more than justifies the additional expense. Warehouses are too commonly designed with a drab appearance. Decorative but functional canopies can do much to improve the appearance at relatively little additional cost.

Door Designs and Materials

While it is normal to give little concern to the warehouse doors, they are functionally very important. An improper door over the life of a warehouse facility can be very costly. For instance suppose that a door is too low or too narrow to permit passage of certain large inventory items or pieces of warehousing equipment. The result is that an unnecessary obstacle is constructed into the building and will continue to cause problems and damage until expensive remodeling is undertaken—or worse, the fault remains for the life of the building.

There are several features of warehouse doors that should be considered during the design phase of the building.

- Width and height
- Design and material
- Manual versus powered
- Number for personnel, truck, and rail use
- Location

The height and width of doors should be decided in relation to their use. If it is intended that road trucks will pass through a door, there must be sufficient clearance for the trucks and the highest and widest loads. Normally this door should be 14 feet high and a minimum of 10 feet wide. Wider doors will be required if it is necessary for the truck to enter the door at an angle. If the doors are at truck-bed height and not intended for road truck passage, they probably should be 10 feet high and at least 8 feet wide. If it is intended to have the back of the truck cover the door opening for reasons of security or to seal against the weather, the door dimensions should correspond to the width and height of the vehicles used. Unless this or other compelling reasons justify narrow doors, they should be constructed as wide as necessary to avoid the lost time incurred in requiring precise spotting of the trucks and rail cars. If oversized objects must pass through the warehouse, the doors should be at least two feet wider than the widest object to pass through them.

The size of the door has a bearing on its cost, but larger doors generally do not cost proportionately more. A part of the door cost is for the installation; this remains constant except for extremes. Also as the size of the door is increased, a like amount of the wall is decreased. The trade-off in materials reduces the cost difference. Thus it is generally better economics to be generous in the size and number of doors installed during initial construction; later remodeling is far more expensive.

There are many different door designs, and there are several different materials commonly used in their construction. Unfortunately the selection of the type door is commonly left to the architect. However, because doors are an integral part of the operation, their selection should be of prime concern to the operating personnel.

Most warehouse doors are opened and closed at least once each working day and perhaps many times. This constitutes either a minor or major operating cost, depending on opening and closing efficiency and frequency. Also doors have an important part in the security of a warehouse. They are the most convenient means for thieves to enter and leave with their booty.

There are two basic truck and rail warehouse door designs: those that open sideways and those that open upward. (See Figure 5.12.) There are many advocates for each type, and both can be practical and efficient. Probably the most commonly used is the upward opening type. It is common to hear it has the advantage of occupying the minimum usable space when open. Side opening doors take a like space along the wall. This space is in one of the busiest areas in the warehouse—the docks. On the other hand, side moving doors can lose the least usable space depending on the type door and use of space beside the door. The side moving type is more commonly used for very large doors as Figure 5.12 shows.

Materials commonly used in door construction are plywood, pressed-wood, composition, and sheet metal—both aluminum and steel. While functionally all will do the job, certain door materials require less maintenance, are less susceptible to damage, and provide greater security because of their material and design strength. Care should be taken to select the right doors. In warehousing particularly, the type of door has a direct and significant effect on both operating efficiency and the total security of the facility. Few other design considerations comprise this double threat.

Windows can be installed in either the sliding or sectional doors. These have the advantage of providing a view of the outside to check whether a trailer or rail car is spotted, without opening the door. In some warehouse operations this can prove to be a valuable convenience and time-saver. The windows should be small enough to prevent entry, or they should be protected by wrought iron bars.

It is possible to equip all doors with powered opening and closing mechanisms. While motorized doors add to construction and maintenance costs, they can reduce operating costs. If they are prudently selected and maintained, they may remain trouble-free for many years. They often prove to be a very worthwhile convenience, particularly if the doors are opened and closed often and if the doors are large and heavy. A definite advantage of powered doors is the feature that they can be remotely operated. For example, a door in a common passageway for lift truck travel can be operated by the lift truck operator pulling a rope switch as she or he passes under it. The door can be equipped with an electronically operated device like those in common use to open home garage doors or the self opening type used for grocery stores. These remote controls can save considerable time and effort compared to the operator dismounting and manually opening and closing the door.

FIGURE 5.12 Warehouse Doors

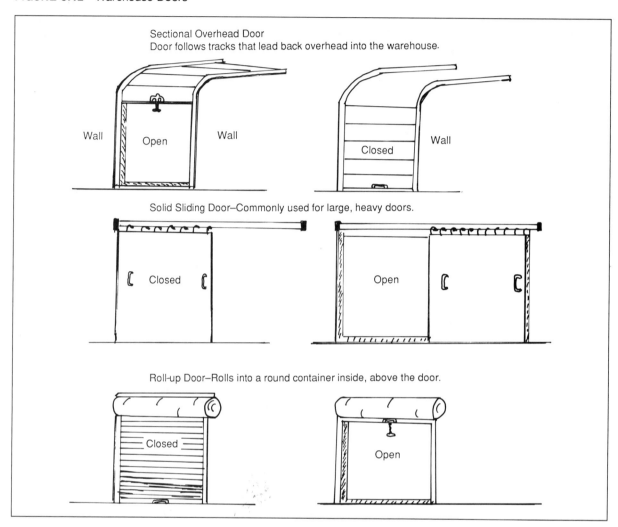

Sectional Overhead Door
Door follows tracks that lead back overhead into the warehouse.

Wall   Open   Wall

Closed   Wall

Solid Sliding Door—Commonly used for large, heavy doors.

Closed

Open

Roll-up Door—Rolls into a round container inside, above the door.

Closed

Open

The Case of the Wrong-Way Hinge   I was idly gazing at a warehouse personnel door, listening to tales of woe from a location manager, when I noticed hinges that looked surprisingly familiar. I had recently removed a door at home to cut off the bottom to fit a new carpet. I had pulled the hinge pins out to free the door. Then I realized that the door I was looking at had the same feature—the hinges were on the outside. Anyone could remove and replace the door as I had done at home. When I called the manager's attention to it, he was flabbergasted. He had been the manager of the facility over ten years from the time it was built and had never noticed this. Needless to say, he had the problem corrected right away.

The point of this story is, of course, to have either the outside personnel doors installed with the hinges on the inside or have the type that cannot have the pins removed.

Fire Sprinkler Systems

The initial cost of a fire sprinkler system is quite high, running between 5 to 15 percent of the total facility construction costs. However, the added protection such a system provides over the life of the building and the lower fire insurance rates it permits generally (but not always) make it a good investment. Many factors have a bearing on the justification of a fire sprinkler system other than the fact that it reduces the hazard of fire damage. The initial cost is very important. The immediate cash position of a company may dictate that it cannot afford the initial high cost and could better afford higher insurance rates for a time and then install the system at a later date, or never.

Many advocates announce that anyone questioning the need for a sprinkler system is stupid or has a few marbles missing. But unless specified by code, it is a decision that can go either way. Fire insurance companies need to make a profit, and they hope to average more money coming in than goes out. If your facility is a low-risk one, you might opt for insurance with a high deductible. Exercise caution about what is best. But also avoid the trap of thinking that if you have a sprinkler system, you will not have a fire. Fires start quite independently from sprinkler systems or insurance. With a sprinkler system you hope the damage will be minimized.

Building code requirements may dictate that a sprinkler system of a certain rating is required. Commonly buildings over 20,000 square feet are required to have such a system and of a specified rating depending on what will be stored. Large buildings are often required to have fire walls at specified intervals, perhaps every 40,000 square feet. High rack storage often requires in-rack as well as overhead sprinkler systems.

When determining the initial cost of the facility, these requirements for fire damage protection may seem an insurmountable burden for companies struggling to get by. They are requirements that do not contribute much to the "bottom line" except for lower fire insurance. There is a strong tendency to get by with the very minimum and trust that there will not be a fire, or if there is one that the fire insurance will cover the loss.

This is a little like the ostrich that puts its head in the sand so it will not be seen. The fire-extinguishing sprinkler system gives peace of mind, qualifies for low insurance rates, and increases the value of the real estate. Furthermore, whether it is installed or not in most localities is not a choice. It is required by law for the general good of the neighborhood.

On the other hand, fire sprinklers have their dark side: water damage often costs more than fire damage. Still, if there were no sprinkler system, the unchecked fire could cause much greater damage than the combination of fire and water in a sprinklered building.

Sprinkler systems that are engineered to confine the water to the specified areas where there is fire are obviously the best. When one hot extinguisher head causes a series of heads to sprinkle, the result can easily lead to more damage by water than by fire. Warehouses that involve dense storage of cartoned inventories are particularly susceptible to the hazard of water damage. Each sprinkler head should operate independently. If you are already occupying a building which is equipped with a sprinkler system, management should investigate what type of sprinkler heads are used and make certain they are appropriate for the areas they protect.

Another incidental caution about sprinkler systems is that the "off" and "on" valves are in operative condition and under proper control. When I am walking through any warehouse and see the main sprinkler system valve chained and locked, questions come to mind. "Is the system locked on or off? And who knows this? When was the last time anyone checked the system to see if it really works? Do the right employees know where the key to the lock is? How about the swing and graveyard shifts—do these employees know what to do in case of fire?"

The confusion often caused by real emergencies would be comical if not so full of potential tragedy. Warehouse management should exercise extra care to assign responsibilities for such emergencies including a system of follow-up to make certain what to do is known and that related systems are operable. Have serious drills as frequently as necessary to make certain that if a fire does occur everyone knows what to do and does it in an expeditious manner.

Aside from what is required by the local code, there are a number of things that should influence whether to have a sprinkler system and if so what type to have. For example, inventories of structural steel are obviously far less of a fire hazard than inventories of paper products. The height of storage and the type storage racks used also have a bearing. The more flammable inventories carried in a warehouse, the greater the fire hazard. Other very important factors are the local building code requirements and the attitude of the local fire marshal. Many localities require sprinkler systems. Some even require them inside the racks as well as overhead. High racks (over 25 feet) are commonly required to have sprinkler systems built into them. If the inventories are combustible you should consider inside sprinklers for racks less than 25 feet even though the code does not require it.

An important yet often unrecognized feature of warehouse design is that of the superstructure of the roof (steel beams, trusses, etc.) will lose its strength, sag, and bring the roof down with it at a lower temperature than will a wooden structure burn. The difference is substantial—about 900°F for steel to 1400°F for wood.

There are published standards for sprinkler systems and warehouse storage; however, these standards are difficult to apply fairly because of the many variable influencing factors. Numerous things affect the hazards of fire in a warehouse. How best to install a sprinkler system to be most effective is a complex problem particularly when the science and practice of high storage is still relatively new.

Listed here are some of the factors that affect a fire hazard environment:

○ Height of storage
○ Depth of storage
○ Density of storage
○ Flammability of inventories
○ Aisle widths
○ Size and number of staging areas
○ Use and placement of fire extinguishers
○ Type of extinguishers
○ Roof and wall construction and materials
○ Fire walls, ability to confine areas
○ Ventilation system
○ Alarm system
○ Response time of local fire department
○ Attitude and expertise of fire chief
○ Availability and pressure of fire hydrants or other fire-fighting water supply
○ Training of warehouse personnel
○ Number and quality of fire practice drills
○ Maximum loss exposure
○ Smoke chimneys
○ Fire barriers built into the ceiling

○ Whether smoking is permitted if so and where

○ Proper butt containers for smokers

○ Extent of hazard that neighboring operations and buildings comprise

Roof Support Columns—Warehousing's Enemy Number One

This building feature is another one of those factors that are just too important to leave to an architect. Input from warehouse operations is of dire importance. What will seem to the architect to be right and proper could well be wrong and very improper from the warehouser's point of view. There is nothing to be gained by saying too late "the architect should have known." Why? Because this is proprietary information known mostly by knowledgeable and experienced warehousers. Just as warehousing experts are not expected to know the physics of stresses and strains, so architects should not be expected to know the effect on operations of roof support columns.

The great dream warehouse in the sky has no roof support columns. Only the walls support the roof and even the roof support columns in the walls do not protrude into the warehouse space. If they have to protrude at all, they do so on the outside of the walls. There are no vertical obstacles in the warehouse areas—except the roof.

The reason why professional designers of warehouses so often lean toward more roof support columns is that the initial cost of the building is lower. Upper management, who approves the design, is more concerned with total cost and square footage than the "details" of operational problems. Warehousing management can be a lot to blame here. Probably the problem has never been researched and possibly warehouse management's exposure has been only to space cluttered with roof support columns. Another reason (but not a very good one) is that warehouse management assumes that the architect and top management know a lot more about the subject than they do. Also factories often make up a large share of industrial architect's work, and column spacing there is generally less important than it is in warehousing.

The only operational value roof support columns could have is to provide something on which to hang fire extinguishers. This is next to no value at all. The extinguishers can be hung on storage racks or fixtures designed specifically for this purpose.

It is not true that "all" roof support columns are severe obstacles; some are only minor obstacles. Warehousing that involves bulk storage (without storage racks) can exercise enough freedom in layout to minimize the adverse effect of the columns (provided there are not too many). Even then they are still obstacles but are not as severe. How undesirable they are depends on how the inventories are stored and the layout of aisles and staging areas. The higher the utilization of storage racks, the worse the effect of roof support columns. The best is that the columns can be tucked between the blind side of two rows of pallet racks (see Figure 5.13). The worst is that the columns are so placed that they are extremely hazardous obstacles in aisleways and staging areas.

Columns are more than just a nuisance; they hold up the roof! The cost of construction generally increases as the columns decrease. To construct without any may be too costly (if not impractical) depending on the size and configuration of the building. If the warehousing requirements have to be compromised, the cost of the compromise should be known. It definitely costs in loss of usable space, in material handling obstacles, in safety hazards, and in real estate value. If ever the facility is sold, the price obtained will reflect the quality of

FIGURE 5.13 Roof Support Columns in Warehousing Space (overhead view of warehousing's enemy no. 1)

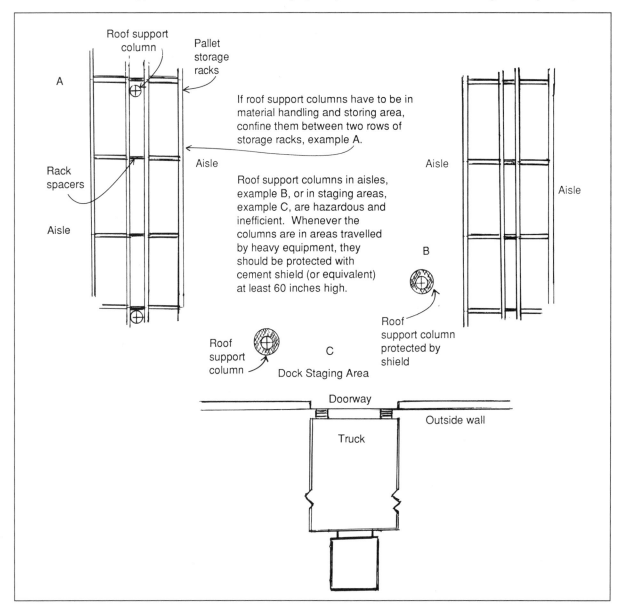

the facility. A forest of columns translates to low-quality space. The fewer the columns, the higher the quality, and the higher the quality, the greater the justifiable price.

The roof support columns are an integral part of the roof system. They are not something that can be eliminated at will. Building with fewer columns means the horizontal beams that support the roof must be increased in support capability. The trade-off is one of columns versus stronger roof trusses. From the standpoint of warehouse operations, it is better to absorb the one-time extra cost of putting in stronger beams rather than to live with the obstacles over the long life of the building (probably about 40 years).

A value should be assigned to the negative aspects of roof support columns to permit comparisons with the additional construction costs to omit them. Make a realistic assumption of the building cost for space, including land and improvements. For sake of illustration, let's assume a cost of $1.00 per cubic foot. Relate this cost to the average loss of space by each column (for example, 10 sq. ft. by 27 ft. high). This converts to a one-time cost of $270 per column ($1.00/cu. ft. × 10 sq. ft. × 27 ft. high).

To reinforce this cost, convert the lost space to what a public warehouse charges for space. Let us assume it is $0.10 per cubic foot per month, or $1.20 per year. This translates to a loss of $324 worth of space annually ($0.10/cu. ft. per month × 270 ft. per column × 12 months).

Another concern about these columns is that of their size. Some are made of steel pipe, others of "I-beams" or square beams and still others of reinforced concrete. From the point of view of losing the least amount of space, the one taking the least space is preferable, provided the capacity to hold up the roof is still adequate. This normally translates into a preference ranking of pipe, square, I-beam, and cement column as a last choice. To meet capacity requirements, cement columns become space pigs. The nominal figure of 10 square feet of space lost cited earlier is not enough. Twenty square feet is more appropriate for cement columns.

On the other hand, the cement column can take a heavier impact than pipe or beams; therefore, it can be considered safer. Concrete columns also are far more resistant to fire. If pipe or beams are used, and they are located in aisles or staging areas where they are better targets, they should be surrounded with steel reinforced cement with a diameter of about 20 to 30 inches.

In summary these estimates of values indicate that roof support columns left in the design will cost about $300 each annually. So if your company wants to recover its investment over five years (which is pretty high expectations) the cost of deleting columns can cost as much as $1,500 each ($300/column/year × 5 years) to comply with the company's policy for return on investment. This does not take into account the loss in handling efficiency or the hazard of knocking down columns if they are located in aisleways or in staging areas. Assume for the sake of comparison that the hazard of knocking them down and the potential for bodily injury comprise a value equal to the value of lost space (though it should be more). The cost of each column then equates to $3,000 annual or $15,000 for 5 years (2 × $1,500/column × 5 years).

I personally experienced a column being knocked down by a "cowboy" lift truck operator. With the column came about 2,000 square feet of roof. Perhaps this is why I continue to wage war against roof support columns and consider them warehousing's number one enemy.

Truck and Rail Dock Designs

No other part of a warehouse is used as much as the docks. The appropriate design for the type and volume of merchandise going across them has a direct relationship to operating efficiency. It would be amusing if it were not so pathetic to see to what extremes some operations are forced to go to transfer freight between the warehouse and the carrier.

A not unusual way of transfer is for a lift truck to be used to move pallet loads from a ground-level warehouse and place them in the doorway of a rail car or truck where the pallets are unloaded and stacked manually in the carrier. This is not all that bad if the material has to be hand stacked in the carrier for some good reason and the "lumpers" (those who load or unload by hand) have the use of pallet movers inside the carrier.

There are as many ways employed to transfer goods between the docks and carriers as the mind can conjure. One that I witnessed stands out as contender for the least efficient. It was for one lift truck to bring the load from storage and place it at the edge of an elevated dock. Another lift truck, operating at ground level, picks the load from the dock and transfers it to the doorway of the rail car. Another lift truck inside the car picks up the load and transfers it to a point where lumpers restack it for transport. Good questions about this horribly inefficient means are: Why did they not use a pallet jack to move loads inside the carrier? How did the second lift truck get from the elevated warehouse floor to ground level, and how did the third lift truck get into the rail car? Further, how did these two lift trucks get back into the warehouse after the carrier was loaded or unloaded (the same process was used in reverse for unloading).

The answer to the first question is that they had tried various pallet jacks, and none worked as well as the small lift truck. The pallet loads consisted of heavy refractory brick. The second lift truck got to the outside ground level by a very common method—an outside ramp. Yet there are many elevated warehouses that do not provide ramps to the outside ground level. In their absence, the operating team has to improvise to get their work done.

In this case the landlord had provided a wooden ramp consisting of salvaged planks from dismantling an old church. The ramp did not hold up to the high loads imposed on it by lift trucks—but that is another story.

How the third lift truck got into and out of the rail car was a lot more ingenious. A large high-capacity lift truck literally picked up the smaller lift truck and placed it in the rail car. The reverse procedure was used to receive merchandise into the warehouse from inbound carriers. This bewildering means is justified—even laudable—to overcome an emergency, but this particular warehouse had operated this way for several years.

The objective of dock design is to make the transport of materials between the warehouse and the bed of the carrier as safely and efficiently as possible. Since the carrier bed is elevated by the carrier's wheel and axle structure to permit transport, the warehouse floor must be brought to the same level to permit material handling equipment to traverse back and forth over a bridge, dock plate, or dock leveler connecting the two. The floor can be brought to the carrier bed level by two means, either by elevating the warehouse floor or by depressing the level of the carrier. The latter means is commonly referred to as a truck or rail "well." The well is accomplished by gradually depressing the driveway or rail siding until the bed of the carrier matches the level of the floor of the warehouse. Most dock wells are for truck use, but there are some rail wells. Their grade has to be even less than those for trucks. Definitely the applicable rail company should be consulted for their specifications for rail wells.

The motivation to use truck and rail wells is that the cost is often less (occasionally substantially less) than elevating the warehouse floor to 48 to perhaps 52 inches, the usual height range. This requires that a lot of fill has to be brought in and compacted. Occasionally the topography of the site can be utilized to reduce the amount of new fill required. This cost should be taken into consideration in determining the total cost of the site to compare with alternative sites when the land is first being evaluated for purchase.

Truck wells entail certain limitations compared to the raised floor method. The grade must not be too steep, and there must be provision to remove rain or snow water that drains to the bottom of the well. Following are some of the main problems encountered with wells that are too steep.

○ Trucks with heavy loads cannot pull out or dangerously spin their wheels trying.

○ Loads in the truck may slip back or topple.

○ There is a need to remove the rain or snow water from the truck or rail well using a sump pump. It will be fortunate if there is a storm drain lower than the bottom of the well permitting the rain water to be carried off by gravity through underground pipes.

○ Ice and snow reduce traction sufficiently to prohibit pulling away from the dock.

The configuration of a truck well is illustrated in Figure 5.14A. The type of trucks serving the warehouse should influence the grade. The level distance in front of the dock should allow for the back wheels to rest on the level pad. The incline section should have as little rise as the area available permits but not to exceed 10 degrees. It is best to keep the rise below 7 degrees.

FIGURE 5.14   Truck Well (depressed dock)

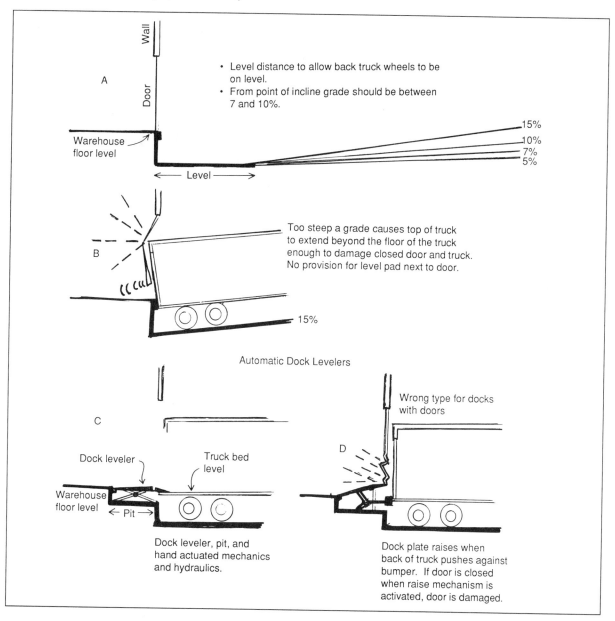

The height of the dock should agree with the type of trucks serving the facility—with an eye to the future. Over the years the beds of trucks have been increasing in height along with length. "Spec" warehouses (those built in anticipation of leasing or selling) normally provide for a 48-in.-high dock. There are, however, situations where 50-in. to 52-in. heights are better. In the range of 48 in. to 52 in. the dock plate (bridge from dock to truck bed) will normally take up the differences in truck bed levels without grade problems particularly when the longer dock boards (60 to 72 in.) are used. Beds of small delivery trucks are lower and occasionally much lower than the big rigs. If this is the case designated doors or a part of the dock should be constructed and equipped for this.

Keep in mind that any truck well will cause the entry end of the truck bed to be slightly lower than when measured on level ground. The steeper the grade of the well the more the back edge of the bed is lowered with the top of the van thrust correspondingly forward. This phenomenon can result in damage to the door and building if the grade is too steep as Figure 5.14B shows.

The design and features of rail docks require the same degree of attention given truck docks. The difference is there are fewer alternatives from which to choose.

The number of rail doors for accessing the rail siding is important. Generally, you should provide as many as possible then securely lock and store in front of those not needed. The additional cost of doors compared with solid walls is not great when installed during the construction phase. To put them through existing walls later is far more expensive. To plan that there will never be a need for more doors than the number the present business requires is foolhardy unless all possible positions along the wall facing the siding or truck dock have door access already. Buildings last many years, probably much beyond the duration of the type warehousing initially practiced. The building may be sold several times during its useful life. To have many doors is an investment that probably will be recovered by a better sales price later. For greater handling efficiency, inbound merchandise should arrive at a door closest to where it will be put into storage. The same in reverse order is true for outbound shipments. For this reason, the trend is for more doors not fewer for factories as well as warehouses. Having too many rail or truck doors for that matter should never be considered a limitation. The tenant can always secure and store in front of the ones not needed.

When more rail car positions are needed than can be made available by using the entire rail side of the building the problem can be solved in two ways: (1) get more frequent switching through the railroad company or provide it with your own equipment and (2) install a double siding where rail cars can be lined up two deep at each door. By using portable dock plates to bridge between the outer door of the closest car to the nearest door of the outer car both cars can be loaded or unloaded from one warehouse rail door.

The most flexibility for handling rail cars or trucks is provided with outside platform docks running the full side of the building. The same can be achieved if the rail siding is put inside the building, but this, of course, incurs loss of inside space. This is justified however if there is considerable freight activity or if an inside overhead bridge crane is used to unload or load carriers and transport through the warehouse. The rails on which the crane rides can extend over the siding and a recessed truck dock.

Actually, having an inside rail dock does not cost significantly more than having it outside. A roof, a floor, an outside wall, and siding are required just as for inside warehouse space. While an inside rail dock constitutes at least some additional construction cost, it may be money well spent.

Most often the reasons to control the temperature and humidity of warehouse space apply as well to that of the rail cars and the space between the outside of the building to the car door. For instance, if the only reason to heat the warehouse space is for the benefit of the workers, this also applies to those working the rail car. Further, if the reason to control temperature and humidity is to maintain a proper environment for temperature-controlled storage, this again applies to working the rail cars. On the other hand, there are means to enclose the dock door, the dock leveler, and the rail car door so that the temperature-controlled warehouse space extends into the rail cars that constitutes a means of controlling these areas without physically locating the siding inside the building. A common way is for accordion pleated hoods that are affixed around the warehouse door and extend to and secure the outside of rail car door.

Dock Levelers Dock levelers for both rail and truck can be separate units that can be positioned with the aid of lift trucks, or they can be semiautomatic and built into the edge of the dock. When they are built in, they become an inseparable part of the facility. (See Figure 5.14C.) To install them after the warehouse floor is laid adds substantially to their costs because the concrete floor must be sawed and jack hammered away to create a pit for the dock leveler mechanism. Then new concrete must be laid to encase the levelers and their mechanisms. An even greater expense is incurred if the wrong dock levelers are installed during construction and later have to be removed and the right ones put in. The type that were all wrong for the use intended is illustrated in Figure 5.14D.

Mechanical dock levelers are efficient if they are properly designed for the function intended, are of good quality, and are purchased and maintained by a company that is going to stay in business and has a record of responsive, high-quality service. Because of the extreme abuse dock levelers take from heavy lift and road trucks, repairs are common. Some dock levelers are designed to withstand this extreme punishment better than others, and some can be repaired more easily than others.

Mechanical dock plates are normally set into specifically designed concrete pits that are recessed into the dock. Different types require different dimension pits, so interchangeability is not characteristic. It is far better to buy right the first time. It is also best to buy all dock plates from the same manufacturer and vendor, provided of course that they are right for the purpose intended. This provides leverage to negotiate the best prices and simplifies repairs and maintenance.

Some mechanical dock plates are mounted at the edge of the dock not requiring a specially designed pit. These fold in the center to collapse out of the way when not in use and fold out to form the bridge when needed. This type does not extend as far as the conventional type making them less versatile in bridging the range of truck bed heights. They are more commonly used for rail dock levelers where the level of the rail cars does not vary as much as for over-the-road trucks.

A poor place to economize is in the acquisition of dock levelers. This is particularly so when the operations will include handling large objects where wide dock levelers are needed and in bridging to a substantial range of truck bed heights where long plates are needed. Not recommended is to buy without hard negotiations. Do sufficient research to find high-quality dock levelers that will effectively and efficiently do the job. Preferably get competitive quotations from at least three different suppliers and then equate their total costs (including guarantees and their maintenance and repair service policies and reputations). It would also help if you can determine the chances of the companies staying in business, but this is very difficult. Probably the best that can be done is avoid what appears to be shaky suppliers in favor of those with solid long-term histories. Becoming a manufacturer of dock levelers is relatively easy (it is believed) compared to most other businesses. As a result many small ones get started for this reason, which results in a corresponding number that go out of business because of undercapitalization and many other reasons.

Paint and Esthetics

There is probably no instance when an attractive facility is not an asset, even when a company wants the least public exposure. Well-painted facilities with harmonious hues contribute to better employee morale and customer and public relations. An initial advantage of a metal-covered building is that the siding and the roofing can be purchased with long-lasting factory-applied paint in many colors. With the right color scheme, which should be complimentary to the landscaping and the building, an attractive facility is assured for a long time.

While quality paint is an initial advantage of metal-covered buildings, these buildings are easily damaged. A lift truck gouging the walls with its forks or a high stack of palletized merchandise tumbling against a wall can severely dent or tear the metal sheathing. Whenever the paint and galvanized protective coatings of steel sheets is scraped away, oxidation will occur.

Aluminum does not prevent the rust problem. It actually oxidizes even quicker initially, but the thin layer of oxidized aluminum serves as a barrier to further oxidation. This is not true of steel which continues to oxidize until all the metal is converted to rust. However, aluminum sheeting for the same gauge is even less resistive to denting or tearing.

Painting concrete or block walls is important mostly for esthetic purposes. Depending on atmospheric conditions, the quality of paint, and its application, these buildings should be repainted every 5 to 15 years. This should be done religiously though, because if left up to the warehouse personnel, they are likely to just not see the need.

An opposing viewpoint regarding painted masonry buildings is that bare masonry can be more attractive than painted, so why paint it? True, there are many attractive buildings with only exposed masonry. Some of the ways to make these buildings more attractive are the artful use of landscaping, designs cast into the concrete panels, exposed aggregate, and decorative blocks and bricks (of which there are many shapes, colors and finishes).

An important consideration about paint is how it can play an important role inside the warehouse. Commonly the expression "painting a warehouse" seems to imply only the outside of the building. The inside is just as important to employees and visitors. It is impressive to have all surfaces that are frequently seen (not having stored inventories blocking the view) painted in a cheerful color or combinations of colors. Perhaps a color specialist should be enlisted to advise if no one in-house has this expertise.

One area in particular that has more than a psychological effect is the ceiling. Most warehouse ceilings have the dull brown appearance that exposed wood takes on with age. If the superstructure of trusses and beams is made of wood it has that same dull exposure. If they are of steel, normally a dull red rust-preventive paint greets the eye. It does not have to be this way. At a relatively small cost the ceiling can be painted white or a whitish blue and the support beams and trusses painted the same or some other complimentary color.

Another place for a good application of paint, or at least a high-grade sealer, is the warehouse floor. Nothing else makes a warehouse look as sharp as clean shiny floors. This is best achieved as a feature of facility design by specifying the floor finish—including the maintenance program necessary to keep it clean and shiny.

If you move into an existing building, you will have to contend with what you find. You should first get rid of the old grit, grime, oil, and tire marks. Then you can seal and paint, or apply some other attractive finish guaranteed by a reputable vendor.

When I was managing a network of warehouses across the country, I insisted that every warehouse get its floors in order and shine them monthly. Time was allowed in the work standards for this. Every warehouse had good engineered layouts so only the aisles and staging areas needed frequent rejuvenation. A few hours each month with a wide mop did the job for the open areas in a warehouse of perhaps 50,000 square feet. With mechanized cleaning and mopping, very large warehouse floors were maintained in about the same time.

Environment and Energy Confrontations

A direct effect of environmental concerns is to construct, equip, and insulate buildings so that they use less fuel. This includes everything from devising ways to avoid pilot lights to better insulation throughout. Many of these means for conserving energy are required by law. All are intended to minimize dependence on fuel and as such should be given favorable consideration. How best to insulate warehouse buildings is not clear. Once concrete walls were thought to be inherently good insulators, but this notion was thoroughly dispensed with by some rather elementary scientific tests. Now it is realized that additional insulation material must be a part of the concrete or an insulation coating added to it to reach significantly favorable "R" insulation ratings. Actually metal-clad walls and ceilings with the desired "R"-rated layer of nonhazardous insulation materials affixed to the metal is one of the most practical means. If the ceiling is constructed of wood, the insulation is affixed to this. For cement walls blown-on insulation or sheets of insulation are sandwiched within or added on to increase the "R" ratings. Insulation wraps and sleeves are used to confine cold and heat to pipes. The era of energy conservation has arrived. The era of wasting fuel is on its way out—kicking, fussing, and cheating but irrevocably on its way out.

Here again the designer of warehouse facilities should enlist help from experts. The reality for the long term is that all that is legally required and economically feasible should be done to avoid wasting energy. Conversely any economically feasible ways to generate energy utilizing the sun, wind, and water waves (nature's free energy sources) should be employed.

COMPARATIVE COST BREAKDOWN OF WAREHOUSE FACILITY

Methodology

While considering different facility design concepts, it is helpful to know the magnitude and relationship of the many different cost factors which comprise the total. (See Figure 5.15.) Without such orientation, it is easy to assign unrealistic importance to this or that or many factors. The effect is to under or overemphasize certain design components. For example, as discussed earlier,

FIGURE 5.15 Comparative Cost Breakdown of Warehouse Facility, 40,000 ft²

Elements	Size	Unit Cost	Total Cost	Percent Total
Land, 2+ acres	88,000 ft²	$ 3/ft²	$ 264,000	16.5%
Drawings and specifications	—	—	30,000	1.9
Building permits and fees	—	—	20,000	1.3
Site preparation	88,000 ft²	1/ft²	88,000	5.5
Warehouse building				
Fill and compaction	40,000 ft²	2/ft²	80,000	5.0
Concrete floor	40,000 ft²	4/ft²	160,000	10.0
Concrete tilt wall	800 ft × 30 ft	4/ft²	96,000	6.0
Roof (20-year bondable) system	42,000 ft²	4/ft²	168,000	10.5
Electrical 110 and 220 volts	—	—	40,000	2.5
Plumbing including office	—	—	30,000	1.9
Truck doors (4)	8 ft × 10 ft	1,500 ea	6,000	0.4
Rail doors (4)	10 ft × 10 ft	2,000 ea	8,000	0.5
Canopies for (8) doors	8 × 14 ft	500 ea	4,000	0.2
Fire sprinkler system	41,000 ft²	3/ft²	123,000	7.7
Total			$ 715,000	44.7%
Office, inside warehouse building	1,000 ft²	70/ft²	70,000	4.4
Yards				
Truck area	10,000 ft²	4/ft²	40,000	2.5
Auto parking area	5,000 ft²	2/ft²	10,000	0.6
Perimeter fence and gates	1,100 ft	7/ft	8,000	0.5
Landscaping	10,000 ft²	2/ft	20,000	1.3
Outside lighting	—	—	4,000	0.3
Total			$ 82,000	5.2%
Railspur and turnout	400 ft	80/ft	32,000	2.0
Loan acquisition costs				
Construction loan points and fees	1,500,000		75,000	4.7
Take-out loan points and fees	1,500,000		75,000	4.7
Total			$ 150,000	9.4%
Total facility costs			$1,451,000	90.9%
Contingency, 10%			145,000	9.1
Total			$1,596,000	100.0%

the cost of increasing the height of a warehouse is generally not as expensive as commonly thought, at least not in comparison to the amount of additional cubic space it makes available.

Another example of misplaced priorities due to not understanding the cost relationship of the different components is that a premium location that fits the company's needs best (and inherently has a better real estate value) may be passed over because it by itself appears too expensive.

When requesting construction contractors to provide competitive quotations, they should be asked to provide a detailed cost schedule that supports their quotation. They also should be advised of the reason you are requesting it: "to assist in evaluating trade-offs" (a good nonthreatening reason to which most contractors will relate). You should let them know that any changes you are considering will be fully described, and they will have the opportunity to requote. Obviously you should not and cannot with precise validly interpolate their costs to different conditions. Component costs that contractors provide to support their quotations should be used as indicative, not absolute. Some figures may validly stand alone, but this is not for you to judge. You would have to know all they know (including their intentions) to determine the effects of changing specifications; and this is totally impractical, just as it would be for building contractors to tell you how to run your warehouse.

If contractors refuse to provide you the cost detail to prepare your own comparative cost schedule even after you swear to confidentiality, you should look to other contractors that will. If none can be found to provide this, then you can always pay a contractor to cost it as you wish. Many contractors will provide this service using published standard costs. These nominal standards indicate the costs to do about anything related to construction, and they are credible for the purpose you will be using them. Your intention is not to determine precise costs. What you need is "cost building blocks" that you can arrange, rearrange, and trade-off generally to design the most economical, yet high-quality facility that will serve the purposes intended. Later you will get formal competitive construction quotations, but by then you will be a lot smarter about what you want and generally what it will cost. Further, you will know whether your cost budget for the facility is realistic.

HOW TO MAKE THE COMPARATIVE COMPONENT-COST SCHEDULE WORK FOR YOU

Floor and Compaction

As an introduction to how a comparative cost schedule can be constructively used, suppose you learn that 6-inch-thick reinforced concrete floor costs $3 per square foot. Simple arithmetic reveals that a 100,000-square foot floor will cost $300,000. The formula is right as far as it goes, but it isolates the concrete slab from other related costs that must be included to have a complete floor. These other costs include such major components as excavation, fill, compaction, and other site preparation costs. It could be extended to include part of boundary and topography surveys, architecture, permits, and even the land. The actual cost of the floor may be closer to $8, $9, or $10 per square foot, depending on what you are intending to do with the figure. If you are using it to compare with alternative sites, you will want all site-related costs for each comparison.

This example is given to demonstrate the importance of examining the component costs in relation to other component costs, and these in relation to total costs. This way of seeing costs provides a perspective that is lacking when dealing with components separately as isolated factors. A schedule like that in Figure 5.15 or one in even greater detail, puts component costs in perspective. Things you thought were relatively minor costs you may find are major, and vice versa.

This schedule also provides insight into potential trade-offs. Assume you learn that to get a 95 pounds per square-inch (psi) fill compaction to support the concrete floor you will have to pay an additional $0.50 per square foot. You get 80 psi for $3.00 per square foot. You know that 80 psi is risky, really not enough, but for the 40,000 square feet building, you will be adding $20,000 ($0.50/sq. ft. × 40,000 sq. ft.). In isolation this cost looks substantial. If it were in your paycheck it would be. Yet, when related to other construction cost factors that will be affected, it does not seem so formidable.

With only 80 psi the entire floor is put at risk. In a larger sense, you are putting the entire facility at risk because you know that the condition of the floor in your type of warehousing is very important, even critical. If the floor goes, the facility loses its value both for warehouse operations and for its real estate value if it is sold. If it is leased to another company, assuming the lessee is a novice and does not know how important floors are, you may be setting up your company for big problems. When the lessee realizes the floor problem your company could be confronted with claims for everything from the costs of moving inventories to disruption of operations and possibly the toll that strain, pain, and anguish have taken on the lessee company's employees and owners.

Therefore the extra $0.50 per square foot to assure the best floor looks like a lot in isolation, but not much in relation to the total cost of the facility and very little in relation to the risks and contingencies involved.

Figure 5.15 is intended to help with this type of perspective. In this case the $0.50-per-square-foot figure is only about one-fourth the fill and compaction cost which in total is only 5.0 percent, one-twentieth of the total facility cost. For $0.50 per square foot more, you should go for the 95-psi compaction. Without the ability to relate the extra $20,000 to other costs and the total, the wrong decision could be made very easily—with nothing but good intentions.

Another way to evaluate the additional $20,000 is to compare it to the amount of contingency allowed in the cost schedule. In Figure 5.15, the amount of contingency is 10 percent of all identified costs, $145,000 (over seven times the $20,000 in question), which is for eventualities that are not even known or are too insignificant to identify separately. "The 10 percent contingency factor" is commonly used in such cost schedules.

Walls, the Most Important Single Variable

If the various components of the facility were appraised separately, probably there would be agreement that spacial capacity to handle and store inventories is most important, and that this capacity can be changed most economically by varying the height of the walls. Using the same $4 per square foot used in the cost breakdown regardless of height (a fair assumption as explained later), the wall height is of singular importance. For instance, if the height were reduced one third from 30 to 20 feet, the cost would reduce $32,000 ($96,000 ÷ 3); but comparing this to the total facility cost, this constitutes only a 2 percent cost reduction ($32,000 ÷ $159,600). On the other hand if the height were increased one third from 30 to 40 feet, you would be getting a 33 percent increase in capacity for a 2 percent increase in cost. This should make believers out of the most hard-nosed skeptics.

True, this is not the whole story. More has to be taken into consideration but the reality is not far off. Actually, the extra 10 feet will cost less per square foot than the first 30 feet because the costly set up will be amortized over more square feet. But the cost of footings to hold up the heavier wall will be higher. And the cost of equipment to utilize the top 10 feet will be higher, but since the warehouse would now be a good candidate for some form of ASRS, the aisles could be much narrower; this translates into better space utilization and lower cost—which at the very least constitutes a swell example of trade-offs in warehouse design.

Roof Alternatives

The roof system cost is substantial, $168,000. This is based on an asphalt-felt composition roof. How about using sheet metal? There are designs that span the rafters and avoid the need for a plywood base altogether. Since no one can see the roof except from a low-flying airplane or helicopter, why not have the under side painted white at the factory but leave the top unpainted. Painting the top has no redeeming qualities. The amount of savings here will depend on the painting process employed. It is possible that painting will have to be foregone altogether if significant savings are to be realized. In this case, you may be willing for the bright aluminum to show inside.

Loan Cost Innovations

The total of the loan acquisition costs (construction plus take out) in Figure 5.15 is $150,000, over 9 percent of the total. Has this really been worked over? How hard has it been shopped? Would a foreign loan cost less? Many countries do not have as high interest rates as the United States. The points and fees are a big part of the initial costs; why should an intermediary get this cut just to be the go-between? You may, however, have to pay because you cannot find the best sources without their help. Loan brokers and lending institutions need to cover their costs and make a profit too. How about packaging together a lease on the land and a loan on the improvements? Perhaps this will make a more attractive total package, which could appeal to less expensive sources of money.

A variation of the lease-loan combination for a lender is to have separate sources for the land and the improvements. Acquire the land on a 40- to 50-year lease through sources that are not interested in tax shelter (religious and non-profit organizations are examples). Then the remaining amount will provide a better tax shelter because the cost of land cannot be depreciated or written off anyway but lease payments can be expensed. It is worth checking out. Make modifications as necessary to reach agreement as long as the carrot of tax avoidance stays in the arrangement. It is an indirect way of getting the government (both state and federal) to subsidize the transaction. Because of this, make certain you determine what income tax laws currently apply. Because it is a big plumb at government's expense, the rules may be changed or modified. If such change is enacted, it will always take effect in the future. Retroactive (ex post facto) laws are illegal.

Office Alternatives

The 1,000-square foot office in the building in Figure 5.15 is inside the warehouse building and costs $70 per square foot. Possibly it would cost less if located contiguous to but outside of the warehouse building, even though additional floor, walls, roof, and so on would be required. This, of course, would release more inside space. Which way to go is a quandary. More information is needed to make a prudent decision.

Compounding the quandary is that the figure $70 per square foot used is illusive, one that cannot be dealt with in isolation because the inside office space interfaces with the available warehouse space. The 1,000-square-foot office is deducted from the 40,000-square-foot warehouse leaving, 39,000 square feet of usable warehouse space. A realistic cost of an inside office would include the warehouse cost of 1,000 square feet of roof and floor and the area of walls used for the office. The cost of the warehouse floor should be deducted and put back at office floor cost, because what is needed for an office is less costly than the heavy-duty floor required for a warehouse.

A simple way to determine the total cost of having the office inside the warehouse building is to add the cost of the inside office space to the cost of the lost warehouse space (by having the office inside). Using Figure 5.15, this would be $70 per square foot plus $40 per square foot (total facility costs of $1,596,000 ÷ 40,000 sq. ft.) for a total of $110 per square foot. This is not entirely true because other factors affect the equation, such as construction of the office to allow storage above it or buying more land because you now have a building of 41,000 square feet compared to 40,000 square feet if the office is outside. These and other factors influence the equation, but going beyond the simple one used here is perhaps refining the equation beyond the rule of significant numbers. Simpler and more reliable would be to get competitive quotations for the alternatives.

Drawings and Specifications

The cost for these, $30,000, in Figure 5.15 is high for a simple warehouse design. While $30,000 is not all that important in relation to the total cost of the facility, every component should be examined and cost avoidance taken wherever found—provided that in the process it does not adversely affect other important things. Then, if opposing values are involved, a comparative analysis should be made, and the most favorable alternative adopted.

Quality input of advice, drawings, and specifications is definitely needed, but these should be provided at a cost less than the $30,000 indicated in Figure 5.15. An architect should not charge the same percentage (which is the common way architects charge) as for designing other more complex commercial and industrial buildings. How much less is hard to say. What is the right price for expertise? Probably the least you have to pay to get what you want.

BUILDING SIZE OPPORTUNITY

During the process of determining the size of the facility and acquiring the land, consideration should be given to building a structure larger than is initially needed. The reason for this is to determine whether the additional space constitutes such a profitable investment that it is too good for the company to pass up. It could be. A golden opportunity may be staring you in the face. You created it. The least you should do is examine it. The opportunity exists to construct additional space at the same time as your initial requirements are being constructed, partition the extra space from your space, and then lease it on relatively short-term leases until you need it or long-term lease if and when expansion for your own company is out of the question.

Referring again to Figure 5.15 the cost schedule shows a total of $1,596,000 to bring about a new facility of 40,000 square feet, 30 feet high. This converts to about $40 per square foot and about $1.48 per cubic foot: $1,596,000 facility cost ÷ (40,000 sq. ft. × 27 ft. usable height). Note that a building with 30 feet of inside clearance nets about 27 feet usable height because about 3 feet will be needed for the sprinkler system (or just because the building code requires it).

Assume that your research shows there is a good market for leased warehouse space. Now suppose that you determine costs to add another 20,000 square feet to the initial building, the best plan seems to be to put the extra space at the opposite end of the building from your office. This will disturb your operations the least. Put in a separate electrical meter and fuse panel for the extra space. Rough-in the plumbing for restrooms but leave the actual restroom and office design to the tenant. Amortize the actual office and restroom costs over the term of the lease in addition to the base lease for warehouse space. For example, if you can profitably lease the extra 20,000 square feet for $0.50 a square foot per month (without the additional electrical, plumbing, and office and restroom construction costs), you would add these costs amortized over the term of the lease. In this example, let us assume the total of these costs is $30,000, and the lease term is five years. The total lease rate would be the base rate of $0.50 per square foot per month plus the amortized portion of $500 per month ($30,000 ÷ 60 months).

In summary, the purpose of the additional 20,000 square feet (it could be more or less) is to provide for future requirements but to be available for lease to some other company at a profitable rate (adjusted periodically to the cost of living index or some other government index that adjusts with the prime interest rate charged the most preferred customers). This should be a very profitable venture because you probably will be able to lease the additional space at close to comparable rates for stand-alone 20,000-square-foot buildings. However, it will cost much less because it is constructed as an add-on to the initial 40,000-square-foot facility (which theoretically absorbs most of the fixed costs common to constructing any facility). You are reaping the benefits of what is commonly called "economy of scale."

The economy of scale phenomenon yields savings in nearly every cost component of the relative cost schedule (Figure 5.15), except possibly land.

Even with land there could be less cost per square foot for the additional 20,000 square feet. If not, there is still some savings on closing costs when it is run through the title company for their doings because some of their charges are the same no matter how big the purchase.

Each cost component will be affected differently, but mostly the economy is related to what may be called setup costs such as bringing in and taking away the heavy-duty crane to lift and position the tilt walls. Without going over each component to describe how each will be affected, let's assume here a cost reduction of 20 percent per square foot for the added 20,000 square feet. This seems conservative enough when you consider the walls (the largest cost) will involve putting up only three sides instead of four.

Taking these assumptions as being realistic, the added 20,000 square feet can be put up for $32 per square foot (100% − 20% or 80% of $40/sq ft). This amounts to a cost reduction of $160,000 ($8/sq. ft. × 20,000 sq. ft.). The financial value of the difference is actually more than the cost reduction of 20 percent. If someone set out to build a stand-alone 20,000-square-foot building, all the setup costs would have to be absorbed by this 20,000 square feet as compared to 40,000 square feet. Therefore, a separate 20,000-square-foot building could easily cost 20 percent per square foot more than the 40,000 square foot of the initial facility. This, added to the lower cost of $160,000 to build, will provide a total cost difference of $320,000.

This assumes that a 20,000-square-foot adjoining building is worth the same as an equal area in a separate building. This really is not true. On the other hand, there are advantages to having contiguous space. For the sake of simplicity this difference is overlooked here—whatever it may be. Granted that the total cost reduction for the additional space is something less than $320,000. Actually the true value will be the lease income capitalized at the going interest rate. For example, if you choose to value the 20,000-square-foot building as though it were a separate building—$960,000 ($48/sq. ft. × 20,000 sq. ft.)—and charge 1 percent per month on a triple net lease (lessee pays all utilities, taxes, insurance, repairs, etc.), the lease rate would be $9,600 per month (1% × $960,000). If you are able to lease it at this rate and this income stream is capitalized ($9,600/month at 1%/month) the value of the extra 20,000 square feet is $960,000.

This arithmetic covers the cost and lease value of the warehouse space, but it does not cover the added costs of the office and restrooms. These are covered by amortizing their cost over the term of the lease. Assume that it is five years in this example. Probably the lessor will realize a profit on this, but it is not certain. Suppose the next tenant (this could be your own company) does not want this office space. If this happens, you have at least recovered your initial cost.

There may be top-level opposition to this type investment for valid business reasons even though the return looks very good. It is best, therefore, to prepare the proposal carefully so that it demonstrates objectivity but has the best chance for approval the first try. Add to the financial return attraction a pitch for what a great idea it is to provide for future expansion. With conviction and clarity, explain how logical it would be to expand into adjacent space rather than having separate operations or moving to larger quarters. Generally, top management is receptive to objective, logical propositions that are based on optimism about their company's future growth.

OTHER DESIGN CONCERNS

It would be too tall an order to try to cover all warehouse design features in this one chapter. Even if the whole book were devoted to the subject, it would not be enough. What is covered is designed to put you in the driver's seat while cruising through the labyrinth of warehouse design and, equally important, to acquaint top management with the fact that there is a lot more to warehousing than stuffing goods into a building.

Many of the major design concerns are dealt with in the preceding part of this chapter. Here are several more factors of commonly less importance to round out the subject with at least cursory treatment.

Outside Security

We begin with outside security. This involves strong perimeter fencing, 6 feet high with coiled barbed wire at the top—or the equivalent—and good lighting at all entrance ways. Electronic eye surveillance may be justified. Even well-trained guard dogs in the fenced enclosure may be required. Keep in mind the best security is that which discourages thieves and vandals from entering the premises, not that which is geared to catch them. Catching criminals in the act is extremely dangerous business.

Ramps

When warehouse floors are elevated to approximate the height of truck and rail car beds, a ramp is needed to move lift trucks and other heavy equipment to and from the outside ground level and the raised inside warehouse floor. This seems obvious to an experienced warehouse, but many warehouse buildings are constructed without the input from experienced warehousers.

In the largest development of warehouse space in this country, accounting for 80 million square feet, ramps were not included as part of the standard building package. Those leasing or buying the buildings had to accept an extra charge for installing ramps as they did for offices (also not a part of the initial package).

Ramps should be constructed to last as long as the building to which they are attached. The incline of the ramps should be no greater than what can accommodate the material handling equipment required to traverse with safety and undue strain. Normally the ramps should be 30 to 40 feet long depending on the use to which they will be put and the elevation they are required to overcome.

Fueling and Charging Material Handling Equipment and In-house Personnel Carriers

Gasoline pumps and liquid propane gas tank racks must be located outside the warehouse building and according to National Fire Protection Code standards. The reason for this is the hazard of fumes and fire when located in an enclosure.

Battery recharging can be accommodated in a separate room designed for this purpose or at a station or stations located conveniently in the general warehouse area. The recharge room is normally used when operations are multishift and equipment is in nearly continuous use. When an operator realizes the battery is low, the equipment is driven to the recharge room where batteries are exchanged. The battery room should have forced ventilation, a water supply, eye wash and shower, floor drainage, and fire extinguishers equipped to fight both electrical and nonelectrical fires.

If operating only one shift, equipment can be parked during the off-shifts for recharging without switching batteries. The station for this should be away from the warehouse traffic but close and convenient to the operator's check-in-and-out location.

The battery charging room permits more extensive use of the company assets, the electrically powered handling equipment in this case. For instance for each dollar tied up in equipment the company gets a certain return for one shift, twice and three times for the second and third shift. One might question this arithmetic with the observation that the equipment will wear out twice or three times faster. This is true. To reinforce opposition to continuous operation of equipment is that repair and maintenance time will be taken from operating time; consequently repair and maintenance costs more.

On the other hand, let us view the situation from the owner's point of view. If $500,000 is invested in 10 pieces of equipment and the gross margin of return (income less cost) on this investment is $25 per unit per operating hour, it follows that the return on all the equipment will be $250 per hour ($25 per hour $\times$ 10 units). If the equipment is operated one 8-hour shift, the return will be $2,000 (8 hours $\times$ $250 per hour). If operated for two shifts, the return will be $4,000 per day, and so on. The gross return on the $500,000 invested in equipment is as follows, assuming 240 working days a year:

Schedule	Number of Shifts Worked per Year	Gross Return		Return on $500,000
		Per Shift	Per Year	
One shift	240	$2,000	$ 480,000	96%
Two shifts	480	2,000	960,000	192
Three shifts	720	2,000	1,440,000	288

This is not the complete story because many factors have been omitted such as downtime, shift-differential wages, supervision, amortizing purchase price of the equipment, repair and maintenance, and even whether the warehouse has productive work for more than one shift. It is generally true as far as it goes and makes use of a recharge room appear less costly when viewed in relation to the return on equipment investment.

Regardless of how the batteries are recharged, the appropriate electrical power supply must be specified during the design process to assure that the power will be where it will be needed.

Truck Maneuvering Room

The space left for truck maneuvering and parking is commonly slighted because the dominant concern is directed toward building size and this tends to subordinate requirements for trucks. Even when the ratio of land to building is only 1 to 1 (50% building coverage), the building can be so located as not to leave enough room for trucks. Of course the number and size trucks handled should influence the area left for them, but these should not be the only criteria. Keep in mind that the building will probably have several different tenants over its life (unless it is highly specialized for one company).

To determine the amount of room to leave for truck maneuvering and parking is difficult because innovative drivers of truck and trailer rigs can get by with less space than the uninitiated would expect. Whether to cause them to get by "or else" may cause sufficient employee strife, delays, and damage so that more space is economically justified.

If truckers and warehousers had their way, there would be 125 feet of paved area in front of the truck docks. With a lot of big-rig trucking, this could well be the most economical thing to do.

If the facility receives only by rail and ships only by small local delivery trucks, about 50 to 60 feet in front of the docks is all that is needed. Certainly from operation's point of view the range wanted would be between 100 and 130 feet for all warehouses served by trucks.

While plenty of space is needed, there are unfortunately many examples of factories and warehouses that have *no* truck maneuvering and parking areas except that of the city street. Trucks park parallel or extend out, which causes other trucks and vehicles to weave off the roadway to pass. This absurdity is all too common in sections of large old cities like Los Angeles, San Francisco and New York. To the extent warehousers can influence how much space should be left we should cast our vote righteously for adequate space. However keep in mind there are strong forces pressing for short term profits and providing adequate truck maneuvering and parking areas requires a long-term view of profits as well as real concern for the continued health of the company.

Chapter 6

How to Develop a High-Quality Warehouse Layout

CHAPTER HIGHLIGHTS

This chapter starts with a determination of the parameters of what should be included in the warehouse layouts, through the implementation and follow-up phases, to the continuing maintenance of a high-quality layout. Nine major elements should be considered in designing a high-quality layout or in evaluating an existing one. There is one particular method of storing that could favorably influence unit-load, bulk storage through the world: diagonal storage.

The plan for the warehouse layout should be completed before the facility is acquired—but it rarely is. Predetermined should be the ideal layout for the optimum combination of handling and storing functions in relation to the warehousing objectives. This data should then be translated to the facility specifications, including square feet, height, roof support columns, docks, doors, and so on. Simply the facility should be acquired to fit the layout, not the other way around.

Acknowledged, however, is that more often than not the facility is acquired before the layout is determined. This is because more existing facilities are acquired for warehousing than new ones designed and constructed to accommodate preplanned layouts. Further, those who acquire buildings in a company often do not appreciate how important good layout and design are to efficient and effective warehouse operations. Then, too, the company's warehousing group may not have the necessary layout expertise, or if they do—they are reluctant to stick out their necks. If this latter reason is the case, top management would do well to draw out from warehouse management what is needed. A qualified industrial engineer should be appropriate for this. *Do not* plan to acquire a building with blind faith that it somehow will be made into a good warehouse.

In addition, when warehousing is not given the status it deserves, the result can be high operating costs and lost sales.

In fact, a bad layout will require two to three times more time and effort as measured in costs, errors, damage, hazards, and responsiveness to service requirements.

How can layout improve service? By making little tasks out of big chores. Suppose, in one warehouse, that it takes two hours to fill an order. Then consider a layout in which the same order takes eight minutes to fill. If the order is received late in the afternoon, the supervisor of warehouse 1 may easily postpone shipping the order until the next day, whereas the supervisor of warehouse 2 will get the order on its way immediately.

When employees know what they are doing in a good layout, order picking is easy, and without interruptions (like searching for a lost store keeping unit), they zip through the task without as much as a groan or moan. This is why layout permits high-quality service at a respectable low cost.

WAREHOUSE LAYOUT DON'TS

Do Not Treat Material Handling Efficiency Separately from Space Utilization

The goal of "maximizing material handling efficiency" really does not say much except as a vague intention of "do good." This is because in warehousing, material handling is inseparable from space utilization. Efficiencies in space utilization can be easily sacrificed in achieving "maximum material handling efficiency." Literally you could store only one pallet high, which would be a boon for handling efficiency but disastrous to space utilization. In truck terminals and flowthrough warehouses, material handling is the dominant concern, but even in these extremes space utilization plays a part that cannot be ignored.

Do Not Establish Space Utilization Objectives Separately

If you were to treat space utilization in isolation, you could literally fill a warehouse facility as though it were a giant box car stuffed to capacity. Then when you open the doors, you are faced with a wall of merchandise and you cannot get to different SKUs except by removing all the other SKUs in front. Ridiculous! Simply, you cannot deal with space utilization without affecting handling efficiency, and vice versa.

Do Not Reduce Material Handling Costs Until You Know What It Will Do to Service

Maximizing efficiency and minimizing cost are different concerns. For instance, if minimizing costs were the sole objective, you might be tempted to reduce salaries and wages, lay off personnel, avoid equipment maintenance, and so on, without regard to the work load and what it would do to service. For the short term at least, costs would be reduced and progress would be made in achieving the goal. This is not as outlandish as it first appears. This is the modis operandi (M.O.) of too many managers and owners. "Turn it around, take our gains, and get out" is a common business concept, followed with "let someone else pick up the pieces." There are many more examples of impractical objectives that could be included, but these three illustrate the foolishness and waste of time of establishing unrealistic goals for warehouse layout.

About everything to do with physical distribution or logistics management and warehousing as a part thereof involves trade-offs—and layout is no exception. Components cannot be dealt with in isolation. This is particularly true of warehousing, because it has both line and staff functions and is supposed to be both efficient and service responsive.

EXAMPLES OF HOW LAYOUT GOALS SHOULD BE ESTABLISHED

1. Increase storage capacity of Section A of warehouse 3 by 20,000 cubic feet without increasing the hazard of product damage, reducing handling efficiency, or changing SKUs and quantities stored there.

2. Provide a layout for aisles and storage areas of the Acme warehouse using narrow-aisle, stand-up lift trucks in place of conventional sit-down type. Plan to use the narrow-aisle units for travel to and from staging but conventional lift trucks for carrier loading and unloading. Compare storage capacity and standard material handling time for present layout and the new one you design.

3. Without reducing space utilization, lay out storage areas to take maximum advantage of the last 12 months activity experience by SKU. Plan for the most active SKUs to require the least travel. Use standard operating times to determine the total time to operate in the present and new layouts.

4. Lay out the Central Warehouse to optimize material handling efficiency and space utilization. Use the following:
    ○ SKU inventory by quantity and turnover—12-month average.
    ○ Shipping by order size and frequency—12-month average.
    ○ Shipping performance of 90 percent within 24 hours and remaining 10 percent within 48 hours.
    ○ Control of inbound and outbound carrier scheduling.
    ○ Zero error rate.
    ○ Include assumptions you make.

    Base material handling and space utilization on engineered standards, factored to average performance for last 12 months.

These sample layout assignments should demonstrate that layout projects should be defined in terms of what is expected (objectives) and based on specified data and parameters. To expect quality layouts without this may get some results but not much better than throwing darts. Admittedly many layout projects have to be carried out with big voids in clarification and information; otherwise nothing would ever get done. More important, it follows that the better the input, the higher the quality of layout that will result—provided the quality of expertise in using the input is commensurate with the high-quality data.

If a layout is effective and efficient within the context of its objectives, it is a good layout. If it is effective and efficient, but does not comply with the objectives, it is a bad layout. A good layout is not achieved by just hard work. It results from a thorough knowledge of material handling and storing processes related to personnel and equipment availability, and the objectives of the layout—then, a lot of, if not hard, dedicated work.

HOW FLEXIBILITY IN LAYOUT CAN BE A MAJOR PITFALL

A common but wrong approach to layout is based on a misunderstanding of the concept "flexibility." Certainly it is important to allow for flexibility in planning the layout. But the otherwise respectable word "flexibility" is often used to cover up bad handling and storing practices. Too easily it becomes an excuse for not marking aisles, because they might change; not designating specific areas for particular inventories, because these areas will not hold during peak inventories; and not doing many other things that make for an orderly and efficient warehouse. Flexibility should be recognized in any layout plan, but because it is a natural coverup for poor warehouse management, it should be used with caution that it does not become a shield to deflect things that really should be done.

HOW TO PREPARE THE LAYOUT PLAN

Step 1: Determine Parameters

The first step in any layout plan is to establish what will and will not be included. Is the plan to be for a family of products at one warehouse? Or is it a plan for an entire warehouse? Or is it a master plan for many warehouses? Will it be limited to only existing space and equipment? Or will it take into consideration all that which will generate a payback within the constraints of the company's policy for new equipment and space investments?

Will the effects of a new layout influence the handling and storing of other inventory? Or can the plan be limited to only that inventory involved in the layout?

These and many other questions require answers to establish realistic parameters for the layout project. Without these boundaries the study may wander astray—stretching out indefinitely, risking that some of the first information gathered will become obsolete before the last data is in.

The time devoted to the layout plan must agree with when it is needed. Use of a chart to show what has to be done by function, the time allocated for each component, and progress against schedule is a good way to keep the project on track (see Figure 6.1).

Step 2: Establish Objectives

While establishing the project's parameters, the objectives may become evident. This is because "what" is to be studied (within the parameters) is inseparable from "why" (the objectives).

The objectives of warehouse layout are not entirely self-evident because what you think should be the objectives may be quite different from what the company's chief executive officer wants them to be. Following are some of the overall objectives that pertain to warehouse operations and some that relate specifically to individual layout programs. The entire list would not apply to any one warehouse.

The list only illustrates widely different types of objectives.

OVERALL OBJECTIVES FOR WAREHOUSE LAYOUT

- ○ Provide minimum-cost warehousing, even though service may be sacrificed.
- ○ Provide minimum-cost warehousing while maintaining the established level of service.

FIGURE 6.1 Progress Against Schedule

LAYOUT PROJECT

Function	Allocated Workdays	April			May			June		
		$\frac{1}{4}$	$\frac{1}{2}$	$\frac{3}{4}$	$\frac{1}{4}$	$\frac{1}{2}$	$\frac{3}{4}$	$\frac{1}{4}$	$\frac{1}{2}$	$\frac{3}{4}$
Parameters Progress	2 days	▪								
Objectives Progress	3 days	▪								
Gather information Progress	16 days		▬▬▬							
Analyze the information Progress	18 days				▬▬▬					
Formulate plan Progress	12 days						▬▬			
Implement Progress	8 days								▬▬	
△ Actual progress										
▲ Actual time										

The schedule is indicated by heavy horizontal lines by major component of the project.

Actual progress is indicated by hollow pyramids on the dotted line compared with the solid pyramids by quarter as reference points.

The arrows connecting the actual time pyramids with the appropriate actual progress pyramids show at a glance whether the project is ahead or behind schedule and by how much.

○ Provide better (quantified) service than competition regardless of costs.

○ Provide competitive (quantified) service at the lowest possible cost.

○ Provide a level of housekeeping and storage (quantified) that will result in a "showcase" for the company's products.

SPECIFIC LAYOUT OBJECTIVES FOR STORAGE LAYOUT PROGRAM

○ Improve space utilization by 20 percent over last year's average without reducing operating efficiency.

○ Provide for most efficient handling regardless of the effect on space utilization.

○ Optimize space utilization in relation to the costs of equipment, space, damage, and handling labor.

○ Make the warehouse a model of good housekeeping with secondary importance given to space utilization and operating efficiency—but provide how much more for both it will cost.

Step 3: Gather Relevant Information

With the parameters and objective of the layout plan established the next step is to gather relevant information to determine how best to conform to these directives.

As with any complex problem the solution becomes easier in direct relationship to the amount of relevant information you have. It is exceedingly difficult to make the right decision if very little is known, but as more valid information is acquired, the easier the right decision becomes. The weaker alternatives drop away, and eventually the right choice emerges with unexpected clarity. This is what happens with the complex considerations in layout. Even the most difficult decisions become manageable if enough valid information is brought to bear.

EXAMPLE: WHERE A WAREHOUSE IS HANDLING A PRODUCT LINE THAT IS PALLETIZED AND STORED IN PALLET RACKS

Customer purchases increase to the extent that several of the SKUs now move in pallet load quantity. The products cannot be stored in bulk because, when stacked two pallets high, damage results to the products on the lower pallet. The question is whether to store these high-volume SKUs two pallets *deep* with special two-deep racks using a deep-reach lift truck or install drive-through gravity fed racks four pallets deep. The inventory required to support the large quantity SKUs is enough to justify using either type rack system. New specialized racks must be acquired for either alternative. A deep-reach lift truck will have to be acquired to use the two-pallet-deep racks. The already-owned conventional-design lift trucks can be used for the drive-in racks.

As more information was gathered, the case for the drive-in rack system strengthened. The clincher came when the high cost was learned of lift trucks that can handle two pallets deep. The extra reach capacity does not come cheap.

The warehouse manager with support from the division's industrial engineer determined that the required new deep-reach lift truck would be only partially utilized for this work. With all facts considered they became convinced to stay away from the specialized handling equipment until the case for it was conclusive and this requirement was at best borderline, not at all conclusive.

This is not to imply that lift trucks with the double reach feature are not good. To the contrary they definitely have a place in material handling and under many circumstances they are far superior to other alternatives.

Measure the Exact Dimensions of the Warehouse Facility Obtain a copy of the original construction drawings to assist in determining the facility specifications, but keep in mind that these drawings are not a holy writ. Architects are prone to human fallibility as well. Also, the drawings contain a lot of information that is not relevant to layout planning. They do contain, however, some vital information on floor composition and soil compaction that is of critical concern to layout that cannot be found elsewhere. Mostly, however, the construction drawings serve as a cross-check against the dimensions you determine with the layout analyst's best and most trusted friend, the common tape measure.

Expect some variances in comparing actual dimensions with the construction drawings. Construction contractors are fallible too even though their finished products look right. Most of their errors are covered over by finishing material or cannot be detected without a tape measure.

Prepare a drawing of those things which are important to layout planning. Keep it as simple as possible yet include all relevant data. The drawing should result from carefully taken measurements which are later cross-checked with the contractor's drawings. Discrepancies should be reconciled. If any of your measurements are different from those on the contractor's drawings, remeasure and measure again until you are satisfied that your specifications are the right ones. Then, use these.

Valid discrepancies should be evaluated with reference to whether the differences are significant. If any are, decide with other responsible persons in your company the best course of action. This may include going back to the owner if the facility is leased and you are paying for something you are not getting or going back to the contractor if your company had the facility constructed. What you should not do is keep such discrepancies as your own little secret. On the other hand, do not proceed like a bull in a china closet either. Pointing out costly errors to those who made them, or did not catch them, is a little like poking a hornet's nest with the end of a short stick.

Include at least the following in the basics of your layout drawing:

○ Area dimensions, including storage heights
○ Roof support columns and their diameters
○ Storage-rack type and capacities
○ Fixed equipment and fixtures
○ Fire-fighting implements and water source
○ Warehouse office and work stations
○ Doors, docks, ventilators, water fountains
○ Fuel supply station(s)
○ Fuse panel box(es), voltage, and amperage
○ Rail siding
○ Truck maneuvering and parking area
○ Repair and maintenance shop
○ Rest and lunch rooms
○ First-aid provisions

○ Any other features of the building and property which will influence receiving, storing, order picking, shipping, and personnel concerns.

Determine Product Mix   Layout planners must have the best information available for receiving, shipping, and inventories to translate it into physical and employee requirements. This information should come through the company's formal system for providing it, as discussed in Chapter 3. Once the CEO says, "This is the plan we work by," warehousing should lock in and go for it. Warehousing should never go it alone; warehousing is an integral part of the company plan not something apart.

Handling and Storing Equipment   The physical and activity characteristics of the product mix largely dictate (or at least indicate) the type and quantity of equipment that breathes life into the layout.

The only additional considerations are the company's policies that relate to the financial and service aspects of warehousing. If the company is committed only to top-quality customer service and requires warehousing to do its part in the most efficient manner, these directives clearly point the way for the type of layout required. However, if the company requires of warehousing only to serve as a reservoir to absorb excess inventory (resulting from the most economical production runs) and gives only incidental importance to customer service, these directives as well clearly point the way to the type of layout needed. Both types of directives, although quite opposite, can be appropriate—depending on the company's objectives.

Step 4: Analyze the Information

None of the information gathered should be ignored. Decide it is irrelevant or assign it a quantitative value, but do not ignore it. Also watch out you do not assign it a higher quantitative value than it deserves. Unrealistically high or low values can lead to some outlandish results. As mentioned before, it is quite possible to attain near-maximum space utilization but be unable to find the products when it comes time to ship them. On the other hand, all materials may be stored separately in easy-to-find little stacks no higher than an employee can reach. This type of storage will probably save handling time but will also dramatically increase the overall costs through poor space utilization.

Handling Time and Space Utilization Standards   Handling time and space utilization standards are indispensable to developing good layout.

HANDLING TIME STANDARDS.   An example of a handling time standard is the time required to get, move a certain distance, and deposit a SKU of a given quantity at the rate of a fair day's work. This rate is officially equivalent to walking 3 miles an hour. It takes into consideration the complexity of the task, personal allowance, fatigue allowance, interference, and so on, and is attainable without pushing. Handling time standards should cover all activity, including receiving instructions and sending information necessary to the work. This may at first appear formidable, but it is not.

Such standards have been in use for many decades, in most cases with remarkable results. Now with computerization, discussed a little later, the use of standards involves a fraction of the time they did before. Further, performance measure with the use of a bar-code system can be on a real time basis if this is considered worthwhile.

SPACE UTILIZATION STANDARDS. These standards are as effective as handling time standards for their purpose. An example is the cubic space required to store a specific SKU in a given manner with certain equipment using a prescribed method of storing. Actually, space utilization standards are easier to develop and easier to use than are handling time standards. They are not as common, however, but considering the valuable contribution they can make to *objective* management, they should be. They too are indispensable to the proper layout of a warehouse.

EXAMPLES OF HANDLING TIME AND SPACE UTILIZATION STANDARDS

Time	Standards
0.26 hours	To open a rail car door.
0.06 hours	To position a pallet load into pallet racks.
0.01 hours	To hand stack a one cubic foot case of a certain weight on a specified pallet.

Space Utilization Standards

5.02 pounds per cubic foot per SKU _____

1.20 cases per cubic foot per SKU _____

9.30 cases per square foot of floor space per SKU _____

Such standards put planning and management on an objective basis. They are worth many times their cost—even when they are manually computed and used. With a computer and a bar-coding system the time and cost to develop and use drops dramatically, while their value increases inversely.

These tools in the hands of layout planners permit them to simulate any reasonable theories and tell their effects almost immediately. Minor errors in the design stage can become gross errors when implemented. Moving tens of thousands of cases and millions of pounds along with the accompanying storage racks becomes far too costly just to see how it looks. It is not like rearranging furniture in your living room.

To decide which layout plan to accept is now a relatively simple matter. You have theorized and hypothesized many different plans using accurate and relevant information. At this point the alternatives should be tested again as to how well they harmonize with the overall objectives for warehousing.

Make compromises as necessary. Any plan will involve some compromising. It is the nature of the work. Trade-offs are inherent in planning layout.

Use of a Layout Model Also indispensable or nearly indispensable is a model of the warehouse and its layout components so that the planning is visual and rearranging is convenient. Probably its greatest value is that it permits everyone to more likely see it the same. This does not negate the old adage that "we see things as we are, not as they are," but it does provide the best means there is of closing the gap. If we see the same layout in model form and still do not see precisely the same thing, what are the chances if we only discuss it? A compromise is to use blueprints of the plan, but this is a poor compromise because blueprints are so inflexible. Using a computerized layout software is a help, but this still falls way short of having miniature look-a-likes of the real thing.

Do not assume that if you have layout software and a computer that a good layout is assured. The same input of objectives, space, equipment, SKU data, timing, theorizing and hypothesizing, and so on go into producing a good layout regardless. With all the costs of progressing to this stage of the plan, a complete model is deserving. Here is where all that has been learned comes together. It is a very poor place to economize.

Where you get models of this nature may present a problem but not an insurmountable one. Miniature lift trucks can be purchased at toy stores, but they may not be close enough to scale for your use. One sure way to get the model components is to design them yourself then have them constructed and painted by anyone handy at this sort of thing. A call to a local artist association might be a good place to start. Another is the teacher of a high school or an adult wood-working class. Sure this is a little unconventional, but these models can be used repeatedly. The models are like the frosting on a cake. Who knows—the inventiveness displayed in creating the models will not hurt your career. Certainly it will not go unnoticed by your boss and other top management.

An alternative way to make a model for layout purposes is to start with a polyester film with a grid of lines making squares 4, 8, or 10 to the inch. The squares provide the scale to relate to the actual building walls and so on. All the lines, letters and numbers are made with self-adhesive units available in many colors. All materials were purchased at a store that caters to illustrating and drafting.

When the plan, using models, is complete, photographs of it will be invaluable for the implementation phase. Even though the plan appears to be the best in every respect, keep the models intact at least until the implementation and follow-up are complete. Then if you want the models for other purposes, dismantle them; you can always get a blown-up photograph of the layout. The likelihood will be, however, that you will want to keep everything intact. It can serve as a working tool to use as layout changes are necessary. Also, it could be justified only as a constant representative of your type of business acumen—of which there will always be a need.

Step 5: Implement the Layout Plan

The project is not complete when the best plan is devised, even when it is in blueprint, polyester or miniature model form. Implementation is the next step.

The Least Costly Way to Implement a Layout   The effective, efficient, and most orderly way in which to implement a layout is to start with an empty building that has all the storage racks and other fixtures installed and the floors sealed and aisles properly lined. Then as the inventories arrive, they are put away according to preestablished plan. No outbound shipments are made until the inventories and paperwork systems are in place and ready to go. The amount of work involved can still be substantial. Just how much depends on how many SKUs and quantities are involved plus how much hand sorting and stacking is required.

A whole new dimension of difficulty opens up when a warehouse is being emptied, transferring its inventories to a new warehouse, and continues customer shipments all at the same time. A further complexity is added when the new warehouse must start customer shipments as soon as it has received the appropriate SKUs. The difficulty of implementing the layout grows in geometric proportions with each new dimension introduced.

Another type of layout implementation relates to an operating warehouse that wants to change its existing layout. This too can be very complex if the warehouse is required to continue receiving and shipping while the change takes place. If the new layout affects only a small part of the warehouse, this may be accomplished with overtime of the regular crew. If the new layout encompasses all or even a large part of the warehouse, part-time help must be brought in and the regulars may be required to put in excessive overtime, working longer hours than they prudently should. The complexity of this type of layout grows commensurate with size of the layout, number of SKUs involved, and volume of receiving and shipping activity during the process.

The air float process of moving loaded storage racks discussed and illustrated in chapter 9 can be invaluable in changing layout of an operating warehouse.

Now that the difficulties of implementing a layout are covered, how these difficulties should be overcome is considered. Treat the changeover as you might organize the logistics of a battle plan. The following list suggests the things you will probably encounter.

1. *Establish a leader.* Determine who will head up the planning and actual implementation.

2. *Decide on the things that have to be done.* Make a complete list of everything that has to be done even what by itself would be trivial.

3. *Organize the requisite activities.* List all the things that have to be done in a chronological sequence. This is called an "algorithm" or a "linear program." Some functions will have to be forced into sequence because in reality they will happen the same time.

4. *Reorganize the planned activities.* Convert the algorithm into a scheduling chart showing how functions will overlap and are being done simultaneously with other functions.

5. *Refine your plan.* Get input from those who will be involved. Organize it by subject.

6. *Assign jobs.* Assign work responsibilities and make certain all know the big picture as well as their own assignments. Establish secondary functions to those whose primary functions may be completed sooner than scheduled. Do not have idle watchers hanging around. Arrange for information about progress and unexpected problems to flow back to the project leader. This is indispensable in any good battle plan.

7. *Make a schedule.* Depending on how big and how complex the project is, allow for overtime and stop receiving and shipping while the project is carried out. If you can see a crisis in the making, rearrange the plan to avoid it.

8. *Go for it.* Make it an organized crash program. Force it to completion in the shortest time possible. Do not string it out. Doing it along with the regular shipping and receiving is the surest way of screwing up the plan and the first crisis will probably be loss of inventory accountability—which is the worst that can happen. Just when everyone is the busiest you do not know what inventory you have—or nearly as bad, where it is.

Step 6: Review the Initial Plan

When the program leader believes the layout is complete, go over the initial plan and reconcile any differences.

If it had been a real honest-to-goodness battle, this is the time citations and medals would be issued, which is not such a bad thing to do here. At the least, issue some type of trophy. At the very, very least, issue a memo singling out participants with a hearty *Job Well Done.*

NINE MAJOR ELEMENTS OF A GOOD LAYOUT AND HOW TO PLAN THEM FOR GREATEST EFFICIENCY

1. Rack Storage

The purposes of rack storage are to improve space utilization, reduce product damage, and increase product accessibility. Products that should be stored in racks have one or more of the following characteristics.

- Too low quantity to palletize and stack multiple pallet loads high.
- Fragile packaging which will not support multiple pallet loads high.
- Irregular configuration that prohibits stacking one on another for economical bulk storage.
- Those products that belong in order-picking racks to improve order-picking efficiency.
- Increase accessibility when SKUs are in too low quantity to put them in bulk storage but they do not qualify for order-picking racks.

Commonly, a combination of products in order-picking racks backed up by unitized loads in bulk storage or high-density storage racks optimize handling efficiency and dense storage. The only problem with this combination is that all inventory taken from bulk storage to supply the order-picking racks is handled twice. The improved efficiency gained by using order-picking racks should more than offset the increased work of double handling the inventories.

There is a great variety of different storage rack designs and a great many rack suppliers. This combination adds to the complexity of what to buy but it also presents the opportunity to find bargains and drive hard deals. Much more is said about storage racks in Chapter 10.

2. Bulk Storage

The name for this type of storage is not very helpful in describing what it is. It is a name given to dense storage without the support of racks. Depending on the strength of the materials and packaging to support loads above, it can be stored any number of units high.

The big advantage of this type of storage is it permits maximum storage density. Normally the products are unitized on pallets or slip sheets. This generally permits storing higher than without the pallets or sheets by rebalancing the stack and tying the unitized loads together.

It is not necessary to use pallets or slip sheets for all products. Some can be handled with squeeze clamps, which are fixtures attached to lift trucks for this purpose. When products can be handled in this manner without causing additional damage, it is the lowest-cost, most efficient combination of handling and storing possible.

Bulk storage with or without pallets should be used wherever it is applicable because as just mentioned, it is the most efficient handling and storing combination. But it does require planning and attention, or it may wind up as a maze where only a mouse can survive. If lift truck operators are just turned loose to stack inbound inventories wherever they can find space, it is more likely than not that this part of the warehouse will turn into a maze. (See Figure 6.2.)

To use bulk storage effectively, aisles must be marked at intervals that are even multiples of the unit loads deep. For example, the depth of a row of unitized loads such as 3, 5, 8, 10, and so on, relates to the number of stacks of unitized loads you can put in that row. The depth should not provide for fractions of unitized loads such as 3½, 8⅓. If this is done, the only way to utilize the fractional space is to put a full unitized load in it, and there goes your layout, the aisle, safety, and about everything else good about the storage plan. Without careful planning and discipline, even the best operators will turn the storage into a maze. For example, when unloading a carrier the operator will search out an area that looks like it will take the quantity of an inbound SKU. Oops, it doesn't. The guess was wrong so the operator has a choice: (1) to keep coming out with additional stacks which obstructs the area intended for an aisle or (2) put the extra material in a different slot in another area which probably only partially fills that space. Both are poor choices. Still, it is not the

FIGURE 6.2 Comparison of Storage Layouts (same building)

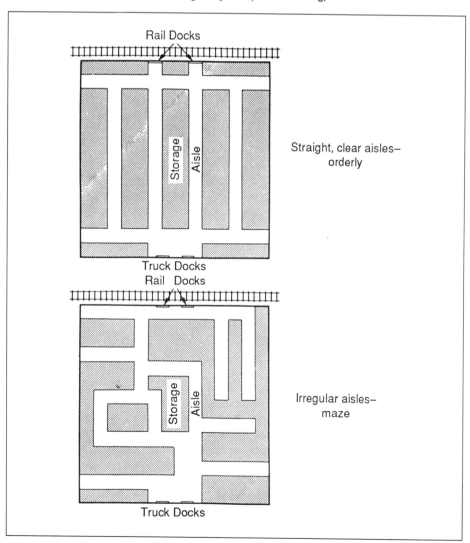

operator's fault; it is the fault of the warehouse supervision for not providing standard operating procedures and having such an undisciplined layout. To operate a lift truck and make engineering calculations about how much to put where at the same time is beyond anyone's capabilities. Being a good lift truck operator is a full job in itself.

Another important consideration about bulk storage is how many unitized-load stacks deep are provided from the access aisle. Already covered is that whatever number it is it should not be a fraction, but this does not tell how many load positions should be provided. The deeper they are, the better the space utilization will be, that is, if accessibility to different SKUs is ignored. But to ignore accessibility is one of the most serious crimes that can be committed in warehousing. The least that can happen is that the pallet stacks in front of a needed SKU will have to be moved and replaced not just once but whenever the hidden (blocked-out) SKU is needed. This is only loss of time and effort, but when the location of hidden SKUs is forgotten, the search until it is found can cause shipping promises to be broken and an inordinate waste of personnel and equipment time.

Sometimes the only realistic way to find the lost items is to walk the tops of the unitized-load stacks. Anyone seeing for the first time an employee do this will rub their eyes in disbelief. The alternative, however, is to keep emptying and refilling rows of stacked merchandise until the lost inventory is found. Neither is a satisfactory solution. Walking the tops of stacked unitized loads can be dangerous. Whenever it looks even remotely dangerous, forget this alternative.

Figure 6.3 shows that in the circumstance illustrated, better space utilization would result by adding another aisle and reducing the depth of bulk storage. In this case there is not enough inventory of most of the individual SKUs to justify such deep slots and maintain access to all SKUs. A good way to see how much storage space is being lost in bulk storage is to show space utilization from a top view as depicted by plan A, then turn each side of the aisle for a vertical view. If it looks like New York City's skyline, perhaps another aisle should be established.

Another caution about bulk storage is the extra control that is necessary to assure the inventory is used chronologically by when it is received. The two most often used methods of inventory usage go by the acronyms FIFO and LIFO, inventory control jargon for "first-in, first-out" and "last-in, first-out." If aging of inventories is a concern, and it is for most general merchandise, some form of FIFO must be practiced. With bulk storage this is not as easy as it is with rack storage. A standard operating procedure for how to accomplish this and the discipline to follow it is necessary. For instance, the last-in stock should not be stored in front of older stock. If it is, it must be removed to get at the first-in (oldest) stock for shipment. The inventories can be arranged to make FIFO easier to practice such as the block design illustrated in Figure 6.4, but this is more applicable to substantial quantities of an SKU. A good compromise is to use the block plan for high-turnover SKUs and shallow slots or pallet racks for low-quantity, slow-turnover SKUs.

The logic used to establish which method will be used (FIFO or LIFO) should be very sound, because if either should be practiced and is not, substantial inventories could be put in jeopardy. Or faulty logic that would require FIFO when it was not really necessary would cause a lot of extra work and loss of space but would gain nothing. Who would do such a thing? Probably some well-meaning executive who did not realize what she or he was doing, and "the way the warehouse manager was arguing against it told the suspicious insecure executive it must be a good thing." Good, secure warehouse managers will argue against FIFO unless it is certain that without a doubt it is necessary.

FIGURE 6.3   Comparison between the Use of Aisles in Two Different Bulk Storage
Layouts (many different products)

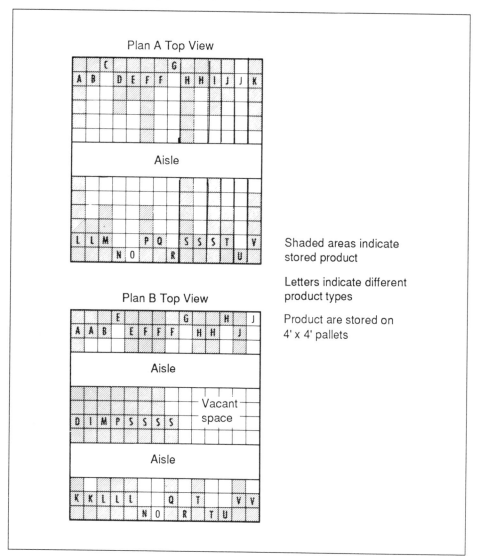

Shaded areas indicate
stored product

Letters indicate different
product types

Product are stored on
4' x 4' pallets

Here, again, experience pays off. You will find much written about FIFO
and LIFO but little written on the costs of rigidly adhering to these rules. To
some decision makers the type of reasoning that prevails, when not enough
information is known to make a rational decision, is "When in doubt, do it; it
can't hurt anyone." True, it is not going to hurt anyone physically in this instance; however, the decision maker should know it costs more.

A good way to accomplish FIFO or LIFO is to have the stock locator system identify storage by date received or production date, whichever is applicable, as well as by location. Even more important is to make certain FIFO is
needed in the first place. If so, determine with engineering precision how long
stock can be in storage without any sign of deterioration or obsolescence or
whatever reason FIFO was required in the first place. With this information
make choices about which stock to ship based on efficient handling and storing
until the danger time approaches; then of course ship the oldest. Keeping such
records manually would be a big chore, but entering the data in the computer
with other information that is necessary would make the routine far less costly,

FIGURE 6.4 Bulk "Block" Storage (for one SKU) to Permit FIFO Inventory Control

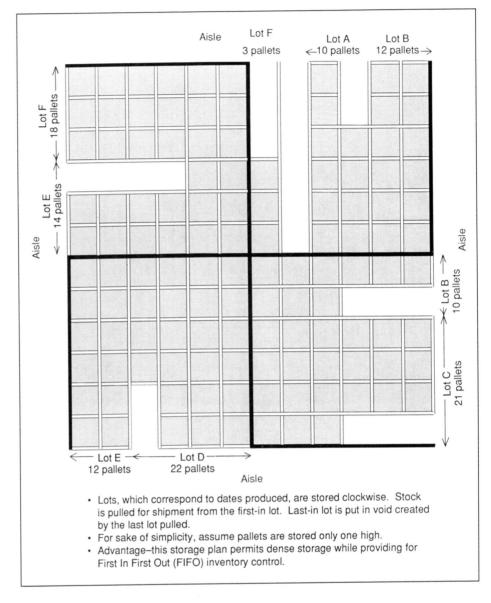

- Lots, which correspond to dates produced, are stored clockwise. Stock is pulled for shipment from the first-in lot. Last-in lot is put in void created by the last lot pulled.
- For sake of simplicity, assume pallets are stored only one high.
- Advantage–this storage plan permits dense storage while providing for First In First Out (FIFO) inventory control.

more timely, and far more accurate. Let the computer do the work of advising what and when to ship. Any handling and storing efficiencies that can be realized while still adhering to FIFO where applicable is that much the better.

3. Diagonal Bulk Storage

Something new in warehousing is laying out the rows of pallets diagonally rather than at right angles to the aisle (Figure 6.5). Certainly diagonal storage is not uncommon. For example, diagonal parking for automobiles along some city streets and in parking lots is quite common. This is done to reduce the needed width of the street or the total amount of space for a given number of parking spaces. The same reasoning applies to diagonal storage in warehousing.

When I was the CEO of a public warehouse company dealing largely in cased wine storage, we laid out all unitized loads diagonally—except for rack

FIGURE 6.5 Diagonal Bulk Storage

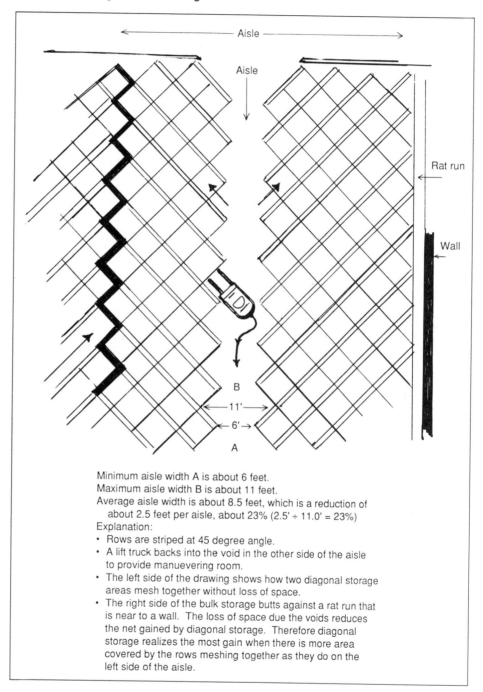

Minimum aisle width A is about 6 feet.
Maximum aisle width B is about 11 feet.
Average aisle width is about 8.5 feet, which is a reduction of
about 2.5 feet per aisle, about 23% (2.5' ÷ 11.0' = 23%)
Explanation:
- Rows are striped at 45 degree angle.
- A lift truck backs into the void in the other side of the aisle to provide manuevering room.
- The left side of the drawing shows how two diagonal storage areas mesh together without loss of space.
- The right side of the bulk storage butts against a rat run that is near to a wall. The loss of space due the voids reduces the net gained by diagonal storage. Therefore diagonal storage realizes the most gain when there is more area covered by the rows meshing together as they do on the left side of the aisle.

storage for less than unit loads. While improving space utilization and accommodating the lift truck operators who preferred it, two additional advantages emerged. (1) It improved material handling efficiency; it takes less time to deposit or pick a load in, say, a 45-degree angle than it does at a 90-degree (perpendicular) angle. (2) It contributed to employee pride about their warehouse. "We do things different." Judging from all the "Oh's," "Ah's," and "Gee whizzes" from customers and visitors when they saw it for the first time, it also added favorably to customer and public relations. It gave the impression: "These people are innovators, they know what they're doing."

I do not want to hold out that diagonal bulk storage will reduce aisle space 30 percent as Figure 6.5 indicates. It shows the results of storage at a 45-degree diagonal. Different degree angles will result in different space utilization. Also there is some lost space with this pattern against walls and the ends of aisles. We reduced this loss by storing in these triangular voids things of less depth and width than the standard unitized loads.

4. Aisles

Aisles demand equal engineering attention as storage areas and both have to be planned together to arrive at a functionally efficient warehouse. As indicated in Figure 6.3 attempts to maximize space utilization for storage can result in a bad layout and poorer space utilization, plan A. Saying it another way, the storage system employed must be appropriate to the product mix. You cannot expect an ideal layout for 10 SKUs to be satisfactory for 100 SKUs, just as one for 100 SKUs would not be right for 1,000 SKUs. Change nearly anything about warehousing, its objectives, its product configurations, its product mix, its volume, its inventory quantities, and so on, and you change the type of layout that will serve best.

Probably the single most important element affecting aisles is the handling equipment employed. This being the case, the aisle characteristics are being formed way back when the means of storing and handling are being decided. If, however, the plans for storing and handling lead to too much space being devoted to aisles, it may be necessary to back up and change the handling equipment to permit narrower aisles. This is not bad in itself. Everything about warehousing seems to involve trade-offs and compromises. That is why warehousing is such an exciting profession, very little stays the same except change.

A worthy objective of a layout should be to lose the least space possible. This is why narrow-aisle lift trucks, side loaders, 180-degree turret lifts, deep-reach forks, stacker cranes, and so on, came about—mainly to minimize space consumed in aisles.

It is not possible to predict in advance how wide and how many aisles a warehouse should have until all the influencing factors are determined, analyzed, and brought together to optimize the layout to satisfy the warehouse objectives. Now with all these qualifiers the following general guide for aisle widths is timidly offered. It relates to using a General Services Administration (GSA) standard size pallet, 40 inches deep by 48 inches wide.

Handling Equipment	Lift Capacity (pounds)	Aisle Width (feet)
Conventional, sit-down lift truck	2,000	10
Conventional, sit-down lift truck	4,000	11
Conventional, sit-down lift truck	6,000	12
Narrow aisle stand-up lift truck	2,000	7
Narrow aisle stand-up lift truck	4,000	8
Narrow aisle stand-up lift truck	6,000	9

Side-loader lift truck 2 feet wider than the load is deep.
Stacker-overhead crane with guides, 1 foot wider than the load is deep.
Crane in an ASRS system, 9 inches wider than the load is deep.

These aisle widths should be taken only as indications because different manufacturers have different designs. Just as in automobiles, all 6- or 8-cylinder models do not react the same.

The basic feature about any lift truck that manufacturers have to reckon with is that more weight must be behind the fulcrum point (the front wheels) than ahead of it. This means that the weight behind the fulcrum must exceed the weight of the truck beyond the front wheels plus the load. This is why the conventional sit-down lift truck takes wider aisles because the load is entirely beyond the front wheels. Narrow-aisle, stand-up lift trucks can operate in narrower aisles because the front wheels extend under or beside the load. Crane-type material handlers are designed entirely different and are able to operate in aisles only a few inches wider than the load. All these material handlers are discussed and illustrated in Chapters 9 and 11.

Make Complete Use of Aisles   An important consideration about aisles is illustrated in Figure 6.6, that both sides of the aisle should access stored merchandise. Since you have to have aisles anyway, take full advantage of them. A glaring example of violating this principle is having an aisle running along the side of a wall. This is a pathetic waste of space; see layout A. Obviously storage should be on both sides of the aisle as illustrated in layouts B and C.

Another all too common violation of this principle is using a single row of pallet racks with aisles on both sides of the rack. Obviously these storage racks should be back to back so that aisles permit access to racks on both sides. Truly the only time a single row of racks is good layout is when the single row backs to a wall, which then enables the aisle to serve access to storage on both sides. Oh, yes, a single row of racks may be a good layout when bulk storage backs to the single row of racks, but this cannot be recommended except with reservations. First, a single row of racks other than against a wall (to which it should be secured) is far more difficult to make secure compared to back-to-back racks. Second, bulk storage is normally used for large quantities per SKU. The bulk storage illustrated in layout C would be difficult to use efficiently. If every stack were a different SKU, it would be better space utilization to put the stock in racks. If, however, one SKU takes several rack positions, this is very poor utilization of aisle access. Accessibility to SKUs is like money; spend it wisely.

5. Staging Areas

Layout must provide for staging areas for both receiving and shipping. The size of the staging areas depends on how much merchandise will accumulate there while it is counted and inspected before putting it in storage or loading it on an outbound carrier. Rack storage against the walls bordering the staging area can be used to hold staged merchandise or regular inventory. If they are used to hold inventory, the SKUs put there should be low quantity and slow moving so that interruption of staging work is minimal. Both uses should be considered, and the one that contributes most is the right way. The major concern about installing racks here is that they can negatively affect use of the staging area. Probably the best, if applicable, is using them for supplies consumed in staging—or packaging, if this is part of warehousing and is located in or near the staging area.

6. Bridging Between Rows of Racks

Figure 6.7 illustrates how additional storage rack space may be gained by bridging over the aisles with pallet racks. Obviously the bridge should be high enough

FIGURE 6.6 Use of Both Sides of Aisles (overhead view)

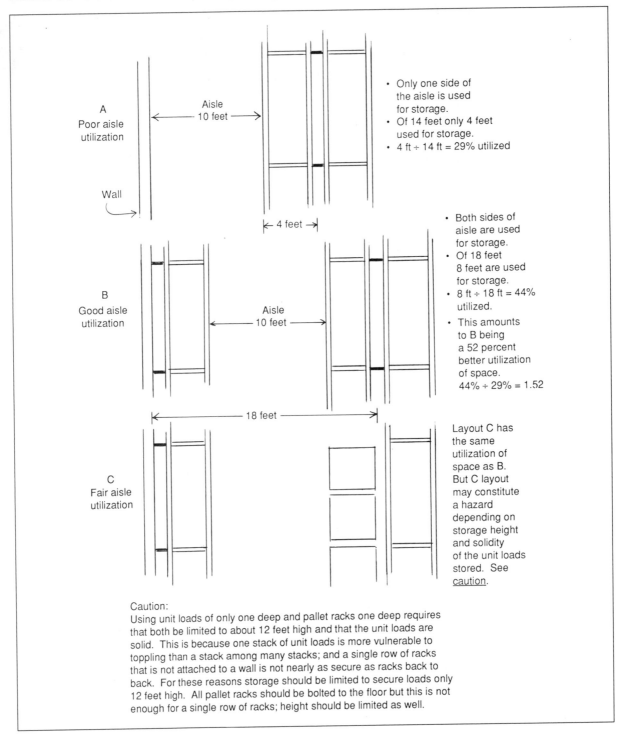

A
Poor aisle utilization

Aisle
10 feet

Wall

- Only one side of the aisle is used for storage.
- Of 14 feet only 4 feet used for storage.
- 4 ft ÷ 14 ft = 29% utilized

4 feet

B
Good aisle utilization

Aisle
10 feet

- Both sides of aisle are used for storage.
- Of 18 feet 8 feet are used for storage.
- 8 ft ÷ 18 ft = 44% utilized.
- This amounts to B being a 52 percent better utilization of space.
  44% ÷ 29% = 1.52

18 feet

C
Fair aisle utilization

Layout C has the same utilization of space as B. But C layout may constitute a hazard depending on storage height and solidity of the unit loads stored. See <u>caution</u>.

Caution:
Using unit loads of only one deep and pallet racks one deep requires that both be limited to about 12 feet high and that the unit loads are solid. This is because one stack of unit loads is more vulnerable to toppling than a stack among many stacks; and a single row of racks that is not attached to a wall is not nearly as secure as racks back to back. For these reasons storage should be limited to secure loads only 12 feet high. All pallet racks should be bolted to the floor but this is not enough for a single row of racks; height should be limited as well.

for load-carrying equipment to clear. Lift trucks are supposed to move loads with the forks lowered for many reasons, but primarily for safety. However, if there is a chance for things to go wrong, they eventually will, but this is true of many common practices such as a pedestrian being hit by an automobile that should not be there. Bridging has become a fairly common practice.

FIGURE 6.7 Bridging to Store Over Aisles

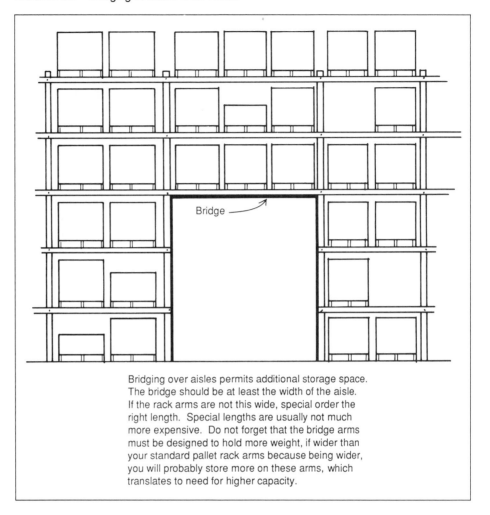

Bridging over aisles permits additional storage space. The bridge should be at least the width of the aisle. If the rack arms are not this wide, special order the right length. Special lengths are usually not much more expensive. Do not forget that the bridge arms must be designed to hold more weight, if wider than your standard pallet rack arms because being wider, you will probably store more on these arms, which translates to need for higher capacity.

7. High-Rise and Automated Layouts

Layout for high-rise and automated warehouses is quite different from that for conventional warehouse facilities. The concern for space utilization and efficient material handling is designed into the structure. Discipline and standardization are inseparable component features.

Chapter 5 has presented the principles of a cube configuration and why it is the most efficient. Here we are concerned about the material handling systems in relation to space utilization.

The size and capacity of the various storage positions in the system must come from the warehouse manager, for example, "We need 436 50 in. × 48 in. × 48 in. cubbyholes for the electrical parts alone," and so on. Vendors commonly will push toward complete standardization of these cubbyholes and this will be the size that will take the largest load handled. They do this because they know that invariably, the warehouser's requirements will change many times over the life of the storage system. "Just as well make all the same, since requirements will change anyway." The warehousers' point of view is that if there are savings involved in being a little less standard, they want to at least investigate the possibilities. If more capacity can be achieved by various-sized load openings, perhaps there is a chance to scale back the system and reduce its costs. Again, business in the United States is commonly tied to quick payoffs. It seems basic to private enterprise: "Why worry about what things will be after 10, 15, 20 years from now; we probably won't be here anyway." The reality of this is that contemporary business leaders wish that more did worry 10, 15, 20 years *ago* about how things would be today.

A viable compromise in the storage system is to make compartments large enough for your largest unitized load and then use dividers that may be put in or taken out as product mix changes.

Some companies will have need for cantilever racks (with arms cantilevered out from the main column, described and illustrated in Chapter 10). If this is the case, make certain it is possible to move, add, or remove arms to accommodate changes in product mix. Also provide that the arms have the capability of being decked, converting them to huge shelves that will accommodate individual packages or unitized loads. Cantilever racks that can be decked are more flexible than are pallet racks and have a definite advantage. They have no vertical obstruction like the uprights of pallet racks.

Of course, quotations for cantilever racks versus pallet racks should be secured. Occasionally the vendor will quote to favor one over the other because her or his source is better for one or the other. A simple check of the total rack *weight* will tell a lot when compared to prices. Even though it may not seem this way, the basic cost of steel used for the racks legitimately influences prices more than any other single component.

Commonly, receipts are taken in at one end of the storage system and shipped out the other. Both ends require enough staging area to do the most efficient unloading and loading. A common feature of each area is that the height of the storage area is not needed in either staging area; this is because the handling equipment in the staging areas probably needs no more than 15 feet clearance while the storage area will commonly be twice to several times that.

Do not arbitrarily drop the ceiling in these areas though. Thoroughly investigate the staging areas' equipment possibilities to make certain they do not and probably will not require the greater heights. You may want the crane mechanism to place outbound loads at a midpoint of the height of the storage area on an elevator or conveyor to bring them to floor level, thereby reducing the vertical distance the more costly crane must travel to get to or put loads in the staging areas.

8. Orient Storage to SKU Activity

SKUs that are shipped in the greatest volume should be stored in the most efficient area for material handling. This simple notion can probably reduce some warehouse's material handling travel by up to 50 percent. It is so important that it could justly be elevated to *the golden rule of warehouse efficiency.*

"If this concept is so fantastic, why does not every warehouse do it?" This is one of the mysteries of life. Probably the reason why this phenomenon is not given its due recognition is that a warehouse is often a frantic place and for employees to look busy is quite enough for many supervisors. To be most productive as well requires far better supervision.

Figure 6.8 indicates that products that are the most active should be stored to permit the most efficient material handling. This most efficient area is in a direct line from the receiving to the shipping dock—and stored nearest the shipping door. This assumes, of course, that there are no physical obstacles such as corners of building or posts that obstruct passage along this line.

FIGURE 6.8 Comparison of Handling Times for Different Storage Areas

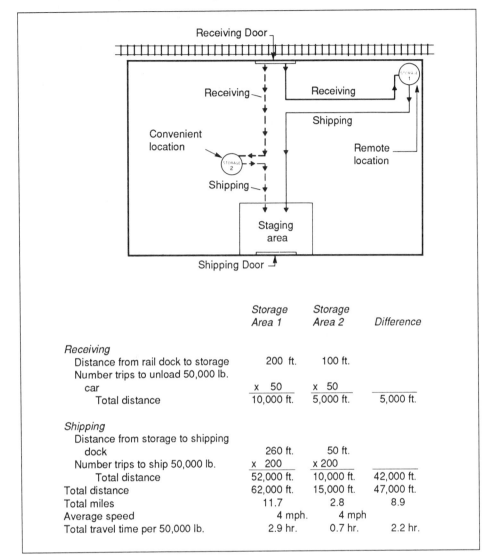

	Storage Area 1	Storage Area 2	Difference
Receiving			
Distance from rail dock to storage	200 ft.	100 ft.	
Number trips to unload 50,000 lb. car	x 50	x 50	
Total distance	10,000 ft.	5,000 ft.	5,000 ft.
Shipping			
Distance from storage to shipping dock	260 ft.	50 ft.	
Number trips to ship 50,000 lb.	x 200	x 200	
Total distance	52,000 ft.	10,000 ft.	42,000 ft.
Total distance	62,000 ft.	15,000 ft.	47,000 ft.
Total miles	11.7	2.8	8.9
Average speed	4 mph.	4 mph	
Total travel time per 50,000 lb.	2.9 hr.	0.7 hr.	2.2 hr.

The reason for making the point "to store the material as close as possible to the shipping door" is because products normally come into warehouses in unitized loads and go out in less than the unitized load. This results in fewer long trips from the receiving dock to the point of storage, with more short trips from that point to the shipping dock.

Figure 6.8 compares the time required to handle an amount of inventory when stored in the most remote area of the warehouse with that stored in a more efficient area. The comparison shows a difference of 2.2 hours of travel time required to handle one rail carload of stock. If the warehouse were to process 30 carloads of this product a month, there would be a difference of 66 hours of travel time. Although this comparison is extreme (it could have been made even more extreme by locating the storage 10 feet from the shipping dock instead of 50) it serves to illustrate the substantial increase in operating efficiency that can be attained from applying the golden rule.

9. Orient Storage to Load Size

This phenomenon is an extension of the preceding one about placing the load most efficiently in relation to shipping activity. This one focuses attention on receiving and shipping load sizes—regardless of shipping activity.

The SKU size loads received, unloaded, and put into storage compared with the size loads of the same SKU shipments directly affects productivity (real accomplishment). The two following examples show that these load ratios can greatly affect real operating efficiencies and illustrate the methodology for determining the optimum locations for all storage.

EXAMPLE A

Canned goods are received by rail, 6,000 cases per car. The cases are palletized in loads of 100 cases each. A lift truck operator can take a full pallet load directly from the car to the storage area without intermittent staging. It takes 60 trips to unload the car. However, because the average customer order is for 4 cases, it requires 1,500 trips to take the 6,000 cases to the staging area for shipment. The ratio of receiving loads to shipping loads is 60 to 1,500, or 1 to 25. You are right! Obviously, the product should be stored as close as possible to the shipping dock. There are 25 times as many shipping trips as receiving trips.

Assuming that the storage area is midway between the receiving and shipping points, and 3 min. are required per trip, the total travel time required for 1 carload would be as follows:

Receiving:	60 trips at 3 min. each =	180 min./car
Shipping:	1,500 trips at 3 min. each =	4,500 min./car
	Total =	4,680 min./car or
		78 hrs./car

Now assume that the storage area is located closer to the shipping dock, so that it takes 5 min. per trip to receive merchandise and put it in storage and only 1 min. per trip to the staging area for shipping.

Receiving:	60 trips at 5 min. per trip =	300 min./car
Shipping:	1,500 trips at 1 min. per trip =	1,500 min./car
	Total =	1,800 min./car or
		30 hrs./car

The difference for the two storage areas is 48 hr. per car (78 hr. versus 30 hr.).

This example is obviously extreme and rarely would you find a similar situation. However the method of using extremes to illustrate a point or to test validity is appropriate and valid. It makes its point.

Normally the warehouse order pickers would pick several SKUs on a trip. This would reduce the huge difference cited of 48 hr. per car, and it would require extensive arithmetic to determine just how much a savings each trip. There are many ways to group or consolidate order picking, but the example, while extreme, serves to illustrate the principle that the load-size ratio between inbound and outbound shipments is very important.

EXAMPLE B

Refrigerators are received by rail, 60 per car. Only one at a time can be transported by lift truck. The load-size ratio is 60 to 60, or 1 to 1. In this example it makes no difference where the product is stored in the warehouse as far as the load-size ratio can influence efficient handling. It should be stored in the most remote area, thereby making room near the shipping dock for products that can benefit most from this prime location, such as the one described in Example A, before.

To demonstrate that a 1-to-1 load ratio gains nothing from being stored near the shipping dock, assume the product is stored midway between the point of receiving and the point of shipping. The total travel time per car is as follows.

Receiving:	60 trips at 3 min. each =	180 min./car
Shipping:	60 trips at 3 min. each =	180 min./car
	Total =	360 min./car or
		6 hr./car

Now assume that the storage area is moved closer to shipping and equally farther from receiving. It now takes 5 min. to get from receiving to the point of storage and only 1 min. to get from there to outbound staging. The travel time required for a carload in this case would be

Receiving:	60 trips at 5 min. each =	300 min./car
Shipping:	60 trips at 1 min. each =	60 min./car
	Total =	360 min./car or
		6 hr./car

It takes 6 hr. travel time regardless of whether the storage area is moved closer to the shipping area, provided that the same distance that is subtracted from the shipping trip is added to the receiving trip.

Caution is suggested in using this phenomenon literally without further investigation. As in Example B of using refrigerators as the product that can only be transported one at a time, this is not always true. An attachment to the lift truck will permit lifting and moving more than one at a time. Depending on how many different models and colors there are in the rail car and how they are shipped (as to colors and models), the arithmetic should be modified accordingly. The principle is right nevertheless. How right depends on these other influencing factors.

10. Storage Height

Discussed extensively in Chapter 5 is the importance of building height, which translates to storage height. Height is as important (perhaps more important) as width and depth in determining total storage capacity. Further, changing this dimension has the least effect on building costs for the same increase in capacity.

Until fairly recently it was unusual to find merchandise stacked over 10 feet high, and most storage was kept within the easy reach of the worker. It is still this way in many parts of the world. Even if the advantage of high storage were recognized in the past, it was not possible to implement because equipment manufacturers did not provide for reaching higher. Since there was little customer demand for high lift equipment, it was slow to be offered.

A further restraint on storage height continues to be the fact that labor is considered cheap in undeveloped countries. The economics, payback, interal rate of return, and so on that apply in industrially advanced countries does not make any sense in these cheap labor markets. Another factor less recognized but nearly as important is the cost of land and buildings. With these differences, it is no surprise that the advantages of high-rise warehouses do not apply everywhere.

Where high-cube economics do apply, the following example illustrates the economics of high storage:

Problem. It is necessary to store 100,000 cubic feet of inventory. Which building design will most economically provide the necessary capacity? For this particular type of storage it has already been determined that 40 percent of the total floor area will be allowed for aisles.

Building I, Low Ceiling. The ceiling is 14 feet high, but because of the overhead sprinkler system and fire code restrictions, storage height is limited to 10 feet. Allowing 40 percent for aisles, a total warehouse area of 16,667 square feet is needed to provide space for the 100,000 cubic feet inventory. Assuming the building costs to be $30 per square foot (relating all land and utilities to the useable warehouse space), the building's square feet and cost would be determined as follows:

$$\frac{100,000 \text{ cu. ft.}}{10 \text{ ft. high} \times 60\% \text{ utilization}} = 16,667 \text{ sq. ft.}$$

16,667 sq. ft. bldg. × $30.00/sq. ft. = $500,000

Building II, High Ceiling. The ceiling is 30 feet high with an effective 26-foot storage height after allowance for the sprinkler system and fire code. The same allowance of 40 percent aisle space is made. A total of only 6,420 square feet of warehouse area is required to provide storage of 100,000 cubic feet of inventory. Assuming the building costs to be $40 per square foot (relating all land and utilities to the useable warehouse space), the building's square feet and cost would be determined as follows:

$$\frac{100,000 \text{ cu. ft.}}{26 \text{ ft. high} \times 60\% \text{ utilization}} = 6,140 \text{ sq. ft.}$$

6,410 sq. ft. bldg. × $40.00/sq. ft. = $256,400

Building II would cost $243,600 less than building I, yet the same amount could be stored in each. Building II costs $10 per square foot more to construct because of the higher walls, but it requires only a little over 38 percent of the square footage area required in building I.

It would be necessary to buy more expensive lift trucks to handle the high cube, but at the height required of about 22 feet, they would be standard, not special. You might ask how a 26-foot height is going to be stacked by a 22-foot lift truck? Assuming a load height of 4.5 feet, the lift truck has to reach only about 22 feet since loads are picked up from the bottom, except for lift trucks with clamp attachments, which are comparatively few. Whatever the additional equipment costs, it would be a small part of the building cost savings of $243,600.

Building I	$500,000
Building II	256,400
Savings	$243,600

This comparison is based on bulk storage (without racks). If racks were included, the savings would remain about the same. The same number of pallet positions would be needed in either case.

LAYOUT MAINTENANCE

Most warehouses are subject to changing demands. Many changes do not cause the layout to be rearranged, but some do. Suppose a packaged SKU were palletized and stored in pallet racks and the company decided to discontinue the item and replace it with another SKU that should also be stored on pallets in pallet racks. There may not be a requirement to change the layout, particularly if the firm ships out the new unit at about the same rate as before. But if the new SKU shipping rate is faster, installing storage racks nearer the shipping dock to reduce the travel time would be recommended. This would probably not affect the layout unless it is a substantially greater quantity and requires installing more storage racks.

A tool essential to layout maintenance is the master layout, whether it is a drawing or a model. The master should be changed only with the authorization of the manager. The actual layout should conform to the master; any change should be planned on the master layout first. Mistakes are easily observed and corrected there; they are far more difficult to detect and much more costly to correct when dealing with actual inventories.

A good layout provides a storage plan for everything, with everything stored according to plan. It also requires disciplined housekeeping practices to maintain the warehouse in good order. A combination of the two will result in efficient, orderly storage. This combination is the foundation on which efficient material handling procedures and responsive customer service can be built. Without it, handling efficiency and good service are impaired by double handling, search for lost inventories, and low employee morale.

No deviation from the master plan should be made by the floor supervision. The need for change should be brought to the attention of the manager or to whomever this responsibility is delegated. If the change is warranted, then the change will be worked out using the master plan. Occasionally there will *appear* to be a need for change, for example, a huge buildup in inventory of a certain family of SKUs, indicating that sales is expecting a big increase in customer orders. Perhaps a major advertising campaign is about to break. Or a line of products is being discontinued, and all inventories are being brought to this one warehouse for a quick close-out sale. If sales had not communicated this big change of plans to the warehouse manager, she or he would have to determine the reason for the buildup or curtailment by calling the sales manager. No one should stand on principle or hide behind responsibility and let the company get in trouble.

Follow-up on layout and housekeeping is an indispensable and regular part of warehouse management. This can be done with spotchecks, but unless conducted seriously, frequently, and systematically, the results will not be lasting. The Layout and Housekeeping Report in Figure 6.9 illustrates one way to follow up on a regular basis. The report should be tailored to specific warehouse conditions and key points that are applicable to those conditions. This report calls for corrective action for any "no" ratings and a target date for correction. Such a report would be appropriate for discussion at the regular warehouse operations meetings. Not only is it intended to police layout and housekeeping, it does the same for repair and maintenance. An all too common malady in production and warehouse operations is for the maintenance and repair department to be behind in their work because they are not monitored as closely as operations. The surest way for this part of layout and housekeeping to lose impetus is for reported problems to not have timely response and action taken. This applies to warehouse management as well. Reported problems should be responded to promptly or eventually they will not be reported. If there is no intention of correcting a reported problem, then this answer with a reasonable explanation should be forthcoming. There will be occasions when doing nothing is doing the right thing, but leaving the reported problem up in the air is certainly not the right way to handle it.

FIGURE 6.9 Layout and Housekeeping Report

Warehouse Operations					
LAYOUT AND HOUSEKEEPING REPORT					
Warehouse				**Building/Area No.**	
NO.	**QUESTION**	**YES**	**NO**	**CORRECTIVE ACTION***	**DATE**
1	Is there a warehouse layout drawing?				
2	Is storage per drawing?				
3	Does whse. drawing agree with Master?				
4	Are aisle borders marked?				
5	Are aisles clean?				
6	Are aisles and staging areas sealed?				
7	Are storage areas identified?				
8	Is storage neat and proper?				
9	Are racks in good condition?				
10	Is damage in specified area?				
11	Is damage identified?				
12	Are truck and rail areas clean?				
13	Are all pallets in good condition?				
14	Are empty pallets stored neatly?				
15	Is building secure from rain?				
16	Are authorized bldg. repairs complete?				
17	Are door locks adequate?				
18	Are windows clean?				
19	Are light bulbs operable?				
20	Are yards clean and neat?				
21	Is office clean and neat?				

*For any NO answer indicate corrective action to be taken. Use additional space below when needed. Reference to appropriate question number.

_____

_____

_____

_____

_____   _____
        Inspected by   Date

Chapter 7

Stock Locator Systems: How to Maintain Location Information Efficiently

CHAPTER HIGHLIGHTS

One of the most important components of efficient warehouse operations is the stock locator system. Though such a system may be superfluous for warehouses having few different SKUs, it is imperative for warehouses having many. Included in the discussion in this Chapter are the pros and cons of the fixed and random location systems and how many warehouses have good reason to employ both. Provided also are step-by-step guidelines for designing and implementing a random locator system, the most common system in most modern warehouse operations. Emphasis is given to how bar coding and computerization have dramatically reduced the amount of work to set up, use, and maintain locator systems, while at the same time greatly increasing accuracy and speed.

Some warehouses have no real need for a stock locator system because the warehouse is so small, has so few SKUs, and does not have a need for production lot or aging control. Being small is not enough. A records and documents warehouse, for example, could have thousands of SKUs in a few hundred square feet, and here more than with most warehouses a stock locator is needed. When files are lost in a records and documents warehouse, they are really lost.

Before computerization there were some fairly valid reasons for not having a stock locator system. It involved a lot of work to set up and maintain; it could be very complex, with lots of errors, including lack of paper flow control. It is not that way today. Computerization is here and at a cost at which almost any warehousing will benefit. Making stock locators work reliably is a major technological advance for warehousing. But it may not be given the importance it deserves because the marvels of bar coding and computerized records and reports have everyone so enamored that it may take a while actually to confront the age-old warehousing problem expressed in these too common phrases: "Where is it?" "I can't find it," and "I don't care what the inventory records say, we don't have it."

Another reason for not rushing to install a locator system is that a number of warehouse operators and supervisors take great pride in having good memories. Their memories are so good that they can keep track of a great many SKUs. The problems arise in the memory system when these employees do not come to work due to illness, vacation, or whatever. Even more important than relying on operations personnel is that the management should have control of operations. Directions and guidance should flow from the office to the floor, not the other way around. Memories that are so important to operations should be in computer storage with instant recall.

The addressing of storage areas is important to layout, material handling, and space utilization. With all this importance, one would expect every warehouse to be addressed, yet few are. Another reason is what might be called "psychological procrastination." It is most commonly manifest in not making roof repairs when it is raining because it is damp and dangerous and not doing it when the sun is out because it is not needed. The same psychological forces are at work with a stock locator system. When a warehouse is operating smoothly, the locator system seems unnecessary, and when it is not, there seems no time to set it up. But with the advent of low-cost computerization and bar coding, our excuses no longer hold water.

In warehouses that carry a large number of different items, SKUs, a lot of time and effort are sacrificed looking for stock—if there is no effective stock locator system. It is not unusual for order pickers to spend as much time locating the stock as they take filling the orders. Nothing is so wasteful as "hunt" time. It is nonproductive and it is demoralizing to the individuals doing it. Also the problem of misplaced or lost inventories can become so severe as to affect the level of warehouse service.

Good housekeeping can reduce the problem, but for a multi-item warehouse; good housekeeping is not enough; nor is reliance on good memories.

While the main purpose of a stock locator system is to provide an efficient way to locate stock, it can do a lot more. When the system is integrated into the warehouse's receiving, storing, and shipping procedures, it makes possible controls and additional handling efficiencies that would not be possible otherwise.

Most locator systems could be justified on the singular basis that they assist order pickers in finding stock. Simply, this is to say its feature of assisting order pickers will more than justify the system. And, if integrated into the other basic functions of warehousing, it will provide inventory accountability.

TWO BASIC TYPES OF STOCK LOCATOR SYSTEMS

Of the two basic kinds of stock locator systems described here, the first serves mainly to locate stocks, and the second incorporates the feature of maximizing space utilization. When integrated into the other warehousing systems, they can do a lot more—as discussed shortly.

Fixed Location System: Advantages, Disadvantages, and Occasion of Best Use

To have a stock locator system, all that is really required is a fixed place for each store keeping unit. The storage location stays the same as long as the SKU is carried in inventory.

A detailed drawing of the stock location serves as a map for the order pickers. Before long, many of the employees will commit to memory where most of the stock is. For warehouses of any size and complexity, it adds to overall efficiency to have the stock locations by SKU showing on receiving and shipping documents or CRT viewers. This eliminates, or at least reduces, the need to rely on memories or to interpret the location map. The efficiency of the system can be further improved by including the locations as a part of the inventory record and as a part of the fixed product information in the data processing system. This permits the stock location to be automatically printed on the receiving and shipping documents.

A fixed location system has the big advantage of being simple and thus easy to use. If stock is always put at the same address, there is little room for error. Even if the address is entered incorrectly on the receiving and shipping documents, the employee putting the stock away or filling an order will probably catch and correct the error. Memory is a valuable aid in the use of a fixed location system. Even if the employee does not remember or has never learned the correct location for a commodity, it is a simple matter to find it by going to the nearest location map or make an inquiry of the computerized address system. This simple process of correcting errors does not apply as well to the other locator system.

Although the fixed location system has the advantage of simplicity, it also has a disadvantage. Its use does not permit good space utilization. To allow sufficient space to store all of an SKU in the same location all the time requires leaving enough room to hold the maximum amount. Nearly twice the amount of space must be left than the average requirement. See Figure 7.1 which illustrates this severe disadvantage.

The illustration shows the profile of space utilization for one SKU. This example is for a certain refrigerator brand, size, color, capacity, and specific accessories. The inventory control policy provides for expected changes of on-hand inventory between 10 and 40 for such refrigerators. Then it provides for 10 units reserve stock to cover higher than usual outbound shipments. Also, space for an extra 10 is kept available in case sales are slower than usual and more inventory backs up.

The inventory activity is described by week showing description of transaction, quantity in the transaction, and the cumulative quantity resulting from the

FIGURE 7.1 How a Fixed Storage Location System Uses Much More Space

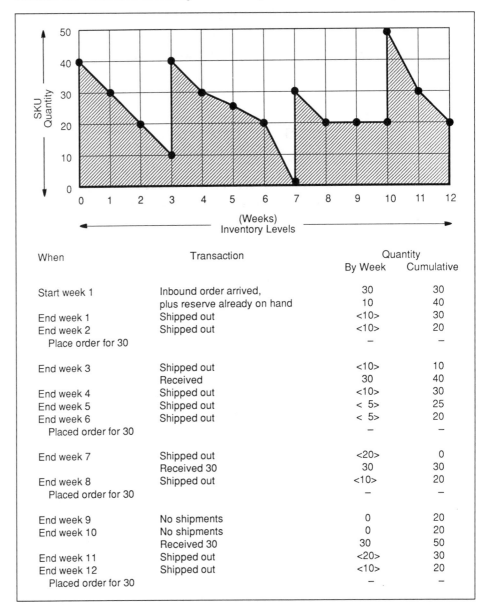

When	Transaction	Quantity	
		By Week	Cumulative
Start week 1	Inbound order arrived,	30	30
	plus reserve already on hand	10	40
End week 1	Shipped out	<10>	30
End week 2	Shipped out	<10>	20
Place order for 30		–	–
End week 3	Shipped out	<10>	10
	Received	30	40
End week 4	Shipped out	<10>	30
End week 5	Shipped out	< 5>	25
End week 6	Shipped out	< 5>	20
Placed order for 30		–	–
End week 7	Shipped out	<20>	0
	Received 30	30	30
End week 8	Shipped out	<10>	20
Placed order for 30		–	–
End week 9	No shipments	0	20
End week 10	No shipments	0	20
	Received 30	30	50
End week 11	Shipped out	<20>	30
End week 12	Shipped out	<10>	20
Placed order for 30		–	–

transactions. The purpose is to show the vacant space resulting from a fixed location system. In this example, average utilization is about 50 percent. Reality could be a lower or higher space utilization, but in most such fixed location systems, the average utilization comes out about the same, 50 percent. This is before deducting for aisles, staging area, and so on. If these also take 50 percent of the total space, this 50 percent added to the 50 percent of that allocated for storage, the net utilization of floor space is about 25 percent. For instance, if the building were 100,000 square feet, arithmetic would show 25,000 square feet net utilized storage space (100,000 sq. ft. × 50 percent for storage × 50 percent space utilization = 25,000 sq. ft.). Therefore, adopting fixed locations for storage is more than a casual decision, it is a very important decision.

Random Locator System: Advantages, Disadvantages, and Occasion of Best Use

To the uninitiated random storage seems to evoke pictures of uncontrolled, helter-skelter inventories. "Random" as a word denotes complete lack of order, and so on. But in warehouse layout it is quite the opposite. Inherent in the random storage system is to know precisely where every SKU is by quantity and whatever other data is important such as production lot number, date produced, and so on. This part of the system does not seem random, and it is not. In fact all this information is the same for both the fixed location and random location systems. The big difference is that with the fixed location all the SKU inventory is at one place, whereas with the random locator system the SKU inventory when received is put just about anywhere there is appropriate storage for it. For example, if palletized and stored in pallet storage racks, it can be stored anywhere in these racks. For reasons other than just a place to store it, the system should direct to store it near a certain shipping door because it is a very fast mover or just the opposite, in a remote part of the warehouse because it is a slow mover.

The whole thing about the random locator system is that it permits far superior utilization of space. When the SKU is on its way in or just as it arrives, the receiving personnel are advised where to store it. Someone (preferably a computer) sorts through all available empty storage spaces (appropriate to this SKU) and advises precisely where to put it. If there is more inventory than the first indicated space can take, receiving is advised how much should be stored at each of several locations if necessary; if for no other reason than to assist order picking, the product should be stored with like inventory. Even though stored at random, the rule of storing like together should be observed. Just because it is random does not mean it can not have rational guidelines.

This does not mean that if the like-product rule is in a random locator system, the system is no longer random. It simply means that if an order for a certain SKU calls for more than the quantity in one location, the operator should not have to travel to the other end of the warehouse to get more to complete the order unless there is absolutely no appropriate storage space nearer. Further, for example, it is more efficient to stay in one area to order pick, say, plumbing supplies, than it is to go a great distance to where mostly canned food is stored to fill the remainder of the plumbing-supplies order. Figure 7.2 shows how effective the space utilization is, but it also makes clear that there has to be a foolproof way to know and remember where things are. This Figure illustrates the mechanics of a random stock locator by showing how pallet rack storage can change to accommodate different SKUs to maintain high-space utilization.

In the random location system, the computer (it will work manually if necessary) has in its memory the complete description of all pertinent information about every SKU. In addition it has the quantity and address where every SKU is stored. As customer orders are filled from these locations, they are depleted in the sequence of FIFO or LIFO or by production lot or any other characteristic desired. This leaves vacant slots, so that when the same SKU is received again, or most important, any other SKU that required the same type storage (pallet or cantilever racks or bulk, or etc.), it can be put into any or all of the empty slots. Where each part of the SKU is stored is retained in the computer's memory so that it can be called up in sequence when outbound orders are filled. When an order is given to an employee to fill, it will include

FIGURE 7.2   Random Storage in the Same Storage Racks

RANDOM STORAGE LAYOUT

- Showing how random storage plan permits maximum utilization of space.
- Addressing system:
  - Aisles = Alphabetic, A to Z
  - Sides of aisles = Numeric with left side odd numbers and right side even numbers
  - Level = Numeric - 1, 2, 3, . . .
  - Address components labeled both in numbers or alphabetic and corresponding bar codes

Typical Address—B23–4 = Aisle B, 23 positions back on left side, fourth level

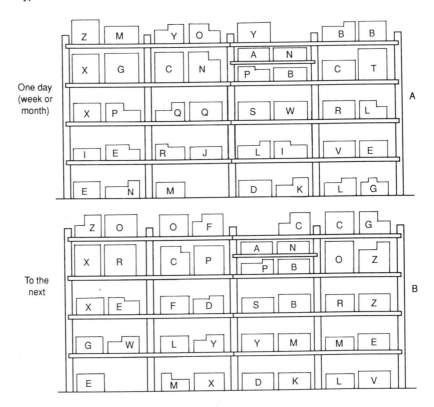

- Alphabet used to denote SKUs and same SKUs in different locations for this exhibit only
- Should be only one partial pallet load per SKU
- Space utilization can be increased further by more extensive use of divider arms to half the standard size pallet slot. This should be made an easy change by using a fixture that can be slipped over the forks on a lift truck.

    The operator communicates to the computer the intention to make a half slot. The computer determines what the new address should be and examines any limitations that has been imposed in creating another slot such as rack capacity. If all is well permission is granted with the change of address from one slot to two half slots—like changing a house to a smaller duplex.

    The illustration shows in the "one-day" layout that two slots have divided. In the "next-day" layout shows two half-slots have been converted back to one full slot. Full-size slots should be easily converted to half-size and back to full-size to maximize space utilization and to keep like stock together.

the address where the order quantity will be found. The order can be on paper, on a fixed or portable CRT viewer, or as voice instructions. The data the operator will receive will be similar to the following:

Order No.: 783-121
For: Acme Metals, Inc.
SKU: 34568
Go to Aisle B, Position *10,* Level *3.*
Scan SKU number of slot.
Correct!
Pick: 10 cases.
Enter: 10 cases.
How many cases remain in the slot?
Enter: 20 cases.
Correct! Now proceed to next SKU

- -

SKU: 47651
For total of: 24 cases
Go to Aisle C, Position *9,* Level *2.*
Scan SKU number of slot.
Correct!
Pick: 6 cases.
Enter: 6 cases.
How many cases remain in the slot?
Enter: 0.
Correct! You need 18 more cases to complete order.
Go to Aisle C, Position *11,* Level *2.*
Scan SKU number of slot.
Correct!
Pick: 18 cases.
Enter: 18 cases.
How many cases remain in the slot?
Enter: 15 cases.
Correct! Order No. 783-121 is complete.
Go to staging conveyor 121.
Scan conveyor number.
Correct!
Deposit load.

- -

NEXT ORDER . . .

Checks and balances are built into the system to ensure the utmost accuracy. In this example the quantities that were suppose to be at the locations were there as the computer memory claimed. Had there been a difference, the computer would have politely asked for a recount. If the difference persisted, the computer would ask the operator to check adjacent storage slots to see if the missing units were accidentaly put there. If the difference still persists, the computer would accept the operator's count, adding this to an Inventory Discrepancy List (to be reconciled by a staff employee at regular intervals). The computer would then direct the operator to another location where this same SKU was stored to take enough to complete the order. The missing quantity may be there. If so, the computer adds this byte of information to the Inventory Discrepancy List to offset the previous input of the missing quantity.

Should the quantities be of substantially more than discussed in this example, a modification of the verification method would have to be made.

Systems should be rational and workable. No one should expect an order picker to verify the count of many units. "Many" in this instance may be more than can be counted in 1 or 2 minutes.

This is a simplified system of locating the right stock. In practice "batch" order picking may be practiced in which the total quantity of this SKU for an interval of time, say, a shift, is transferred to staging at once. Or the operator may be filling more than one order at a time and the computer is guiding the operation through the shortest route.

STEP-BY-STEP GUIDELINES FOR DESIGNING AND IMPLEMENTING A RANDOM LOCATOR SYSTEM

The benefits of random locator systems are too great to be ignored. However, they are not easy to start up and get functioning properly. Your warehouse probably will need better controls, discipline, and supervision than ever it had before. Without this, the locator records will become inaccurate. "Inaccurate" in this sense means that the records do not show where the stock really is. It loses credibility. As this happens, the random stock locator system quickly becomes a liability. When large numbers of SKUs and inventory quantities are involved, the results can be more than a severe inventory problem and very disheartening. It can delay shipments, which translates to bad customer relations, and it can consume lots of excess employee and equipment time. Far better to overdo when first implementing with more supervision and more operations personnel until it is certain that it will operate with less attention.

Following are suggested guidelines for the design and implementation of a random location system.

1. *Investigate random storage literature and visit warehouses actually using it.* Become knowledgeable about random storage systems firsthand. Find the pitfalls as well as the good points. Probably you will find that those using it will say "they couldn't do without it."

Keep in mind it comes with the price of discipline. The substantial improvement that will come in material handling and space utilization—along with far more accuracy—will make it all worth while. Be cognizant though, you are just going to get tangled up unless it is done right. It has an unforgiving nature.

2. *Develop a drawing (or use models if you have them) of the warehouse being considered for the random storage.* To handle change effectively, you must know where you were before. It is the point of departure. You really cannot make transition without knowing where you are and where you are going.

3. *Document present methods and procedures for handling and storing inventories in writing and with flow diagrams.* With a drawing or model of the present layout describe in writing how to determine where to put stock, discussed above, and how to find it to fill orders. For certain include how instructions are given and what needs to be known to follow them. This detail is needed to learn all that is wrong with the present system, to focus on potential trouble spots of the random location system, to provide bridges to get from existing to new, and most important to assure that management will be effective and respected in leading the change over. Nothing demonstrates management's ineptness more than to be ill prepared in changing from a fixed location system where everything is comparatively obvious to a random system that depends on unseen forces to make it work.

4. *Make a list of problems with the present layout.* When the present way of doing things is clearly displayed, it is generally not hard to find better ways, and each better way exposes a hidden problem of the present. You may very well confront what is commonly the initial obstacle which is expressed as "Why change when it seems everything is going OK? Who's complaining anyway?" There are many answers to this, but perhaps the best immediate one is that the present way costs too much in space, handling time, and errors—and be able to cite figures to support your answer.

5. *Compute the space not used in the present layout.* This is necessary to give substance to "Why change?" It is not difficult. Go through the whole storage area listing and evaluating how much space is not being used. Include the aisles and staging areas even though you do not intend to change them. For pallet storage racks, evaluate each pallet slot as to full, empty, or a percentage used such as 25 percent, 50 percent, 75 percent, and so on. Watch out you may discover the space left for pallet loads at present is not right. Perhaps another layer of cartons could be added to the pallet loads to better utilize the space that is being left for them—a serendipity, no less.

If bulk storage is being evaluated, determine how many columns of the unitized loads could be added to fill the area completely. Much of what you see will be spaces being held in reserve for when inventory is up to capacity, which is characteristic of the fixed storage system.

Some claim to be able to determine the space lost easier by viewing the profile of bulk storage upside down. (See Figure 7.3.) The unused space does seem to glare at you when examining it from upside down. If you use this technique, you should take pictures and turn them upside down. Do not try to evaluate by standing on your head.

6. *Survey to find the most appropriate software and bar coding for the random locator system.* Consider the company whose computer was controlled absolutely by accounting. Accounting kept it their province for a long while. Too often they would get top management to agree that warehousing should discontinue their hand-posted records, that one set of inventory records should be all that is necessary and theirs had to be more accurate because it was computerized. They would provide warehousing a daily record of activity and inventories. It all sounded good. Later, accounting would generously put one of "their" CRT viewers in the warehouse office so the warehouse staff could inquire on its own as to what inventories were at anytime.

When the warehouse showed differences in accounting's records and theirs (or in accountings records and physical inventories), who was at fault?

It is normal for accounting to be behind in their postings, and there is nothing that says that shipments should not be posted before receipts. Except at the end of the month everything must be brought up to the cutoff date so that the month can be closed, say, the fifth or tenth of the next month. Warehousing's inventories have to be current at all times. Their work is in the real world, were an SKU has substance and utility. Warehousing cannot work with inventories that reflect accounting's priorities and work habits.

Now that computers have improved in quantum leaps and costs have dropped correspondingly, warehousing can have its "own" computers, and accounting can tap in for their information if they want. Warehousing's inventory information is more accurate and timely than theirs can ever be. They have to be for warehousing to effectively operate.

7. *Prepare preliminary design of proposed random stock locator system.* Should you start the new stock locator design with a committee or go it alone until there is enough of a skeleton to see what in total it will comprise? In most projects it is best that everyone be in on the development, but the initial

FIGURE 7.3 Different Ways to View Unused Space

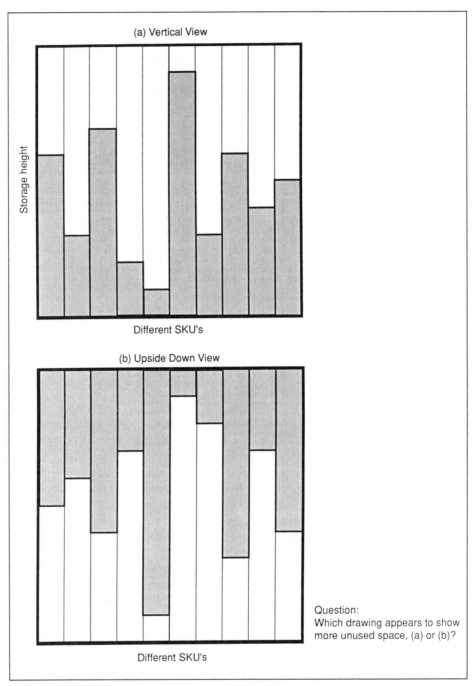

(a) Vertical View

Storage height

Different SKU's

(b) Upside Down View

Different SKU's

Question:
Which drawing appears to show
more unused space, (a) or (b)?

design of a random stock-locator system should involve only a two- or three-employee team. There is no reason for the blind to lead the blind at the outset.

Address plan. There is no one right way to address a warehouse. First, if there is more than one building, then each should be assigned a distinguishing identification, as simple as 1, 2, 3 or A, B, C. A mixture of alphabetic and numeric helps to remember. Most car license plates have alphanumeric for the same reason.

After the building is identified, the aisles and storage areas must be given addresses. One way is for each row of racks to be numbered consecutive from a starting point and direction. Each bay of racks is given another set of numbers and the levels another. But there is no magic in how it is done. Use of female and male names like those assigned hurricanes would even work if the computer can manage it.

Addressing bulk storage is another matter. Perhaps the best is to establish a grid of equal squares and hang signs from above telling block numbers such as 21 East, 14 South. You will probably come up with something better.

Verify what is received. A key element in any warehousing program is the receiving operation. This is the point at which warehousing accepts responsibility for the merchandise.

The random layout system calls for receiving to be advised that an inbound shipment is on its way and when to expect it. When it arrives the delivering carrier's responsibility is signed off and warehousing's responsibility starts.

The merchandise is unloaded and staged and counted by SKU. This data is forwarded to the computer to match with what was suppose to have been shipped. When this input of what was ordered, shipped, and received is reconciled, the computer advises where to put the merchandise and the most efficient route to take. When the inbound merchandise has been put in its specified place, the computer is again advised where it was put and another reconciliation takes place—where it was supposed to be stored and where it actually was stored.

Verify orders picked. The instructions and verifications that the right stock is pulled for the order is assured by the order picker "wanding" units picked to show the SKU and number of units that have been pulled are as instructed. An alternative to wanding each unit pulled is to wand an auxiliary code for the total picked. The bar code information is transmitted to the computer memory for which there is a match or reconciliation is made. Then as a further test the computer requests the order picker to transmit how many of the SKU are left. This then has to agree or be reconciled. The exchange of data also provides the very important function of executing a physical inventory of that SKU. In fact, this—if functioning as it should—can take the place of so-called "official" physical inventories. It performs a physical inventory by SKU every time an order is picked. What a big help this is to accurate inventories and warehousing's accountability for them.

Verify staged orders. While the employee is staging the order for shipment, the merchandise, SKUs, and quantities are again wanded and the information is transmitted to the computer for another match and possible reconciliation.

Many warehouses ship unitized loads as well as by carton or package count. The unitized load is not disassembled and wanded piece by piece. The employee knows by pallet pattern how many units there are, and this unit count is transmitted as a unitized load of so many units, the same as is done at the checkout line for groceries for several of one SKU.

Any pallet pattern of unitized loads that can conceal voids must be changed to a pattern that cannot. Otherwise, the employee who is verifying the order must disassemble the load until the right count can be discerned or some other means must be devised to check that the total units are correct. One way is to weigh the unitized load, and if it weighs correct, probably the count is correct. This is not 100 percent valid because something without value weighing the same can be substituted. At the first detection of foul play, bells should ring and sirens blare. You should overly dramatize the incident so that the culprit will be less prone to try that again.

8. *Have meetings with the employees who will implement and operate the plan.* Record everyone's questions and suggestions regardless of how bizarre. No criticism is permitted during this phase. Then the things brought up are organized into subject areas. Then the same group criticizes everything. Everyone's previous suggestions are critically ripped apart. No one's feelings are hurt. Every subject of the project gets the same. What is left is formed into a plan. Everyone is a contributor so it follows that everyone supports the plan.

9. *Design and Redesign until all who are participating in it are satisfied this is the best plan to go with.* The first try to arrive at a plan will have some weaknesses. Recall the planning committee even after it seems the best plan is already established. This round of discussion will bring out those who were most cautious the first time around. Now that they see it is for real, they will be more concerned and bring up more considerations, some genuine and some to make certain that their names are also etched for posterity in the records as contributors to the founding of this marvelous system.

10. *Input the software which will drive it.* Earlier in the plan's development a search was made to determine computer and bar-coding hardware requirements. As the committee progresses with the plan, the capabilities of the hard and software were recurring issues. Now these have been decided and the computer and bar-code hardware have been acquired. The software that was available involved too many compromises, so the committee agreed to have a system that was a modification of a standard program. Customizing to their own requirements seemed a necessity, even though this programming cost almost as much as the total hardware acquired. Now is the time to go for it. The system's software is loaded. Next is to load the SKU descriptions and quantities. During the discussion stage the subject of which quantities to start with, record or physical inventory, brought out more stubborn opinions than any other issue. No doubt some will express righteous indignation about using the records as the source of quantities. Others, who may be more practical than righteous, will say, "Let's be practical. Taking a physical and jumping into the system too is just too much. In the past it has taken days to reconcile the physical to record. Let's take a physical only to the extent to determine SKU locations so the program can be loaded with this essential information. Then, let the system correct itself. Remember, this is one of the main reasons why most of us gave the system our support in the first place."

11. *Address the warehouse with the system agreed upon.* The addressing need not wait until this late in the system development. It is, however, the first physical change to be made due to the program. For this, it is important to massage it thoroughly, to make certain it ties into the other features of the locator system before freezing it. When given the final examination and all holds together, do it. Then or before, get the address system into the fixed data of the computer.

12. *Require suppliers to bar code the inbound merchandise. Until they do, code it yourself.* The story is told about Henry Ford's power over his suppliers. A supplier of one of the items his company bought was crated with wood to protect it in transit. Mr. Ford told the supplier to continue packaging as before but to cut a hole a certain size in a specific position on each of the four side panels. The supplier did not want to add to its work so at first put up an argument. Mr. Ford was suppose to have said in effect: "If you want my business, cut the holes as I ask." The supplier did just that and later learned why. The panels with the holes cut just right became the floor boards of the enormously successful Model T's.

Not many companies have the clout that Henry Ford had over his suppliers, but more certainly have enough to force the application of a bar code on the merchandise your company buys from them, particularly when the bar code is the one that has been formally adopted by spokesmen of the industry. Give up any idea of designing a new bar code system; just adopt the one that is already in existence for your type of merchandise.

Until all your suppliers can pick up the bar coding (many will have already put it on their products), affix it yourselves. It is not a big deal. It would be best, however, to get any suppliers not using it to agree to put it on by a certain date. If they do not put it on by then, agree, with their concurrence, to charge back to them the cost of your warehouse putting it on. Much more is said about bar codes in Chapter 13.

13. *Ready, set, go—start program.* All has been done that could be done to prepare for "D" Day. Start operating the new locator system. The problems you expected will probably occur, and the things you expected to run smoothly probably will. These are the indicators of thorough preparation. Few surprises occur in a well-designed system.

14. *Assure successful implementation.* Have extra help on hand to get the system back on track if it gets derailed. Get the help from industrial engineering, production control, accounting, and so on, who have been well briefed on the system and can give the competent temporary hands-on help needed. The extra helpers should appreciate it is warehouse operations' systems that is being installed. It is not accounting's, purchasing's, or some other division's system. It is warehousing's and through warehousing, theirs and the company's.

Make certain follow-up continues until the system is working well on its own. Conduct brief meetings of all concerned just before or at ends of each shift to learn the snags and snafus and find group-agreed means for correcting them. You may have to limit the meetings only to the really tough problems, or you may find them taking far more time than necessary. Probably you will get a lot of questions that are not so much problems as that individuals want to be heard to let others know they are in there fighting. This is all right. These will fade away after the first few meetings.

15. *Throw a victory celebration.* Throw a victory celebration when all is going well with the system. Do not wait until everything is going 100 percent right. This may put too much time between the implementation and celebration. If you do, you will find the connection between the successful installation and the rejoicing has dimmed.

Pay for any overtime the nonexempt personnel put in. See that the exempt people get a hearty personal thanks for their giving of their time. It would be good to put it in writing with a copy to their personnel file.

Some memento should be given to every participant, a special badge, for example, "that will be worth millions a hundred years from now." If not a badge, something else that can be worn such as a cap with a victory slogan, so that when others see it they will realize it must have been quite an accomplishment—and that it was. Warehousing will not be the same at this company ever again.

THE ADVANTAGES OF USING A COMBINATION OF LOCATOR SYSTEMS

Most warehouses have part fixed and part random locator systems. Order-picking sites consisting of many small quantities from one case to lots of perhaps 10 to 20 cases (depending on package size) should be in a fixed location

FIGURE 7.4 Two-Zone Warehouse: Order picking from flow-through racks, back-up
stock in bulk random storage

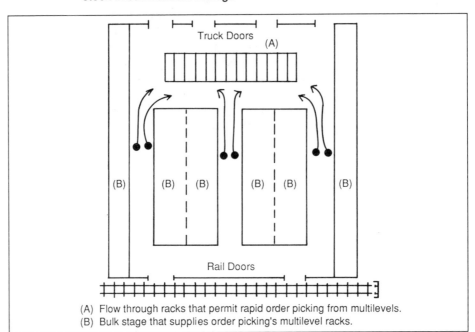

(A) Flow through racks that permit rapid order picking from multilevels.
(B) Bulk stage that supplies order picking's multilevel racks.

environment—almost without exception. Many conveyor storage systems will
provide continuous SKU access within easy reach, one case at a time—with
another case slipping into the exposed position the moment the front one is
removed. This tied into a bar code and a conveyor system that sorts by customer order and transportation mode is one that is hard to beat. How the
backup stock is handled to get it into the fixed location system is another
matter. See Figure 7.4, which presents a fixed locator system for efficient
order picking with a large backup of inventories stored according to a random
locator system. One job function is to keep the order-picking section supplied
from the backup inventory. Another is to rapid order pick.

Where parts of some customer orders are for larger quantities per SKU
than is efficient to send through the aforementioned order-picking system, another means of order picking is needed. This can be from the backup inventory
whose main purpose is to supply the fast small quantity order-picking system.
The backup inventory can be used for both purposes. The locator system for
the backup inventory should definitely be random. This combination for those
warehouses with two types of order picking is better than either one locator
system in total.

USING A ZONE LAYOUT SYSTEM

Some warehouses, usually larger ones, can adopt multizone layouts for their
inventories and order picking. This means to divide the inventories by type so
that specialization is better applied. The previous section, on combination locator systems, is a form of zone layout, two zones, in fact. But when thinking
of zone layout in general, it refers to more zones and specializing by commodity
type such as (1) small electrical appliances; (2) large electrical appliances;

(3) nuts, bolts, and fasteners; (4) caps, aprons, and gloves; and so on. Each zone is designed around the fewest employees possible for the most efficient storing and handling of the limited number of products in the zone. Usually there is a mobile conveyance to link the zones to a common or specialized staging and loading area.

What the zone layout is intended to achieve is that by specializing by products handled, equipment, and standard operating methods, the work accomplished will be far more efficient. In theory this is true. No lost motion. No waiting for others because commonly there is only one employee per zone. If there are more, the intention is to organize them into compatible teams that work together to achieve more and to take pride in the team accomplishment.

Extra caution should be exercised, however, in adopting this layout. History has not been kind to this type of warehousing. All can appear as though it will be a winner, then the employees rebel. Apparently they feel they are being treated more like machines than human beings. Something inspiring employee cooperation is necessary to increase the likelihood of making it a success. This would indicate that warehouses having poor employee relations change this before imposing zone layout on the situation. For those with good employee relations, make certain everything is done to maintain these good relations. The system holds the potential of major cost reduction, but first it must be made to work.

Chapter 8

Warehouse Equipment and How to Learn What Is Available, Evaluate, Justify, and Maintain It

CHAPTER HIGHLIGHTS

There are many concerns involved in equipping and maintaining a warehouse with the necessary hardware to perform its operations in an efficient, top-quality manner. In this chapter we (1) learn what is available, (2) evaluate what is best for a particular situation, and (3) then justify its acquisition. Then, once the equipment is acquired, we consider how to keep it in good order. Less than thorough treatment of all the elements jeopardizes operations, since the right equipment in proper condition is essential to efficient, modern warehouse operations. And that it constitutes a large part of its costs as well: looked at another way you pay for the equipment you need when you do not have it—the cost is higher operating costs and poor customer service. Finally, it is established that the cost of anticipated repair and maintenance is as important to evaluation, selection, and justification as the initial purchase price, a fact that too often gets short shrift.

Although equipment can be found to assist in or actually do almost any warehousing function, it should be kept in mind that many of the operations can also be performed manually. Managers who have become entirely equipment oriented make the erroneous assumption that if a function is performed manually, it is inefficient. This is not the case. Some material handling functions are still, and possibly always will be, most economically performed manually. Equipment should only replace or assist when it is the best alternative.

Used wisely, equipment can increase many times an individual's ability to do things. Consider, for example, a person attempting to unload and store a carload of canned goods without the assistance of equipment. The worker would probably pick up three cases at a time from the car, carry them to the designated storage area inside the warehouse, and stack them within arms reach high. Assuming that there were 3,000 cases in the car, it would take 1,000 trips. If 5 minutes per trip were allowed and a 5-minute rest after every five trips achieved would be 30 cases an hour. Unloading would take 100 hours of material handling time per car. Stacking the cases, say, 7 feet high, it would take about 400 square feet of floor space for the one carload. If this were representative of how canned goods were handled and stored today, half the population would have to move from the cities back to the farms. People would have to raise most of their own food, as they did back at the turn of the century. The cost of distribution would force the cost of food to rise so high that only the very rich could afford to buy in stores.

Using this same example, let's assume that the worker employs a four-wheel handcart to assist in transferring the canned goods from the rail car to the point of storage inside the warehouse. Now the worker can move 20 cases each trip. The number of trips would be reduced from 1,000 to 150. If it took 10 minutes per trip with a 10-minute rest after each five trips, it will now take only 30 hours of material handling time per car as opposed to 100 hours without the cart.

Now let's assume that the cases are already palletized into loads of 100 cases per pallet when they arrive and that a lift truck is used to unload, transport, and stack them. The number of trips would be reduced to 30. The time per trip would be about 4 minutes. The total time to unload and store would be reduced to 2 1/4 hours, even allowing one 15-minute rest time. Furthermore, with a lift truck the cases could be stacked at least three pallet loads high, reducing the floor space used from 400 to 133 square feet.

Thus, it is shown that for the very common task of unloading and storing carloads of canned goods, the handling time can be reduced from 100 hours to 30 hours by using a very simple piece of equipment, the four-wheel car. It can be reduced from 30 hours to only 2 1/4 hours by palletizing the cases and using a lift truck. In addition, floor space requirements can be cut by at least 67 percent from 400 to 133 square feet by using the lift truck. When this type of material handling and storing efficiency is employed, people can afford to buy their food from stores and live in cities remote from where the food is produced.

This example is applicable to thousands of other items of commerce. For some things, the improvement has not been as dramatic; for others, it has been greater. Many items being handled in warehouses today are either too heavy or too large to handle without modern powered equipment. Further, equipment has made warehouse work easier. With appropriate equipment, more by far can be accomplished with less effort and with greater safety. Much of the work has shifted from hard, unskilled labor to that of skilled both female and male equipment operators. The change has improved the warehouse employee's living standard while at the same time it has contributed to the general welfare of others by reducing the cost of the products they buy.

HOW TO LEARN WHAT WAREHOUSING EQUIPMENT IS AVAILABLE

The proper selection of equipment depends on a comprehensive knowledge of what equipment is available. There are hundreds of equipment suppliers offering hundreds and maybe thousands of different items applicable to the handling, storing, and information functions of warehousing. The problem of knowing the equipment that is available is all the greater because new types are constantly being developed. The number of suppliers and the types of equipment are not static. Many are added and many are withdrawn from the field each year. To keep abreast of developments and changes requires deliberate and constant attention.

Successful warehousing organizations must have, or have access to, equipment expertise. To acquire equipment without this expertise is to hazard the wasting of large sums of money in the initial purchases and possibly to incur excess costs throughout the life of the equipment by using tools that are less than satisfactory for the job they were acquired to do.

Inadequate knowledge of equipment can lead to very expensive mistakes. Many warehouse managers have had the painful experience of acquiring the wrong equipment. One of the main reasons for these mistakes is not knowing what equipment is available and what it will do. The reason for not knowing can be attributed in large part to an often unrecognized effect of tight money—due mainly to the required quick paybacks imposed. The warehouse manager lets the objective of getting the scarce money take priority over the thoroughness of the study to determine really what is needed and whether a particular purchase would be very best value for the money.

The three main sources of information on equipment are suppliers, consultants, and expertise within one's own warehousing organization. A general discussion of each, including advantages and disadvantages, follows.

Equipment Suppliers

The principal source of all information on equipment is equipment suppliers. They know best what the equipment is capable of doing because they make it or represent the companies that do. Further, they are anxious to tell others what it will do because they want to sell it. Part of this information is lost in translation between designers, manufacturers, and sales representatives, but the chain of communication still provides the most reliable source of data about any specific equipment. Provided that the suppliers are reputable, as the greatest number are, their specifications are the most accurate that are available. They are accurate because the equipment was designed to meet these specifications in the first place; then the specifications are field tested and retested in the production and quality control process; finally there is a constant feedback from satisfied and unsatisfied customers who are using the equipment in actual warehousing conditions. To determine the best information about any one item of equipment, there is probably no better source than those who make and supply it.

The best way to become knowledgeable about equipment availability without becoming too indebted to the salesperson is to subscribe to several trade journals where equipment suppliers advertise. This provides the opportunity to keep up with the latest because suppliers devote most advertising to their latest. Fortunately, you can probably get these journals free. The publishers are so anxious to build their circulation to get more advertising that they are very liberal about giving subscriptions to anyone who is a potential equipment buyer or advertiser.

The disadvantage of using suppliers as the only source of equipment information is that they are biased. One should not expect equipment suppliers to give equal salesmanship to the limitations of their own products. Nor should one expect them to recommend another company's product over their own. When asking equipment suppliers for their advice, it should be recognized that their counsel will not be objective. For a while they may strive to give objective advice to win over the potential buyer's confidence, but the need to sell their own product will eventually prevail over objectivity.

Another limitation to using suppliers for equipment information is that it is an imposition to take up too much of the supplier's time without his or her making a sale to recover this investment. If a supplier is repeatedly called upon for advice and the purchases are made from other companies, it will not be long before the advisors will need to devote their time to better use. This is only fair. Suppliers have to sell their equipment to stay in business. If they were in the business of offering unlimited advice, they should charge consulting fees.

Equipment Consultants

Equipment consultants are in the business of offering advice, and they charge for it. Advice is their product. Consultants play an important role in modern business, and the trend toward using their services is up. The big advantage they have over equipment suppliers is that they can be objective. Their motivation is to do the best job they can for their client. This builds their reputation, and reputation is a consultant's most valuable asset. Reputable consultants also are either experienced in the type of work about which they offer advice or have experience within their firm from which they can draw.

Consultants can do the job better sometimes than others with the same abilities within the warehousing organization. They can be truly objective, while anyone within the organization approaches problems with some bias, even if it is only the result of doing what is perceived as what the boss wants. Further, some companies will act on the advice of consultants but will not act on the same advice if offered by someone within their organization. This is so because consultants are recognized experts, and people within the company are generally not given this recognition, even though they may be equally or better qualified. Also, consultants charge relatively high fees for the counsel, and there is a tendency to put a higher value on advice that costs more.

Although consulting service can be very valuable, it has its limitations. Possibly the biggest one is that it is expensive. Well-known consulting firms charge many times as much as the cost of an employee for the same period. Also, it could take the consultants much longer to do the same job. Although they may have a superior knowledge of the equipment available and its uses, they have to take time to learn the particular warehousing situation in which they will apply this knowledge. While they are learning, they are being paid, and a considerable bill will run up before they are ready to offer any constructive advice.

Another limitation of using consultants is that they do not guarantee results. They are paid for their time, not results. Many companies have gone the route of paying high fees for sophisticated consulting services and have found nothing in the consultants' attractively prepared reports to justify their investment. Of course, consulting firms cannot continue to produce unproductive reports indefinitely, but they do not have to satisfy every customer, either. This is the chance a company takes when procuring this type of service.

Expertise Within the Company

The third means, and generally the optimum, is to have equipment expertise within the warehousing organization. This seems to be obvious, but while it may be recognized, its application is the exception rather than the rule. Warehousing people, like many in other professions, rarely take the time to master their profession, possibly because most have had enough of their profession after putting in 8 to 12 hours on the job plus an hour or two on the freeways or toll roads commuting to and from it. They are ready for a diversion after fulfilling the pressing demands of their work.

To become an expert in any field requires putting extra time and effort into it. This is true of learning any subject, including warehousing equipment. It happens, however, that equipment availability and utilization is a field of knowledge which almost anyone in warehousing can master if they are willing to put in extra time and effort. Handling and storing equipment as a formal academic course is not generally offered, although it probably should be. To become an expert on warehousing equipment requires the initiative to organize one's own program of learning and the self-discipline to follow it through.

The main advantage of having expert knowledge within the warehousing organization is the convenience of having it available when needed. Equipment expertise is not just required on special projects, it is needed continually in all but the very smallest warehouse operations. There is a constant need in a warehouse that is regularly taking on a variety of new merchandise to monitor the use of equipment and suggest particular equipment for specific routines. This is necessary, if for no other reason than to make certain the standard storage procedures (SSPs) are current and are being followed—and of course to evaluate and recommend on any investments in additions, replacements, and major repairs before the money is spent. This evaluation requires an expert knowledge of equipment. Other advantages of this intrawarehousing knowledge are that the advice is generally based on a more genuine concern for long-range good results. Also, it will be based on a frame of reference that includes a familiarity with the particular warehouse's problems, organization, present equipment, financial situation, and management objectives. Equipment suppliers and consultants have to take the time to develop a comparable frame of reference to enable them to do a comparable job.

On major equipment projects, it is not uncommon for suppliers, consultants, and company experts to all offer advice on the selection and utilization of equipment.

For example, if a large warehouse were to undertake a program of automating its material handling, and a huge investment in equipment were anticipated, the program might well require assistance from all three sources. Qualified personnel within the warehousing organization could establish the objectives, analyze the present material handling processes, and, with the help of many different equipment suppliers, design the proposed automated system, including specifications and cost of equipment. Then a consulting firm could be employed to check out the proposal for its soundness and to suggest improvements. This approach would permit using company personnel, suppliers, and consultants to their greatest advantage. It would bring consultants into the program after much of the time-consuming groundwork had been done, thus keeping the consultants' fee to a minimum but still providing for their important contribution of expertise and objectivity.

List of Sources

The following sources of equipment information should prove helpful:

1. Equipment suppliers.
2. Equipment consultants.
3. Trade journals and textbooks covering material handling, transportation, warehousing, and so on.
4. Government publications.
5. Visits to other warehouses.
6. Visits to production facilities.
7. Association with others in materials handling and warehousing fields through professional organizations.
8. General knowledge of the design and application of handling and storing equipment used for any purpose: domestic, business, science, and so on— and translating this knowledge to warehousing.

STEPS TO EQUIPMENT EVALUATION

Equipment, just because it is equipment, is not a panacea for the problems of material handling and storing. Generally, an investment in equipment represents a significant capital expenditure. Such an expenditure should be thoroughly analyzed and evaluated before it is made. Not only is the initial investment important; the continuing costs of operating and maintaining the equipment can have a major effect on the total cost of the warehouse operation. Decisions regarding equipment will be some of the most important ones that warehouse management will make. Discussed here are guidelines for selecting warehouse equipment.

Guidelines for Determining the Job to Be Done

The job should be first analyzed to determine the essential elements. All too frequently equipment is acquired before there is a thorough understanding of what it is to be used for. For instance, it is a waste of money to purchase equipment with much more or less capacity than is really needed. A considerable amount of idle equipment in warehouses today stands as monuments to not thoroughly investigating before purchase. The equipment lies idle for many reasons. Soon after acquisition, a better way was found, or the equipment did not have sufficient capacity, or specialized equipment that had a useful life of 10 years was purchased to do a job that ended in 10 months. The following are some pertinent questions to answer before acquiring equipment.

1. Is the equipment really necessary? Can other things be done that will make the job unnecessary?
2. How long will the job last? If it is a short job, can equipment be acquired on a temporary basis, or can extra personnel alone handle it? If so, which costs less?

3. Can present equipment be better utilized so there will be time available for the new work?

4. What are the specifications of the material being concerned? Will they change?

5. What about the related factors: floor capacity, clearance, fumes, moisture, heat, cold, dirt, auxiliary equipment, and so on.?

6. Would the use or nonuse of equipment change the workers' job classifications? Has the labor union been consulted or advised?

Guidelines for Determining Safety Requirements

Some equipment can be justified simply because it is needed for employees' safety. There are times when a reduction of insurance costs can be directly related to the purchase of safety equipment, such as a sprinkler system for fire protection, but in most cases, safety equipment must be justified simply because it contributes to a safer environment and the well-being of personnel. In the long range, safe working conditions pay off, but it is difficult to economically justify each piece of safety equipment separately. Because this difficulty is commonly recognized, management frequently does not ask for the same thoroughness in the analysis of this type of equipment that it expects for equipment that can be directly related to dollar savings. This can be an error on management's part, and the error can be compounded when follow-up is not requested to make certain that the safety equipment is accomplishing what was expected of it. Management generally follows up on equipment that was justified on the basis of savings. Why not a follow-up on safety equipment? Because of this rather unscientific approach, there is a proportionately large amount of money wasted on wrong purchases of safety equipment. Another cause of wasted money is that many times safety equipment is purchased and never used. Management should give safety equipment the same careful analysis and evaluation it gives to any other type of equipment.

The following are examples of representative errors made in purchasing safety equipment:

1. Incorrectly designed overhead guards for lift trucks that add the hazard of pinching either arms, legs, or neck between the supporting posts of the guard and building columns, stacked material, and so on.

2. Fire extinguishers filled with an extinguishing agent that is not appropriate to fight the type of fires for which they are intended. Many water-type extinguishers are erroneously positioned where they might be used to extinguish electrical fires. Expensive chemical extinguishers are put in areas where inexpensive water extinguishers would be as effective.

3. Sprinkler systems are installed in areas where water would do more damage than fire.

4. Sprinkler systems are installed properly, but stock is stored so close to the sprinkler heads that they could not be effective if they were set off.

5. Oxygen units are made available, but personnel are not trained to use them.

6. Equipment guards for shears, saws, cutting tools, and so on are poorly designed, making it too hard to use them. They are removed, leaving the danger points exposed, and, ironically, then after the equipment is used, they are put back on.

7. First-aid kits are installed, but no provision is made to replenish the supplies.

8. Safety scoreboards, such as those indicating "number of days without a lost-time accident," are installed but are not maintained—or are not a valid means for measuring safety performance.

9. Safety helmets are provided, but they are not used because they are too heavy, poorly designed, or just plain uncomfortable.

10. Grounded electrical outlets are provided, but nongrounded-type extension cords are used. Additional money is spent for adapters so that the two-prong plugs can be used with the three-hole (grounded) receptacles. This, of course, defeats the purpose of the grounded outlets.

The fact that many bad purchases of safety equipment have been made in the past is not a good reason to avoid purchasing safety equipment in the future. Actually, it should take priority over other types; however, suggested is that its selection and maintenance should be given more attention than it normally receives.

Guidelines for Determining the Right Equipment for the Job

After establishing the requirements of the job, the right equipment to do the job must be determined. This one-two process is only simple logic, but often the sequence is reversed. Interesting equipment is discovered; then an application for it is found. Occasionally this reverse logic turns out fine, but it should not be used as a normal routine. As a rule, the problem should be defined before a solution is sought.

Listed here are guides to the right selection of equipment. Most of them apply to both handling and storing equipment; some, however, apply to only one or the other. The reader should have no difficulty relating the guides to the right types of equipment.

1. *There is a price range that is appropriate for each job.* Total cost of the equipment is of primary importance as a guide to determining the right equipment. It would be a waste of time to spend very much effort investigating equipment that was outside the appropriate price range. For example, if a warehouse were to get a new account that involved about two rail carloads a month of packaged articles that could be handled manually, it would not be appropriate to consider very expensive equipment to handle it. There is not enough labor involved to justify a large expenditure for equipment. On the other hand, if the job involved handling 20 carloads a month, the price range of equipment that could be considered would be substantially more. One does not use a BB gun to hunt elephants, nor does one use an elephant gun to hunt sparrows. This same relationship of magnitudes applies to the price of equipment and the job to be done.

A realistic approach should be taken to what the total cost of the equipment really is. The one amount that the total cost is not is the list price. To begin with, warehouse management should try to get the equipment for less than list price just as individuals try to get the best price they can when buying a personal automobile or home. Some equipment suppliers will not, or cannot, deviate from their published prices; others are susceptible to bargaining. Storage-rack suppliers in particular are able to lower their prices through quantity discounts and in many cases are induced to just by some good old-fashioned jawboning.

The purchase price of equipment is not its final cost. There are other costs related to the purchase that should be added in to arrive at the total cost. These include sales tax, freight from supplier, installation costs, and so on. When the equipment is put into operation, there will be operating and maintenance costs and property taxes. For storage racks there are no operating costs, but there will be repairs, even though these may be negligible. For powered equipment, such as cranes and lift trucks, the operating and maintenance costs are significant. Warehouse management should make certain that these costs are investigated and added to the price of the equipment in determining its total cost.

2. *Capacity is possibly the one most important specification of warehouse equipment.* To provide for more capacity than is really needed is a waste of money because the cost generally increases in direct proportion to the capacity. Also, the size of equipment generally increases proportionately with capacity. For instance, a conventional lift truck with 6,000 pounds of lifting capacity requires about 2 feet more turning radius than one with 4,000 pounds capacity. This means that aisles with access to storage must be made 2 feet wider wherever the larger unit is used. The larger lift truck will probably require power steering, whereas it may be possible to get by without it on a smaller unit. Fuel costs will be greater. Not only is the initial cost higher, but so is the cost of using it.

Although equipment should not have too much capacity, neither should it have less capacity than is required. Lift trucks that are used to move loads greater than they were designed to handle will wear out much faster and can even be dangerous to operate.

Storage racks that are under capacity for the job are definitely dangerous. Anyone who has been associated with warehousing for long has seen the effects of rack failures. It happens far too often. The reasons for these failures include overload, poor design, and use of the racks for purposes different from what the supplier intended. Because a low-capacity rack does not look very different from one that has high capacity, the person specifying which racks to buy too often opts for the low price. The difference in capacity is just not obvious, as it is with most other types of equipment. Use of different strength steel will affect size of uprights and arms, causing appearance to be deceptive. Also, some racks are poorly designed because unqualified companies produced them.

Racks last a long time. The person who provided the specifications when they were purchased initially may have provided the appropriate specifications for the use at hand. Several years later, and probably under different management, much heavier loads may be put into them. The result: Collapse! The sight of a warehouse where racks have given way is a disheartening one. Generally, the collapse causes a chain reaction. Large areas of racks have been known to topple as a result of one rack giving way.

3. *The dilemma involved in attaining higher storage.* Of particular importance in warehousing is the height dimension. There is a trend in modern warehousing to build higher buildings, to send racks higher and higher, and to specify cranes and lift trucks to use this greater height.

The warehousing industry as a whole is converting from square feet to cubic feet as a focus of attention. Actually, this conversion would be made at a faster rate except that handling and storing equipment are frequently purchased separately. Warehouse management may want to be able to store higher, but the investment must be made in both the handling and the storing equipment in order for either to be of value. For instance, suppose that a warehouse is ready to buy another lift truck. Management would like to buy one this time that will lift loads to a height of 28 feet. The problem it faces is that it has an entire warehouse full of racks that permit storing only 14 feet high. Should the firm pay extra for a lift truck that will reach 28 feet when all that can be used effectively is one that will service 14 feet?

If management does not buy the higher lift truck now, when it comes time to buy more racks it will be faced with the problem of not having a high lift to use with higher racks. The dilemma becomes even worse if the building does not have clearance for higher storage. Should management buy a lift truck to reach 28 feet when neither the present building nor the racks will permit use of this high reach? The problem is similar to the one of the chicken and the egg: Which comes first?

The forward-looking approach is to purchase the lift truck, racks, or building at the height that will be reached eventually, even though the one cannot be used until the other two are acquired. Of course, the high-clearance building should come first, to erect the racks inside when they are purchased. For some racks, however, it is possible to buy extensions, which permits buying the racks first. However, there are limits to how high the extensions can be used because the uprights have to have the capacity to take the cumulative heavier loads.

If a high lift is acquired first, it may be necessary to install a limiting device or governor that will prevent extending the mast through the roof. The important thing is that, with the purchase of a building, lift trucks, or racks, the desired height should be acquired even though it cannot be used until the companion items are purchased. Although this may appear to be a temporary waste of money, the first step must be taken to later permit taking the second and third steps. Obviously, this problem is not present when the building, lift truck, and racks are all purchased at the same time, but this is an opportunity that does not occur often. When it does, seize it and treat it for what it is, a chance to make a big breakthrough in storing efficiency.

Guidelines for Standardizing Equipment

Most warehouses have an unnecessarily large variety of equipment. There may have been a sound reason for acquiring each different item—at least, the reason appeared sound at the time to the person who selected the equipment. But, now the warehouse is paying a high price in operating and maintenance. The variety referred to here is mainly lift trucks and racks, which are the two most basic types of warehousing equipment.

Warehouse personnel have personal preferences in lift trucks just as people have preferences in the automobiles they drive. As one person will argue that a Ford is the only car to buy, his neighbor will argue that a Chevrolet is far superior, so will warehouse operators argue about brand X and brand Y lift trucks. Actually, most standard cars are good, and so are most standard types of lift trucks. The strong preferences that exist are based more on individual experience than on genuine differences.

As in the automobile field, different lift trucks are designed to do basically different things, and they fall into different cost ranges accordingly. It is not fair to compare the power and comfort of a Cadillac with that of a sports car. A Cadillac was designed for power and comfort and is priced accordingly. The sports car was designed for dash, flash, and fun. Many of both types are sold, and both have many satisfied customers. The same type of comparison applies to lift trucks.

Equipment should fit the job to be done, but it should also be as standard as possible within a single warehouse and within a single warehousing system. Fitting the job and standardization are not always compatible, but the closer the two concepts are brought together, the closer will warehousing equipment approach the ideal.

Following are advantages of equipment standardization:

1. More flexibility in using equipment is made possible. When a piece of equipment cannot be used because of breakdown, repair, and so on, other

equipment can be used in its place. When there are temporary, extra-heavy workloads for one product line, extra pieces of equipment can be diverted to help out.

2. Better utilization of equipment is possible. For example, rarely can an arm of one brand of storage rack be connected to the upright of another type of rack, but it would be far more efficient if all were of the same design so they could.

3. Repair and maintenance programs are more effective and cost less. The same repair and maintenance skills and the same spare parts can be used on the same make of equipment.

4. Quantity discounts can be given by suppliers when a larger amount of the same equipment is purchased.

5. Problems of operator's personal preferences for different types of equipment will be avoided.

Guidelines for Determining Realistic Operating Costs

The purchase price of the equipment is only the initial cost. There will be operating and maintenance cost for the equipment when used. The operating and maintenance cost for powered equipment will be far greater than for nonpowered equipment, but such costs exist to some extent for any equipment. Even storage racks need occasional repair. Racks will be bent and broken as a result of infrequent, but inevitable, bunting by lift trucks or other mobile equipment. The operating costs for powered equipment constitute a significant factor in the evaluation of equipment and may in some cases be enough to offset the expected savings. These costs should be included in any evaluation that compares the alternatives of using equipment and performing the function manually or comparing one type equipment with another.

Two other important costs inherent to equipment are depreciation and obsolescence. "Depreciation" refers to a lowering of value because of the wearing-out process. "Obsolescence" refers to a lowering of value because of the process of becoming outdated. Both, though commonly thought of as just two accounting terms are very real. Even a well-maintained lift truck receiving normal warehouse use has a useful life of only 5 to 10 years. Some wear out much sooner; a few last longer. Electrically powered lift trucks generally have a longer useful life than do gas-powered units, but they have costly batteries that must be replaced every few years. Racks have a longer life than powered equipment, but even they do not last indefinitely. Old racks will not bear the loads they could safely support when they were new. This is the result of damage and general weakening referred to as fatigue that takes place over many years of hard use.

Lift trucks, racks, and other warehouse equipment also lose value because they become obsolete. Obsolescence has many causes. Equipment that is specialized to handle a specific kind of commodity will become obsolete automatically if this commodity is discontinued. Capacity and height are two factors in particular that cause obsolescence. As products are palletized, or just packaged in larger containers, new equipment with greater capacity is required for both handling and storing. The equipment that was used before the change becomes obsolete. It may still be in good condition, but its value has decreased because it is out of date with reference to the new handling and storing requirements.

The storage height for warehousing in general has been increasing at a relatively rapid rate. Until after World War II, most of industry stored only to heights of about 10 feet. Since then the height has been steadily going up. Storage to 28 feet is now common using standard catalog-offered equipment. With specially designed equipment high-rise operations are on the threshold of becoming common. There are many warehouses in the 40- to 80-foot range and some over 100 feet high. This has caused major changes in handling and storing equipment. With these changes has come a mass obsolescence of the equipment that was designed for the lower storage. Many warehouses have been caught with lift trucks and racks and so on that are still in good condition but are limited to low-level storage. The increasing costs of property, buildings, and labor have made it mandatory for warehousing to go higher. Equipment that cannot be used for this new elevation has become uneconomical to use. It has become out of date with reference to current warehousing requirements. Present equipment buyers may rationalize that the present storage height is as high as it will go. This may be true, but those equipment buyers who 20 years ago thought the same thing have been proven wrong.

The following is a list of factors that influence the operating cost of equipment.

EQUIPMENT OPERATING COST FACTORS

1. Total direct labor costs for operating the equipment.
2. Job classifications due to changes in required skills.
3. Indirect labor costs related to the equipment, such as an operator's helper and need for more or less supervision and clerical support.
4. Increase or decrease in dimensions of aisles, doorways, and other overhead clearances.
5. Increase or decrease in safety measures required by new operating conditions.
6. Maintenance and repair costs and cost of keeping spare parts.
7. Additional costs that will be incurred to do the work another way while equipment is down for repair or down for other reasons.
8. Power supply costs for electricity, gas, or diesel.

Guidelines for Determining If New Equipment Obsoletes Any Existing Equipment

If the new takes the place of existing equipment, this should be so noted and the decision made for what to do with the surplus equipment. Can it be put to productive use elsewhere, or can it be traded in or sold as is? If none of these possibilities exists, should it be sold for scrap value? What you should not do, which is all too common, is to store it outside without disposition instructions. Maybe it should be protectively stored for a possible future use. Nothing is wrong with this, provided it is a conscious decision and is so recorded in the written justification for the new replacement equipment. If put in storage, a schedule of reviews should be in the written justification, for example, "Review this stored equipment quarterly to determine if it can be productively used until _____ (date). At that time sell it for what can be realized even if it is for only scrap value. Or, if it does not have any value, pay to have it hauled away to the dump."

One particular disposition where extra caution should be exercised is if a company employee asks to buy the obsolete equipment. Company employees should not be discriminated against nor should they be individually favored. If the best value can be realized by selling to an employee, all well and good, but such an action should be clearly authorized by the highest practical authority. Perhaps even post the opportunity to buy and the financial terms so that all employees will have the same opportunity. Beware that the equipment is not quietly sold at a low price to a favored employee. It can come back at a later date and haunt the participants. Whoever sold and bought under these conditions will probably come to wish they never heard of the equipment.

GUIDELINES FOR DETERMINING WHETHER THE EQUIPMENT IS ECONOMICALLY JUSTIFIED

The main reason for acquiring warehouse equipment is to reduce costs. There are other reasons, which include safety, no other possible way, employee morale, and so on, but the purpose of most equipment is to save money. If it is to be acquired for this reason, the economic justification should be sound. For most warehouse managers, the task of preparing a report on the economical justification is very difficult, yet such a report is a prerequisite to obtaining capital funds in most companies. The report is required to convince top management that the purchase is a good investment and to provide the proper information for accounting to set up the depreciation schedules, to record the assets, to classify expenditures, and to provide a means for holding accountable.

It is difficult to prepare a good economic justification report because it requires considerable time and a good knowledge of business economics to make a proper analysis and logical presentation. The line of reasoning that has to be overcome is embodied in the following common expression: "The need is obvious; why must it be written down?" The fact is that the need may be obvious only to the warehouse manager, and even if it happens to be obvious to all concerned, the need still must be written down to provide a record of why the thing was acquired. If it is acquired, the person who justified it should be held accountable to make good the claims contained in the justification and with a lot more seriousness than politicians are held accountable for their campaign promises.

An example of the different logic used in justifying equipment by two different levels of management is portrayed in this situation:

A warehouse manager asks for authorization to buy a new lift truck. For the economic justification, she or he reports that a time study has been made showing that an average of 8 hours a day are wasted by workers waiting for lift trucks. Reported is that the cost of this wasted labor in one year is almost enough to pay for the additional truck. To the local manager this is an airtight case. To him or her, "They will have to be blind to not see it." On the other hand, let's see how the manager's boss might view the case. If there is the equivalent of one operator waiting for lift trucks, the obvious answer to the problem is that the warehouse is carrying one too many operators—one should be laid off.

Possibly the warehouse manager really needs the lift truck to handle an increased work load and the warehouse level of service has fallen off due to the lack of lift truck capacity. This is a more sound reason than the one given, but even this reason should be supported by detail. For example, how long will the increased work load last, what evidence is there that the service level is dropping, what alternatives were considered, and should another shift be added to get better use of present equipment?

It is unfortunate that many requests for equipment are turned down because the warehouse manager cannot convincingly package the justification when much of this equipment is truly needed and could be justified if properly presented.

Listed here are points of logic to be considered in determining the economic justification of warehouse equipment:

1. *Define the Problem.* Analyze the job that has to be done. For instance, if the problem is the need for more storage space, determine what products or situation caused this need and what are the effects of not having the space. How to define the problem is covered previously in this chapter under the title, "Guidelines for Determining the Job to Be Done."

2. *Describe the Alternatives.* After defining the problem, all the main alternative solutions should be considered. If the problem relates to a shortage of handling equipment, consideration should be given to getting extra capacity by adding employees or going to a second or third shift. If the equipment problem relates to a shortage of storage space, the alternatives of acquiring additional usable space should be explored including acquisition of storage racks and handling equipment that will permit storing higher.

3. *Specify the Savings.* It should be made clear how the savings that are claimed will be realized. If worker's time will be reduced, the number of hours should be stated. The cost of this time should be given, including base wage plus fringe benefits, overtime costs, and effect on administrative costs, if any. The operating and maintenance cost of the new equipment should be declared. If floor space is to be gained, determine the value of the space. The cost of utilities, insurance, taxes, and so on should be included in the cost of space. If the equipment selected will reduce damage, the amount of reduction should be indicated. Give the basis for determining the cost of damage, such as the actual cost or list price less the salvage or scrap value. The writer who is preparing the justification should put himself or herself inside the mind of who will be approving or rejecting the request. Determine what is necessary from this point of view to authorize the acquisition and then do it.

4. *Relate the Savings to the Investment.* The net savings to be realized should be compared to the total cost of the requested equipment. This comparison should be made for all of the alternatives. Generally, the alternative with the best return on the amount invested should be the one selected; however, the expected life of the equipment and the possible risk of obsolescence should be given due consideration. Specialized types of equipment should have a much quicker return on investment than versatile equipment requires. For example, the purchase of general-purpose pallet racks having a four-year return on investment could be a better investment than specialized racks having a two-year return on investment.

There exist different formulas used in financial evaluation other than annual net savings divided into total cost. "Net present value" is one that discounts cash flow of the future back to present value. "Internal rate of return" is one that provides for getting a specified return on the money saved as it is saved. You will, of course, have to tailor your equipment justification to the method used in your company.

There is no one best universal guide for what the return on investment should be to justify equipment purchase. Companies have different standards. Differences exist even between divisions within a company. Also, the formulas used to determine return on investment differ. In most cases, these differences are quite legitimate. They exist because companies try to show different things with the return-on-investment concept.

Differences exist in company objectives, financial position, and many other influencing factors. For instance, variations in these factors can make a five-year return on investment for a specific type of equipment seem attractive for one company while another company would require a one-year return to be equally attractive. It is of serious concern that companies in the United States generally require much quicker payoffs of investments in capital equipment expenditures than do their main foreign competitors.

5. *Include Other Factors That Will Influence the Investment.* In the process of determining the economic justification of equipment, there will be factors that are very difficult or impractical to assign a dollar value, yet they should be considered in the final decision of whether or not to buy. Some of these factors are employee safety, goodwill, capacity for future growth, employee morale, security, image, and public relations. These may not be the main reason for the investment; however, they should be given full consideration as to their positive or negative value. It is quite possible to have an excellent monetary return on investment and yet have other factors make the acquisition unfavorable. On the other hand, a poor monetary return can become a very good overall investment if other factors are favorable.

6. *Provide Detailed Equipment Specifications and Price Quotations.* It is not enough to say that the investment is for a general classification of equipment, such as "lift truck" or "racks." The detailed specifications must be analyzed, determined, and specified. Many times warehouse managers have been surprised to find that they receive something quite different from what they expected particularly when the job of buying it is turned over to the purchasing department. Suppliers who quote on equipment should be asked to provide detailed information about it. A cross-check of different suppliers' quotations and equipment specifications will provide valuable information for determining the right specifications for the intended equipment.

EXAMPLE OF A FORMAL REQUEST FOR CAPITAL EXPENDITURE

The previous section dealt with the principles involved in the proper selection of equipment. This section takes up the application of those guidelines using an example of a request and justification for a stacker crane system. The case is presented as a formal request for a capital expenditure. Most companies have a similar procedure to obtain top-management or board of directors' approval for appropriation of capital funds. The presentation here will treat very briefly what most companies would actually require but in much greater detail. However, the format and consideration are common to those required in many companies.

I.   SUMMARY

The sum of $590,000 is requested to purchase and install a stacker crane system at the company warehouse in San Francisco.

At present the materials are manually stocked in and picked from 7-foot-high bin racks. With the proposed equipment the materials will be stocked and picked by an operator riding a stacker crane that services bin racks 30 feet high.

The annual cost savings resulting from use of the stacker crane system compared to the present level of costs is $437,000 before income tax. The payout period is 1.35 years.

II. DESCRIPTION

A. *Present Operation.* The San Francisco warehouse was established 10 years ago to supply the West Coast with automotive repair parts. The increase in volume through the warehouse has paralleled the growth of the company's business, which has been about 6 percent per year. Until now the warehouse has been able to absorb the increased volume and inventories by improving work practices, adding racks, improving storage layout, and increasing inventory turnover.

With the present storing and handling system, the warehouse is no longer able to hold the required inventories and permit efficient handling. Aisle storage has become necessary as a routine. This practice, while giving temporary relief, now prevents making many shipments on time and causes excessive rehandling with loss of worker efficiency, high damage, and a reduction in safety.

B. *Proposed Operation.* The proposed system consists of 30-foot-high bin racks along both sides of two 100-foot aisles. A stacker crane for each aisle rides on a steel rail in the center of aisle secured to the floor and connects to an overhead rail above the racks, attached to the roof trusses for further stability providing rapid access to all bins. Each stacker is equipped with a carriage for an operator to ride and to direct the crane. A convenient two-bin rack is a part of the carriage. The rack holds materials for restocking the bins and for order-picking operations. The operator can deliver new stock on the way to pick orders.

The proposed rack system will replace the present 7-foot-high order picking bins. The building has a 34-foot-high clearance, which provides adequate clearance for the proposed new 30-foot-high racks. The actual floor space used for the new system will be 4,000 square feet, compared to the 10,000 square feet now used. The new system will provide for 80,000 cubic feet of storage, compared to the present 50,000 cubic feet. An area of 6,000 square feet will be made available for later expansion or other use.

The stacker crane system will permit reducing the number of workers to handle present volume from 10 to 4. It will also permit warehouse operation to provide much closer the level of service that was established as basic for the success of the company marketing program, 100 percent of the orders out within 24 hours. The present service level is 65 percent. Before the warehouse became so congested by the overstocked condition, the 100 percent level was attainable and averaged 97 percent. The proposed system should enable performance very near 100 percent, 99 percent routinely. In addition, the stacker crane system will permit a reduction of handling damage from the present level of 1.0 percent to 0.05 percent, from $60,000 to $3,000 annually.

III. PROJECT COSTS

The following is a summary of costs to change from present to proposed system.

	Capital (000s)
A. *Installation*	
Remove existing racks	$ 10
Install new racks	20
Install crane system	10
Rehandle stocks	20
Total	$ 60
B. *Equipment*	
Racks	$230
Cranes (2)	200
Electrical	20

	Capital (000s)
Sales tax	25
Freight	25
Total	$500
Subtotal	$560
Contingency, 10%	56
Salvage of present racks	(26)
Total project cost	$590

C. *Alternatives*

Alternatives that were explored but were found to be more expensive when both the initial project and continuing costs were included:

1. Build or lease larger building in another location and move the entire warehouse operation. Present building cannot be enlarged.

2. Build or lease another small building in another location and split the operations.

3. Increase height of present storage racks and handle materials with step ladders or with operator-up order-picking lift trucks. This was considered not feasible due to hazards of carrying materials up and down ladders and interference with order picking by workers on the floor and those riding the lift trucks at the same time in the same area.

IV. OPERATING COSTS

The following is a comparison of operating costs for the present and proposed systems.

	Annual Costs (000s)
A. *Present*	
Workers (10)	$500
Maintenance (racks and 5 platform lowboy trucks)	15
Space at lease cost, 10,000 sq. ft. (50,000 cu. ft. storage)	72
Utilities (area heating and electric trucks)	15
Inventory damage, 1.0%	60
Housekeeping	20
Depreciation	5
Total	$687
B. *Proposed*	
Workers (4)	$220
Maintenance (racks, bins, and cranes)	10
Space at lease cost, 3,000 sq. ft. (70,000 cu. ft.)	22
Utilities (area heating and cranes)	10
Inventory damage, 0.05%	3
Housekeeping	5
Depreciation	30
Subtotal	$300
Less: Value of space freed for other use	50
Total	$250

V. ANNUAL COST SAVINGS

Present	$687
Less: Proposed	250
Net Difference	$437

VI. PAYOUT CALCULATION

Total project costs ÷ total annual savings = payout period

$590 ÷ $437 = 1.35 years

VII. OTHER CONSIDERATIONS

    A. The same type stacker crane system is in use at three other warehouse operations in the San Francisco Bay Area. Each was visited, and conferences with the managers were held to explore how they felt about the system. Each in their own way volunteered raving reviews. After the initial shakedowns, which varied from 2 to 4 months, the systems were equal to or exceeded expectations. The same expectations were used in the operating costs for this proposal. The operations visited were

        Cyclops Eye Remedies, Oakland

        Hydra Glove Manufacturing, San Mateo

        Titan Toys, San Francisco

    The Cyclops and Hydra companies had installations larger and Titan had smaller than the one proposed here.

    B. The company's employer relations manager after comparing the operating requirements between the present and proposed systems suggested that the crane operators warrant a 10 percent premium over the present order-picker wages. This increase has been provided for in the calculations for the proposed system.

    C. The four crane operators needed in the proposed system will be selected by seniority and their preference from the present work force. The surplused workers resulting from the new system will be accounted for by laying them off with the least seniority but first an attempt will be made to absorb them into openings resulting from normal attrition in both production and warehousing. If they are laid off they will be given priority when the company hires in the future.

    D. The chief safety officer has critically examined the new system for hazards and contends it meets or exceeds the company's most stringent safety requirements and importantly it will get away from the frequent back and arm strains associated with the present 7-foot-high order-picking racks.

VIII. COMPLETION SCHEDULE

    The project can be completed 8 months after approval of this request. Changeover from the present to the new system will be planned to cause minimum disruption of warehouse service.

    Figure 8.1 is a transmittal and summary form showing at a glance the information commonly included in a request for capital expenditure. All blanks are not filled in for every request. The form is intended to be a help as a checklist of the main management concerns for most requests for capital expenditures.

WHAT A GOOD EQUIPMENT MAINTENANCE PROGRAM INCLUDES

    Basically, there are two different approaches to equipment maintenance: (1) to have a program of preventive maintenance and (2) to make repairs only when needed. Most who are responsible for equipment operation would, if asked, say that the preventive approach is best and that the reasons are obvious; yet there is probably as much equipment operated under the don't-fix-it-'til-it's-broke concept as there is under the preventive plan. In the same way, people believe preventive medicine is right, but many will not take the time to get regular physical checkups or shots to immunize them against diseases—even when the service is free. For equipment maintenance there is always a direct and payable charge, and the well-being of machines is not as important as that of people; the

FIGURE 8.1 Capital Expenditure Request

```
CAPITAL EXPENDITURE REQUEST
        (CER)                                        CER. No. _____
                                                     Date _____
Warehouse Name: _____     Location _____
Summary:



Changes in Capacities and Availabilities:

Capital Requested:                                            $_____
Noncapital Expenditure Requested:                             $_____
  Total Cost:                                                 $_____
Salvage Value of Facilities to be Retired:                    $_____
NEW MONEY REQUIRED:                                           $_____
Current Book Value of Facilities to Be Retired                $_____
Annual Net  ☐ Savings  ☐ Profit                              $_____
Payout _____ years              Return on Investment _____%
Commencement Date _____     Completion Date _____
Depreciation Method _____   Life (in years) _____
Review and Approval:

Warehouse Mgr      _____          Controller _____
Nat'l Warehouse Mgr _____         Division V.P. _____
Engineering Mgr    _____          President _____
```

result is that effective maintenance for equipment is not nearly as common as it would seem it should be.

The size of the warehouse operation affects the importance of a preventive maintenance program. In large operations that have a considerable amount of equipment and a full-time maintenance crew, it may not be very important if individual pieces of equipment unexpectedly break down. Other equipment can be diverted to do the essential work, and mechanics are available to make quick repairs to the unit that is down. In small warehouse operations, any equipment breakdown may be critical. Work may have to stop until repairs can be made, and additional time is lost in getting a mechanic to the warehouse or in sending the machine out to a repair shop. If an effective preventive maintenance program is deemed important for large warehouses, it should be deemed indispensable for small ones.

Computerizing and Bar Coding R (Repair) and M (Maintenance)

Repair and maintenance (R and M) of warehouse equipment provides a fertile area to get the very best from a marriage between computerizing and bar coding. All the good data that supervision needed before to manage this tricky area properly can now be provided—accurately and in a timely fashion. Most of it can be gleaned from data that is reported and accumulated (and justified) for other reasons such as the material handling time standards and performance measure. The little additional information needed is trivial compared to the value to be derived from effectively managing warehousing's equipment.

Note that the usual context of R and M is expanded here to include managing equipment as well as repairs and maintenance. It is expanded by design because how equipment is used directly influences R and M and how well equipment is maintained affects all other phases of warehousing: operator safety and well-being, productivity, customer services, and so on. Excepting personnel, it can be argued that equipment and how it is used and maintained may be singularly the most important component of warehousing.

By the simple introduction of bar coding and computer interface, all important information about equipment can be accumulated, massaged, and reported in a manner to give management what it always wanted to most effectively manage equipment. It is done like this. Each operator and R and M mechanic, electrician, and electronics expert—and each piece of equipment—has an exclusive bar code. Also each type of work is bar coded. Further each part used in the process of repairing or rebuilding is bar coded. Together, all this with proper computer software tells what is needed to best manage a warehouse's equipment, which should include office equipment as well as that used in operations. In summary it provides the following very useful data.

1. Description of equipment, when and from whom acquired, new or used, capacity, initial cost, guarantees, and the manufacturer's recommended maintenance.
2. Nature of R and M work on it, costs, when and by whom.
3. Hours operated in total and since last preventive maintenance and when next is scheduled.
4. Correlations and performance measurement—using standard times where appropriate.

The remainder of this section is presented in terms of doing things without computerization and bar coding so that what is said will be meaningful to those without the benefits of computers and bar coding. Those with them should translate without much difficulty.

Benefits of Preventive Maintenance

Listed here are some of the benefits that can be expected from a preventive maintenance program compared to the repair-as-needed way:

Less expensive repairs

Longer operating life

More economic performance

More reliable performance

Safer operation

Higher operator confidence and morale

Though these factors are all favorable, it does not mean that all preventive maintenance programs are good. Many programs have been discontinued because the expected benefits have not materialized or because the program cost was greater than the cost of keeping extra replacement units available and making repairs only as needed. The actual worth of a preventive maintenance program depends on how well it is designed and implemented in relation to the particular warehousing circumstances. There are situations where a maximum program is justified, there are those cases where a minimum program is best, and there are times when the repair-as-needed approach is the wisest course to follow—but this is quite rare.

Six Basic Requirements of a Preventive Maintenance Program

Certain requirements are basic to an effective preventive maintenance program. These are applicable regardless of the type of equipment involved, as long as the equipment is of sufficient importance to be included in the program. Following are some of the more important ones.

1. *Equipment identification.* An identification code number should be assigned and affixed with a metal tag to, or permanently stenciled on, each unit. The number is needed for purposes of accountability, correlation with handling-time standards, R and M records, and reports regarding each piece of equipment.

2. *Equipment file.* A file should be set up and maintained for each unit. The file should include the manufacturer's equipment specifications, guarantees, inspection and maintenance schedule, and a history of maintenance and repairs. Also, the file should include a copy of the maintenance contract if the service is being performed by another company. The primary function of the file is to assist in planning, scheduling, and better management decisions.

3. *Operating-hour meter.* Most powered handling equipment, such as lift trucks, cranes, and material moving robots, should have an operating-hour meter attached to each unit. An accurate accounting of operating and R and M hours is necessary to analyze and to evaluate maintenance, repairs, operating, and total performance.

4. *Operator instructions and training.* The equipment operators should be recognized as playing a key role in the success of a preventive maintenance program. First, they should operate the equipment according to the manufacturer's operating instructions; second, they should perform certain inspection and maintenance routines daily. These include proper fueling or charging batteries and checking oil and hydraulic fluid levels, brakes, tires, steering, cables, chains, motor, and hoists to make certain all are in safe and good working order.

5. *Schedules for inspection and maintenance.* A rigid schedule for inspection and maintenance should be established for each unit of equipment. An engineered checklist form should be provided for the mechanics to assure that the proper parts and mechanisms are checked, adjusted, replaced, and lubricated. Equipment manufacturers provide specific R and M procedures, check lists, and schedules with each piece of their equipment. These should be religiously followed by the operators and R and M. Copies should be retained in the R and M department for ready reference and in the warehouse office for administration and performance measurement, and that which is pertinent to operators plasticized and securely attached to the equipment. A history of all R and M and who operates the equipment should be included as a permanent record in the equipment files.

6. *The importance of manufacturers' guarantees.* These must be common knowledge as well as copies in both files. This is necessary to make certain nothing is done, or not done, that will void the equipment guarantees and, further, to make certain that any problems that are covered by guarantee will corrected at the supplier's expense.

Checklists for Lift Truck and Crane Maintenance

For the maintenance checklist form to be most effective, its design should be based on data obtained from several sources, including the equipment manufacturer, the mechanics who perform the work, and the experience of the warehouse personnel who operate the equipment. Also, the warehouse management's objectives for the preventive maintenance program, and how much it is willing to pay, should play an important part in the design of the maintenance checklist. The entire R and M program will revolve around this list; care should be taken to design it to do what is really wanted, not more, not less. Design it for utility not to impress the personnel department or top management.

Presented here are examples of maintenance checklists for two of warehousing's most common types of handling equipment: lift trucks and cranes. The frequency of checking or performing the different functions will depend on the type of equipment, the time and way it is used, and the physical environment in which the equipment operates. Important, however, is that the checklist be designed to conform to the specific piece of equipment for which it is intended.

CHECKLIST FOR LIFT TRUCK MAINTENANCE

1. Lubricate in accordance with manufacturer's recommendations.
2. Change motor oil.
3. Clean or replace air filter.
4. Blow out radiator core.
5. Tighten nuts and bolts, including electrical connections.
6. Adjust steering assembly.
7. Check and take corrective action for

    Distributor points and spark plugs (if LPG)

    Battery terminals and water level

    Oil in hydraulic system

    Mast assembly

    Brakes

    Clutch

    Engine mounts

    Engine

    Electrical system

    Tire condition and pressure

    Fan and fan belt

    Wheel bearings

8. Clean exterior of equipment thoroughly, removing all dirt, rust, and excess grease.

9. Annually (or semiannually, depending on usage) perform the following:

    Test truck under load

    Repair wheel bearings, universal joints and steering gear units

    Change lubricants in differential and gear housings

    Paint exterior and undercarriage if required

CHECKLIST FOR CRANE MAINTENANCE

1. Lubricate in accordance with manufacturer's recommendations.
2. Tighten nuts and bolts, including electrical connections.
3. Check and take corrective action for

    Track alignment and fastenings

    Wheels, flat spots—end play

    Bearings

    Brakes

    Motor supports

    Motors, bridge—hoist—trolley

    Hoist mechanics

    Limit switches

    Electrical system

    Walkway, railing, ladder

4. Clean exterior of equipment thoroughly, removing all dirt, rust, and excess grease.
5. Annually (or semiannually, depending on usage) perform the following:

    Test crane under load

    Repack bearings

    Change lubricants in gear housings

    Paint exterior if required

PROS AND CONS OF BUYING USED STORING EQUIPMENT

Buying used storing equipment can be an alternative but one fraught with danger. Probably it is easier to make a big boner in buying used storage racks than it is for any other type of warehouse equipment. This is no reason to say "forget it" to what appears to be a good buy, because if all the cautions are acknowledged and provided for, a right-quality purchase can be made. Recognize though that when it comes to buying used storing racks, it is a lot easier to make a wrong purchase decision than it is to make a good one. This being fairly well recognized by potential buyers may be the reason that there are few companies that sell used storage racks. And, rack-producing companies rarely have used racks to sell. If they do, it is in their own brand.

Extra care should be taken to buy only used racks that meet your specifications.

Following are some important considerations of buying used storage racks.

1. Find out the specifications of the used racks you are considering. For pallet racks this means

Height and capacity of uprights

Width and capacity of arms

Distance (depth) between pairs of arms

2. Is the company that made the racks still in business? If it is, who is it and where is it located? Can you buy more of exactly the same design if ever needed?

3. Do the racks include row spacers, wall attachments, base plates, and so on?

4. Is there any damage? If so, what is it and how much of it? Is it repairable?

5. Is sales tax charged on sale of used racks as it is on new racks? If so, how much is it?

6. Does the seller guarantee anything about the racks? If so, can you get it in writing?

7. Are the racks compatible with any other brand? If so, specifically how do the other brand's arms fit into the uprights of the used racks you are considering?

8. How old is the racks and for what were they used?

9. Are the racks rusting? If so, where and how much?

10. Is delivery included? If not, what will it cost.

11. Can you buy just what you need or must you take the whole lot?

12. Is the appearance of the racks acceptable, or do they need to be repainted?

13. What is their total price (purchase, tax, delivery, and installation) and how does this compare with the same quantity of new racks?

There is a uniqueness about buying new storage racks that I think does not apply to any other warehouse equipment. It is this: *hard negotiations can yield surprisingly good results.* That is my experience anyway. Apparently there is a much greater range of discount that a rack company can work on than there is for, say, lift trucks. I never bought new storage racks for less than 35 percent discount and many for 48 percent. If you buy a small quantity and buy them through a broker rather than through the company that makes them, you will probably pay list or near list price. But if you buy in quantity directly from the company that produces, then you can probably get them for much less.

This discount that can be negotiated with rack suppliers causes used storage rack prices to lose some of their charm. Their prices may look great compared to list prices, but list prices generally should not be used in the comparison. The best hard negotiated price of both the used as well as the new rack prices should be compared.

Another tool of storing that is commonly used that does much better in the used-equipment market than storage racks is the common wood pallet. The principal reason for this is because they can be bought by the used-pallet dealers relatively low and can be sold relatively high. This results in a wide margin for the dealers. The main reasons why the dealers can buy cheap in relation to their value is because there are a lot of them that become available from becoming obsolete by the companies that used them. And, there are many pallet-using companies that go out of business by moving off-shore or declaring bankruptcy.

Obsolescence is the primary source of used pallets. For instance, visualize the huge pile of pallets that automatically become obsolete when warehousing or production of a large canned-goods company converts from pallets to slip-sheets or clamp handling as many of them have and many more will. When companies obsolete pallets for whatever reasons, they generally want to get rid of them in a hurry, as they should. Often they are susceptible to a used pallet dealer's offer "to take them all off their hands tomorrow," and the dealer will take them all even those that are broken so the company will not have to bother with taking them to the dump themselves. Which brings to light another source of used pallets. All used-pallet dealers are set up to repair broken pallets, but many users of pallets are not. A company will keep stacking their broken pallets in a corner of the warehouse or more likely outside in the yard until there is a truckload then call a used-pallet dealer to come get them.

Another reason for the rather brisk market in used pallets is that the price of new pallets has climbed right along with the escalation in the price of wood. This gives rise to such comments as, "Do you realize what we're paying for pallets? It's plain robbery. Next time let's try used ones. We can't do worse." There are, however, pitfalls in buying used pallets. Here are but a few.

1. Used-pallet dealers are reluctant to answer questions about their pallets. "Come on down and pick out what you want." Buyers of used pallets should have an expertise in pallets and know what they are going to be used for.

2. Pallet size can be a problem. Suppose you need 38" × 48" pallets for a new product. You buy the pallets and they arrive just in time for their intended use. Then a lift truck operator announces, "Joe, you've really done it this time. We need pallets with the stringers going the 48" side. What you got runs the 38" side. All our racks are for 48" deep. What you got will fall through. What do we do now?" This can only be worse if the same mistake were made in new pallets you order. At least if it happened with used-pallets, you probably got a good price on the wrong ones.

3. It is easy to find used pallets to buy, but it is not so easy to buy the right design, construction, material, and size you need. If the type you want is common, you will no doubt have to pay more for them.

4. Concern should be given to whether the used pallets are sound enough for the use intended. Have a few pallets give way while in storage or break up while being moved, and you will be sorry you ever got such a "good deal" on them.

5. Pallets stored outside, as they usually are at used-pallet dealers' places of business, become unsightly from weathering before long. Physically, they can be all right, but do you want your product to be seen on them?

Chapter 9

How Efficient Material Handling Equipment Makes the Big Difference in Productivity

CHAPTER HIGHLIGHTS

Material handling equipment used in modern warehousing ranges from the most basic two-wheel handcart through lift trucks, conveyors, and cranes, to the ultimate heavy-load material mover that is at the leading edge of technology. You will see with the use of illustrations how human capabilities and productivity can be multiplied many times over by material handling equipment and that the most dramatic is the latest—hardly out of the design stage. Yet some equipment such as the carousel and the pneumatic tubes are being rediscovered with greater appreciation than ever before.

TYPES OF MATERIAL HANDLING EQUIPMENT, THEIR CHARACTERISTICS AND USES

The previous chapter covers the importance of proper equipment evaluation. This chapter deals with the types of material handling equipment available to modern warehousing. Included are descriptions, illustrations and suggested applications.

Because of the many different types of equipment available, it is difficult to make certain that even the right general type of equipment is being considered for a particular material handling function. There are many different mechanical ways of moving materials, and for that matter there are many different types of racks to assist in storing them. It is easy to spend all one's time investigating the wrong kind of equipment and, after purchase has been made, to find that an entirely different type or combination would have been more efficient and cost less.

A complete investigation of all the different types of warehousing equipment available would be almost endless. Fortunately, however, most of the equipment falls within a fairly manageable list of basic types. Within each group there are many variations which are very important and should be given consideration before the final selection is made.

Following are checklists of equipment used in warehousing. The purpose of these checklists is to provide in a fairly complete listing of the range of equipment that should be given consideration. The checklists are not intended to be all-inclusive since new items and variations of present ones are coming onto the market all the time. However, they will serve to prompt investigation into equipment that would not be otherwise considered, and to assure that the main types of equipment have been considered. Characteristics, advantages, disadvantages, and applications of some of the most common equipment are discussed.

No one warehouse or system of warehouses would or should use all items of equipment in the following checklists. It is desirable to standardize the minimum types of equipment used in a particular warehousing operation. Having too wide a variety of specialized equipment will hinder flexibility and result in low utilization. Although there are many different types of equipment available to warehousing, most of them can be considered variations of the main grouping shown in the following checklists. These individual variations, however, are very important in determining the equipment requirements for a warehouse. It is not enough to specify, for instance, lift trucks, conveyors, and cranes. The specific types of lift trucks, conveyors, and cranes must be determined and the detailed specifications given for each. This is obvious to those who are aware of the many variations in warehousing equipment, but there are many examples in warehousing of the wrong type of equipment being pressed into service, or sitting idle, because those who acquired it were unfamiliar with these variations. A good example that seems to catch the unwary is to acquire narrow-aisle, non-telescopic straddle lift trucks and then realize that they can only be used with single-wing pallets and the distribution system uses only the conventional double-face pallets. Ouch!

Checklist of 23 Types of Lift Trucks and Their Uses

- ☐ Operator sit
- ☐ Operator stand

- Operator walk behind
- Conventional counterbalance
- Narrow-aisle straddle-arm
- Narrow-aisle telescopic
- Four-directional
- Side-load move sideways
- Fork carrier with only few inches of lift
- Platform carrier with only few inches lift
- Manual power
- Battery power
- Gasoline power
- Compressed-gas power
- Diesel power
- Hydraulic lift
- Chain-drive lift
- Telescopic mast
- Double-deep telescopic mast
- Nontelescopic mast
- Turret, 180 degrees
- Hands-on control
- Remote control

The lift truck, also called the forklift or power lift, is the workhorse of warehousing. It is the most versatile single piece of material handling equipment used in warehousing. It can move things horizontally and vertically; it can travel about freely; and with attachments, it can pick up, turn, push, and pull all types and shapes of objects. It is mostly reliable and relatively easy to operate. It can do many things that other types of handling equipment can do, but any one other type can do very few of the things it can do. Without the lift truck, the warehousing industry would not be at all what it is today, nor would it have the prospects of the bright and growing future that it has. Much of the value of warehousing depends on its handling equipment, and the lift truck is the "king" of this equipment. Because of the importance the lift truck plays in material handling, considerable effort and money have been invested in modifying its basic design to make it do more things. Now there is an extremely broad selection of different designs from which to choose, as well as many more accessory attachments that extend the utility and versatility of the basic machines. Discussed here are the general purpose, characteristics, advantages, disadvantages, and applications of the more common types of lift trucks and attachments. Some of them are illustrated in Figure 9.1.

Conventional Counterbalance Type.   This was the first type of lift truck to become widely used in materials handling and probably still is the most widely used. (See Figure 9.1A.) It is designed to utilize the principle of "counterbalance," which is to oppose with equal weight or force. The principle is the same as that used in a child's teeter-totter, or seesaw. The weight at one end exerts a force via a fulcrum that opposes the force of the weight at the other end. The fulcrum in the case of the counterbalance lift truck is the front

FIGURE 9.1 Representative Types of Lift Trucks

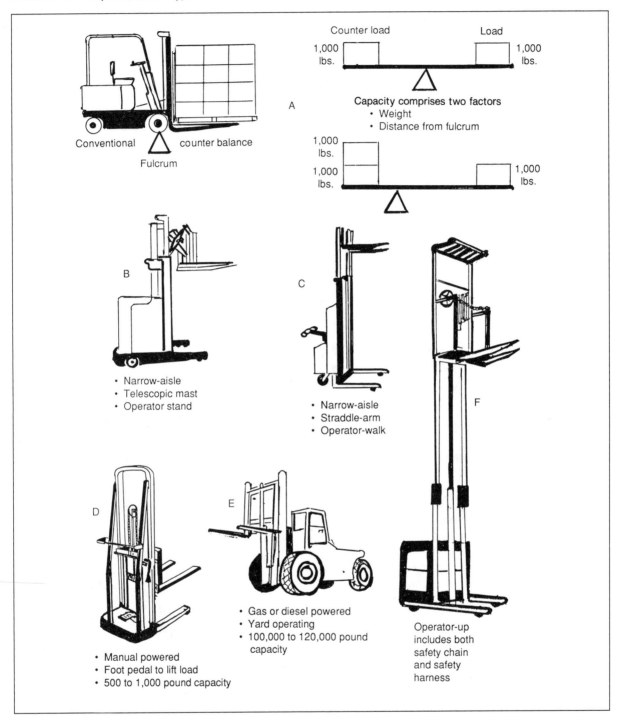

wheels. The machine is designed so that the weight behind the front wheels is greater than the weight in front of them. The weight behind includes the weight of the rear wheels, power unit, chassis, body, additional deadweight, and the weight of the operator. The weight in front includes the weight of the lifting mechanism and the load that is being carried. Understanding this principle makes it obvious that the more weight that is added to the back end, the

FIGURE 9.1 Continued

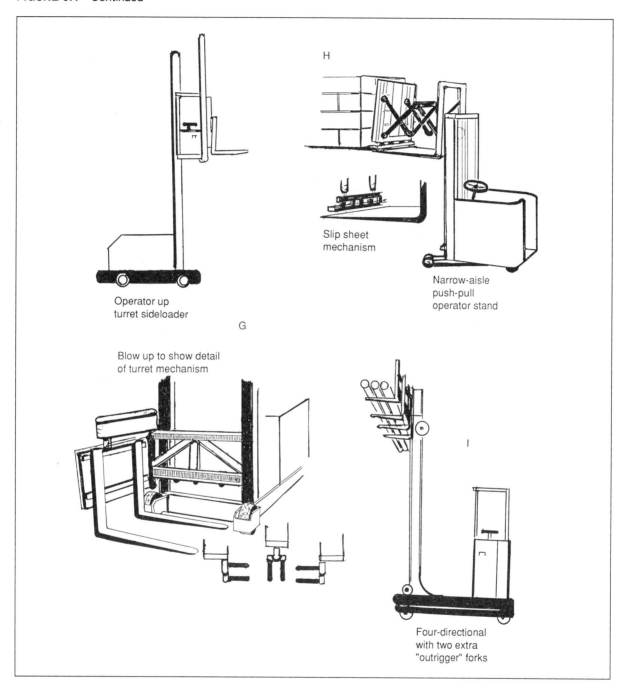

Operator up
turret sideloader

H

Slip sheet
mechanism

Narrow-aisle
push-pull
operator stand

G

Blow up to show detail
of turret mechanism

I

Four-directional
with two extra
"outrigger" forks

heavier can be the load carried at the front. Of course, the power unit and design must be compatible to effectively increase the lift truck's capacity.

The counterbalance design permits lift trucks to be made with almost unlimited lift capacity and reach height. The usual lift capacities for inside warehousing range from 2,000 to 7,000 pounds. The reach heights ranging from a few feet to, say, 28 feet. Lift trucks can be obtained that will lift more and reach much higher, but they are outside the scope of what is normally used in the warehousing industry. Actually, lift trucks of over 7,000 pounds capacity are unusual for inside warehouse work. They are too large, heavy, and awkward to be used effectively inside most buildings. Too much space must be allowed for aisles, and the floor capacity of most warehouses is not sufficient to hold up under such heavy loads. Lift trucks having over, say, 7,000 to 100,000 pounds (yes, lift trucks are available with this phenomenal capacity) are generally confined to outside warehousing, where aisle space and surface capacity are not limiting factors. The height that lift trucks can reach is also limited more by what is operationally practical than by what equipment manufacturers can make. However, with the aid of computer-controlled guidance, lift truck type vehicles can operate safely and efficiently at heights in the 40- to 50-foot range as discussed later in Chapter 11 under high-rise and ASRS equipment.

Even though the conventional counterbalance lift truck is the most versatile and most commonly used, it does have an important disadvantage. It requires much wider aisles than the other types that were designed specifically to operate in narrow aisles. For the same capacity, the conventional, operator-sit type requires 25 to 50 percent more turning radius and correspondingly wider aisles.

Narrow-Aisle Straddle-Arm Type. Actually there are only two basic designs used in the construction of lift trucks: the conventional counterbalance type just discussed above and the narrow-aisle straddle-arm type discussed here. (See Figure 9.1B and C.) The names of these designs refer to the means by which the load leverage is accomplished. The counterbalance type gets its leverage, as the name implies, by counterbalancing the weight of the lift truck against the weight of the load. The straddle-arm type gets its leverage from arms with wheels that extend forward under the load. There are many different variations of these two designs, but all lift trucks use either one design or the other.

The main advantage of the straddle-arm lift trucks is that they have a much shorter turning radius; therefore, the aisles can be narrower, permitting greater utilization of warehouse space for storage. In fact, this type of truck is commonly referred to as the "narrow-aisle lift truck."

Although the counterbalance lift truck is still used more widely, the use of the straddle-arm lift trucks has grown at a faster rate in recent years. The high cost of storage space has brought about a greater interest in lift trucks that will operate with less aisle space. The straddle-arm type will operate in aisles as narrow as 6 to 8 feet, depending on the capacity of lift truck and the dimensions of the loads carried where the conventional type requires, say, 9- to 14-foot-wide aisles, depending on the capacity and dimensions of the load.

The disadvantages of the standard, nonreach straddle-arm truck, which keep it from being even more popular, are directly related to the extended arms that are required to give it leverage and balance. All storage in the warehouse must allow space for these arms to roll under to pick up loads. To make the most effective use of the trucks, all racks must be designed to permit this clearance, and only single-wing pallets can be used. Also, the trucks should have a smooth and level surface on which to travel. The wheels on the extended arms must be kept small so that the clearance necessary for the arms can be kept to a minimum. The small wheels combined with the short overall wheelbase of the truck do not permit convenient travel over rough or steep surfaces. For example, straddle-arm lift trucks generally are not used to load or unload trucks or rail cars. Travel over dock plates and rough surfaces of carrier beds is often too much for this type of lift truck. Also, the short wheelbase of the straddle-arm lift truck does not provide the balance necessary to reach as high as the conventional counterbalance lift trucks. Because of this balancing problem, most straddle-arm trucks are limited to lift heights of less than 25 feet. When these lift trucks are designed to go as high as counterbalance trucks, they have to be made with a longer wheelbase, which reduces their advantage as narrow-aisle trucks. In summary, straddle-arm trucks have the advantage of permitting narrower aisles, but they are not as versatile as the conventional counterbalance trucks.

A modification of the straddle-arm lift truck that increases its versatility is the addition of a telescopic mechanism to extend the fork unit out 3 or 4 feet to pick up loads. The forks can be extended to pick up and position loads and can be withdrawn to the normal position for travel. The telescopic fork unit adds versatility to the straddle-arm truck, but it also reduces its lift capacity. When the fork unit is extended, the lift truck is really working on the conventional counterbalance principle. The capacity to lift then depends on the amount of weight behind the front wheels just as it does with a counterbalance lift truck.

Four-Directional Type. The four-directional lift truck is designed to operate in exceptionally narrow aisles. (See Figure 9.1I.) It is unique in that it will move sideways as well as forward and backward. This feature permits aisles to be only a few inches wider than the lift truck plus the load. This lift truck uses the straddle-arm principle for leverage and can be equipped with telescopic forks like the straddle-arm lift trucks.

Four-directional trucks are particularly suited for hauling long loads such as pipe, rod, bar, and lumber. Such objects, which may be 20 to 30 feet long, can be carried along an aisle as little as 6 feet wide. The lift truck moves sideways down the aisle, then moves forward to put the load in the rack. An attachment will provide for another set of forks making four in all that are used to support very long loads. The *outrigger* forks can be positioned, say, 5 feet out from the usual forks and can be automatically extended and folded back when not needed.

A four-directional lift truck can do many of the things a stacker-crane can do, but for the same capacity, it will generally cost considerably less. The disadvantages of a four-directional lift truck are those of any straddle-arm vehicle; also, it requires more skill to operate than do conventional lift trucks.

Side-Load Type. The side-load truck is also designed to carry long objects down narrow aisles. (See Figure 9.1G.) The main difference between this and the four-directional truck is that it drives like a conventional counterbalance unit, that is, forward and backward, but it has the lift-fork unit on the side instead of the front. The fork unit moves out and back on rails and can be equipped with outrigger forks as well.

Because of their counterbalance design, side-load lift trucks have a higher capacity than do four-directional trucks. In the past, they have been used mainly outside, in lumber and steel warehousing, but smaller, more versatile models with fork-extension mechanics are now being used more and more for inside warehouse work.

Double-Deep Pallet Reach. With double-deep pallet racks instead of just the one pallet facing the aisle, there is provision for a second behind the first. This permits a major increase in space utilization.

For comparison, say, a 12-foot-wide aisle is bordered by one-deep 4-foot-deep pallet position on each side. This translates to 8 feet of storage for 12 feet of aisle: 4-foot-deep storage on one side, a 12-foot-wide aisle, and 4-foot-deep storage on the other—or 40 percent space utilization (8 feet ÷ 20 feet).

Now assume the lift truck has scissor extenders that will permit reaching another 4 feet and the storage racks are so designed to accommodate two pallets deep. This now translates to 4 feet plus 4 feet storage, 12 feet aisle, and 4 feet plus 4 feet storage. This permits 16 feet of storage for a 12-foot wide aisle, or 57 percent space utilization (16 ft. ÷ 28 ft.). What is given up for this basic advantage is capacity. The center of gravity in front of the fulcrum (front wheels) moves out causing loss of lift truck capacity.

The advantages are obvious. The procedural concern however is that there is a very good stock locator system to avoid losing one SKU behind another.

Order-Picker, Operator-Up. This is an adaptation of the lift truck for the operator to ride in a cab with the lift carriage. (See Figure 9.1F.) The controls of the lift truck are built into the cab so that the operator can manipulate the vehicle the same as when riding in the usual position at floor level.

Incidentally what was just described is commonly called "operator up," meaning the operator rides with the load lifting assembly in a cab. This variation of lift truck is used when the stock to be selected is small and weighs only enough to be conveniently lifted and moved by the operator. There are four distinct advantages of the operator-up, order-picking lift truck.

- Aisles can be narrow.
- Stock picking is in the *golden zone,* from waist to shoulder requiring least strain.
- Stock picking is always near eye level.
- Operator is never under the load. And most operators would prefer to have the load at the side or in front to avoid neck strain if nothing else.

Turret Sideloader. This is an innovative means to put in or take out loads from very narrow aisles bordered with storage racks—using a conventional, operator-sit lift truck. (See Figure 9.1G.) In many ways this combines the best of two worlds—that of using the convenient, operator sit, conventional lift truck and narrow aisles.

The limitation of this type of lift truck is relatively minor. Some of its capacity is lost to permit depositing and retrieving loads perpendicular to the direction of lift truck travel. The side wheels become the fulcrum, making the narrower width of the chassis the counterbalance rather than the length of the chassis. As with a teeter-totter, if two children are of equal size and sit equal distance from the fulcrum the counterbalance is equal. But if one child moves closer and the other stays put, the mechanism is out of balance—no fun.

This is what happens when the side wheels of a conventional lift truck become the fulcrum; the center of gravity of the chassis shortens. To attain equilibrium again the load must be reduced. Thus the reason for loss of capacity. Some of this loss can be overcome by design of the lift truck but the counterbalance phenomena must be accommodated one way or another. What this all means is that a heavier, higher-powered lift truck must be used to get the same capacity of a conventional lift truck. And, what this means is that the cost per pound of capacity will be greater.

This limitation is important but not prohibitive compared to the better utilization of space it makes possible. When the unit's advantage can be fully exploited in the right warehouse situation, it definitely fills a void and is probably destined to play an increasingly larger role in warehouse-type material handling.

Manual Power Lift Trucks. It is easy to get carried away with high-powered, high-reach lift trucks and entirely overlook that there are manually powered lift trucks that occasionally have a useful place in warehousing (see Figure 9.10). In moderation (perhaps severe moderation is more appropriate), they can do some things the electric- or fuel-powered units can do and a few things better. Their advantages relate to two features. They can operate in very tight quarters and comparatively their cost is minimal. Because they cost so little, you can buy a dozen or more for the cost of one of their big and powerful cousins.

Their low cost suggests they can be stationed in a confined area for functions requiring little capacity and height, where it would be more cost effective to have one standby for occasional use than to borrow the services of a usually busy high-powered unit. Appropriate places for them may be in an isolated recoup, fuel room, and light repackaging and finishing operations areas.

Representative specifications for hand crank or foot pedal lift, manually pushed, units are lift capacity of 1,000 pounds at 18-inch load center and to a height of a little above 6 feet. One occupies a space of about 8 square feet.

From these humble manually powered lift trucks, there is a fairly constant progression in power and capacity to surprisingly large and high-capacity units that can move seagoing containers—with a corresponding progression in costs. One of the preferable talents of management is to fit the equipment appropriately to the task to be performed. Do not use a chain saw to cut butter.

Checklist of 20 Types of Accessories for Lift Trucks and Their Uses

- ▢ Crane
- ▢ Clamp
- ▢ Push pull
- ▢ Shovel
- ▢ Boom
- ▢ Ram
- ▢ Scoop
- ▢ Power steering
- ▢ Power brakes
- ▢ Hard, soft, balloon tires
- ▢ Appliance holder
- ▢ Computer terminal with CRT screen
- ▢ Spotlight
- ▢ Fire extinguisher
- ▢ Overhead guard
- ▢ Side shifter
- ▢ Multiple forks
- ▢ Rotating forks
- ▢ Fork extensions
- ▢ Weigh scale

The usefulness and effectiveness of the basic lift truck can be enhanced and extended with accessories. For instance, there are many different types of material handling devices that can be used in place of the conventional forks. These can be made a permanent part of the lift truck, which will limit its use, or they may be removable so that the truck may be used with other attachments or with the regular forks, as needed. Most accessories are so designed that they may be secured or removed with little effort and time. See Figure 9.2 for representative types of lift truck attachments, followed by a brief discussion of the most common and most unique ones.

Crane Attachment.   A very common accessory for lift trucks is a crane attachment. Many warehouses have at least a limited need for a crane, preferably one that is mobile. Rather than invest in a mobile crane per se, which can be

FIGURE 9.2   Representative Types of Lift Truck Attachments

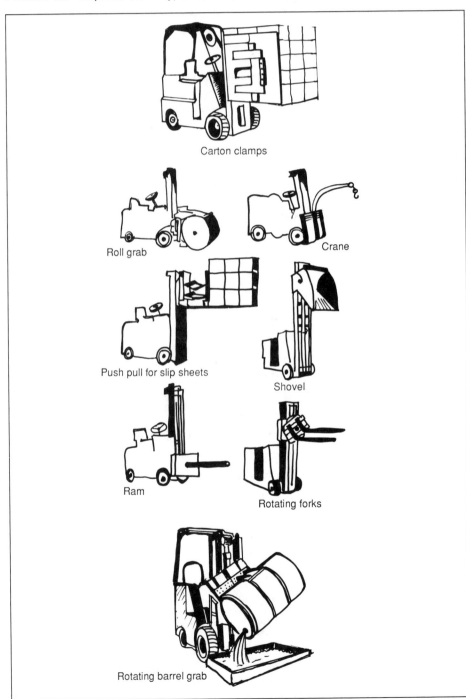

used only as a crane, it is frequently more economical to procure a crane attachment for the lift truck. Although the attachment will not be quite as efficient as a specialized mobile crane unit, it costs only a fraction of what the separate mobile crane would cost.

Clamps, Multiple Saber Forks, Push-Pull Attachments. Other common accessories for lift trucks are those that are used to handle palletless, unitized loads. These include clamps, multiple saber forks, and push-pull attachments. Palletless load handling plays a big part in the handling of packaged goods, particularly in canned and bottled food warehousing. This method retains the benefits of handling pallet loads without the actual use of pallets. The built-up loads are moved on sheets of pressboard or are held together with clamps instead of on the conventional pallets. Now more canned goods are handled using the palletless method than are handled on pallets. This has brought about a large market for accessory attachments related to this type of material handling.

Both slip-sheet and clamp handling where applicable are big improvements over use of pallets, mainly because empty pallet handling and storing are at best a big nuisance. Further, they are costly both in initial purchase and later repairs. Repairs and taking the empty pallets back to suppliers can be avoided by using cheaper one-way pallets, but the cost per unit load often is more than the reusable pallets and their extra handling and return.

Side Shifter. An accessory that is so common some vendors include it as a standard part of the lift truck is the side shifter. This enables the operator to move the forks or other attachment a few inches to the right or left—and what a time and effort saver this is. Rather than move the whole lift truck to jockey into final position, the side shifter accomplishes this. It is used both in positioning to pick up and to deposit loads. "Because it provides such a basic function, is a lift truck really complete without it?" Actually, yes. Some types of material handling do not require it, and occasionally when close positioning is needed some operators become so skilled they can precisely position the first try without need for adjustment. But as a rule the side shifter should be considered a basic part of the initial lift truck purchase.

Appliance Handler. One accessory that illustrates how specialized equipment can become is what is commonly called the "basiloid," named after Basiloid Products Corporation, the company that mainly produces them. Probably most warehouse professionals have never heard of it and for good reason—it is used only in moving large appliances like refrigerators, stoves, and washers, and it relates to how these are packaged.

A rectangular cardboard encases the appliances with possibly some inside fixture made of cardboard or wood to keep the unit from joggling about. The feature that relates to a basiloid is the top of the container. It is a separate high-strength, card-board hood that covers the top and extends down the sides a short distance.

The lift truck forks are removed and the basiloid is attached. It is a steel fixture shaped in a manner to slip under the hood cap that extends down the sides a few inches. When the fixture lip is inserted behind the cap, the mast and fixture are raised and up comes the appliance ready for transport. The basiloid is a highly efficient way to handle appliances. It is also available to handle multiple appliances at a time.

While for a long time the basiloid seemed the one best way to handle appliances, but it now has a challenger. Many warehouses prefer using clamps. Which means is best is similar to the controversy over the slip sheet and/or load clamps discussed before. What truly is best is what works best in a specific cycle of handling. What would be ideal is levitation. Short of that, both these are respectable contenders.

Other lift truck accessory items include shovels to move loose materials; rams (or booms) to handle carpet rolls, culvert, and coils; and barrel grabs to handle cylindrical objects. Employment of specialized attachments has greatly extended the use of the basic lift truck and has done much to justify its being called the "workhorse" of warehousing.

Checklist of 9 Types of Manual Carts and Trucks and Their Uses

☐ Two-wheel vertical truck

☐ Three-wheel tow truck

☐ Four-wheel platform trailer or truck

☐ Bin stock picker truck

☐ Bin stock picker truck with ladder

☐ Manual lift truck

☐ Two-wheel pallet, used with hand-lift jack

☐ Pallet rollers, dollies

☐ Wheelbarrow

A complete list of manual equipment for material handling would be almost endless. Apparently because this equipment is relatively cheap, an extremely large variety of items has been developed. Distributors and brokers for manual equipment manufacturers are good sources for such information. However, the problem of where to use manual equipment does seem appropriate for discussion here. Some illustrations are shown in Figure 9.3.

There seem to be two extremes with regard to the extent manual handling equipment is used in warehousing. At one extreme, many warehouses throughout the world still use only manual equipment. To acquire an electrical or gasoline-powered lift truck for these warehouses would be considered a quantum leap into automation. At the other extreme, many warehouses have only powered equipment. Regardless of the size load, it is moved by powered lift truck, conveyor, or crane. Warehouse workers even jump on lift trucks to ride from one part of the warehouse to another for lunch or coffee breaks rather than walk. These employees seem to have a compulsion for powered equipment. Their concept seems to be "anything that is work should be done by machine." Both extremes are wastefully wrong. It would be difficult to assess which practice, manual or machine, is being abused more. For health's sake a little more manual probably would be best.

There is definitely a place for manual equipment in modern warehousing. Many jobs can be accomplished faster and with less effort by using a manual cart or truck than they can be by using powered equipment. When the work to be performed is light and of low volume, there is a good chance it can be done more economically with manual tools. For instance, many order-picking operations can be performed more efficiently with the aid of manually pushed bin trucks than they can be with powered lift trucks and conveyors. Powered equipment costs more initially, it requires time to maintain, it involves higher operating and maintenance costs, and it generally takes up more space. Unless these limitations can be offset by the advantages of powered equipment, the work

FIGURE 9.3   Representative Types of Manually Powered Equipment

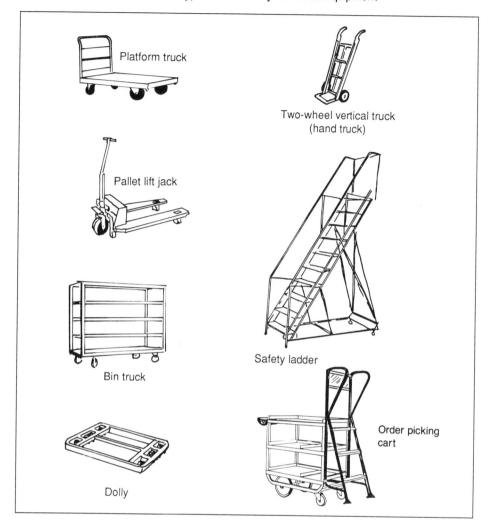

should be performed manually. Every function in warehousing should be considered first as a manual operation and then examined to see how much better it might be done with powered equipment. For some, like handling high storage, powered equipment is essential, but the test for doing manual should be given if only in fun. For example, "Perhaps monkeys could be trained to . . .".

Checklist of 17 Types of Conveyors and Their Uses

- ☐ Gravity power
- ☐ Motor power
- ☐ Air float
- ☐ Skate wheel
- ☐ Roller bearing
- ☐ Roller
- ☐ Belt

- □ Slat
- □ Screw
- □ Chain
- □ Oscillating
- □ Portable
- □ Fixed
- □ Horizontal
- □ Inclined
- □ Spiral
- □ Overhead

While lift trucks are the most common type of warehouse handling equipment, the second most common type is conveyors, at least for relatively small items. Cranes take second place for large objects. Conveyors are best used for high-volume items with a fairly constant flow along a fixed route. Most conveyor systems are tailored to fit the specific warehousing function they are intended to serve. There are, however, a few types that are standard and can be purchased as regular catalog items. These are mainly the portable variety and they find wide application in the loading and unloading operations. See Figure 9.4 for representative types of conveyors.

One characteristic of conveyors that has made them such a valuable tool for materials handling is that they are relatively easy to equip with automatic control devices. Automatic controls for sorting, squaring off, and weighing are frequently built into conveyor systems. Baggage handling at airline terminals and package handling in large postal centers make extensive use of automatic-sorting conveyor systems. Some warehouse operations that have a large volume of small shipments use similar systems. These, for example, may involve many spur conveyors that feed from individual packaging stations into a main conveyor line. An operator at a central control station on the main line reads the destination address of each package as it passes by. She or he programs the central control panel to activate "gates" and "traffic cops" that are located along the route of the conveyor which automatically divert the packages to their appropriate cumulating centers. These centers may be for the purpose of consolidating freight or for gathering items to make up multi-item orders, or the system may be used in the receiving operation to send commodities to different parts of the warehouse for storage.

An obvious improvement in such conveyor systems is to use bar coding to direct the packages to their particular destinations. This requires a very disciplined system as described in Chapter 13, but the benefits to be derived can be dramatic.

There are many different types of conveyors, and they can be installed in many different ways: in the floor, above the floor, suspended from overhead, inclined or spiraled from one floor to another, on truck beds, on elevator tables, and almost any other way material regularly moves. Conveyors can be gravity or motor powered, or a combination of both. When powered by gravity, a drop of about ½ inch per foot is suggested to keep the load in motion.

The power equipment depends on the type of conveyor, the loads to be moved, and the plane in which the load is to be moved. Steep inclines obviously require more power than do horizontal planes. In any case, the power requirements are generally less than is first expected by those not fully acquainted with powered conveyors. The high reduction ratio of gears used in these power

FIGURE 9.4 Representative Types of Conveyors

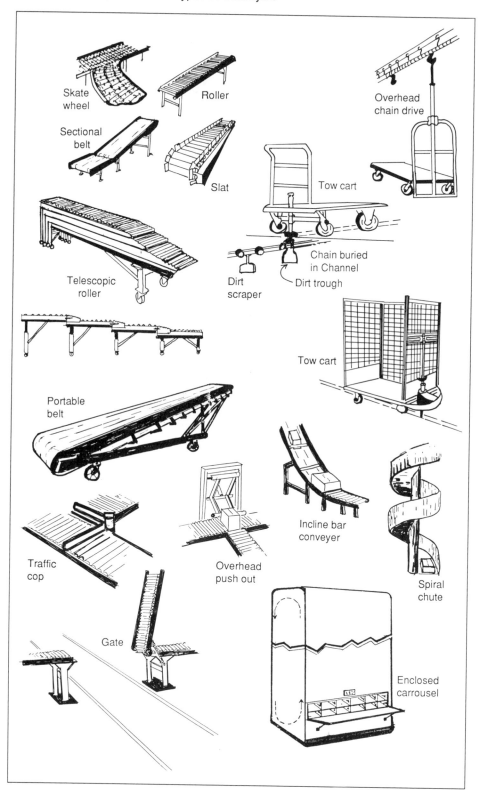

systems permits relatively low-horsepower motors to move large masses of merchandise.

Discussed next are the main types of conveyors used in warehousing; examples of applications are included.

Wheel Conveyor. Frequently referred to as a "skate wheel conveyor," this type has small steel or plastic wheels that turn on ball bearings or sleeves. (See Figure 9.4.) The spacing of the wheels is in an alternating pattern that is designed to support the load on three or more wheels at all times. This type of conveyor is laid horizontally, and loads are manually pushed along or they are declined and gravity powered. The conveyor line is built in standard straight and curved sections, from 5 to 20 feet long. Articles transferred on the wheel conveyor must have a flat, relatively smooth surface.

The gravity-powered wheel conveyor finds wide application in warehousing because of its versatility, its ready availability from suppliers in standard sizes, and its relatively low cost. Using standard lengths, it is a simple matter for a warehouse to construct its own conveyor system. Such a system can be very efficient in loading and unloading carriers when there is a large volume of small packaged items that are not unitized. The conveyor line can be put together or dismantled in a few minutes, yet it can save hours in the materials handling of a single shipment.

The gravity-powered wheel conveyor is also commonly used in highly sophisticated conveyor systems. Frequently, it is used in combination with motor-driven roller and belt conveyors. Part of almost any powered system can operate by the force of gravity. The articles being transported are moved up short inclines with powered conveyors and then move down long distances with less costly gravity-powered wheel conveyors. To provide motor power for the entire system is costly and generally not necessary.

Roller Conveyor. The roller conveyor is similar to the wheel conveyor, except that it is made up of rollers instead of wheels. (See Figure 9.4.) The diameter of the rolls, which extend across the full width of the conveyor, is generally between 1 and 3 inches. Like the wheel conveyor, it can be purchased in standard lengths and in straight and curved sections. It is frequently used in gravity-powered systems but can be motor powered.

An interesting application of the roller conveyor is its use in a two-part system for rapid mass loading and unloading of trucks. One part of the system consists of a large, powered roller conveyor the width and length of the bed of a truck. This conveyor is installed at the edge of the loading dock. Actually it extends beyond the edge about 2 feet to align with the edge of the truck bed. The other part of the system consists of a powered conveyor that covers, and is mounted to, the bed of the truck. Pallets of material are staged on the loading dock conveyor in the pattern in which they are to be carried in the truck. The truck backs up to the dock and aligns its conveyor with the dock conveyor. The two-part conveyor system is then activated, moving the load intact from the dock inside the truck. The conveyor inside the truck is locked and the load is secured for travel. Using this method, the entire truck can be loaded in a matter of a few minutes. The same method in reverse can be used to unload.

Belt, Slat, and Screw Conveyors. The names of these conveyors describe their design, which is based on the type of materials they are designed to move. (See Figure 9.4.) The belt conveyor consists of a continuous belt on which articles are transferred. It is probably the most versatile of all conveyors; it can be used to move sand, gravel, bags, small cartons, large packages, and almost any other materials. It can also be used to move several different types of materials on the same line at the same time. Belt conveyors also are made in portable motor-driven units that are useful in many warehousing operations. These units can be adjustable, so that they can be tilted to operate in progressively higher elevations, which is particularly handy when stacking long items in bulk or unloading such items vehicles that have been loaded in bulk.

The slat conveyor is used in place of the belt conveyor when the weight or mass of the articles to be moved requires a strong, rigid carrying surface. The slats are made of metal or wood and are connected to two lines of motor-driven chain.

The screw conveyor consists of a tube or trough in which a coarse screw rotates to push the material along. It is very effective in handling loose sand, gravel, grain, cement, and so on. The screw conveyor is an example of specialization to perform a specific function most effectively. Other conveyors of this nature include the chain, ribbon, and oscillating designs. These special-purpose conveyors find application more in the industries of food processing, mining, milling, and production than they do in general merchandise warehousing.

Checklist of 15 Types of Cranes and Their Uses

- ☐ Stacker
- ☐ Bridge
- ☐ Jib
- ☐ Gantry
- ☐ Truck mounted
- ☐ Trailer mounted
- ☐ Lift-truck attachment
- ☐ Monorail
- ☐ Portable
- ☐ Cab controlled
- ☐ Floor controlled
- ☐ Remote controlled
- ☐ Hand-chain hoist
- ☐ Gas-powered hoist
- ☐ Electric-powered hoist

Cranes, along with lift trucks and conveyors, constitute one of the three principal types of equipment for material handling in warehousing. Generally, lift trucks provide versatile handling from the floor surface. Conveyors provide fixed-route transfer at any elevation. Cranes provide versatile handling overhead. All three are important to warehouse operations, and each can perform certain types of material handling best.

The main advantage of some cranes is that they can operate quite independently of the warehouse floor. Aisles for maneuvering the equipment are not required as they are for lift trucks; materials can be transported over the top of floor working and storage areas. Their other very important advantage is that they can handle loads at high elevations with greater safety and with more efficiency, thus permitting better utilization of vertical warehouse space. Cranes may appropriately be given credit for adding the full benefits of the vertical dimension to warehousing.

A further advantage of cranes that really has nothing to do with height is their ability to handle unwieldy loads. Cranes are mounted on trucks, tractors, and even rail cars to make use of this unique feature. The purpose of these mobile cranes is to handle articles that cannot be handled by other means or that, if handled by lift truck or conveyor, would prove to be exceedingly awkward. Cranes have the unique ability to pick up and carry things from above. This ability makes them essential in certain warehousing operations.

There are many different types of cranes. They can be powered entirely manually or entirely by motor. Or they can move manually but use a motorized hoist. Or they can move by motor power but have a manual hoist. They can be designed to follow a fixed route or to serve a specific area, and they can be mobile, portable, or stationary. Discussed here are some of the main types of cranes used to serve modern warehousing. See Figure 9.5 for representative types of cranes.

Bridge Crane. The main characteristic of this crane is that it has a horizontal structure called a "bridge" spanning the storage and work area. (See Figure 9.5.) The bridge travels back and forth on wheels riding on rails that are secured to the roof support columns. A vertical hoist travels across the bridge on wheels riding on rails that are secured to the movable bridge structure. This arrangement enables an all-directional movement of materials over the area covered by the crane.

Bridge cranes can be entirely motorized, entirely manual, or a combination of motor and manual. The motorized cranes can be controlled from a cab suspended from the bridge or from the floor with a pendant pushbutton control box, or with electronic remote controls. The cab cranes permit the operator to have an overhead view of the entire storage and work area below, but they also have the disadvantage of keeping the operator from doing anything other than operating the crane. Of course when there is a lot of work to do, operating the crane is a full-time job requiring constant attention. The floor-controlled crane, while not as convenient for the operator, permits the operator to do the supporting work on the floor for the crane as well as to operate it. Many cab cranes have been converted to floor control in recent years to permit better utilization of personnel.

The main purpose of bridge cranes is to give complete overhead crane service to a large rectangular area. It makes possible the moving of items over the top of work and storage areas without regard to aisles. It permits very high utilization of floor space because aisleways can be as narrow as 2 feet, just wide enough to walk, and working areas do not have to include allowances for floor-based handling equipment.

Stacker Crane. More research and development work has been done in recent years on the stacker crane (Figure 9.5) than on any other type of warehouse equipment. Apparently, this is because the stacker crane has been recognized for its advantages in providing very efficient storage at high levels with minimum loss of aisle space and with a relatively high degree of safety. It does not have the versatility of a forklift, but for the one function of storing at high levels in a limited area, it is generally acknowledged to be superior. Many warehousing companies are now using stacker cranes to attain greater space utilization.

The first stacker cranes were made by securing the combination of a rigid vertical mast and a turntable to a conventional overhead bridge crane. A turntable, which permitted the mast to turn 360 degrees, was built into the bed of the trolley. A load-carrying carriage was attached to the hoist that rode up and down the rigid mast. The crane was operated by an operator who walked beside the mast with a pushbutton control box. This arrangement permitted the crane

FIGURE 9.5 Representative Types of Cranes

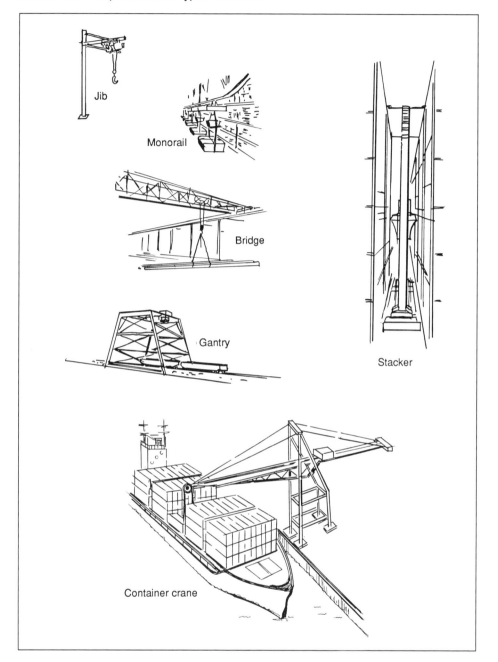

to be used much like a lift truck. A fork attachment on the carriage would raise and lower loads in the same way that a fork and mast arrangement works on a lift truck. The advantage of the stacker crane, however, was that it required much less aisle width. The aisles needed to be only the depth of the load plus the carriage and clearance. For a 48-inch pallet, the aisle could be less than 6 feet, leaving ample clearance on both sides of the load. The result was a reduction of aisle widths by up to 50 percent. Few equipment innovations for material handling have been so dramatic.

The first major improvement in the stacker crane idea was to attach a cab, with the controls in it, to the carriage, so that the operator could ride with the load. The cab was put beside the carriage so that little or no additional width was added to the unit. This arrangement permitted the operator to be always close to the load. No longer was time lost while the operator slowly positioned the loads at heights far above. The operator could now ride up and down with the load, remaining close enough to see it clearly at all times. Even more important, the operator was safely away from the load in case it should accidentally topple. The safety hazard of the stacker crane was greatly reduced when the operator was able to ride with the load rather than direct it from below.

The second innovative attempt was to suspend a much lighter crane from a bridge running on rails attached to the top of the storage racks, usually one crane for each aisle or a means of transferring a crane between aisles. This means served fine for installations involving relatively light loads.

The next big improvement was to support the crane from a steel rail or pair of rails attached to the floor and a rail or pair of rails suspended from the superstructure of the roof system to steady the crane. This innovation largely got away from vibrating the racks and cost less than a comparatively heavy bridge suspended from the building columns along a bay or having the racks support rails on which the bridge travels.

The last big improvement in the stacker crane concept was to design a complete handling and storing process that combined racks and crane and computer control into one complementary handling and storing system. This constituted a giant step toward the now-famous automatic storage and retrieval system, ASRS, which is discussed in some detail in Chapter 11.

Other Cranes. While the bridge crane is the most versatile of all overhead cranes, there are other types of cranes that are designed to do certain things with the high efficiency that only specialization will give. (See Figure 9.5.)

Gantry cranes are like bridge cranes except that the structure that supports the bridge and hoist rests on wheels that travel over steel rails secured to the floor or ground. The entire structure moves along a fixed route. Gantry cranes are generally used for outdoor movement of materials and are frequently found at wharves, railroad yards, metal storage yards, and terminals that process heavy commodities.

The jib crane consists of a hoist that travels along a free-swinging arm called a jib. The pivotal part of the jib can be mounted to a column of a building, to a freestanding column, or to a mobile piece of equipment. The jib crane is used where the material handling function is limited to a relatively small and defined area. The area served can be described as an arc or circle whose radius is the length of the jib. Jib cranes are used in warehousing to transfer cargo from gondola or flat cars to the dock and to move loads from the fixed route of one crane to the fixed route of another. The jib crane provides a means of interfacing two fixed-route crane systems.

Monorail cranes consist basically of an "I" beam suspended from overhead and a hoist that has wheels which ride on top of the lower horizontal part of the beam. The crane gets its name from the monorail that provides the track to support and guide the hoist. These cranes are made in a great variety of shapes and sizes and for many different purposes. In fact, there is a difference of opinion among material handling authorities as to whether the monorail system should be classified as a crane or as a conveyor, or whether it is really separate, neither one nor the other. For warehouse management, it is not very important which family of equipment it belongs to. The important thing is to understand how a monorail system works and how to apply it to warehouse operations.

The Carousel and Its Use

The carousel is one of the most ingenious material handling devices ever invented yet so very little is made of it in warehousing or production. Dry-cleaning stores have been using it for ages. The position is recorded on the copy of the receipt retained by the store—or the clothes are hung in strict alphabetic order. When the customer comes back for the cleaned clothes, the clerk punches the proper location designation and the carousel moves around until the right clothes are at his or her fingertips. (See Figure 9.4.)

The carousel has a lot going for it because it is reliable, simple, and highly efficient. The density of storage is exceptionally high, and often it can be put in the least desirable space such as overhead, as in the dry-cleaning stores. Further it has the big advantage of bringing the inventory to the order picker instead of the order picker traveling to the inventory.

Pneumatic Tube System and Its Uses

Like the carousel, it is surprising, at least to me, that more has not been done with pneumatic tube systems in warehousing and production. (See Figure 9.6.) I have designed it into warehouses to link sales officers to the warehouse office and from there to operations supervisors' workstations in the warehouse. It is a great way to move paperwork, but as I have learned, it can do a lot more than that.

I had the good fortune to visit a huge repair and maintenance facility consisting of many buildings scattered across the landscape. From a central ASRS for small parts, pneumatic tubes linked various workstations and buildings throughout the complex. Robot material movers and tow carts that hooked to a buried chain moved the large parts and small parts in large quantity. Small parts in small quantities moved via an extensive pneumatic tube system.

In this case the canisters that carried the parts were all the same size, about 10 inches diameter and a foot long. An order received at the ASRS workstation was picked, packed, coded and put into the canister, and transported to a outlying building workstation in something less than 5 minutes.

The worker who took things from the ASRS and sent them on the pneumatic way said of the system. "We love it. You should have seen it around here before. I hated to come to work."

Pneumatic tube systems can theoretically be made in any size. Certainly lengths to several feet and diameters to a few feet are within present technology, though its application in rapid, reliable, and economical moving of materials seems relatively undeveloped.

Pneumatic tube systems are not applicable to all material movement, but where they are, a real breakthrough is possible in reducing transfer time and improving reliability. This translates to lower inventories along with reduced handling and storing costs. This is quite a lot for a system that is as old as pneumatics and one that most people still think of as a paperwork mover.

Air Float System (Floating on Air) and Its Uses

A revolution underway in the short-distance material handling of heavy objects is rapidly taking over the movement of things in the heavy-weight class, say, from 20,000 to 300,000 pounds, and it is only a matter of time until it is common in warehousing. Loads of up to 300,000 pounds are floated on a thin film of air generally with an air pressure of from 10 to 50 pounds per square inch. (See Figure 9.6.)

FIGURE 9.6 Air Powered Material Movers

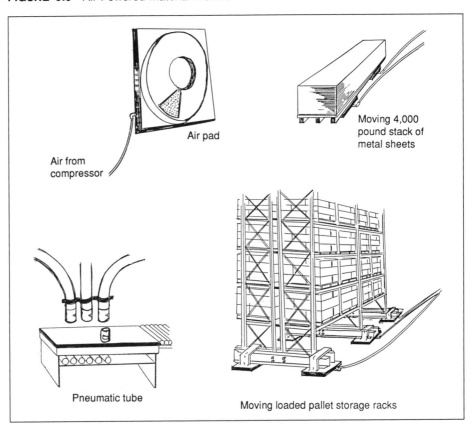

To operate, a solid frame, say, 2 inches high and 2 feet wide is made of sheet metal. A coupling is put on one side to an attached air hose leading from a small air compressor, portable or stationary. The sides and top are securely sealed. The bottom, however, has many little holes through which the air escapes at a paltry 10 to 50 psi (pounds per square inch). When the air compressor is turned on, the air streams out the many little holes against a hard, flat, smooth surface, usually the floor. The sheet metal frame raises about ¼ inch.

Let us assume there is a 1,000-pound object resting on top the frame. No strain. The frame lifts the object as though it were not there—or probably more like it was as light as a feather. Through controlled testing it has been established that a horizontal push of 1 pound will move 1,000 pounds so elevated. A 100-pound push will move a 100,000-pound load and so on. It is claimed that applying the same principle there is no limit to the weight and size that can be so lifted and moved.

There have been modifications of the float system for improvements. Plastic casters fitted into the bottom of the metal frame to hold and provide the air streams are now used. For the heavy-weight versions of the float, oil seems to be better than air.

The float system requires a smooth surface against which the air (or oil) streams push. If the floor has pit holes and cracks, the air under the object being lifted will escape, reducing or stopping the lift. This is remedied by laying a flat sturdy metal sheet along the line of travel. Use of epoxy to fill in the pit holes and cracks has, it is reported, also met with success.

Three of the primary advantages of the system other than its miraculous lifting power are these:

1. Often the costs are a small fraction of the alternatives. They are not even in the same range of magnitude.
2. Often an object can be set up and moved by the time a crane or high-capacity lift truck can be brought in to do the job.
3. The float permits turning the object around, or moving it back and forth in any direction in the horizontal plane. It is ideally suited as a turntable for large airplanes and boats.

One of the uses of the air float system that enables warehousing to do that which was not practical before is to move fully assembled and loaded storage racks as illustrated in Figure 9.6.

A common need in warehousing is to move pallet or cantilever racks to provide narrower or occasionally wider aisles. This arises because a warehouse acquires narrow-aisle material handling equipment and must move the racks closer to achieve its objective of functional narrow aisles. Or the warehouse is required to open aisles farther to accommodate larger units of inventory. The usual practice is to unload the racks, store the material somewhere else in the meantime, disassemble the racks, reassemble them in the new position, and restock them. Depending on the size project this could take days to weeks of hard work.

An air float system can make the move of fully loaded racks in a fraction of that time. For pallet racks, steel beams are horizontally attached to the upright columns just high enough to allow an air float to be inserted at each end of the beams. The floats are activated. The racks float and are manually pushed to the new location, the air is turned off, pads and horizontal lifting beams removed, and the fully loaded racks are ready for use. The same process is used for cantilever racks except in this case since there is already cross beams at the base of the racks, these can be elevated with a lift truck, or if too heavy for this a jack. The air float pads are inserted and the same process is followed as for the pallet racks. There are, or if not there should be, companies that specialized in offering this storage-rack moving services to warehouses. The horizontal lifting beams are the only specialized equipment. The float pads for this can be used over and over again for this type or other moving chores.

Another use of the air float system is for conveyors. This is particularly advantageous for very fragile merchandise. The articles can glide along on self air-generating pads or the bed of the conveyor can be so constructed to have the air jets flow up against the bottom of the article being transported.

Since the usual conveyors are already efficient the air float type are not causing a revolutionary change over but the new air technology offers a viable alternative in special circumstances.

Air Float Pallet Mover and Its Use

The remarkable air float system is available in the design of a special pallet mover (see Figure 9.6), special because the pallets (more appropriately called skids) and the mover are designed to function together. The clearance between the top of the mover and the bottom side of the skid platform must be close enough so that the small rise of the mover when activated will be enough elevated the skid.

The air float device has a means to move it in any direction built into the bottom of the frame between the air pads. When the air lift is activated, the mover mechanism engages the floor surface with a small, electric motor-driven hard-tire wheel that can turn 360 degrees and moves the combined unit in any direction.

A control panel is situated at a convenient level for the operator who walks behind it. The electrical source is a cable that plugs into an electrical outlet. Some units carry their own power supply. The air float skidmover is not intended to compete with the conventional low-boys discussed a few pages further on. It is quite enough for it to turn the previous, horrendously difficult tasks of moving almost immovable objects with gigantic gantry or overhead cranes into a task performed in comparative leisure with a contraption that probably costs less than a second-hand lift truck. That is real technological progress at its best—levitating the heaviest objects with a few psi's of *air* and moving them through frictionless space. Could this be the process used by the ancients to levitate and move the monoliths of Stonehenge, and of the Inca and Egyptian cultures? Seems the combination of a simple system of bellows, tubes, and air bladders made from parts of the local flora and fauna—with a hearty but solemn incantation or two, might very well have been how these long pondered, astonishing things were actually accomplished. What do you think?

Vacuum and Magnetic Hoists and Their Uses

Many inventory items can be lifted and moved better by vacuum or magnetism than by forks, hooks, or slings. A vacuum pad or an electrical magnet is hung from the hoist of a crane with a simple on and off switch. The holding device is hung from an overhead crane to provide coverage of a large area or from a jib crane providing a relatively small arc of coverage.

A big advantage of a magnet used with an overhead crane is that an operator in a cab can operate without another worker on the floor to position the forks or slings to lift the material. Simply putting the magnet over the material and turning on the switch does it. The limitation of the magnet is, of course, that the material to be moved must be magnetic; this means it can be used to move only iron and steel merchandise.

The vacuum lifts are usually confined to jib cranes where the source of the vacuum, compressor, can remain fixed and the arc of the arm of the crane limits the access area. A particularly good application of this combination is to remove individual sheets of metal from a stack of sheets. When the sheets are very thin, not rigid, or large, say, over 8 feet, several vacuum cups in tandem on one arm are used.

Floor-Operated Material Movers and Their Use

A good companion to fork lifts and cranes is the floor-operated platform merchandise movers often referred to as "low boys." There are many variations: short, long, with platform to slip under long skids, forks to move pallets, operator ride or walk behind, and low and high capacity. The lift power is by electric motor, infrequently by gas, or manual power aided by hydraulics and leverage.

One common application of low boys is their use in loading and unloading carriers where lifting of only a few inches is required. Yet they are highly maneuverable and capable of moving pallets or skids across the dock to or from staging and the carrier in the same and often less total time than with a lift truck.

Representative Types of Dock Levelers and Their Uses

There are two types of dock levelers, nonmechanical and mechanical. (See Figure 9.7.) The purpose of both is to provide a bridge from the edge of the

FIGURE 9.7   Representative Types of Dock Levelers

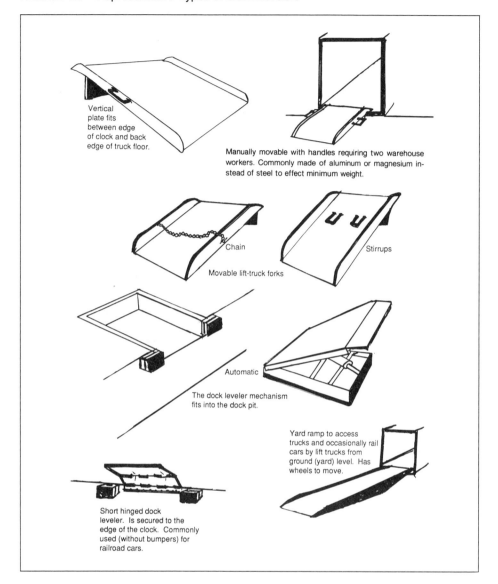

Vertical plate fits between edge of clock and back edge of truck floor.

Manually movable with handles requiring two warehouse workers. Commonly made of aluminum or magnesium instead of steel to effect minimum weight.

Chain

Stirrups

Movable lift-truck forks

Automatic

The dock leveler mechanism fits into the dock pit.

Yard ramp to access trucks and occasionally rail cars by lift trucks from ground (yard) level. Has wheels to move.

Short hinged dock leveler. Is secured to the edge of the clock. Commonly used (without bumpers) for railroad cars.

warehouse floor to the bed of a carrier—a container, truck, or rail car. The nonmechanical type is portable and is moved into place either manually or with a lift truck or crane. The larger dock plates, which are intended to be moved with the aid of equipment, have stirrups or chain to use in picking them up by lift truck or crane.

Nonmechanical dock plates cost less initially, but they are not as efficient as the mechanical plates. The nonmechanical kind are made of aluminum, magnesium, or steel. The mechanical kind are generally made only of steel. All nonmechanical dock plates should have a safety lip or pin arrangement that fits against the side of the carrier or dock or both to prevent slippage. Nonmechanical dock plates generally have a very long, useful life, and they rarely need repairs.

Mechanical dock plates are far more efficient to use, but their initial cost is greater and their maintenance cost is much higher—so high that maintenance cost is an important factor. Because of the heavy abuse a dock plate must take, particularly from trucks ramming into it, repairs are not uncommon. Some automatic dock plates are designed to withstand this punishment better than others. Also, some can be repaired more easily than others. If ever it is necessary to change from one type of automatic dock plate to another, the change can be very expensive. Automatic dock plates are normally set into specially designed concrete pits that are recessed into the dock. A change in plate design could require a change in pit dimensions that can be quite expensive.

Another caution regarding automatic dock plates is that the length and width of the plate are important. Too narrow a plate will restrict the turning radius of the lift truck. Too short a plate could cause too steep an incline for the lift truck to travel safely. A thorough investigation should be made before purchasing any automatic dock plate.

Mechanical Tractor-Train and Carts and Their Characteristics

The basic tractor-train used for transporting materials in warehousing consists of a powered tractor and a set of four-wheel carts that are equipped with front and rear coupling devices. When the tractor and carts are linked together, they form a train, similar to a small railroad train. The tractor-train may run on steel tracks or use rubber wheels and be free to maneuver throughout the warehousing area. The tractor provides the moving power for many carts. Orders are staged on the carts in the order-picking areas and are taken to the shipping area by the tractor, or the carts are loaded at the receiving area and delivered by the tractor to their respective points of storage. Tractor-trains are particularly effective in large warehousing operations involving many different order-picking and storage areas. Under certain conditions an operator driving a tractor-train has a transportation capacity equivalent to that of several lift trucks; thus, a significant savings is achieved in both labor and the cost of equipment.

An important improvement in the tractor-train concept is the use of driverless carts. Each cart is equipped with a mechanical device that grasps a drag chain laid in the floor. (See Figure 9.4.) The chain is laid in a prescribed path throughout the warehouse. Along the path, signal contacts can be fixed that will cause the cart to stop, and even to blow a horn to call attention. After the load is removed or a new load is put on, a start mechanism is engaged, and the cart goes on its way. Sidings can be added to the circuit path that accept carts for later handling.

Robot Material Mover and Its Uses

The robot mover is similar to the drag-chain cart just discussed but is electronically guided and fully automated. It is commonly referred to as an AGV, automated guidance vehicle. (See Figure 11.1.) It has its own battery power and its own electronics that interface with a host computer. It operates according to its unique instructions independent of its fellow robots. A network of wires buried in the floor and computer-programmed instructions provide the robot the most efficient routing, including the pickup and delivery functions—all without human intervention.

These robots are bidirectional, which enables them to enter a dead-end spur, pick up or deposit a load, reverse direction, and return to the main guide path. With the help of a host computer, they follow the most efficient route from where they are to where instructed to go. They will move off the main line onto a siding to let robots with higher-priority loads pass and then resume their journey. This feature, along with the one of picking up and depositing while shunted off on a spur, goes a long way to avoid traffic congestion. The host computer monitors all the robots in the system by continuous communications with each vehicle.

If it is necessary to remove a robot from the system an operator can plug in a hand-held set of controls that permits manually steering the robot to any location away from the guide path.

The method used to pick up and deposit loads is nothing short of ingenious and particularly so due to its simplicity. At locations along the main guide path, there are sidings with a fixture to suspend the load just above the lowered height of the robot's lifting mechanism. The robot moves between the sides of the fixture that suspends the load. After slight automatic positioning to assure correct alignment, the robot hydraulically lifts the load to clear the holding fixture and starts on its way to where it is to deposit the load in reverse sequence. Figure 11.1 also illustrates this. The robot can return empty to pick up another load, pick up a nearby load to make a productive back haul, or do whatever it is signaled to do.

Should the robot meet another robot or other material handling vehicle so equipped at an intersection, each can sense the other coming. With impulses back to the computer, the question is answered who has the right-of-way. One is instructed to stop, to yield the right-of-way to the other. When the one with higher priority passes, the other resumes its journey.

Following are suggested applications of these robot material movers in warehousing. It is assumed at each load or unload station, there is a conveyorized means of accumulating unit loads.

- Take loads from receiving to storage or directly to shipping if orders are awaiting the particular materials.
- Take loads from storage to the appropriate staging area for shipping—or if the warehouse is a part of a production facility, directly to the workstation where the material will be used.
- Take loads from manufacturing to storage in warehouse—or to shipping if orders are waiting.
- Take loads from receiving or storing through a weigh-count station to verify quantity and right SKU before shipping.
- Take loads from receiving through a square-up station to assure loads are ready to put into storage.

PROS AND CONS OF BUYING USED MATERIAL HANDLING EQUIPMENT

Buying used material handling equipment is a viable alternative to buying new. It has the indisputable advantage of costing less. This alone is enough to cause it to be the best value acquisition for many applications. It has its limitations, but unlike the purchase of used storing equipment discussed in the next chapter, these are more obvious and more easily dealt with. Because of this the company seeking to acquire handling equipment has a big market from which to choose. And the company no longer needing it has a easier time selling it. This is one reason why the difference in price of used and new material handling equipment is generally not as great as the potential buyer might expect or hope for. In addition, style is not an important factor, except in the case of how high a lift truck can reach, but this is not so important because there are many applications for lift trucks that do not require high reach.

Another reason for the narrow price spread between new and used is that the operating condition is fairly easy to check; therefore, the used equipment offered is more likely to be in good working order. A lift truck maintenance professional can usually make a valid appraisal of the condition and should be used for checking out other used handling equipment as well before a deal is made.

Oh, yes, there is one more characteristic about powered warehouse equipment that should be mentioned. Companies that make and sell lift trucks in particular do not leave much room for negotiation. At least that has been my experience. To get 5 percent off on purchase of one lift truck is pretty good. Getting 10 percent off on three to five lift trucks bought at a time is very good. Buying many more at a time will probably get even a better price, but not much better than 15 percent, and I'm not certain of that. At least I have not witnessed better.

There are many used handling equipment dealers and this is often all they sell. Also new lift truck outlets usually deal in used equipment as well. This is definitely a source that should be checked before actual purchase is made. Too, they will probably accept as trade-in any similar handling equipment that the new equipment will surplus.

10

Storage Techniques for Reducing Space Costs, Material Handling Costs, and Product Damage

CHAPTER HIGHLIGHTS

This chapter concerns the storing techniques and equipment that are best for virtually all warehousing situations. Appropriate specifications of the equipment for the specific job to be done are also given, though this information is not intended to supplant an engineering evaluation or the suppliers' role in this process.

The focus here is on how storage techniques interface with material handling; how to unitize pallet, skid, slip-sheet, and clamp loads; and why it is best to determine first what will be stored then determine the best way to store it.

Numerous techniques exist for storing inventories, some of which are better than others. The most common and the best one by far is storing in bulk if conditions permit. For purposes here bulk storage refers to stacking one unit load on top another and another until a limit is reached. The limit can be any of the following:

○ Height lift truck can reach
○ Weight of top load too heavy for bottom load to support
○ Height of the roof trusses and the clearance required
○ Height of the fire extinguishing heads and the clearance required
○ The amount of inventory carried not being large enough to benefit from bulk storage

The only equipment used for bulk storage are pallets and skids, and these are regularly used with storage racks as well. First we consider the storage techniques made possible with different types of storage racks including how to determine their specifications. Next we consider the most common pallets and skids, followed by how to unitize loads for storing in bulk or in racks.

TYPES OF PALLETS AND SKIDS AND HOW TO USE THEM TO BEST ADVANTAGE

Pallets and Skids

There exists some confusion in both production and warehousing over the difference between a pallet and a skid. (See Figure 10.1.) Some use the terms interchangeably; others seem quite clear about the differences. A comparison of warehouse personnel from various geographic areas confirms that there is little agreement on standard terminology. The following are my definitions:

Pallet: An elevated platform used for transporting and storing articles. It is designed to permit vertical stacking of one pallet load on another, and used for several to many store keeping units that are characteristically similar, with a flat surface top and bottom.

Skid: A set of legs or runners used in combination with a platform and possibly a set of wheels to elevate and to transport materials. It is custom designed specifically for products whose characteristics are not compatible with standard pallets. Skids are not designed to be stackable, one skid load on another.

Because there are so many different kinds of pallets and skids, certain types of one can closely resemble certain types of the other. The one type of pallet most often called a skid is the single-faced pallet. It consists of two or three runners attached to a platform. So far this description fits both a pallet and a skid; however, if the runners are constructed and spaced to permit tiering, the unit is a pallet. If the purpose of the runners is only to elevate for moving it, the unit is a skid.

Double-Faced Pallet. The double-faced pallet is the most familiar of all pallets used in warehousing. It consists of two or three runners, generally 2 by 4's

FIGURE 10.1   Representative Pallets and Skids

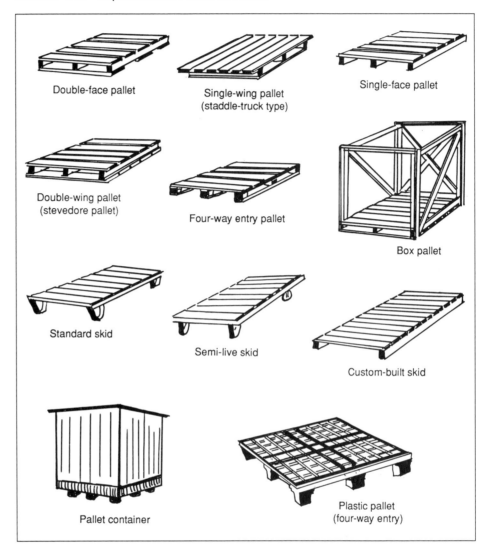

or 3 by 4's attached to an upper and lower deck, generally made up of 1- by 4-inch or 1- by 6-inch boards. The runners provide openings of a suitable size for the forks of a lift truck to enter between the decks. The upper and lower decks provide the necessary surfaces to store one palletized load on another to obtain better utilization of vertical space.

Single-Faced Pallet.   The single-faced pallet consists of two or three runners attached to an upper deck. It does not have a lower deck. This design costs less than the double-faced kind, but it is restricted when used for tier stacking to even and solid loads that will support the concentrated pressure of the runners of the unit load above.

Four-Way Pallet.   The four-way entry pallet is designed to permit forks to enter at any of its four sides. This is accomplished by using short supports, generally 4- by 4-inch blocks, in place of the full-length runners that are used with the standard two-way entry pallets. The four-way entry can also be achieved by notching the regular runners to allow the forks to enter. This kind of pallet provides greater handling and storing flexibility since it can be picked up from any side.

Standard Skid.   This is designed for general purpose floor use, not for stacking one load on another. Usually the legs and frame are made of steel with a deck of hard wood. They are designed to take many years of hard use and abuse.

Semilive Skid.   This is designed the same as the standard skid except it has two rugged wheels that replace one set of legs. The wheels provide easier maneuverability for manually moving the unit. It is designed to be handled with a lift truck and crane, or manually pushed on the floor.

Single-Wing Pallet.   This is like a single-faced pallet except it has wings. It is used with an overhead crane and sling. The sling fits under the two wings. Its most common use in warehousing is with narrow-aisle straddle trucks. The extended arms and wheels of this type truck slip under the pallet wings, straddling the runners and elevation is accomplished by lifting pressure of the forks against the wings.

Double-Wing Pallet.   This design is also referred to as the stevedore pallet. Its design also permits crane and sling handling. It is constructed like the double-faced pallet except for its wings, which are necessary for sling handling.

Box Pallet.   This design is constructed with a superstructure to protect the product being carried and stored from damage and to support pallets above. Tier racks provide the same functions, but if the structure is not returned after shipment, the box costs considerably less than a metal tier rack.

Custom-Built Skid.   Skids are custom built for specific product configurations. While pallets are usually confined to rectangular dimensions that range between 2 and 5 feet and a height of between 4 and 7 inches, skids can be almost any size. For example, some skids used for metal roofing sheet will be over 20 feet long. They can be made in any shape that enables the load to be elevated for transport.

TYPES OF STORAGE RACKS AND REQUIREMENTS FOR STORING EQUIPMENT

The storing equipment is often as important to the total cost and success of warehouse operations as is the handling equipment, though companies generally give more attention to the way their inventories will be handled than to the way they will be stored. Management will spend considerable time on what type of lift trucks, conveyors, and cranes to buy; they will even bring in equipment specialists to give them expert advice on handling equipment. But they will hold back on storage racks to "see how things develop" or "see if racks are really needed."

This off-handed approach to racks may stem from the fact that the need for handling equipment is much more obvious than is the need for storing equipment. For example, it is obvious even to the casual observer that some type of handling equipment is necessary to warehouse, say, 1,000-pound motors. It is also just as clear that it is necessary to have floor space on which to store them. It is not as obvious that storage racks are needed. The motors can always be stored side by side, one high, on the floor. Yet, if the situation were analyzed, it might well be found that the cost of the extra floor space to store the motors one high would be much greater than the amortized cost of handling equipment.

Some accounting systems unfortunately contribute to the error of ignoring space costs. The systems will provide for collecting and issuing cost data on labor, supplies, and equipment operation but leave out the cost of space. A common reason given for this is that "space doesn't cost us anything; we own the building." This is wrong, and it displays a lack of common sense in one's approach to accounting.

At the very minimum, space is worth the amount for which it could be leased, and this amount annually is somewhere in the neighborhood of 10 percent of its replacement cost. For example, warehouse facilities that cost $40.00 per square foot generally lease for about $4.00 per square foot per year.

While better utilization of space is probably the primary reason for storage racks, there are two other very important reasons. These are to improve handling efficiency and to avoid material damage. In some warehousing situations either of these reasons may be more important than better utilization of space. In any evaluation of storage racks, it is important to give consideration to all three factors: utilization of space, efficiency in handling, and material damage. In some cases, all three factors will be favorably affected, in others it is possible that only one or two will be positively affected, while the other will be negatively affected. For instance, there are many times when some handling efficiency must be sacrificed for more significant savings in space or reduction of material damage. Decisions regarding storage equipment should be based on the net improvement to the warehouse operation. And net improvement must take into consideration less tangible essentials such as customer service and worker safety. The most efficient low-cost warehouse is to no avail if it gives poor service or is a dangerous place to work. This is where the concept of quality comes in. Quality encompasses all these performance measures.

The main types of storage racks used in warehousing are discussed here, and representative types are illustrated in Figure 10.2.

Pallet Racks

Pallet racks get their name from their main purpose, which is to hold pallet loads of material. The racks consist of upright columns, load-supporting arms (bars, or beams), and horizontal and diagonal bracing. Pallets span the front and back arms with a few inches of overhang for safety.

The length of pallet arms is based on (1) the width of pallets used, (2) the number of pallets per section or bay, (3) the clearance left around the pallets for maneuvering, and (4) the combined weight of the pallet loads. If weight could be ignored, the most efficient and least expensive pallet racks would be those with the longest arms. There would be fewer uprights to interfere with pallet placement, and less money would be invested in the uprights, whose only purpose is to support the arms that support the loads. The weight of the materials to be stored, however, cannot be ignored. On the contrary, the design and structural material used in the fabricating of the racks, as well as the spacing of the uprights, are all directly related to the weight put in the racks. Load capacity can be increased by using stronger structural material or better rack design, or by reducing the width between the uprights which reduces the length of the load-bearing arms.

Pallet racks are available in standard and custom sizes from many different suppliers, and each supplier generally has its own patented designs. Some

FIGURE 10.2   Representative Types of Storage Racks

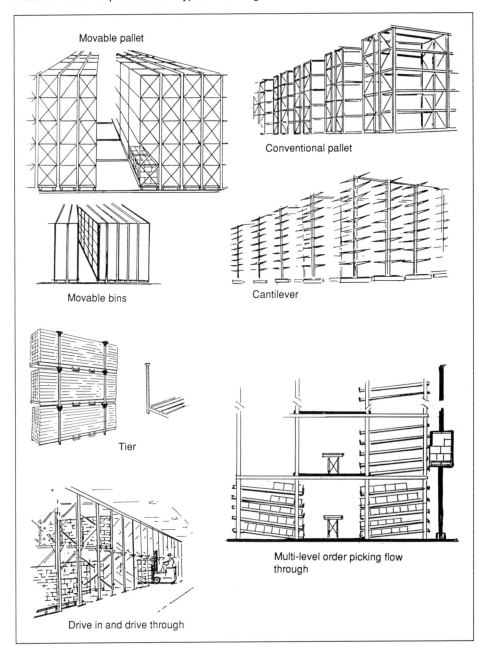

racks are designed so that they can be erected by warehouse workers very quickly. Other racks require considerable time and effort to put together, and may require special tools and special mechanical skills. Warehouse management should compare not only the purchase price of different storage racks but also the cost of erecting them.

A particularly desirable feature of some rack designs is adjustable arms. They are constructed so that the arms can be fitted into position or dismantled with relative ease. There are no nuts and bolts to remove or welds to break. This feature is achieved by slots in either the arms or the uprights and protruding lips or buttons on the other member. Also, an extra, specially designed, wedge is sometimes used to assure the interlocking connection. Adjustable arms permit changing rack openings to accommodate changing product mix. They also allow for quick disassembly to permit moving the rack to another location when necessary.

Pallet racks are not restricted to storing only pallets. They are just as effective for skids or any commodity that has a supporting surface that will span the two arms. In addition, pallet racks can be used effectively for slip-sheet and clamp unitized loads by decking over the two arms with plywood or sheet steel. Some arm designs provide an inset to accommodate the decking materials.

Use of pallet racks for bin or shelf storage is occasionally appropriate for low-volume order picking that involves one to several cases of an item per shipment. Restocking of the shelves can be accomplished manually by transferring the cases, one at a time, from pallet loads. When setting up racks for this purpose, aisle widths need be only the width of the lift truck, or other material handling device, plus operating clearance of 1 to 2 feet. There is no need to allow room for turning radius, as would be necessary if the handling were in full pallet loads. The shelves will be stocked and picked by hand, and equipment will never have to turn into the racks to deposit a pallet; therefore, no space should be allowed for this maneuver. But this constitutes a flagrant waste of labor and should only be considered when labor is the least cost of the three components—space, equipment, and labor—which is not normally the case in the United States. Better by far is to use a lift truck equipped with turret forks that deposit or retrieve the loads at 90 degrees, perpendicular to the travel direction of the lift truck or employ an operator-up, narrow-aisle, order-picking lift truck. Better still is to use the turret lift truck to stock the racks and the operator-up lift truck to order pick. This combination permits optimum advantage of both the operator-up and the turret lift trucks. These types of equipment are discussed and illustrated later in this chapter.

Cantilever Racks

Cantilever racks get their name from the leverage technique used to support the load-bearing arms, which is "cantilever" and which means "supported at one end." (See Figure 10.2.) The racks consist of a row of single upright columns, spaced several feet apart, with arms extending from one or both sides of the uprights to form supports for storage. The base of the upright rests on the floor and keeps the racks from toppling forward or backward. Horizontal and diagonal bracing between uprights keeps the racks from toppling left or right.

The important advantage of cantilever racks is that they provide long, unobstructed storage support with no uprights to restrict the use of horizontal space. The arms can be covered with a decking of wood or metal, or if the articles to be stored are long and sturdy enough, they can be supported by spanning two or more arms, in which case decking is not needed. Cantilever racks permit the storage of a large variety of shapes and sizes. They are particularly efficient for commodities of long configuration such as sofas, rugs, rod, bar, pipe, and sheet. The racks can be purchased with adjustable arms that have the same advantages for these as discussed before for pallet racks.

Probably the improvements in design and the general use of cantilever racks have been more in modern warehousing than any other type of storage racks. Not too many years ago, cantilever racks were known to only a few warehouse workers, and to these, they were known only as specialized racks for a particular kind of storage and for a limited number of products. However, with the trend toward increased space utilization, and reduced material handling time, the cantilever racks have become common to many warehouse operations. Their big advantage of not requiring upright frames that obstruct handling and storing permits them to compete favorably with other types of racks for storage of many kinds of commodities.

One type of warehousing that cantilever racks have a demonstrated superiority is in storing a variety of furniture in huge mass merchandising in warehouse-store outlets. With side-load lift trucks the aisles can be kept narrow, moving long loads down the aisles sideways. Then the varied length loads are put into decked cantilever racks. The one storage feature that can be counted on in many lines of furniture is that the configurations will vary to extremes. This is the condition that takes best advantage of cantilever racks that have no vertical obstructions and arms that are comparatively easy to adjust.

Bin Racks

Bin racks, used for a wide variety of products, are available from suppliers in many different designs. (See Figure 10.2.) In appearance and use they are very much like decked pallet racks except for their size. They are generally less than 30 inches deep and are not higher than a person can reach, about 7 feet. The shallow depth, however, is a more constant characteristic than height, since shelves less than 30 inches deep could extend to any height and still be considered bin racks. The low 7-foot-high type of rack is most often used for rapid order picking of small items by workers operating at floor level.

Bin racks are generally made with solid decking. They should also include solid sides and back, and a 2- or 3-inch lip in front, if the articles to be stored in them are of a shape that do not stack securely and may spill out and onto the floor. The shelves of the racks should, when possible, be made adjustable so that the openings can be enlarged or reduced as needed. In addition, the racks should be easy to assemble with no, or the least number of, screws, nuts, and bolts. Some bin racks, like pallet racks, are constructed so that they simply snap together without any additional fastening devices. They can be readily assembled or disassembled with a minimum of labor. Racks that have permanently welded shelves should be acquired with caution, since most warehousing racks are moved several times during their lifetimes and have cause for adjustment far more often.

Typical products stored in bin racks are stationery, small hardware, medical supplies, small tools, and electronic parts, especially when these items are shipped in less than case lots or when the cases are very small—say, under 500 cubic inches. There are a variety of dividers, drawers, and trays that can be used with bin racks to keep the small items segregated, protected, and to improve the utilization of space.

Most warehouses have some inventory that is appropriately stored in bin racks and if this is not a significant amount and turnover is slow they just may constitute the best means available. If possible they should be put in an area where the overhead space is not wasted. The cost of using such bins when they prevent using the space above them gets to be very expensive storage.

A variation of the bin storage is a system of rollaway bins. This is a series of back-to-back bin modules that are on wheels or bearings that can be moved to the right or left. There is only one aisle to access all the modules. When something is needed from an inner module, the ones in front are moved aside. More about rollaway racks appears later in this chapter.

When there is a large active inventory of bin-type stock keeping units (SKUs), the space utilization can be improved by using multilevel bin racks where order pickers can work at each level.

The ultimate warehousing of SKUs that are best stored in bins is to have a small cellular ASRS (automatic storage and retrieval system) specifically for this purpose. This consists of a workstation in front of a set of racks that hold the separate bins. The order picker simply takes the quantity required from a bin that has been automatically taken from the bin racks and brought to rest conveniently before the order picker. The quantity left is confirmed with the host computer and the material handling device automatically returns the bin to its address in the racks.

What and how much to pick and the sequence in which they should be picked can be put into the computer for almost any number of orders. The order picker only does what is instructed on the CRT viewer at the workstation as the corresponding bin comes to rest in front of the worker. Added to this can be a printer next to the CRT that prints a label to show order and SKU numbers, next destination in the warehouse, and customer that ordered it. Included on the label can be bar codes to cover this essential product data and to automate getting the article to its destination via a system of bar-code-controlled conveyors or pneumatic tubes.

This type ASRS captures in one integrated system most of the best of warehousing technology. It has all the fineries of the usual much larger ASRS systems, but it costs much less and it can be fit into small areas that are part of workstations where the materials will be used. Equally and sometimes more important is the accuracy and accountability it enforces. Commonly in modern industry the reliability of having materials available when needed provides the primary economic justification for these cellular modules. Such installations are justified when the bins' capacities are even fractionally used. It is worth, for instance, using a bin for two or three little special shapes when the bin could hold hundreds of them. This is when there is only occasionally need for one of the units but when it is needed it is needed now—or before. More about these cellular modules appears later, in Chapter 11.

Tier Racks

The tier rack is commonly designed to be used with standard wooden pallets. (See Figure 10.2.) The rack consists of four corner posts and horizontal top supports that, when affixed to a pallet, permit another pallet to be stored on top. The upper pallet rests on the frame support of the pallet below. Use of tier racks permits storing several pallets high, with free access to the articles stored in each pallet tier. The articles do not bear the weight of the pallets above, making these racks well suited for storing fragile materials and irregular shapes.

In the receiving operation, a stack of pallets can be spotted near the truck or rail unloading, and the "lumper" can load directly onto the pallets. A tier rack can then be affixed to the pallet, and it is ready to be transported to the tier storage area. The shipping operation works the same way but in reverse order. When the pallet is unloaded, the rack can be removed from the pallet and disassembled, or nested together for compact storage while not in use. The combination of pallet and tier rack makes possible efficient storage for those commodities that are appropriate to this type of handling and storage. Typical of these commodities are automobile tires, coils of wire, motors, pumps, and fragile cased goods such as glassware and ceramics.

There are many different types of tier racks. Some have adjustable corner posts; others have both adjustable posts and adjustable top supports. Some consist of only corner posts without the horizontal top supports. This latter type simply supports the top pallet by four vertical posts that fit into the four corner sleeves permanently affixed to the pallet. A pallet with the corner sleeves serves to secure the top of the four posts of the pallet beneath and to secure the bottom of the posts of the pallet above.

What tier racks are all about is they permit bulk-type storage for pallets of merchandise that otherwise could not be stored one on top another. And very important, they permit order-picking access to each tier of products. Some warehouses use only tier racks for their entire inventories. Most warehouses can make productive use of some if only to store partial pallet loads one atop another.

When investigating the availability of tier racks for purchase, several different suppliers should be contacted. Most rack manufacturers have their own patented designs. One particular combination of price and design will be the best value for a specific warehousing situation. This concept of checking with several suppliers applies, of course, to other types of handling and storing equipment as well as to tier racks.

A variation of the usual wooden pallet tier rack is for the pallet to be made of steel with stirrups welded at the corners to hold the steel posts. The stirrups secure the top of the posts from the rack below as well as the bottoms of the posts for the rack above. Although these tier racks are comparatively expensive what they can achieve makes them near ideal for certain types of handling and storage. A common use is for cartoned long configuration products. The racks with product can be moved in and out of carriers with low-boy platform, electric-powered trucks. Then lifted and positioned several tiers high with conventional lift trucks.

Seeing tier racks used in this manner makes instant converts to this type rack. The advantages are obvious. The racks make a possible efficient handling as well as dense storage. Rack loads can be moved two or three high, depending on weight, throughout the warehouse. They permit good space utilization because unitized loads can be stacked several tiers high. Material damage is held to a minimum by limiting how high each tier rack can be loaded and the perimeter of rack provides protection from bumping. Yes, custom-designed steel tier racks cost more, but where appropriate, the payback of investment can be very short when all three factors—(1) efficient handling, (2) dense storage, and (3) product damage—are given due recognition.

Flowthrough Racks

The primary purpose of flowthrough racks is to provide a rapid means of order picking. (See Figure 10.2.) The racks are similar to bin racks except that provision is included for another item or case to move forward into position when the front item or case is removed. Each bin opening has an inclined chute or a conveyor that feeds the front of the bin rack with a backup of a number of units of the same product. This arrangement permits concentrating the order picking to a small area without the interruption of restocking the bins. The restocking function is performed separately, from the rear of the flowthrough racks.

These racks are used for order picking of pharmaceuticals, books, stationery items, and small commodities of almost any variety when there is a high volume of shipping orders that consist of several different line items (SKUs) each. It may not be economically feasible to provide flowthrough racks for all products in warehouses that carry thousands of different inventory items, since these racks are relatively expensive. However, in many warehouses, when the frequency of shipment by item is analyzed, it is often found that about 20 percent of the SKUs make up 80 percent of the shipments. This being the case, the use of flowthrough racks for just the 20 percent fast movers can result in substantial savings. The remaining slow movers can be stored in, and order picked from, less expensive racks or even from bulk storage.

When warehouses have order picking of case and less-than-case lots (also referred to as split- or broken-case lots), the situation is labor intensive. Many workers can be absorbed all looking busy yet be sadly, very unproductive, traveling between the last SKU picked and the next one coming up. Adopting efficient methods and procedures can result in dramatic productivity improvements from the case where the order pickers travel 75 percent of the time and pick orders only 25 percent of the time to picking orders 75 percent of the time and traveling only 25 percent.

There are basically three approaches to convert a busy-work beehive of activity into a model of efficiency.

1. Install flowthrough racks.
2. Use an operator-up lift truck in conjunction with a stock locator computer system that arranges the stock in the most efficient manner. Then the operator-up is directed to pick the orders manually in the least-travel-required sequence. Or the operator-up lift truck is automatically moved by computer guidance to pick the order materials in the least-travel-required sequence.
3. Use ASRS to bring the stock to the order picker whose sole function is to pick the orders and send them on their way to staging via a bar-code-activated conveyor or pneumatic tube. A viable alternative is for the ASRS to be directed to batch pull stock so that the order picker selects units that are common to several orders at a time.

Drive-Through Racks

Drive-through racks sound similar to the flowthrough racks, but they are entirely different. (See Figure 10.2.) They vary in design, and they are used for a different purpose. Flowthrough racks are designed to assist in rapid order picking; drive-through racks consist of columns that have horizontal rails to support rows of pallets several high that permit each level of pallets to be supported independently of the other. The pallets span from the left side rail to the right side rail over the corridor that is formed by the vertical columns. When the racks are placed so that one end of the corridor is against a wall or another type of storage, they are called "drive-in" racks. When the racks are placed so that there is lift truck access to both ends, they are called "drive-through" racks.

These racks are principally used to attain better utilization of space for pallet storage when the loads are too fragile to support pallet loads above. You may have detected that this type of rack is used for the same purpose as the tier racks discussed before. This is true. While they are of entirely different designs, both are for the same purpose—to support pallet loads above independently from the pallet loads below. It is not uncommon to have to decide between the two rack systems. Drive-through racks have two distinct advantages. They provide for FIFO (first in, first out) inventory control by putting pallet loads in one end and picking them from the other. Also, they do not involve the nuisance of putting together and taking apart the tier racks for each pallet load handled.

"A" Frame Racks

The A-frame rack gets its name from the A-shaped upright structure used in its construction. Two or more "A" frames are connected in tandem with cross and horizontal bracing. A horizontal beam attached to the legs of the "A" may be used for the base of the rack, or the legs alone may serve as the base. Horizontal or inclined arms spaced from a few inches to a foot or more along the "A" frame serve as load-bearing arms for storage.

"A" frame racks have uses similar to those of the cantilever racks. Both are well suited for storing long narrow shapes such as tubing, bar, and rod stock. The "A" frame rack's main advantage is its simplicity. A small rack can be easily constructed by a metal worker, since its design requires less technical knowledge of rack engineering than does the cantilever design. The rack is generally loaded and unloaded by crane or by hand because the wide base prevents convenient access to the upper arms with a lift truck. These racks are not used with stacker cranes because all storage arms must extend to the same horizontal point for the stacker system to operate effectively. Arms of the "A" frame rack extend out farthest at the lowest level and less far with each level going up the A frame. Cantilever rack makers have little to fear from "A" frame rack makers.

Rollaway Racks

Storage racks are usually stationary. In fact, many who have been in warehousing for years have never heard of, let alone seen, racks that are intended to be moved as a part of their storing function. Yet there are such racks, and they are very efficient when appropriately used. The principle on which rollaway racks is based is that aisles are only useful when they are being used; the rest of the time they are wasting good space. Rollaway racks permit the absolute minimum aisle space. (See Figure 10.2.)

These racks have an arrangement of wheels and rails or some other mobile mechanics that permits an entire row of racks to move away from the adjacent row of racks. Usually there are many rows of racks to one rollaway system. Aisle space is left only after several rows of racks, not between each row. As access between rows is needed, the adjacent racks are moved either forward or back to make an aisle opening.

Rollaway racks are relatively expensive in comparison with other types of racks; therefore, they are used mainly where space is very valuable. This type of rack is appropriate and economical in a small book warehouse located within a museum or an educational facility. When using rollaway storage racks, a good, reliable address and stock-locator system is needed. Neither the energy to move the racks nor the workers' time should be wasted in searching for lost SKUs. A good memory is generally not enough with this type of storage.

Another consideration is whether the movement of the racks should be by human effort or by electrically powered mechanics and electronically controlled. Certainly how hard they are to move is an important factor but just because some workers have the strength is not adequate reason to depend on human effort. Perhaps this would be a good application for an air float system discussed in Chapter 9.

Double-Decker Racks

To take full advantage of vertical space, certain types of racks can be double-decked. (See Figure 10.2.) A second working level is particularly appropriate over the bin type of racks that are kept to a height that an order picker can conveniently reach while working from the floor, which is no more than about 7 feet. In a building that has high clearance, it is a waste of overhead space to have racks that use only 7 feet. By placing a floor over these racks, it is possible to have an overhead storage and order-picking area just like the one below. Products can be efficiently lifted to the second deck by crane, elevator, lift truck, or powered conveyor and be lowered by gravity chute or conveyor. With an effective means of getting the products to and from the second level, the utilization of space can be increased 100 percent, and the handling efficiency should not be significantly affected.

While a second deck provides these good things, a third and fourth level can be that much better—provided there is sufficient height and the system is properly engineered. The storage racks or bins for multilevel order picking can be a single stand-alone system with, say, steel grating of the aisles separately supported from the racks at each level. Or each level can be a complete floor extending under the racks at each level. If the multilever system is added to an existing building concern should be that there is adequate lighting and probably a sprinkler system at each of the lower levels, since only the top level will benefit adequately from that which was there before installing the additional levels.

HOW TO DETERMINE STORAGE RACK SPECIFICATIONS AND WHY THEY ARE CRITICAL

The two most common obstacles encountered in dealing with storage racks are

1. what to call the component parts.
2. how to determine what is needed.

Together they constitute the storage rack specifications that must be known to communicate effectively about this large inseparable segment of warehousing. (See Figure 10.3.) How else can instructions be given to warehouse personnel and orders be given to equipment vendors?

The results of not knowing and freely admitting it are not bad—and at times it is refreshing to hear such honesty. Most everyone seems to want to help those who admit not knowing and appear to want to learn. Using confusing and wrong terminology and specifications results in inefficiencies and misunderstandings that can lead to excessive costs and worse—accidents and injuries. Storage racks can be dangerous if misused or abused. Tons of product can come tumbling down with sorry consequences. Explored here is the most common terminology of storage racks and how to determine the particular specifications for pallet and cantilever racks, the two most common storage racks in contemporary warehousing.

Load, as It Applies to All Storage Racks

The type and specifications of storage racks begins with the specifications of the load to be stored.

1. *Height.* The pallet or skid used plus the stored material.
2. *Depth.* The overall depth of the load, which is the length of the pallet stringer (usually of 2-in. × 4-in. wood) plus any overhang of material.
3. *Width.* The overall breadth of the load which includes the width of the pallet plus any overhang of stacked material.
4. *Weight.* Total weight of the material plus the weight of the pallet or skid.

Pallet Rack Specifications

Pallet racks are by far the most common storage racks in warehousing, but the name is something of a misnomer. The name "pallet" was used initially because the racks were designed to hold materials on pallets. Soon after, decks were put across the arms so that small items could be stored on them without falling between the arms. When used in this manner they are more appropriately called "shelves." Then palletless loads were developed. This was accomplished by two totally different means. One consisted of the load resting on what is called a slip sheet, a rectangular sheet of press board impregnated with a strengthener and water repellent. The load was moved and stored on the slip sheet with a special lift truck attachment discussed in the preceding chapter. The other way was to grab the load with a clamp attachment on the lift truck. The process being much like moving a stack of toy blocks with pressure from the palms of one's hands. Now the term "unit load" came into vogue because the new loads were like pallet loads except there were no pallets. Now pallet loads and unit loads along with shelf products were being stored in pallet racks, and the racks had not changed at all. Rather than find a better term than "pallet rack," the gurus of warehousing threw up their hands and decided to revert back to calling them pallet racks. Anyway, for our purposes here pallet racks will hold pallet or skid loads and by decking between or over the arms they hold loads on slip sheets and clamped loads. The following terminology and specifications relate to "pallet" racks.

Uprights. This is the vertical frame including diagonal and horizontal cross bracing from which the horizontal load bearing arms are suspended (Figure 10.3).

To determine the required height of the uprights for a specific rack installation, add together each storage opening plus the height of the load-bearing arms, also called bars and beams. Keep in mind that the upright must extend above the top arm only enough for the connector that secures the arm to the upright to connect to the upright. For example, if the arm were to be bolted to the upright and a hole were drilled through both the arm and the upright to insert the bolt, the top of the upright and the top arm would level.

For the upright to extend above the top arm at all is, at best, a nuisance when putting on or taking off unit loads at the top level. At worst, it can snag the pallet or the load itself causing product damage, or it can cause the lift truck mast to bunt or pull the rack, which can cause a major accident. Fortunately, most lift truck operators display surprising skill in avoiding hazards like this. The point is that most pallet racks are not bolted together. They would be horrible to erect if they were. The designers provide holes in the upright for protrusions (commonly called "tits") on the side of the ends of the arms to slip into and bind the arms to the uprights. Often, for the tits to fit the holes the uprights have to extend above the arms enough to mesh. The objective is to have the two members mesh evenly but if this is not possible have the upright extend up the minimum. Whenever ordering pallet racks, ask your supplier if the uprights can be cut in a way to avoid any extension. When the design permits this, be certain to specify it. For this little extra attention, the nuisance or hazard can be avoided over the long useful life of the racks.

HOW TO CALCULATE THE HEIGHT OF THE UPRIGHTS. The height of the uprights should be determined taking into consideration several influencing factors:

1. The height the lift trucks that service the racks can reach. You may want to acquire racks higher than your present lift trucks will reach with the intention of getting ones that will reach in the future

FIGURE 10.3   Pallet Rack Components

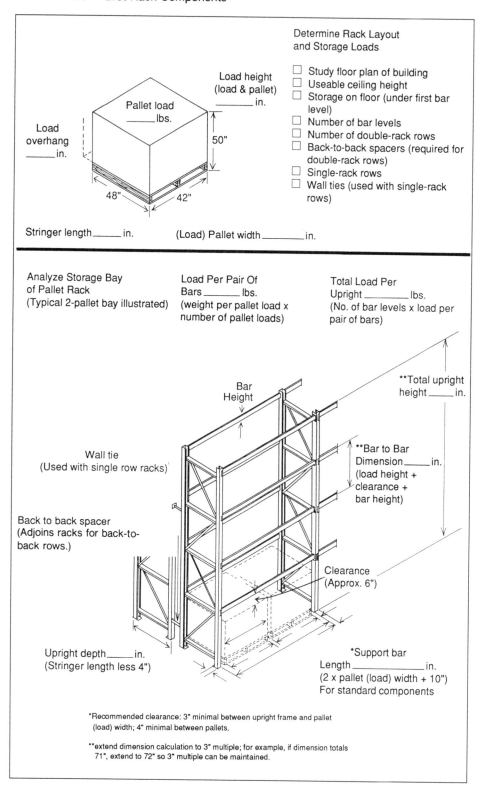

Determine Rack Layout
and Storage Loads

☐ Study floor plan of building
☐ Useable ceiling height
☐ Storage on floor (under first bar level)
☐ Number of bar levels
☐ Number of double-rack rows
☐ Back-to-back spacers (required for double-rack rows)
☐ Single-rack rows
☐ Wall ties (used with single-rack rows)

Load height
(load & pallet)
_____ in.

Pallet load
_____ lbs.

Load overhang
_____ in.

50"

48"   42"

Stringer length _____ in.   (Load) Pallet width _____ in.

Analyze Storage Bay
of Pallet Rack
(Typical 2-pallet bay illustrated)

Load Per Pair Of
Bars _____ lbs.
(weight per pallet load x
number of pallet loads)

Total Load Per
Upright _____ lbs.
(No. of bar levels x load per
pair of bars)

Bar
Height

**Total upright
height _____ in.

**Bar to Bar
Dimension_____ in.
(load height +
clearance +
bar height)

Wall tie
(Used with single row racks)

Back to back spacer
(Adjoins racks for back-to-back rows.)

Clearance
(Approx. 6")

Upright depth_____ in.
(Stringer length less 4")

*Support bar
Length _____ in.
(2 x pallet (load) width + 10")
For standard components

*Recommended clearance: 3" minimal between upright frame and pallet
(load) width; 4" minimal between pallets.

**extend dimension calculation to 3" multiple; for example, if dimension totals
71", extend to 72" so 3" multiple can be maintained.

2. The height of any overhead obstruction such as the trusses or the fire-sprinkler heads. Material cannot be stacked too close to the sprinkler heads or the spray will not have room to spread to the next closest head's spray. Normally 3 feet is enough, but this should be determined by the local fire marshall, the sprinkler supplier, and your fire insurance company. Whatever you do, do not cheat on what is decided. And plenty of pressure can be applied to do this—to utilize as much space as possible. Hold firm. You could, if there were a fire, have the insurance company refuse to make good.

3. The calculated height of the number of loads plus clearances plus rack arm heights is also needed. This is determined like this. Assume you are working with the following factors:

Height of loads	4'-0"
Height of pallet	0'-6"
Vertical clearance needed to maneuver the load into position	0'-6"
Height of arms	0'-6"
Stacking height to 3' of the fire sprinkler	
First pallet load will rest on the floor	

With these factors you can determine how many vertical loads positions can be realized before reaching the sprinkler head or truss limitation at 27'-6".

Vertical Span	Vertical Distance	Cumulative Distance
1. From floor to bottom of first arm: pallet 0'6" + load 4'0" + clearance 0'6" =	5'0"	5'0"
2. From bottom of first arm to bottom of next arm up: arm 0'6" + pallet 0'6" + load 4'0" = clearance 0'6" =	5'6"	10'6"
3. From bottom of second arm to bottom of next arm up: arm 0'6" + pallet 0'6" + load 4'0" = clearance 0'6" =	5'6"	16'0"
4. From bottom of third arm to bottom of next arm up: arm 0'6" + pallet 0'6" + load 4'0" + clearance 0'6" =	5'6"	21'6"
5. Height of top (fourth arm up)	0.6"	22'0"
Height of upright and top of top arm is 22'0"		
6. From top of fourth arm to top of top load: pallet 0'6" + load 4'0" =	4'6"	24'6"
7. Clearance over top load to fire sprinklers: clearance 3'0" =	3'0"	27'6"
Height to fire sprinklers is 27'6".		

The capacity of the upright depends on the weight of the loads, plus the weight of the pallets and the arms they will support. Capacity of the uprights will be discussed after the length, width, and capacity of the arms are dealt with.

HOW TO DETERMINE LENGTH OF THE ARMS (ALSO CALLED BARS OR BEAMS). The length of the arms depends on how many loads across the arms there will be, the width of the loads, and the clearance left for maneuvering the loads on to and off from the arms. Normally two loads 40 or 48 inches wide are used with clearances of 3 inches from the left upright to the load, 4 inches between loads and 3 inches from the second load to the right upright.

Normally storage racks are *not kept* in inventory by the manufacturer. They are built to order so their specifications can be varied according to the buyer's needs without significant penalty—provided a respectable number of racks are ordered at the same time. Because of this, warehouse management should tailor the clearances to its own needs, not accept what is represented as normal. How the loads are put in and taken out, and how the standard load dimensions are held to, dictate the clearances. For example a lift truck with a side shifter that permits the operator to shift the forks to the right or left should not require as much horizontal clearance as one that does not have a shifter—assuming the same operator skill. Another example is the difference in clearance necessary for an operator-up that rides near the load and can position the load more precisely than a lift truck operator that operates at floor level that is trying to judge one or two inches from, say, 20 feet below.

HOW TO DETERMINE DEPTH OF THE ARMS. The distance between the front and back of the load-bearing arms should be something less than the depth of the pallets used. This should be, say, a 3- to 4-inch pallet overhang in the front and back. This means that if the pallets are 48 inches deep (the length of the stringers, sometimes called runners) the distance between the outer edges of the arms should be, say, 40 inches to 42 inches, leaving a 3- to 4-inch overhang front and back. If the arms are intended to support, say, a 36-inch-deep pallet, the distance between the outer edges of the arms should be, say, 28 to 30 inches.

HOW TO DETERMINE THE LOAD-BEARING CAPACITY OF THE ARMS. This is determined by the total of product weight on the pair of arms plus the weight of the pallets (if used) and the weight of the arms. If decking is used between arms this too should be added in. Then to this total should be added the safety factor, whatever it is. The safety factor should be automatically added by the manufacturer without the buyer having to deal with it, but it is so important the supplier should be asked about it.

The design and construction of pallet racks are simple enough and the market for them is so large and divergent it attracts many manufacturers. Do not count on all rack suppliers using the same safety factor. A concern should be that the means of connecting the arms to the uprights is engineered to hold the determined capacity. This is usually the weakest point of arm capacity. Ask the supplier to provide the certified capacity of a pair of arms—and that of the uprights as well.

HOW TO DETERMINE THE CAPACITY OF THE UPRIGHTS. The upright's capacity should be the sum of all the capacities of the arms attached to it divided by 2. The divisor is used because the capacity of each pair of arms is always supported by two uprights. For example, if there were four sets of arms extending from each side of an upright, there would be eight sets of arms connected to each upright (except at the ends of a row of racks which would only have four). But the arms are supported by uprights at each end; therefore the actual capacity in this example would be the sum of 8 pairs of arm capacities divided between two uprights. Then the safety factor should be added to this. Assuming each pair of arms have the rated capacity of 4,000 pounds, the arithmetic to determine the upright capacity would be as follows:

8 pairs of arms × 4,000 pounds per pair ÷ 2 uprights
= 16,000 pounds per upright

Cantilever Rack Specifications

While the purpose of all storage racks is the same—to increase space utilization, to protect inventories, and to improve material handling efficiency—the different designs involve different considerations in determining their specifications. The cantilever rack design is entirely different from the pallet rack just discussed. (See Figure 10.2.)

HOW TO CALCULATE THE HEIGHT OF THE UPRIGHT. The same considerations discussed about the height of pallet racks apply equally to cantilever racks, except what is involved in determining the number of load levels. The cantilever has a heavy base that supports and gives rigidity to the upright and serves in place of the first load-bearing arm. Then the load size, clearances, and height of arms govern the height of the upright. With these factors you can determine how many vertical load positions can be realized before a truss or sprinkler head limits the height.

Vertical Span	Vertical Distance	Cumulative Distance
1. Height of the rack base	1′0″	1′0″
2. From top of base to bottom of first arm: load 2′8″ + clearance 0′4″	3′0″	4′0″
3. From bottom of first arm to bottom of next arm up: arm 0′6″ + load 2′8″ + clearance 0′4″	3′6″	7′6″
4. Repeat (3) above for five more arms	17′6″	25′0″
5. Height of top arm 0′6″	0′6″	25′6″
Height of upright and top of top arm is 25′6″.		
6. From top of top arm to top of load	2′8″	28′2″
7. Clearance over top load for fire sprinklers clearance 3′0″ =	3′0″	31′2″
Height to fire sprinkler is 31′2″.		

HOW TO DETERMINE THE DEPTH OF THE ARMS. The depth of the arms is governed by the depth of the articles stored on them. If an article has a depth of, say, 36 inches, the arms can be a few inches less if there is no problem caused by overhang. If the articles were smaller and were to be stored several deep on the arms, a multiple of the depth of the articles should be selected. For example, if the articles were 1 foot deep, the arms should be say 33 to 35 inches for three deep or 45 to 47 inches for four deep. If the arms were for the same product 30 inches or 42 inches deep, 7 to 8 inches of each arm would not be utilized, because the article at the outer end must have enough arm support to avoid falling off. For instance,

3 units deep × 12 inches deep unit = 36 inches deep for 3 units

If the arm is only 30 inches deep, a third item on the arms would have only 6 inches of its 12 inches on the arm and would fall off with the least vibration.

How to Determine Capacity and Arm Spacing for Cantilever Racks. This depends on the following factors:

- Length of products
- Physical rigidity
- Weight or weights of the inventory

These factors should be considered in combination. They are interrelated. Change one and the others change in turn.

The following examples will demonstrate this and lead to a specific combination that will be best for a specific set of factors.

Inventory: Consists of metal sheets packed 100 sheets per pack in lengths of 8, 12, 16, 20, and 24 feet and all 48 inches wide with weight of 100 pounds per foot of package length. For instance the 10-foot-long package weighs 1,000 pounds (100 lb./ft. × 10 ft. long) and the 24-foot-long package weighs 2,400 pounds. The packs are 10 inches high, including the protective packaging. The packs are rigid enough that support every 4 feet is more than adequate.

Horizontal Arm Spacing: A little arithmetic indicates the horizontal spacing of the arms on 48½-inch centers will do just fine with the actual arm width of 5 inches. This will provide for support every 4 feet with a minimum of 1-inch horizontal clearance between packs.

Vertical Arm Spacing: The packs are 10 inches high. After trying a number of "what-ifs" about inbound and outbound shipments it was determined that stacking 2 packs high with a 3-in. × 3-in. × 48-in. wood divider between the packs is the best compromise without buying another side loader with greater lift capacity. Lifting the 24-foot-long packs that weigh 2,400 pounds is right at the capacity of the present vehicle when 600 pounds is added for the weight for the outrigger fork attachment needed to handle the long length.

The routine to follow to determine the height of the uprights was covered in the first part of this section on cantilever racks.

Specifications for Other Rack Designs

The examples and exercises just covered for the pallet and cantilever racks, which constitute the majority of all storage racks, should indicate how to approach setting specifications for other types of storage racks such as the drive-in, drive-through, flowthrough, and tier racks covered before in this chapter. Start out with the best information available, apply objective reasoning, and build your model. All this can be done for you by the rack salesperson, but you will have a better feeling for and understanding of it all if you do it yourself. Then give the cantilever salesperson the same load specifications you used and ask for the best rack plan he or she can come up with. Check it with your plan selecting the best of each. Investment in storage racks is usually a substantial one, but even more, it establishes how things will be done for a long time to come. Best to do it right the first time, one does not get a second chance.

Storage Rack Accessories and Their Uses

There are many types of rack accessories. Some are essential to the racks, such as the horizontal and vertical cross-bracing required of all uprights, but most is necessary only under special circumstance or is added to obtain additional rack capabilities. Covered here are some of the more common rack accessories and their uses. (See Figure 10.3.)

Base Plates. Used with pallet, drive-in, and drive-through racks, they are put under the uprights' legs to distribute weight of the racks and their contents over a larger floor area. Otherwise, the small area covered the posts of the uprights which are usually in the form of a rectangle or less often in the form of a circle and will dig into the floor, chipping a little away each time the rack vibrates. And the vibration can be caused by as little and be as common as a lift truck passing by. The plates are made of flat steel, usually between ⅜ and ½ inch thick, and between 7 and 10 inches square.

These plates are not as commonly used as they should be probably because with the exceptionally high quality of some floors, the signs of chipping are not evident for several years. Yet many floors show effects within a few months. Normally, for the relatively little extra cost, plates entirely remove this problem with pallet racks. Cantilever racks do not require plates because the base of these racks serve also to distribute weight of the racks and their contents.

Shims. Used with racks that have uprights, they are steel wedges to level the uprights caused most commonly by uneven floors and occasionally uneven racks. When using plates, the shims should be put between the post of the upright and the plate. If put below the plate, the shim could dig into the concrete.

Floor Bolts. Used with any stationary storage racks, they secure the bottom of the uprights to the floor. Commonly, the uprights are made with a means for attaching the bolts to them. When a 90-degree steel angle can be used, one side is attached to the upright and the other to the floor. If a base plate is used, a hole will have to be drilled through it to attach both it and the upright to the floor. The purpose of the bolts is obvious, to keep the racks in place; otherwise, they start to wander.

Decking. Pallet racks commonly require decking between or over the arms to convert the racks to shelving. Cantilever racks are occasionally decked as well. The purpose of decking is to store things on it that would otherwise fall between the arms. Steel decking of various varieties are catalog items with most rack manufacturers. Plywood or tongue and groove planking can be used as well. Pallet rack arms are often designed with a recessed portion to accommodate decking so it will not have to be put over the arms for support. This recessed part means also assures that the decking will stay put without bolts.

Row Spacers. These are used to fix the space left between back-to-back rows of pallet racks. They are made of steel and are designed to be used with a specific design of upright. If row spaces are not used between the rows, the pallet racks will start to wander. If the racks are bolted to the concrete the row spacers are still highly recommended because they add stability to the racks, resulting in less strain on the floor bolts and arm-upright connections. The racks will definitely look better and last longer if row spaces are used.

Wall Supports. When pallet racks are positioned in a single row along a wall there is need for wall supports: (1) to keep the racks far enough away from the wall to accommodate the overhang of the loads, (2) to give critical stability to the stand-alone racks, and (3) to provide space for a "rat run." A rat run is an area between storage and the walls that permits inspection, spraying for insects, and setting traps for rodents. It is a code requirement for many areas of the country and a good idea for most warehouses.

Upright Guards. The legs of uprights of drive-in, drive-through, and pallet racks can be easily knocked and bent by lift trucks. This weakens the racks, which may cause their eventual collapse, destroying a lot of the inventory stored in them. To prevent this or reduce the impact on the racks, steel guards (best painted yellow for caution) are attached to the floor in front of the uprights. Even though a direct hard hit will bend the guards and in turn bend the racks, many lesser hits will be stopped by the guards. Some rack suppliers even recess on an angle the outer legs of the uprights to reduce the hazard.

Again, remember that bent storage racks should be removed and replaced immediately. If new parts are not kept as spares, they will have to be ordered from the supplier. This will take time. In the meantime the products in the damaged racks should be removed and a red sign posted saying to the effect "danger do not use racks." If bent racks can be straightened, keep in mind that the section of the rack is still weakened; therefore, it should be further strengthened by bolting or better welding steel reinforcement.

HOW TO UNITIZE LOADS TO IMPROVE STORING AND HANDLING MATERIAL

There is a continuous warehousing need to *unitize* merchandise for more efficient handling and storing. The term *"unitize"* is often thrown about in ignorance, but when used appropriately, it does constitute a concise description. To start on solid ground, consider what Webster says it is: "to make into a single unit." When used in warehouse jargon, it means to secure a number of separate articles into a single handling and/or storing unit.

There are several ways to unitize merchandise for better handling and storing. These include building the load on a standard raised platform, called a *pallet,* or the reverse, building the platform called a *skid* to fit the load. Both the pallet and skid can be made of wood (the most common), metal, or plastic. Both are also designed to accept the forks of a lift truck and certain designs accept the slings of a crane to elevate and transport. Low-boy material movers equipped with either forks or platform are also used to lift and transport unitized loads. Both pallets and skids are common in most warehousing and production operations. Pallets are used most often when the unitized loads can be standardized, and skids are used most often when the loads are not standard. Further, skids are appropriate where the configuration or specifications of the load are unusual such as a platform specifically designed for unitizing a stack of long metal sheets or to move a large generator assembly.

Two other common means of unitizing are the "slip sheet" on which the load is assembled and the "clamp load," which is conspicuously different. It is a load assembled directly on the floor or other work surface in a manner that broad clamps, hydraulically pressured, one on each side of the load, can elevate and move the unitized load in a manner similar to how you would pick up and move a stack of toy building blocks with pressure between the palms of your hands. Where applicable, the clamp means is least costly because there is no additional material involved such as for pallets, skids, or slip sheets. The clamps are a standard accessory for lift trucks and constitute one of the most widespread improvements in warehouse-type material handling in recent times.

There are many other means for unitizing loads and there are various ways to improve on the effectiveness of the four common means just described: pallet, skid, slip sheet, and clamp. Custom-designed unitizing containers to permit easier inspection and verification of counts are growing in use as attempts are made to reduce cost of inspectors and load checkers. Glue lines between layers of packages of a unitized load are used to hold the load together more securely. Shrink plastic wrap is used extensively to secure the load further and keep the contents free of contaminates,—the most common of which is dust, the number one warehouse nuisance.

The following paragraphs discuss in more detail the pros and cons of the three most common means for unitizing loads in warehousing: pallet, slip sheet, and clamp.

Pros and Cons for Using Pallets

Pallets are probably the most common nonmechanical tools used in the warehousing industry. Nearly every warehouse uses them to some extent. Certain warehouses use pallets in the handling and storing of all their inventories. Even warehouses whose products are not normally packaged use some pallets in their operations. They have become an almost universal warehouse operations tool. They provide a convenient, simple way to stack, transport, and store materials.

Possibly because pallets are in such common use, warehouse management too often takes it for granted that workers know how to use pallets efficiently, yet this is not the case.

Pallet Sizes. One of the most common problems is the lack of size standardization. It is not uncommon to find several different sizes of pallet in the same warehouse. This is all right, provided that each size exists for a good reason and that the use of the pallets is effectively controlled to comply with those reasons. Too often, however, the presence of many different sizes is not the result of good management planning, or, if it is, the controls for their use are not effective.

Warehouses accumulate different pallet sizes because

○ They came in with a certain shipment.
○ The purchasing agent was able to get a good buy on them.
○ The pallets were good for the type of handling equipment the warehouse used to have.
○ Surplus pallets were acquired at a very good price.
○ Specialized pallets were acquired for a special product line that has since been dropped.
○ The choice of pallet size was left up to the individual supervisors.

Probably, the best number of different-size pallets for a warehouse is one. If, however, additional sizes can be clearly justified, of course they should be allowed—under controlled circumstances.

INEFFICIENCIES CAUSED BY TOO MANY SIZES. Following is a list of reasons why too many pallet sizes for one warehouse cause inefficiencies:

○ Handling equipment is often designed to handle only certain-size pallets. Different sizes limit the use of this expensive equipment.

○ Storage racks are designed to accommodate a specific pallet size; using different-size pallets cause low space utilization.

○ Use of different-size pallets is a deterrent to establishing standard procedures for handling and storing.

○ Taking good physical inventories is more difficult when different pallet loads of the same product contain different amounts.

○ Use of different-size pallets contributes to errors in the receiving and shipping operations.

○ Good housekeeping practices are more difficult to enforce.

○ Use of many different pallet sizes prevents, or greatly reduces the effectiveness of, using standard pallet patterns.

Standard Pallet Patterns, Their Purpose and Uses. The term "pallet pattern" has evolved into a misnomer because with the increasing use of other means of unitizing more appropriate would be the term "unitized-load pattern." But, because pallet pattern is so commonly used and conveys what is intended, it continues to be favored by practicing warehousers.

The use of standard pallet patterns (see Figure 10.4) increases handling and storing efficiency. Considerable time is wasted when the worker who is receiving the goods has to stop to figure what pattern to use. The solution to the problem could involve several approaches, including relying on memory for the pattern that was used the last time, going to where some of the same product is already in storage to see how it is stacked, and experimenting to determine a new pattern. All these solutions involve wasted time and the chance of error. Even to have the worker do the experimenting for new products is not as efficient as having the pattern determined in advance by someone in the office.

The process of determining the most efficient pallet patterns requires the use of arithmetic, logic, templates, and drawings. As a general practice, workers who must interrupt their normal work routines to determine proper pallet patterns will waste time and not come up with the best results. Certainly they can be trained to design pallet patterns, but this is better accomplished in the office, where tools are available to do it more efficiently.

A standard pallet patterns means a prescribed way of arranging specific-size material on a specific-size pallet. The optimum pattern will provide for maximum utilization of the pallet for the purpose intended. Generally, this means that the design will provide for the use of as much of the pallet surface as possible, with material extending over the edges a short distance if this does not cause damage. It also means that the load is built to be solid and stable. A solid pallet pattern provides for the maximum material per cubic area, the highest density. A stable pattern permits the load to be transferred and stacked with minimum chance of toppling. Alternating patterns for each tier or layer of the load provides an interlocking effect that adds greatly to the stability. The height of the prescribed pattern also influences stability. Material should be stored to the maximum height that still provides stability, avoids crushing of the bottom material, and is within the capacity and clearance limitations of the handling and storing equipment that will be used. Additional height can be attained in some cases by placing paper or fiberboard binders between tiers. Other techniques include using thin glue lines between tiers or tying the top tier with twine. It is common in warehousing to aim for a pallet pattern that has a gross cube of 64 cubic feet, 4 by 4 by 4 feet, but this is only a general guide, and deviations should be freely introduced whenever there are sufficient advantages to be realized.

FIGURE 10.4   Representative Pallet Patterns

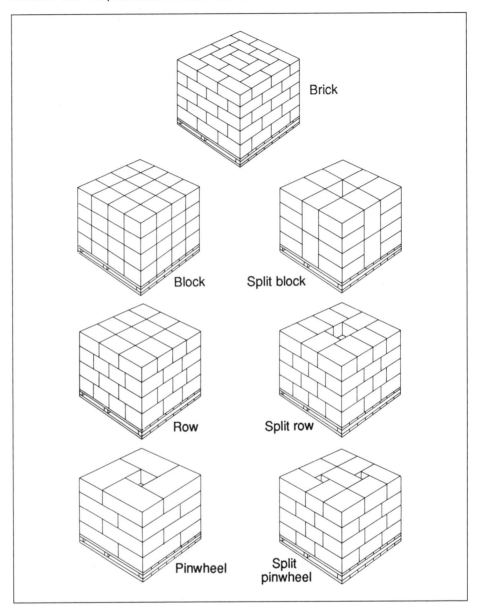

To avoid the pitfalls of uncontrolled pallet patterns, a procedure should be established that requires standard patterns and their use. In small warehouses, the manager or an assistant should have the function of designing and controlling pallet patterns. In large warehouses, this should be the duty of an industrial engineer or equivalent. Once the design has been determined, a simple drawing should be made and a code number assigned to it. A minimum of two manuals containing complete sets of drawings should be maintained: one to be kept by the person who is charged with designing and controlling the patterns, the other to be kept at the receiving workstation. Those who are palletizing the materials should be required to use the warehouse's standard pallet patterns.

Help for and Cautions about Developing Pallet Patterns.   Computer programs exist that can determine the optimum pallet patterns for the product specifications, pallet sizes, and handling and storing equipment that will be used. But these are aids, not gospel. Here are some other concerns:

- What is the strength of the pallet?
- Is the pallet single or double faced (single-faced pallets are not designed to permit stacking one pallet load on another)?
- How many pallet loads will be stacked one on another?
- How high will the product strength permit stacking?
- If storage racks will be used what are the dimensions of the openings?
- If tier racks will be used, what are the inside clearances?
- What is the environmental humidity (high humidity reduces strength of cardboard)?
- How secure should the load be considering the travel to which it will be subjected?

Pros and Cons for Using Slip Sheets

As a means of unitizing loads, slip sheets discussed here and clamp handling that follows are equally used to store as well as to handle inventories. They are explored in this chapter as storing techniques only because they are directly involved in unit loads like pallets and skids, but if the reader prefers to categorize them as handling techniques, so be it. Perhaps the most appropriate classification would be "warehouse mavericks," which only illustrates the difficulty one gets into trying to label things.

A slip sheet (Figure 9.1) is a strong, highly glazed composition sheet of wood fibers commonly used in place of a pallet. One thin, broad (width of load) fork or set of narrow forks is slipped under the slip sheet to provide the necessary support to lift the unitized load. An accessory mechanism of the lift truck called a "push-pull" is an essential part in the use of slip sheets. The following paragraphs describe the slip-sheet process of handling unitized loads.

The merchandise is stacked on a slip sheet the size of a common pallet footprint. The load is unitized in a pallet pattern to provide as secure a load as possible. Often, the layers are glue lined, or a string is used to tie the top layer, or the load is shrink wrapped to add further stability to the load. A flap of the slip sheet extends beyond the load. The lift truck's push-pull mechanism is extended and its gripper engages the flap. The mechanism pulls the load back on the set of broad thin forks. With this the unitized load is snug and secure and ready to be lifted and transported. At its destination the load is positioned slightly above the floor or rack or atop another load, and the push mechanism holds the load in position while the pull mechanism withdraws the fork. The cycle is complete.

The advantages of the slip-sheet process are obvious. Costly pallets, the space they occupy, and the cost to return them are eliminated. The cost of the slip sheet, however, is significant, something between 10 and 20 percent of good wood pallet costs.

Although the slip sheets do not provide as sturdy a load as pallets, they are "some better" than the clamp method discussed next. "How much is this some better?" This is perennially debated by advocates of one or the other. The champions of the clamp method seem to be gaining due to the continued pressure to reduce costs, but it is probably safe to say there are situations where each is better. What usually tips the balance is how much damage results and how costly it is. Dropping a case of jug wine is an annoyance; dropping a case of rare wine would be devastating.

Pros and Cons for Using Hydraulic Clamps

Clamp attachments for lift trucks come in a variety of sizes and features. (See Figure 9.2.) The concept of clamping the load from the sides is applicable to so many different products that a whole family of different clamp mechanisms have been designed. The following are just a few.

Bale clamp. Used to handle bales of cotton, paper, rags, and scrap metal.

Cylinder clamp. Used to handle coils, drums, and rolls.

Crate clamps. Used to handle large creates and packages.

Carton clamps. Used to handle unitized loads of cartoned products.

Variations of these permit rotating, up ending, and carrying double-high loads, where applicable. The clamps are padded and configured as required to protect and to grab the load more securely. There are general-purpose clamps as well as specialized ones. There should be no hesitation in investigating custom design if there is a large volume of such handling involved and a special design would work better. Do not be surprised if you find that what you think is custom is an off-the-shelf item. There are already a surprising number of different designs that are standard catalog items.

The most common generic type is the carton clamp—there are more cartons in commerce than any other type packaging. This type comes with either single or double pads. The single-pad model is primarily used to handle cartoned goods of cans, bottles, and grocery-type products. The double-pad model is designed to handle larger cartons of items such as televisions, washers, stoves, and so on. The following is how the clamp attachment process works for cartoned products.

The cartons are stacked on the floor or other work surface with the same stacking patterns used for pallets and slip sheets. The layers may be glue lined, but a flexible glue should be used; otherwise the slight shift of the cartons will probably break the seal, but it is worthwhile experimenting. If glue is not used, the top row of cartons should probably be tied. Again, experiment to determine what is necessary to prevent the unitized load coming apart. Do not add either glue or string unless more is saved than spent. Most clamped loads are handled and stored without benefit of either. But this should not be the guide either. What may be an acceptable amount of damage to warehouse management may be too costly to the CEO or some other person whose job it is to worry about the total company's economics.

The clamps are positioned at the sides of the unitized load and just the right hydraulic pressure is applied to lift and move the load in tack. The load is placed either in a decked pallet rack or in bulk storage—one clamped unit load on another—just as you would if the loads were on pallets.

11

Automation: The Way to Major Breakthroughs in Cost Savings

CHAPTER HIGHLIGHTS

Presented in this chapter is the type of equipment and disciplines necessary to turn conventional warehousing into a giant efficiency machine while providing better inventory accountability and higher levels of customer service. Included is the unique building design made possible with the high-rise storage racks serving as the superstructure to attach the sides and roof and how this is more efficient to build and how it could have favorable income tax consequences. Also covered is the semiautomated storage and retrieval system that enables an operator to ride in a carriage with the load-lift mechanism in a high-rise environment.

To tie up as many loose ends as possible, a dozen advantages that high-rise automation has over conventional warehousing are offered. Finally, suggestions are offered on how to automate when your financial resources are limited.

Automation means different things to different warehousers. In some warehouses in the less industrialized world, employees would see automation as resulting from the acquisition of their first lift truck, whereas in the more industrialized world, many view the common lift as archaic. Automation, to the latter, is achieved when things are directed or put on track by pushing keys or moving a computer mouse about. As it is dealt with here, automation is the range of things between these two extremes—with a strong leaning toward the second view.

AUTOMATIC STORAGE AND RETRIEVAL

The ultimate in warehousing and a major breakthrough in warehouse handling and storing, the automatic storage and retrieval system (ASRS), illustrated in Figure 11.1, has done more to shake up warehousing than anything else.

Perhaps the best way to treat the subject is to describe it in total and then discuss each of its parts.

ASRS: How It Works

In its narrowest sense ASRS is the automatic means to put into storage, travel, and take out of storage. This does not mean an operator goes along to make it do what it is supposed to; it means that its computer program via electronic signals causes it to automatically perform these most basic warehousing functions under ultracontrolled conditions.

The most common ASRSs in the United States are high-rise storage heights from 30 feet to over 100 feet, and mostly huge installations. In general, the economics of these large systems are better than small ones in relation to what most companies in this country want. But this is not universal. For example, in Japan, there are many more ASRSs, but they are comparatively much smaller. They are often small, cellular-type ASRSs installed next to where the material is used, which reduces handling and transportation; it also aids the application of JIT (just-in-time) inventory flow.

U.S. companies are now looking more favorably at the smaller, cellular-type ASRSs that feed directly into production, but the same ratio of many more smaller installations may never be reached because of differences between U.S. and Japanese business operations.

Two very big differences are (1) in Japan its industry is highly concentrated, while in the United States it is sprawled across the nation, and (2) Japan's raw materials sources and finished goods markets can be directly accessed by ocean freight while much of U.S. supply is located inland.

With these advantages Japan may always favor small ASRSs but the stronger attention given to operations and inventory costs in this country will probably continue the current trend toward the smaller, cellular-type installations being located in the work area where the stored materials will be consumed.

A Marriage of Rigid Storage Racks and Special Material Handling Cranes Characteristically an ASRS consists of banks of storage racks with narrow access aisles. The aisles are only a few inches wider than the material handling device with a load. The handling device carries the load beside it if it consists of one traveling column or between if there are two columns. This permits the narrowest aisles possible.

FIGURE 11.1 High-Rise, Automatic Storage and Retrieval System (ASRS)

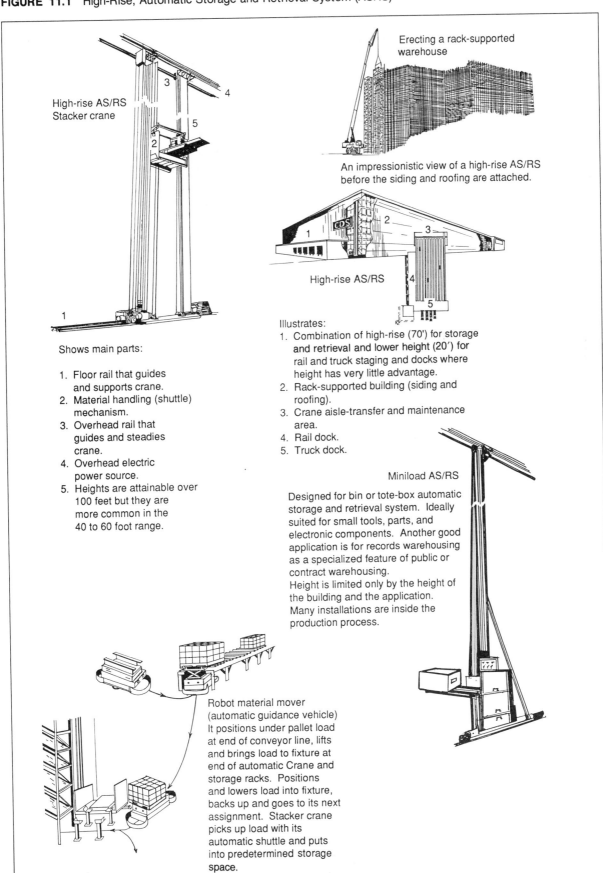

Erecting a rack-supported warehouse

An impressionistic view of a high-rise AS/RS before the siding and roofing are attached.

High-rise AS/RS Stacker crane

Shows main parts:

1. Floor rail that guides and supports crane.
2. Material handling (shuttle) mechanism.
3. Overhead rail that guides and steadies crane.
4. Overhead electric power source.
5. Heights are attainable over 100 feet but they are more common in the 40 to 60 foot range.

High-rise AS/RS

Illustrates:
1. Combination of high-rise (70') for storage and retrieval and lower height (20') for rail and truck staging and docks where height has very little advantage.
2. Rack-supported building (siding and roofing).
3. Crane aisle-transfer and maintenance area.
4. Rail dock.
5. Truck dock.

Miniload AS/RS

Designed for bin or tote-box automatic storage and retrieval system. Ideally suited for small tools, parts, and electronic components. Another good application is for records warehousing as a specialized feature of public or contract warehousing.
Height is limited only by the height of the building and the application. Many installations are inside the production process.

Robot material mover (automatic guidance vehicle) It positions under pallet load at end of conveyor line, lifts and brings load to fixture at end of automatic Crane and storage racks. Positions and lowers load into fixture, backs up and goes to its next assignment. Stacker crane picks up load with its automatic shuttle and puts into predetermined storage space.

The material handler commonly called a crane can be one or two columns having wheels that ride on a steel rail in the center of the aisle set in the floor. A rail suspended from the top of the racks or from the roof structure steadies the crane. It is this top rail that permits the cranes to operate much higher than material movers that do not have it. Some installations have a separate crane for each aisle; thus if there were ten aisles, there would be ten cranes. Or the system can be so designed that the cranes will move to the right or to the left just beyond the racks which permit one crane to handle more than one aisle. However, this ability to move between aisles automatically can be fraught with high costs and technical problems that cause many companies to opt for each aisle to have its own independent crane.

The best building configuration for ASRS with a separate crane for each aisle is high and deep, to get the most out of each aisle-captive crane. It is a narrow, high, and very long rectangle—even though in all other circumstances the shape of the building should be a perfect cube for it to be the most economical to construct and operate—as discussed in Chapter 5. But this changes when costly cranes are confined to one aisle each.

This can be illustrated by comparing two different configurations. First, let us assume a cube-shaped building 100 feet on each of its three directions that yields a total of 1,000,000 cubic feet. To fill an area this size with 4-foot-deep pallet racks and 4.5-foot-wide aisles would result in 16 rows of racks (14 of which are back-to-back) and 8 aisles 4.5 feet wide. (See Figure 11.2.) Although this could be the most economical to build, it would require eight automatic cranes, one for each aisle.

Next let us assume that the cranes are very expensive and it is clear that the cost of the building has less influence on total costs than does the number of cranes. Engineering finds that a building with only three crane aisles and six rows of racks is the most economical. The shape of the building would be 37.5 ft. wide × 100 ft. high × 266.7 ft. long = 1,000,000 cu. ft.

All this adds up to finding the optimum combination of building and crane costs. The amount of land needed in both are the same, but the area of exterior material required to cover the building is different.

	Cubic Shape	Long Rectangular Shape
Roof (100 ft. × 100 ft.)	10,000 sq. ft.	
Roof (37.5 ft. × 266.7 ft.)		10,000 sq. ft.
Two sides (100 ft. × 100 ft.)	20,000	—
Two sides (266.7 ft. × 100 ft.)	—	53,340
Two ends (100 ft. × 100 ft.)	20,000	—
Two ends (37.5 ft. × 100 ft.)	—	7,500
	50,000 sq. ft.	70,840 sq. ft.

The cost of five more cranes for the 8-aisle cube building should be compared to the cost of the additional 20,840 square feet (40 percent more) of siding for the long rectangular building.

Many other things will affect this comparison such as the configurations of the land sites that are available, whether it is a rack-supported building, and the capacity of the cranes. But, taking only the extra five cranes and the 20,840 square feet of additional siding into consideration, the cost comparison definitely favors the long rectangular. Therefore it can be concluded that in general for ASRS-type installations with a separate crane for each aisle you

FIGURE 11.2 High-Rise ASRS Building Configurations when a Crane Is Used for Each Aisle

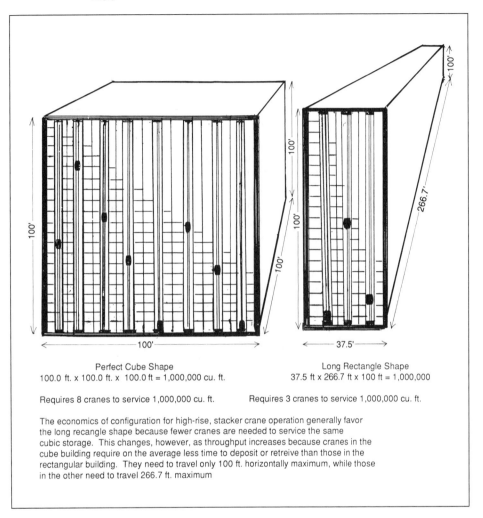

Perfect Cube Shape
100.0 ft. x 100.0 ft. x 100.0 ft = 1,000,000 cu. ft.

Long Rectangle Shape
37.5 ft x 266.7 ft x 100 ft = 1,000,000

Requires 8 cranes to service 1,000,000 cu. ft.

Requires 3 cranes to service 1,000,000 cu. ft.

The economics of configuration for high-rise, stacker crane operation generally favor
the long recangle shape because fewer cranes are needed to service the same
cubic storage. This changes, however, as throughput increases because cranes in the
cube building require on the average less time to deposit or retreive than those in the
rectangular building. They need to travel only 100 ft. horizontally maximum, while those
in the other need to travel 266.7 ft. maximum

will probably want to go with a long rectangular building. Keep in mind, however, that this logic and arithmetic does not apply to an overhead performing crane or to operator-up turret lift truck material handling vehicles, only to ASRS cranes that ride on rails in the aisle and are steadied by an overhead rail.

The cranes require repair and maintenance just like any other mobile equipment but generally less than lift trucks. Most cranes have an expected useful life much longer than lift trucks. Where cranes last 20 to 40 years, the usual life truck has an expected life of, say, 7 to 10 years—if it is electric. If gas, it is not expected to last as long and the maintenance repairs are more.

ASRS cranes require a place where mechanics and electricians can get at them for maintenance and repair. The narrow aisles in which they operate do not provide the room necessary to get at all that has to be got to. Therefore, at the far end of the racks there is a space where the crane can move beyond the racks, giving the mechanics and engineers all the maneuvering room they need. This space is an essential part of an ASRS crane system and must be provided in the design of the building. As well, the cost of this space should be appropriately assigned to the ASRS system.

Needed at the front end of the rack and crane area is a means to input stock into the system and take away what is order picked. The cranes are usually confined to the racks and R and M areas and a short distance in front of the racks to pick up and deposit loads. Commonly this area is highly conveyorized to permit inbound stock to be deposited at a place that is most efficient for the crane to pick up and put it away. Likewise, the crane-picked stock should be deposited where it is most efficient for the crane and let conveyors or some other material mover take it to where it is to be staged for outbound shipments.

Conveyors have all kinds of advantages, but too many can certainly clutter up an area for any other use. The alternatives are to move stock to and from the ASRS cranes by tow carts, conveyors, material-moving robots, and of course the common lift truck. Which is best depends on the particular situation. Important though is to realize that there is or can be a fixed route from the receiving docks to the stacker cranes and from the cranes to the shipping docks. These routings will include the flow of all or most of the inventories handled by the facility. These can be standard routings which should signal that they should be automated. It would be a shame to use lift trucks for moving one or two unit loads at a time. The situation cries out for conveyor, towline carts, or individual robot material movers without worker intervention. There are too many other functions in warehousing where human intellect and skills are needed to waste them here.

Whatever means is used to move stock to and from the cranes, there should be a surge area where loads can back up until they are ready to be handled. This can be a loop conveyor, a carousel, or whatever that will reliably meter the flow of unit loads to any automated part of the cycle, from unit-load receiving to crane storing, and from crane picking to staging and shipping, or to less-than-unit-load order picking, staging, and shipping.

The entire receiving and shipping processes should be done with the minimum human intervention except for an "overlord" watching all movement of materials on an electronically controlled mapboard showing where all material movers are at any time. When something must be changed or there is a problem in the flow, the "overlord" makes the necessary adjustments to get everything going and back on track.

Storage racks in an ASRS can have any design. There can even be different types of racks used for different type products in the same system, provided the crane and the computer program accommodates these differences. Probably the most common racks are those for unitized loads. These may be similar to pallet racks but may as well be flowthrough racks that provide at the opposite end for unit-load or less-than-unit-load order picking. Cantilever racks are also commonly used in automatic storage and retrieval systems.

Slave Pallets   When unitized loads are employed, there is need for a standard platform to support the unit load while being moved by the crane and while being stored in its slot in the racks. Generally, the pallets or slip sheets that are received with the loads cannot be used in automated systems and occasionally not in manually controlled cranes. Instead solid square or rectangular pieces of a good grade of plywood called slave pallets are used. Merchandise received on pallets or slip sheets is usually put intact on the slave pallets. Unless there is good reason not to, the pallets and slip sheets should stay on the slave pallets throughout the receiving-storing-order-picking-staging cycle.

Weigh Counting and Squaring Off Unit Loads   An important concern about receiving loads into the ASRS is that they are the right size for the rack slots in which they will be stored. This involves more than having the suppliers

make up the loads according to specifications. It includes automatically checking to see that the load actually does meet specifications before it is picked up
by the crane. This is usually accomplished by the unit loads traveling by conveyor over a weight-control check and then through a load-sizing apparatus that
makes certain size complies on all four sides and height. Every carton that has
been jostled must be put back in position in the unit load. This becomes evident
when you visualize a crane weighing tons blindly putting a unit load in an opening, say, 80 feet high and a carton is sticking out beyond the dimension of the
slot. The slave pallet and some of the cartons will get into the storage slot, but
some will come crashing down. This will not happen if size control is exercised
before the crane takes possession and nothing happens to shake loose the
squared-off unit load on the crane trip to the assigned stockage-rack slot, which
is usually a pretty smooth ride.

When the unit loads come apart too easily, some warehouses employ shrink
wraps or glue lines between layers of cartons.

Discipline and Standardization   ASRSs require discipline and standardization. It is all right to have a certain number of slots of a specific design for
one type load and another type for a different type load and so on just so that
the system is programmed both as to hardware and software. And, within these
categories there is 100 percent standardization. This should not frighten away
would-be users by forcing discipline and standardization on customers' fluctuating demands. What it means is to discipline and standardize all in-house
operational routines and then attend to those true exceptions.

Sturdy metal bins represent the acme of unit-loads. The most common
way bins are used in ASRS is for the host computer to activate the crane to get
the right bin and bring it to a workstation in front of the storage racks where a
worker removes the quantity of the SKU that is printed on a picking list or
shown on a CRT viewer situated next to where the bin is deposited. The worker
wands the bin SKU code, confirming that the right one is being picked, and
then signals how many are removed for the order and how many are left in the
bin. With computer agreement the crane returns the bin to its addressed slot
and picks the next bin according to computer instructions.

The only limitation for bins in an ASRS is that they are appropriate for
only a small share of the total inventories warehoused. But, if any inventory is
thought of and treated as though it were a disciplined and standard rectangular bin, it can be handled nearly as well as the actual bins. Even long SKUs
such as pipe, bar, and rod can be handled and stored in an ASRS in cantilever
racks—provided that the hardware and software are designed and programmed properly.

A Different Type of Crane, the Overhead Stacker   Another type of crane
used in ASRS and operator-up material handlers is the overhead stacker crane.
Its big advantage over the floor-rail-riding crane is that it has the capability to
move freely in front of and behind the rack system. It consists of a bridge that
spans between the roof support columns of a storage bay. It rides on steel rails
supported by these columns. A carriage with a vertical load support column
rides on the bridge and provides the free horizontal movement on steel rails.
The load-carrying apparatus moves up and down the rigid carriage column.
This type crane has the advantage of not being confined to one aisle or even the
entire rack system. It can maneuver freely wherever the bridge has rails to take
it. And, importantly, it can be locked out of running into the racks or any other
specified area such as an office or restrooms.

There are disadvantages of the overhead stacker crane, but they are not monumental. First, the building must be taller to provide the same storage height as a floor-rail crane or an independent floor-running material mover. Next, the rail system along the building support column, and the sturdy and heavy bridge that spans the storage bay, can be more costly than a crane that rides on floor rails.

I was responsible for two overhead stacker crane installations that were planned, designed, and installed in new warehouse facilities. The two systems were identical, except that one had a longer storage bay with more racks. The bridge of the cranes spanned 60-foot-wide bays and had the capacity of 3 tons. They were operator-up controlled except the operators could not, even if they deliberately tried to, drive the cranes into racks. This precaution was taken by programming each to be able to move freely through the rail receiving and staging area and the same through the truck staging and shipping area. But they could only operate *in the aisles* of the storage rack system.

Both the rail spur and truck loading dock were inside the building. The truck dock was recessed into the building far enough for the crane to load or unload flat bed trucks, which constituted about half of the freight. The crane also extended over the rail siding for the occasional times material arrived or was shipped on flat bed cars.

The cranes could deposit and retrieve stock to a height of about 40 feet in 46-foot-clear buildings. The rest of the warehouse was designed and constructed for storing up to 28 feet for lift truck handling. This because a good share of the inventories were best stored in bulk, without racks, and the stacker crane and racks were determined to be only marginally better, not enough to justify the additional equipment and higher building.

The aisles between racks for the stacker crane system were deliberately made 7 feet wide despite the fact that the crane only needed a little more than 5-foot-wide aisles—and this was clearly understood before designing the facility. "But, if you knew better, why did you do it?" "Hmm . . . another good question, but I'm glad you asked so I can make a better point of it." Stacker cranes of this nature were new to me, and it was back when they were still new to most. Ours was the first such installation on the West Coast. The reasoning behind the wider than necessary aisles was that if the cranes did not work as planned or if it took longer than expected to get the crane back in operation after a breakdown, customer orders would not be delayed. To buy a second crane to stand by seemed outlandish. Then too there was the chance both cranes could be out at the same time. So we decided to provide a side-loader material mover and straddle our bet. The side loader would operate in 7-foot-wide aisles. I had theorized that loss of a little over two feet per aisle was cheap enough insurance to assure that customers would be reliably supplied. We did, however, have to put guides along the base of the racks to prevent the side loader from crashing into the racks.

As the venture turned out we could have avoided purchase of the side loaders. The cranes were and are so reliable they have never needed a back up. And breakdowns were so few and repairs made so quickly these were not a factor. The only saving grace is that we did use both during the heaviest shipping periods to avoid a third shift.

One particularly good thing in the layout was to have the only office door to the warehouse open on a dramatic view of the high-rise stacker crane system. It was an awe-inspiring sight. To add to the effect, all the racks were painted bright white enamel. The ceiling was white, the floors regularly shined, and the yellow lines were freshly painted. The lighting was a little better than necessary. Visitors were definitely impressed!

Unique Building Design: Its Features and Advantages

There is a unique feature of building design that surfaces (Figure 11.1) when serious consideration is given to constructing high-rise automated warehouses. This is that the racks can serve as the framework for the building because the racks are designed to be exceptionally strong. Outside metal siding with proper fixtures can be attached and supported by the racks inside. The roof has the same feature, which does away with the many costly girders and trusses that make up the framework of conventionally designed warehouse buildings.

This feature makes the building inseparable from the storage racks. Since racks are classified by the IRS as equipment, so the metal siding and roofing that cover the racks should also be classed equipment. You certainly cannot remove the rack equipment and use the building for another purpose—again, they are physically inseparable.

This construction technique provides three important advantages.

1. The cost of the facility including the racks and exterior covering can constitute a major cost savings compared to conventional warehouse buildings where the building and the racks are separate.

2. The rack system can be erected much more efficiently. The racks are assembled then the sheet-metal walls and roof are attached and supported by the racks. Erecting high-rise racks within an existing building is much more difficult.

3. The combination of the racks and the shelter that protects the racks should be declared equipment as far as the IRS is concerned. As such it is entitled to the faster depreciation of equipment compared to that allowed for buildings. Also the entire superstructure should qualify for any investment tax credit provided by the government. These serendipities have been sufficient to turn marginal investments in such facilities to good and very good investments.

Caution is suggested, however; a company should not embark on such a facility program assuming there are tax and investment credit savings without first getting legal guidance. The IRS uses depreciation and investments as the proverbial football that gets kicked this and that way. Their many changes are not conducive to including tax and investment credit rules in a text of this nature. Far better is to get such advice from a tax consultant who has specialized in such matters.

Semiautomated Storage and Retrieval Systems

A fully automatic system for storage and retrieval requires rigid discipline and standardization. When these conditions can be met, full automation should be the goal. But this should not become a fanatical goal. Better to have a smooth-running semiautomatic system than a fully automatic one that is filled with stress and strain and never really works as the designers planned.

A semiautomatic system involves an operator-up. Instructions show on a small CRT viewer or a printer or both in the cage. All the checks and balances of inventory are performed as in the fully automatic system. But, how does the crane and order picker know where to move and in what SKU sequence to achieve the most efficient routing? The order picker is advised on the viewer or printer the address of the next SKU location or the crane automatically responds to the electronic impulses from the host computer that determines and automatically takes the best routing. When one assignment is complete, the rider or the crane is directed to take the stock to a deposit fixture outside the racks where conveyors, robot material movers, or manually driven lift trucks take over and move the stock to staging where the goods are assembled for shipment.

Probably more systems should be fully automatic than they are and far more manual systems should be semiautomatic than they are. Yet, generally, when either of these systems is in and running, employees commonly agree: "I just don't know how we ever did it before."

Operator-Up Turret Side Loaders

There are essentially two ways to provide the material handling for high-rise racks with narrow aisles: the crane, as already discussed, and a mobile unit that an operator drives from a cage that travels up and down with the carriage and load. (See Figure 9.1.) There are usually guard rails attached to the floor to assist the driver in keeping the mobile unit within the narrow aisles and true to its course. It rides on hard rubber or plastic tires similar to those of a lift truck. It is powered by batteries. So equipped, it can be driven freely between as well as up and down aisles. And it can be driven away from the rack system for R and M to recharge batteries or for whatever reason. This capability to move about freely is its primarily advantage, and a big advantage it is. Being able to handle the material flow in one or several aisles permits full utilization of the equipment.

Another advantage of these high-rise mobile units is that the long, narrow building that is most economical to house cranes that serve only one aisle, discussed earlier, is no longer the best. In fact if the mobile unit can freely move with its own power source, the economics of the cube design again prevails, as discussed in Chapter 5.

The features of the high-lift, operator-up, turret side-load vehicles are listed here with brief comments about the nature of each. The capacities are indicated in terms of their upper limits where appropriate. The specifications should be taken only as indicative not as absolute. (See Figure 9.1.)

Lift height	Forty feet is considered very high for this type vehicle. Above this, cranes take over because they are secured by a top guide rail.
Lift speeds	Empty, about 80 fpm (feet per minute).
	With a 2,000-pound load, about 70 fpm.
	With a 4,000-pound load, about 65 fpm.
Lowering Speeds	Empty, about 80 fpm.
	With load, about 65 fpm.
Travel speeds	Empty (forks and cab), lowered and forks withdrawn, about 400 fpm.
	Loaded and any other positions, between 85 and 170 fpm.
	(For reference, a good steady pace for an adult to walk is about 260 fpm.)
Fork pivot	A full 180 degrees, permitting pickup and deposit from either side or front.

Electrical source   Some designs utilize only battery power. Others use an electrical source inside the confines of the rack system and use its batteries only when outside the rack system such as to change aisles or move to and from the battery recharge station.

THE ADVANTAGES OF HIGH-RISE AUTOMATION OVER CONVENTIONAL WAREHOUSING

The advantages of high-rise automated warehousing over conventional warehousing should obviously be sufficient to justify making the change or no change should be made. But, for this observation to be valid, the data on which the evaluation is made must be valid and complete.

Sometimes the benefits of high-rise ASRS appear so obvious that those who control such expenditures will authorize based on enthusiastic intuition and little else. But this, fortunately, is the exception. The information on which the decision is based should be prepared carefully and presented professionally. And it must show clearly the proposed system to be significantly better or it should not be authorized.

The glitter and drama of high-rise automated warehousing can have a positive value to employee and customer relations, but rarely should this be the sole basis for acquiring the system, though it should not be ruled out either. Some companies suffer from a dated reputation that repels customers and investors, and dims employee moral, which adversely affects productivity. A new high-rise ASRS may be just the thing to turn such an image around, and it could be the least expensive way to do it.

"The high-rise ASRSs that have been built in the past have mainly been justified by consideration of only employee and floor space reductions," so say leading designers and producers of such systems. Assuming they know what they are talking about, what pathetically inadequate information on which to base such major decisions. Probably there would be far more high-rise ASRSs in operation today if the bigger picture were taken into consideration.

Here is a list of things favorably influenced by such systems followed by a discussion of each.

1. Inventories, reduced by 10 to 30 percent
2. Employees, reduced by 30 to 60 percent
3. Land, reduced by 50 to 60 percent
4. Repair and maintenance, reduced
5. Utilities usage, reduced
6. Pilferage, reduced
7. Product damage, reduced
8. Fire protection, improved
9. Support equipment, improved
10. Housekeeping, improved
11. Customer service, improved

Inventories.   Until it hit home that offshore competition was producing better goods at less cost, true concern about inventories was lacking in this country's business leaders. Then, when the situation had to be faced, the big question was: "What's competition doing that we aren't?" Many things were done differently, but the two that relate most to the subject at hand are (1) less, much less inventory and (2) more, much more automation, including ASRSs and robotics in general.

In comparing attitudes toward inventories, a vast difference separated the two. No doubt both believed more or less that timely customer deliveries were important. Where the difference came was in how much inventory was necessary to support timely deliveries.

The next big question was: "Why was foreign competition able to do more with less?" The answer that came back was contrary to the one they believed kept the good ol' US of A number one for so long. Foreign competition was emphasizing the old-fashioned concept of "reliability," reliability in producing high-quality products by removing causes of error which resulted in superior design and superior workmanship.

How all this relates to high-rise ASRSs is that they are capable of reducing to nil errors in receiving, storing, and shipping. High-rise ASRSs cannot create a better product, but they can make great strides in reducing shipping errors and improving customer relations, which constitute a big share of the total problem. With total reliability in all phases of warehousing, there is no need to carry backup inventories to cover for its errors. Even companies that did not include inventory reduction in their reasons to initially get into high-rise ASRS report 10 to 30 percent inventory reductions. "What does that amount to in dollars and cents?" asks the hard-nosed CEO. "Well, if we accept our industrial engineering department's figures that inventory costs an annual 30 percent and an average of what ASRS users claim they have reduced inventories, say 20 percent, with yesterday's report on how much is in our inventory at cost, about $10.5 million, we should save $630,000 a year. That's nothing to sneeze at, and that figure doesn't include personnel and space savings or any of those other goodies—like stopping theft. I know we've got a problem with this. How big I don't know. The inventory records are too wacky to tell."

"I think we should look into it further; what do you think, boss?"

"Do it!"

Employees. A final figure for this requires detailed comparison of the before and after systems, but probably it can be safely claimed a reduction of 40 to 60 percent of the entire warehouse division's personnel. It affects more than the material handling employees. Its accuracy, reliability, and real-time work and inventory status cut deep into floor supervision, clerks, engineers, and other staff support—and it helps the manager be a better manager.

The automatic crane and rack system compared with conventional warehousing results in fairly obvious employee reduction. But conveyors, robotics, and other automatic features can be just as effective in reducing worker and staff time. Doing things right the first time accounts for a significant part of the personnel reduction, while at the same time resulting in big improvements in accountability and customer service.

Land. The difference in space requirements of high-rise handling and storing compared to conventional lift truck, pallet-rack warehousing are the most obvious and dramatic changes. Aisles are narrower and storage racks are higher. Compared to that needed for conventional sit-down lift trucks, the aisles will reduce from about 12 feet (which is most common for this type of lift truck) to perhaps 5 feet, which is ample for automatic crane handling with 4-foot-deep pallets. This change alone reduces space needed for aisles by 58 percent, from 12 feet to 5 feet.

Added to this is that the high-rise can make better, much better, use of square feet (floor and roof) by racks that permit storing to, say, 75 feet, three times as high as our assumed conventional warehouse of 25 feet. This height is not unusual. High-rise warehouses in the 100-foot range are feasible with examples around to attest to it.

The comparison comes down to this. The high-rise ASRS permits using aisles 5 feet wide instead of 12 feet wide and store three times as high, 25 versus 75 feet. Of course, this comparison is loaded to dramatize the differences, but it is not without precedent. The factor most likely to narrow the difference in the comparison is the aisles. The conventional warehouse could be using narrow-aisle handling equipment and already have narrower aisles, which would reduce this difference. On the other hand, the storage height of the conventional warehouse could be less than the 25 feet used, which would increase the difference. It is necessary to compare specific layouts to determine more precise differences.

It is probably safe to say, though, that a high-rise ASRS warehouse will reduce overall site requirements by, say, 50 to 60 percent, which translates to a sizable savings in land costs. Such land savings may make possible getting a more desirable warehouse location than could be afforded when so much more land area is required with conventional warehouse designs. Or the land saving will go along way toward paying for the more costly handling and storing equipment.

Repair and Maintenance.   There is a significant difference in repair and maintenance in high-rise ASRS and conventional warehousing. This relates mainly to the material handling equipment. First and foremost is that cranes take far longer to wear out than do lift trucks. It is rare that you will see a lift truck over 10 years old that has had continuous use. If you do you will see one that has probably been completely overhauled a few times and has a long, costly record of repairs, replacements, and maintenance. And what you see is probably electrically powered. An LPG lift truck would require even more to keep it going that long.

Yet cranes seem to last forever with less attention. They are of entirely different design. The path they travel is a good example. Movement forward and back is on steel wheels on steel rails (or hard plastic on steel or hard plastic) which have far less resistance than do rubber tires on concrete. Further, these type cranes are not subjected to the pounding and jostling that lift trucks are. All this comes down to perhaps a 7- to 10-year life for lift trucks compared to say a 20- to 40-year life for cranes. Probably there are as many cranes in use over 40 years than there are lift trucks in use over ten years. It is still too soon to know the expectant life of the cranes used in high-rise and automated warehouses because this type warehousing is still too new. But as a class of material handling equipment, cranes' longevity far exceeds that of lift trucks.

Utilities.   Utilities for the high-rise ASRS installation are less than for a comparable amount of activity in a conventional warehouse because there is less area to light, less material handling equipment to operate, and fewer employees to provide for. The reason for less area to light is a particularly interesting one. The high-rise rack area is in total darkness, no lighting. This is because the crane operates automatically without ability or reason to see. This comes as a surprise to those being initiated to an ASRS for the first time—as it did to me.

Pilferage.   Theft losses, when admitted, amount to a hefty part of warehousing costs—at least for those having attractive items that can be easily carried away. Even some warehouses whose inventories seem difficult to carry away and hard to fence are stolen.

The largest caper I have encountered involved a coordinated effort of warehouse workers, truckers, and a fence to dispose of the goods. The material was metal billets used in making extrusions—what appeared to be a highly unlikely thing to steal. Yet the theft continued over many months, involving hundreds of thousands of dollars. As experts already know, any type merchandise that has a value is subject to theft.

The high-rise ASRS provides the single best deterrent to theft in warehousing. It is a by-product of the rigid accountability imposed by computer tracking of every inventory item, and every worker who does anything with it, from placing the order with the supplier to eventual delivery to, and receipt by, the warehouse customer. At each juncture the computer queries who is doing what to which and how many there are and how many are left. If any response is different from what it should be, bells should ring and horns should blow.

Another valuable deterrent is how merchandise is stored in the high-rise racks. Employee access to the stored inventory is virtually impossible. The system is designed to be automatically accessed by a crane, not humans. You could say that it is just not human friendly. The crane will only activate by an authorized code. When the crane moves in the aisle, it is tracked by a CRT. Where the crane stops to deposit or retrieve is also tracked via the CRT, and the bar code of that address must agree with where it is supposed to be.

Further, a beam of light across the front and back of the rack system could activate an alarm if broken to discourage unauthorized entry during off-work times. Even if a thief were to get past this, the total darkness in the rack system would serve as a further deterrent.

No high-rise ASRS is 100 percent pilferageproof. Still, the high-rise ASRS is the best place to build a relatively theft-proof system.

Product Damage. The high-rise ASRS has less chance of damaging inventories than does conventional warehousing. All handling and storing are far more disciplined. A good way to appreciate this difference is to consider the causes of damage in conventional warehousing and how these are dealt with in a high-rise ASRS.

1. Stacking too high for the particular product's strength to support the pressure from above. Bottom items crush. This can cause stacks of unitized loads to topple causing much more damage. Worse, a stack of unitized loads can lean too hard against another stack causing the domino effect, bringing all the neatly lined rows of stacked pallets in harm's way to come crashing down.

   The high-rise ASRS has a separate, independently supported storage slot for each unit load. It is not possible to stack one load on another.

2. Unit loads come apart in the process of picking them up; part to all of the product units fall off causing damage.

   The high-rise automated system requires that unit loads are secure and squared off. Special tests before the crane gets the load assure this. Such a rigid requirement is not commonly imposed in conventional warehousing. Normally it is not necessary—though it may be good practice to enforce it in more warehousing situations than it is.

3. Lift truck jars and tips part to all of the load. This can be caused as simply as accidentally running over a board left in the aisle or a depression in the concrete floor resulting from continuous chipping away by lift

trucks passing over what began as a hairline crack. The crane in the high-rise ASRS provides a consistently smoother ride and the chance of debris being left on the track is extremely remote if not impossible.

4. Bumping the load at a corner of bulk storage or while threading a lift truck in or out of a deep bulk storage lane (with rows of pallet stacks on both sides) is always a possibility. It happens enough to be a recognized source of product damage.

   The precision of automatic crane handling coupled with the damage preventive means it employs makes bumping one load with another extremely remote if not impossible.

Perhaps the most important thing about a high-rise ASRS is that it is as far removed from human frailty as a material handling and storing system can get. As an automobile can be used as an instrument of destruction, so can a lift truck and a lift truck with a load even more so. Any work that requires frequent judgment calls, alertness at all times, exceptional depth perception, and plenty of skill is an accident ready to happen—particularly when a few tons of mass are involved. Anything that will reduce the chances or magnitude of a slip-up should be recognized for its value and a high-rise ASRS virtually eliminates damage from this cause.

Fire Protection.   High-rise storage racks require in-rack fire extinguishers and not uncommonly at every pallet level up. This is as it should be. Fire is warehousing's number one dread. Unchecked, fire in warehousing is devastating.

   Even warehouses that have the usual overhead sprinkler system go up in flames. The sprinkler system can be in complete compliance, but management has the workers store too high, too close to the sprinkler heads to spray far enough to overlap with spray from the next sprinkler heads. Once the roof catches, all that will be left is regrets. Regrets that the fire code was abused to squeeze in a little more inventory than permitted for the system to be as effective as designed.

   Another way to abuse a sprinkler system is to store more flammable inventory than the system was designed for. The sprinkler system may go on just as designed but fail to quench the intensity of fire that emerges. Sprinkler heads and piping are definitely required inside the racks for high-rise warehousing.

   Perhaps part of the cost of an in-rack system can be treated in the economic justification as an improvement over the existing system to help strengthen the total justification. In-rack sprinkler systems are definitely better protection than the usual, single overhead systems in conventional warehouses.

Support Equipment.   A high-rise ASRS should not be imposed on top of a conventional warehousing system. It should replace all or most of it. For the inventories that go through the ASRS, the cranes take the place of lift trucks for depositing and retrieving. But the crane is not as flexible as the lift truck. It can neither zip in and out of rail cars and trucks to load and unload, nor can it move the stock from the receiving dock to the racks. The fact is it cannot do any of material handling outside the confines of the rack system. But a bit surprising is that in a ASRS environment the lift truck is not the best equipment for these functions. Much better to have the stock moved along these relatively fixed routes with automatic conveyances such as conveyers, drag lines, or material moving robots. The fact that lift trucks require operators is a major limitation when thinking or doing automation. Even the loading and unloading of rail cars and trucks is often achieved better with conveyor means in the beds of the vehicles that interface with conveyor means on the dock floor. The conventional warehouse equipment should stay only if it is best for the application. Any excess equipment should be disposed of as best possible.

When you are submitting the justification report for a high-rise ASRS, you should include consideration of automation for handling the goods from unlocking the door of the inbound carrier until the outbound carrier leaves for delivery.

Probably a means for counting by weighing and a unit-load squarer-offer will be part of the support equipment. A lot of the other equipment discussed and illustrated in this chapter should be given serious consideration. Rarely does an ASRS take over all the inventories, and it should not be forced to do other than what it can do best. One of the largest such systems in the United States handles and stores only unitized loads. The loads are transferred to another adjacent building that is set up to order pick by case and less than case quantities with more conventional warehouse equipment and procedures.

Housekeeping. A chore in every warehouse is housekeeping, and often it is done rather poorly. Part of the reason for this is that it is difficult to reconcile two different opinions as to who is responsible for it. Many warehouses solve this dilemma by employing janitors. The lift truck operators and lumpers throw dunnage and trash in little heaps about the warehouse for the janitors to remove. This could very well be the best way. It keeps material handlers handling materials, not doing less demanding housekeeping functions.

Other warehouses go to the other extreme and insist that all workers clean up their own litter. The rational behind this is that if workers know that they must clean up after themselves, they will not litter as much. The rule is that a job is not done until the tidying up has been done. Common areas that are difficult to assign are cleaned up by all workers lending a hand when the supervisor deems it necessary. Often this is done just before the end of the shift. A limitation of the clean-up-after-yourself idea is that certain workers, mainly equipment operators, feel any clean up is a poor use of their talents—or it is below their dignity.

Fortunately the high-rise ASRS has less space to housekeep. Not only does it occupy much less floor space than does conventional warehousing, its high-rise storage has little to no litter due to loads being secure going in and coming out of the system. Further, loads are put in and taken out with greater precision so that less damage is incurred during these operations.

Customer Relations. If you were to specify the most important things for customer service, you would probably develop a list something like this.

> Honesty
> Reliability
> Responsiveness
> Courteousness

The ASRS is designed to accommodate these features. Basic to good customer service, and a feature of automated warehousing, is the ability to know status on a real time basis and the capacity to take on large fluctuations in demand with bogging down.

Safety of Operations. Claiming high-rise automated warehousing is *safer* is like needlessly climbing out on a limb because companies that advertise this equipment do not include *safer* as one of its attributes. At least I have not witnessed it. But it does seem to be safer, considering the many beneficial things claimed for it. Following are characteristics that seem to me to constitute safer operations, but you decide for yourself.

1. Overall fewer employees, fewer accidents.
2. Automatic putting into and taking from storage, two of conventional warehousing's most labor intensive and hazardous functions. No employees, no accidents.
3. Other functions like moving materials to or from storage is automatic. No employees, no accidents.

Caution! Watch out that the commonly used performance measurement of safety—*how many employee days without an accident,* or anything similar—is not used as a measure of an automated warehouse's safety, at least not to compare with the same type record in conventional warehouse. Why? Because an automated warehouse will handle, say, 1,000,000 pounds during 100 safe employee days, while a conventional warehouse that handles precisely the same but only half as productive uses 200 safe employee days. Does this mean that the automated warehouse is just half as safe—because it has gone only half as long without an accident—or does it say there is something wrong with the performance measurement?

Backed up with a truly reliable and responsive system, it's easier to be honest, reliable, responsive and courteous. Without such a system, you cannot even be honest in making promises or accurate in describing the status of this or that. At least you appear to be dishonest or inaccurate to your customers. Top management should provide what is needed to provide the service it expects. ASRS may well be just what is needed.

HOW TO AUTOMATE ON A LOW BUDGET

Addressed here is how to get the most benefits for the least expenditure, or expressed another way, how to get the most bang for the buck.

To begin with only those things that are repetitious and can be disciplined are candidates for automation. But most of warehousing is repetitious and can be disciplined, so it should not take long to dispense with that consideration. Now the question is in what order things should be automated to realize the most return in the shortest time? Simply these are the things that constitute *how to automate on a low budget.*

This is something many warehouses would like to do but hold off doing because of the impression that automation costs a fortune. High-rises with huge banks of racks and automatic cranes and other support equipment do cost a lot, but there are far more warehousing situations that are candidates for automation on a smaller scale.

If I were to be pressed for what automation would yield the most for the least investment, I would say in order of importance the following:

1. *Combine Bar Coding and Computer*

   Introduce a combination of bar coding interfaced with a host computer and remote terminals enabling a warehouse to achieve quantum leaps in productivity, quality of service, and reliability for the following basic functions:

- Managing inventories to get the most with the least.
- Addressing and stock locating interfaced with computerization to permit instant, real-time knowledge of what stock is where at all times.
- Laying out the warehouse for optimum handling and storing efficiencies.
- Directing storing and order picking through terminals with small rugged CRTs on lift trucks and material moving equipment to attain optimum efficiency.

2. *Introduce Standards and Performance Measurement*

Establish and employ handling time and space utilization standards with performance measurement to monitor all systems and to highlight opportunities and problem areas. Spend staff help on exceptions, not on routine that your bar-coding and computer programs can do much better and faster.

3. *Automate Sections of Material Flow*

Identify routes of repetitious material flow through the warehouse and automate with any or all of the following proven winners.

- Dragline
- Pneumatic tube
- Automatic guidance vehicle
- Conveyor
- Monorail

4. *Employ Flowthrough Order-Picking Racks*

For the 20 percent of the SKUs that account for 80 percent of the activity, employ flowthrough order-picking racks. Use operator-up order-picking lift trucks to utilized height. Or install a mezzanine for two (or more) levels. Use monorail, chute, or conveyor to bring picked materials to the staging area. Use conveyor with traffic cops and bar coding to sort and send materials to the right staging area for shipping.

5. *Eliminate Paperwork*

Use terminals throughout the warehouse to communicate between the host computer and the work stations. Print packing lists and bills of lading for carriers through a terminal or terminals at the shipping dock.

6. *Improve Employee Morale*

Devise ways for all employees to benefit from the improvements that they implement and help make winners.

There are many more things that can be done to automate but the foregoing are intended as an extension of Pareto's law—with 20 percent expenditure, 80 percent good can be realized.

Automating warehouses is not all new. It has gone on for decades, and not just selectively.

For those who automated their installations early on, it is time to resume their leadership. What has been learned over the years, with the new tools that have become available, should make getting and maintaining the best that automation has to offer a breeze or at least a lot easier than was taking the initial step.

Chapter 12

How to Measure Warehouse Performance

CHAPTER HIGHLIGHTS

This chapter concerns setting standards and establishing performance measurement for

1. *Material handling.*
2. *Material storing.*
3. *Error-free shipping.*
4. *Promised delivery time.*
5. *Operating costs.*

Included is a case history discussion of a plan for the development and implementation of a performance measurement program for a typical warehouse.

Standards are the foundation of warehouse management. They are essential for objective performance measurement and control, which in turn are necessary to satisfy the warehousing and company goals. Without them, decisions are based on subjective estimates, which are emotional and variable and, therefore, not reliable.

When navigators learned to use a star as a fixed reference point, they were able to determine their position wherever they sailed. A stake in the ground serves the same for surveyors; they need a point of reference for their maps. Warehouse management must also have its star or stake-in-the-ground to guide it in carrying out its plans. With time and space standards, the effectiveness of handling and storing efficiency can be measured and controlled. Without them, performance is based on individuals' judgments, which may be good or bad but never consistently right. Comparisons of warehouses that do not have an effective standards and performance measurement with those that do show big differences.

Also, the productivity of different workers within the uncontrolled warehouse varies far more than those in warehouses that have standard controls. Those with firsthand experience supervising warehouse employees recognize that the best workers can accomplish at least twice as much as the poorest workers. This is to say that if good employees' work were rated at 100 percent, the poor ones would be rated at 50 percent. Translating this to dollars, a project that would cost $100 in labor to accomplish with the best workers will cost $200 using the poorest. If you are more comfortable with larger amounts, add three zeros to each. Now you have $100,000 difference in employees. That should get attention.

The same range of error rates exists between the best and poorest workers. Often the highest producers have the lowest error rates, but not always. Performance reports provide the insight to compliment where warranted and give help where needed—objectively. Performance reports also provide the insight to tell the difference between busyness and productivity. Some employees will drive their lift truck 1,000 feet to pick, say, 3 different SKUs. Another will pick the same SKUs traveling only 500 feet. Often as not, the long-distance traveler does not recognize that he or she travels twice as far as necessary to pick orders. Even when this is recognized, the worker probably does not realize the additional costs being incurred—for certain, it is a lot more than wages.

If a supervisor in a *nonstandard, controlled* warehouse thinks a certain worker is far less productive than another, he or she must point this out with what may be called "circumstantial evidence." About this time the supervisor would surely welcome an objective factual report that reflects the worker's input as to what was achieved compared to what should have been achieved—and a comparison with other workers doing the same. Even better, a comparison with what the worker used to do before the drop in efficiency—if this is the case. "Hey, Joe, let's look at this report together. You may be working too hard for what you are getting done." Far, far better this is than: "Hey, Joe, you either work harder or you're out."

What does it mean when the boss says *"work harder"*? Do not take the authorized rest breaks? Or the boss is having a bad day? "Work harder" is a subjective instruction that has many interpretations.

HANDLING TIME STANDARDS: HOW TO DETERMINE HOW MUCH TIME A WAREHOUSE ACTIVITY SHOULD TAKE

Commonly heard is: "You cannot put time standards on warehouse work; it varies too much and every job has a different priority." It is important to realize that valid time standards can be set on warehouse work—and on any other type of work that has a direct relationship to time, even doctors, dentists, and lawyers.

In the not too distant past, because of the huge amount of time necessary, first, to establish standards and, then, to maintain them, many were poorly developed or out-of-date. Now with a good bar code system and much-higher-power yet lower-cost computers, there should be no excuse for not having valid and current standards in warehouse operations.

It is best to have all work covered by standards. This avoids the problem of how to deal with nonstandard work, which unless very tightly controlled, tends to reduce the effectiveness of the standards. Some warehouses find it too costly to set and maintain standards for certain operations, but they cover all routine work. If this compromise is necessary, the standard work should be clearly isolated, as far as reports and records are concerned, from the nonstandard work. Controls must assure that the time spent on standard work is the exact time spent on that work and that the same is true of nonstandard work. Any variance in the time reporting will adversely affect the usefulness of the entire standards program.

Consider this example:

Actual time related to work *on standard*	5.6 hr.
Standard time earned	4.7 hr.
Performance (4.7 hr. ÷ 5.6 hr.) = 84%	
Actual time worked *on nonstandard*	1.9 hr.
Standard time earned (1.9 hr. × 84%)	1.6 hr.
Total actual time worked	7.5 hr.
Total standard time earned	6.3 hr.
Total performance (6.3 hr. ÷ 7.5 hr.) = 84%	

Another way to deal with the performance of work not on standard is to consider all of it done at 100 percent, though much of the total performance could be distorted this way. Example:

Actual time related to work on standard	3.5 hr.
Standard time earned	2.1 hr.
Performance (2.1 hr. ÷ 3.5 hr.) = 60%	
Actual time worked on nonstandard	4.0 hr.
Standard time earned (4.0 hr. at 100%)	4.0 hr.
Total actual time worked	7.5 hr.
Total standard time earned	6.1 hr.
Total performance (6.1 hr. ÷ 7.5 hr.) = 81%	

The total performance of 81 percent is too high with reference to 60 percent for that covered by standards. The 60 percent is more indicative of the total. When nonstandard work is put in at 100 percent, the temptation for workers to fudge on their time reporting is increased. With the use of bar coding to report time, cheating is more difficult, but it is not impossible. Best to remove or at least decrease the temptation.

The degree of refinement to which the standards are developed is a key to how useful they will be. Standards can be developed in great detail, or they may be kept general. There can be many different parts or elements to each standard, or there can be only one or two. The elements are like toy building blocks. They can be small enough to cover a single motion, such as to turn on the ignition key of a lift truck, or they may be large enough to cover all the motions involved in unloading a rail car.

With small elements, many different standards can be developed, just as many different configurations can be built with many small building blocks. With but a few large elements or blocks, the application of standards is definitely more limited. Without the computerization and bar coding, time necessary to set and maintain detail was formidable, often so much that the refined approach was forsaken for larger elements. With these technological marvels, it is far more economical to go to the more refined elements that add validity to performance measurement and permit more thorough methods analysis to determine better ways to do things. If pay incentive is a part of the standards program, without a doubt you need the most refined standards possible.

The basic purpose of handling time standards is to determine how much time an activity should take to do. To illustrate how this is done, assume that two standards cover the entire work of a warehouse. The first is 2.0 hours to receive and put into storage each inbound shipment. The second is 1.0 hour to order-pick and load each outbound order. If the entire activity for a month consisted of 20 inbound shipments and 460 outbound orders, the computation to determine total standard time would be as follows:

> *Inbound*:
> 20 shipments at standard time of 2.0 hr. each   =   40 hr./mo.
>
> *Outbound*:
> 460 orders at standard time of 1.0 hr. each   = 460 hr./mo.
>
> *Total standard time earned*   500 hr./mo.

Now, if the warehouse actually used 600 hours to perform this work, the handling performance, or efficiency, is expressed as 83 percent (500 standard hours ÷ 600 actual hours).

Nonstandard work was not included in this example, but if it were, its efficiency should be 83 percent also. This method of treating nonstandard work as just discussed helps to reduce its effect on the standard work and provides a more valid overall performance measurement.

How to Set Handling Time Standards

Standards can be established by anyone who knows how or will take the time to learn. It is a technical process though, and care should be taken that whoever takes on the assignment is well qualified.

Another consideration is that the standards are *set objectively* and that this is recognized and accepted throughout the company. This means that warehousing should not be solely responsible for setting its own standards—for the same reason that foxes are not used to guard hen houses. They are not impartial.

If the company has an industrial engineering department or the equivalent, setting and maintaining standards should fall within its province. If it does not have one, the work is important enough to employ outside expertise. A good combination is to have highly qualified leadership from outside warehousing head up the project but use in large part warehouse staff to do the work. Then have this same outside source continue in an advisory and monitoring function, having the maintenance function performed by warehouse staff but directed and monitored by that separate authority that assures the objectivity feature.

The ideal is to have in-house industrial engineers take the assignment with the warehouse manager and one or two warehouse staff members and a lot of input from front-line supervisors. This combination is far better than having one or the other to do it all. To have the industrial engineers develop the standards apart is probably worse than the warehouse doing it all on its own.

Warehouse personnel must understand and honor the standards.

Four-Ways to Develop Handling Time Standards   Basically there are four different ways to develop handling time standards:

1. Historical data
2. Work sampling
3. Predetermined time elements
4. Time study

A brief description of each follows:

HISTORICAL DATA.   This technique involves an analysis of accurate time and work records to determine the average time required to perform specific functions. Provided that the records are available, this is the fastest way to determine standards, and if the records are reliable, the standards can be reliable. This technique offers a simple approach to setting standards that any warehouse can accomplish without an indepth technical knowledge of the subject.

The disadvantage of historical standards is that they are based on the *actual time taken* to perform the work rather than on the time it *should have taken* to do the work. If poor work practices are used, the standards will be based on these poor practices. The other techniques for establishing standards provide for analyzing the work while setting the standards so that the standard times established will be based on the best work practices possible under the existing conditions.

The best way to develop historical data standards is to install a good barcode, computerized time-keeping system to collect time by SKU, quantity, and activity. A few months of history of this will provide much higher-quality basic data to set good historical handling time standards.

WORK SAMPLING.   This is a technique for establishing standards that is based on the law of probability. If a statistically correct number of random samples are taken, the results are the same as though a continuous study were made. Proper work sampling permits setting standards in less time than by the regular time study. First, a survey is made to determine the work elements; then a statistically correct number and frequency of sample observations are made to determine the standard times for these elements.

The technique requires that the frequency of observations be truly random. This can be determined by pulling numbers from a hat, throwing dice, or—a safer method—using a published table of random numbers. The accuracy of the sample increases with the number of observations made. Work sampling is also effectively used to refine historical standards or in conjunction with the techniques of predetermined time elements and time study.

PREDETERMINED TIME ELEMENTS.   Frederick W. Taylor, the father of time study, and Frank B. Gilbreth, the father of motion study, both did developmental work in the use of predetermined time elements to set standards. Taylor's method involved subdividing operations into elements of work and time studying each element to assign the appropriate time. Gilbreth subdivided the work elements into motions, which he named "therbligs" (Gilbreth spelled backward). Handling time standards can be developed from predetermined times for either work elements or motions. Commonly known systems using basic elemental times are called MTM (methods time measurement) and BMT (basic motion time study).

Predetermined time standards are developed, following these steps:

1. Divide operations into essential and most efficient elements or motions.
2. Apply predetermined time elements.
3. Apply appropriate allowances: fatigue, personal, interference, and so on.
4. Calculate the standard time.

Predetermined standards offer the important advantage that very little observing time is required, and this only to determine the necessary elements. It also permits analysis of the operation in extreme detail to determine the most efficient work practice. This technique is often used to establish time standards for office work as well as for production and warehousing.

The technique also permits taking maximum advantage of computerization and bar coding. Using these implements should half the time necessary before their advent.

TIME STUDY.   This is the basic and most common method of setting handling time standards. Even though other techniques are used, there is usually need for some time study to verify or supplement the standards that are developed by the other means. Because this is the most common technique, and because an understanding of time study leads to a greater appreciation for standards in general, a brief description of the steps involved in setting standard this way is discussed here. It is not essential that warehouse management have an expert knowledge of how to develop standards, but it is important that it have sufficient knowledge of how they are developed and their appropriate application to have confidence in their use.

1. *Determine efficient handling practices.* Standards should be established on the best handling practices. To set them on poor practices perpetuates the poor ways of doing things. It would also make the standards so loose that they would become obsolete if the work were ever done right. Time should not be allowed in the standards for things that should not be done.

2. *Let workers and their supervisors know they are being time-studied.* Time study and standards should not be covert. The workers should be told that they are being studied and why. Time standards are simply an objective means of work measurement, just as a yardstick is an objective means of distance measurement. Too frequently, unfounded suspicion and fear of standards are created when these could be avoided entirely with a little early preparatory groundwork. Shame on those who do not do this.

3. *Divide the handling routines into useful elements.* An element in this case is a series of motions that take place within an interval of time. The elements may be large, such as all motions needed to unload a specific-type rail car of a specific commodity, or they may be small, such as the motions needed to start an electric lift truck. Warehouse management should determine the degree of refinement to be built into the standards. The more refined the standards are, the more they will cost to develop and to maintain. On the other hand, the more refined they are, the more useful they will be. It is important to determine the time and cost to establish and

maintain the standards in the context of having a bar code and computer system. You will probably find that you will opt for the best standards possible. The cost difference to go first cabin using bar coding and computerization is not that great.

4. *Determine the basic time required to perform each element.* Enough time studies should be taken, and they should be taken under enough different conditions, to establish the right amount of time needed to perform each work element. A good stopwatch is best for this purpose, but a regular wristwatch with a second hand can also be used and can be much less threatening.

5. *"Effort-rate" the basic time.* While the workers are being time studied, they should also be effort rated. The purpose of effort rating is to relate the pace of work that is being observed to the pace of work that is considered a fair day's work. The classical example of what is considered a fair day's work is an adult walking on a level surface at the rate of 3 miles an hour. The basis of this example is that the average worker can walk at this rate without undue fatigue.

6. *Add personal and fatigue allowances to the work-time data to establish total standard time.* The allowances will be different for different types of work. Heavy work, such as the manual handling of bags of cement or grain, should receive a larger fatigue allowance than driving a lift truck. Also, environmental conditions should be recognized in the allowances. Work that is performed in very hot and humid places should receive a larger allowance than work performed in favorable temperature and atmospheric conditions.

Most warehousing work involves personal and fatigue allowances of between 10 and 20 percent, with an average of about 15 percent. If a high degree of refinement is required in the standards, each element should be analyzed independently to determine the appropriate allowances. A good textbook on time standards will provide suggested allowances for different types of work.

7. *Add time allowances for delays due to interruptions of work.* An allowance should be built into the standards for delays and interruptions that are common to warehouse work. The purpose of the allowance is to give recognition to the reality that more warehouses absorb fluctuations in demand to free production of this so that its operations can be steady and more disciplined. When the allowance does not apply, do not put it in; when it does, include it.

Whoever is charged with responsibility for developing warehouse handling time standards should recognize and provide for this difference in production and warehousing standards—though it may not be covered in other warehousing or standards textbooks.

How to Get the Most from Handling Time Standards

The following are suggestions and principles for developing and using handling time standards:

1. Get a clear charter from top management, the CEO, or profit center manager for the entire scope of the program, including

        □ Computerization and bar coding.

        □ Standards and performance measurement program.

        □ Cooperation from all related divisions.

        □ Equipment and staff requirements.

2.   Install and maintain an effective bar code and computer system to

        □ Assist in developing and maintaining standards.

        □ Retain in computer memory the address and stock locator system.

        □ Have computer determine most efficient travel routes to put away receipts, order pick, stage, and load outbound.

        □ Accumulate in computer memory standard and actual times to provide performance measurement by worker and group of workers, by SKU and family of SKUs, and by function.

        □ Permit real-time access to all standards and performance data noted above.

        □ Permit access to the composition of standards, including each standard operating procedure's elemental times and allowances.

        □ Provide for both hard-copy printing as well as CRT viewing.

3.   Standards should be sufficiently refined to measure performance reliably and validly, regardless of changes in product mix.

4.   Devise means for bridging from existing to revised standards when changes are made so that performance continuity is maintained.

5.   Keep standards current, making changes as products and handling procedures change.

6.   Use standards and performance measurement for every feasible application, recognizing that the more used, the higher the quality they become. Following are some of their main applications.

        □ Calculate warehouse charge rates.

        □ Plan personnel and equipment requirements.

        □ Determine priorities for investigating material handling bottlenecks and efficiency problems.

        □ Promote constructive, good-natured competition among individuals, groups of employees, and warehouse facilities when there is more than one warehouse in the company.

        □ Set objectives and budgets.

        □ Analyze methods to determine optimum standard operating procedures.

        □ Determine efficiency (productivity) ranking of workers.

7.   Use performance measurement as the valuable objective management tool that it is—to train and motivate workers, not as a club to bludgeon and bully.

8.   Recognize and be guided by the simple truth that even the most minor negative reference to performance measurement can be devastating to some workers' egos. Used against the workers, it can be explosive, which can easily negate all its positive values. It is the quickest and surest way to sabotage the whole standards program.

9.   Genuinely enlist the workers and the union to be a constructive part and ally of the standards program.

Distribution of Performance Data

The complete warehouse standards should be in accessible computer memory with all activity reported via bar coding. Then with the right programming, real-time access to performance is a reality. What is going on, how well, and by whom can be accessed from a CRT-equipped terminal and/or with hard-copy performance reports. Determine who needs this information to do their jobs and provide only that which is needed. Do not send copies out for what you think is *business courtesy* or because "so and so" *may be interested.* The distribution of hard copies of reports should be few to none (as in a paperless warehouse).

The best way to distribute data about warehouse performance is with the paperless CRT viewers with access on a need-to-know basis.

The following guidelines are offered:

1. *The warehouse manager* and *assistant manager* should have total access to all warehousing's standards and performance measurement data.

2. *Industrial engineering* should have limited access to information it needs for current warehousing projects and those standards and functions it is charged with monitoring.

3. *Warehouse operations supervisors* should have limited access to all data that directly relates to their areas of authority and responsibility.

4. *The manager's boss* should have limited access to summary data. Any more should be at request to the manager to patch into specific data.

5. *Others* having need for data to perform their specific functions effectively, such as accounting,

   ○ To be aware of "on-order data" to know financial commitments.

   ○ To be aware of receipts to initiate payments.

   ○ To be aware of total inventory to know this part of the company assets.

   ○ To be aware of customer shipments to initiate invoicing for accounts receivable.

     Note that invoicing for shipments may be most effective and efficient if warehousing performs this function for accounting and they have real-time access to this data. Reason? Because warehousing is on real time with real-time customers and accounting is not.

   ○ To be aware of all capital equipment that is used by warehousing—for their assets, depreciation, and other fiscal concerns.

   ○ And any other accounting needs to perform its basic responsibilities.

     But no access should be permitted to give accounting even the hint that they are warehousing's performance watchdog other than for accountability for assets—and this in some companies resides with the treasury division not accounting. "Then who is warehousing responsible to for operating performance, if not accounting or treasury?" The answer is so trite it is somewhat embarrassing to state—*the warehouse manager's boss,* and no one else.

Similar access by other divisions to warehouse data should be made available on a need-to-know basis like that discussed for accounting but in far less scope. Divisions that are permitted access should not get the idea they are monitoring warehousing's performance. Some needs are satisfied best by phone or written inquiry rather than by access to computer memory. Under no condition should other divisions have the ability, let alone the right, *to change* warehousing's computer data. It must be the sole function of warehousing to maintain the continuity of accountability and prevent data chaos.

What Should Be Included in Performance Reports

Whether the performance data is called forth to a CRT viewer or hard copies are printed, how it is presented is almost as important as the data itself. Language and format can confuse or clearly convey the message intended. Why are some business reports so difficult and others so easy to read?

The format and information provided should be viewed through the eyes of the reader. This may require different reports to different people. So be it. If that is what is necessary to convey the message intended, it is far better than to send reports, or provide computer access, that the reader does not understand.

Commonly, simple graphs help readers to understand better than columns of figures or many words. The old adage about a picture being worth . . . is particularly applicable to presenting statistical data. And a computer with good color graphics can present such data efficiently and effectively. (See Figure 12.1 for examples of warehouse reporting of handling time performance.)

Panel (a) shows the combined performance (average) of all departments of warehousing for each of the last 12 months, the last calendar year goal, and this year's goal compared with performance each month for the current year.

Panel (b) compares the cumulative average performance by month and by calendar year.

When warehousing is divided into departments, separate graphs should be maintained for each, as illustrated in (c) and (d) for a two-department warehouse: receiving, which includes unloading inbound carriers, staging, and putting stock in storage, and shipping, which includes order picking, staging, and loading outbound carriers.

There are many advantages to be realized by maintaining performance by components of the total—particularly for medium- to large-sized warehouses. As illustrated by the receiving and shipping graphs in (c) and (d), it breaks down problems and opportunities into more manageable size. One of the important things that separate performance reports show is how each department contributes to the total. For instance in August of the current year the total performance was 100 percent. To average this Receiving had a 104 percent which had to offset Shipping's 97 percent performance. Shipping has more employees; therefore, its performance carries more weight than does receiving's performance. The graphs also show that shipping's performance is commonly lower than receiving's performance, not by a great deal but enough to be concerned. The manager should meet with each of the department supervisors separately to discuss their department's performance. Both are improving, which is positive. For this, both should be congratulated, but both should still be asked how help can be given to help them carry out their responsibilities.

There can be many things that cause shipping's performance to be lower. Following are a few.

1. Neglect in reporting things that would earn more standard hours such as recoup (sort, repair, or scrap) damaged merchandise.

2. Not enough lift trucks resulting in too much wait time—or more is done manually that could be more efficiently done with a lift truck.

3. Peer pressure to dog it a little: "They're getting their money's worth—they're not paying us enough to break our backs."

FIGURE 12.1 Handling-Time Performance Report

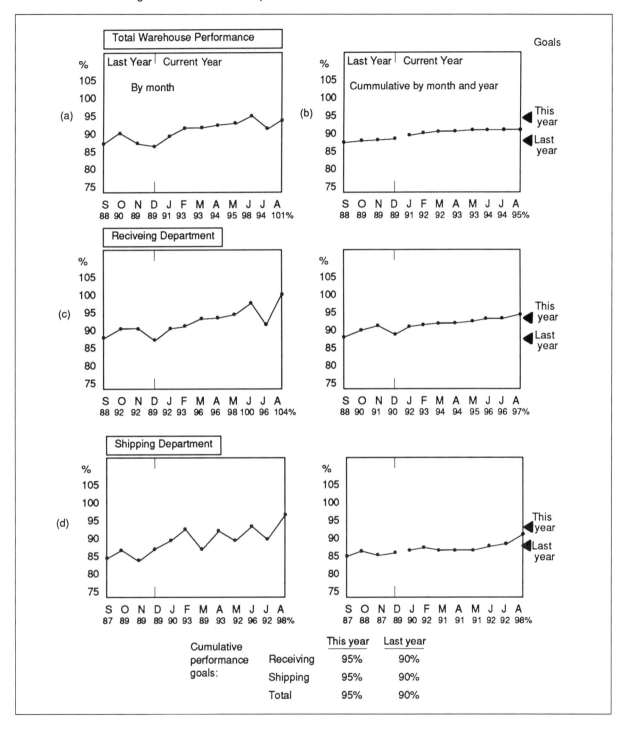

4. The receiving department is putting away inbound merchandise where it will be most efficient for them, not where it will be optimally efficient for both departments.

5. Certain standards covering common functions performed by shipping are mis-applied. An example would be that due to so much trouble with automatic dock plates at the shipping dock, it was decided to use portable dock

plates. This avoids repair costs but increases the time necessary to set up for loading out.

After investigating the lower shipping performance and turning up nothing significant, a good move would be to have the supervisors change responsibilities. This should, after a few months, tell a lot. Even if there were not a consistent difference in performance, it is still a good idea to rotate, cross-train supervisors. Both will bring new ideas to their new responsibility and, it is hoped, shed some of their bad ones on the way. Further, training in both receiving and shipping leads the supervisors closer to manager status. It is the warehouse manager's obligation to train replacements. Rotating supervisors to learn more operations is a big step toward fulfilling that obligation. This will not go unnoticed by upper management. When opportunity occurs for the manager to move up the ladder, far better that the manager is know for developing personnel than one who is indispensable: "Things just don't get done right when ol' George isn't there."

Summary of Advantages of Using the Performance Report Illustrated

1. Illustrates how each department contributes to the whole.
2. Indicates the performance by month when memory is still fresh.
3. Shows that by far the cumulative performance is more important than one or two exceptional months.
4. Shows that any one month's performance becomes more meaningful when related to the goal, past performance, and the performance of other like organizational units using the same set of standards.
5. Illustrates that the goals and progress toward goals are for the same time interval. In this case it is a calendar year because this is used in the company's management-by-objectives program as well as being its fiscal year.
6. Indicates that correlations can be easily seen by the line graph, and the alignment of one graph directly above or below another.
7. Illustrates that the scale used of 75 percent to 105 percent magnifies differences by design, to highlight accomplishment. In contrast, a scale of 0 to 105 percent would not communicate that which is important.
8. Shows that the use of numerical performance below each month adds confidence in analyzing and drawing conclusions about performance.

Probably the biggest advantage of this type performance report is its simplicity. It tells at a glance what is going on in operations and provides clues to what should be investigated. Whether the report is printed for distribution or viewed only on a CRT is another concern. The format is equally applicable for both.

As a serious caution about motivation the idea is to not use a club to motivate when a gentle tap is sufficient. In circumstance reflected by Figure 12.1 both departments are doing well, with cumulative performance of 97 percent and 93 percent, respectively. As a frame of reference, these two percentages are very good compared to most warehouses using valid standards. It is not uncommon for performances to be nearer sixtieth percentile than in the nineties, as in the illustration particularly during the first year the handling time standards are used. The standards setters, or industrial engineers, see *acceptable work performance* quite differently than do workers or even supervisors left to their own ideas of acceptability.

A Five-Year Implementation Plan

There are essentially two different extremes to developing and implementing a handling time standards program. One is to strive for an evolution from old to new over years. The other is a crash program to get it in and running. Both have advantages and disadvantages.

Following is an evolution-type schedule of five years to realize the full potential of the program.

Year	Year-End Performance	Explanation
Minus 1	50%	Determined by retroactive application of standards
1	65	Big improvement (first year on the program)
2	75	Still big improvement
3	85	Improvement more difficult
4	95	Harder still
5	100	Much harder still

This gradual improvement over five years is still comparatively good and is quite achievable—with a lot of attention and hard work. Thinking in terms of five years to fully realize the benefits may seem like a long time to some. Another way of looking at it is to view how the added costs are offset by reduced costs of operations. Assuming no change in the dollar, this is how these costs would be reduced using the year before implementation as a base and that year $1,000,000 was spent on this segment of warehouse operations.

FINANCIAL IMPROVEMENT FROM
HANDLING-TIME STANDARDS PROGRAM
(EXPRESSED IN THOUSANDS OF DOLLARS)

Year	% Performance	Cost per Year	Savings Compared to One Year Before Implementation	
			Annual	Cumulative
Minus 1	50%	$1,000	—	—
1	65	850	150	150
2	75	750	250	400
3	85	650	350	750
4	95	550	450	1,200
5	100	500	500	1,700

The biggest gains will result the first two years then tail off as illustrated. These improvements do not come free. The cost of the task force that designs, implements, and maintains the program reduces the savings. A horseback guess would be something like this—still expressed in thousands.

These costs combined with the savings in the chart on the following page indicate that the design, implementation, and maintenance are recovered early in the third operating year. Thereafter the system nets handsomely.

No doubt anyone actually thinking of going to such a system will have a different circumstance from that assumed here. Usually the less complicated warehousing, such as warehousing only pallet loads of canned goods or handling only 15 to 20 SKUs of salt or sugar, will not be able to realize the savings indicated. With such comparatively simple operations, the warehouse manager has probably already extracted most of the potential savings. On the other hand, the cost of design, implementation, and maintenance for such operations are correspondingly lower.

Year	Task Force Cost	Cumulative Cost
Minus 1	$150	$150
1	150	300
2	150	450
3	100	550
4	100	650
5	100	750

The use of 50 percent performance prior to standards may disturb some as being too inefficient. They will honestly not see how productivity can improve 100 percent. Maybe it cannot for the situations they are thinking of as reference, but to industrial engineers who have been in the standards business long, they will probably not have a problem with the 50 percent. Keep in mind that standard operating and storing procedures are developed first; then the time standards are applied, based on the optimum procedures.

Just the practice of storing inventories more according to efficient travel time and material handling could provide a 20 to 40 percent improvement. Another big gain is realized by bringing the poorer workers' productivity up closer to that of the good workers'. Most experienced warehouse supervisors know there can be two to three times difference in their best and worst workers, and this without assigning value to the quality of work—which usually has a positive correlation with the more productive workers. Production operations normally do not experience such great differences because most of the work is paced by the machines being operated. Warehousing work is not paced by machines. Workers pace themselves with some (all too often) *subjective* prodding from their supervisors.

Another concern about this example is that the cost of design, implementation, and maintenance is too low for the savings claimed. This may come into focus better by saying that these costs are based on fully utilizing computer and bar-code technologies, which substantially reduces engineering and clerical time (as well as worker time) and produces better results. One might ask: "If this is the case, are the costs in there for these technologies as well?" There you have me. But, since the cost of these marvels is not comparatively great, I will say they fall within the latitude taken with guessing the costs and savings of the assumed "typical" handling time standards program.

An Eleven-Month Implementation Plan

Considering the near frantic times for a lot of this country's business due to fierce competition from abroad, five years to realize full benefits may be just too long. And this country's usual impatience for short-term profits does not help a bit. The following list is an outline of requirements for getting a warehousing job done in 11 months.

1. Objectives and Scope. Determine objectives and parameters in enough detail to provide clear orientation throughout the project. The CEO should be in complete agreement.

2. Get the CEO to launch the project giving it his blessings and commitment.

3. Develop a large (4-ft. × 8-ft.) scheduling chart showing by component the time involved in each and the chronological sequence—to complete the project within the 11-month deadline.

4. Staff up to carry the project through. Fill key positions in the project from within the company but use enough outside contract help to assure that participating employees are not laid off at completion of project.

5. Develop flowcharts of present system and procedures across the entire chalkboard in the conference room to assure that the new system and procedures take everything into account and to bridge from *what is* to *what will be,* including

   ○ Material flow and storage.

   ○ Communications and files.

   ○ Equipment description and use.

   ○ Personnel.

6. Obtain short- and long-range forecasts from sales, and translate to order size, shipments, inventories, and receipts by SKU and SKU grouping.

7. Determine the optimum warehouse layout and initiate acquisition of equipment through a special streamlined justification and authorization procedure just for this project.

8. Determine best stock locator and address system.

9. Determine the optimum combination of handling and storing procedures. Then develop corresponding handling time and space utilization standards.

10. Reexamine the entire new plan for completeness and to assure the most effective and efficient procedures and systems.

11. Design performance reports.

12. Implement the new layout including the equipment (new and existing), the stock locator system (including location addressing), the new standard operating and storing procedures—and, the new handling time and space utilization standards.

13. Throw a victory celebration, picnic, or dinner for everyone who participated in the project—giving out classy T-shirts with our own logo and message.

14. Follow up, make adjustments as necessary—always keeping the computer data base current.

SHIPPING ERROR PERFORMANCE MEASUREMENT

Shipping errors are mainly made up of two types: errors made in shipping the wrong material and errors made in leaving out materials. The latter is less common and generally costs less to fix because return freight is not involved, but it is just as damaging to customer relations.

There is actually a third type of shipping error—that of shipping visibly damaged material—that the warehouse should have caught. Concealed damage is generally considered the fault of the manufacturer. That which is obvious should be caught by the warehouse and should be treated the same as shipping the wrong material but should be clearly identified in the performance report to highlight it for what it is. This type error is usually the least common, but it is an error, and it is at least as costly and injurious to customer service as any other shipping error.

An interesting aspect of visible damage getting through the warehouse to the customer is that the responsibility for the damage is entirely that of the warehouse, not the carrier that brought it or production that made it. Warehousing's receiving should have caught it if it arrived damaged. The warehouse or customer may be able to blame outbound carrier, but if not, the warehouse is responsible for two errors: (1) accepting visibly damaged goods or doing the damage and (2) shipping the damage to the customer. The warehouse may wiggle out of actually paying for it, but the warehouse is still responsible for the damage and even worse passing it on to the customer.

Standards for Shipping Errors, Zero!

First, do not call it "standard for shipping errors." To do so is to imply there is an acceptable ratio of shipping errors. "Make no more than this rate of errors, and you are 100% OK." Again, such a mentality expressed by this has singularly been cause for loss of more production to foreign countries than any other single thing. For want of a better term, let us call it "Error-Free Shipping Performance."

To establish the standard is easy enough. It is zero, none. But what ingredients to measure is not so easy. For instance, which of the following should constitute the formula to determine error-free shipping performance?

○ Error-free customer orders per day, week, month, and so on, compared to the total orders shipped.

○ Error-free SKUs per some time interval compared to the total SKUs shipped.

○ The same as either or both of the foregoing except to use the *standard cost* of the products instead of the quantities.

○ The effect of shipping errors on customers.

Just these alternatives are enough to illustrate the difficulty in selecting the right thing to measure. Probably there is no "right" thing to measure—only a "best" thing.

Added to this concern is the reality that only what can be measured can be used as standard. For example, if the number of SKUs is selected for measurement, it is necessary to have the bar code, computer program, or manual system, whichever, collect data by SKU.

The main reason for the difficulty in selecting the best performance formula is in trying to relate warehouse error-free performance to customer priorities. Some things are not too important to the customers. They can be conveniently shipped later if they were overlooked when the order was initially shipped, or they can be replaced later if they were the wrong product or count, both being little more than a nuisance to customers. They were not hurting for the material anyway. But other things not shipped may cost the company and the customers dearly such as even a two-bit part necessary for an assembly. And, if unable to complete the assembly, the customer's production is crippled or shut down. The difference of the two types of shipping errors is infinite. How to show this difference in performance measurement is nearly impossible because it would require knowing far more about customers' businesses than supplying warehouses are privy to know.

Another important difference to consider relates to leaving out a part of a customer order. Whose fault is it? This may not be easily discernible. It could be the result of any of the following reasons.

Then the stock does not arrive and it will not be delivered for some time to come, the customer will split its ordering between two suppliers. The warehouse manager and sales manager of the supplying company may wonder why the ordering of one of their prime customers fell off so badly. "Our competitor must be offering better prices." Just how costly was this inventory error?

On-Time Delivery Performance

The most common purpose for warehousing is to provide on-time customer delivery. Customers want to receive the merchandise in a predictable short time. This they need so they can operate their business more efficiently and reliably to provide responsive service to their customers.

Reliable deliveries have become essential in becoming competitive and maintaining competitiveness. Just-in-time practice is crucially dependent on such service. So dominant a feature of modern business has this become that warehousing is changing its basic characteristic of inventories *at rest* to inventories *in motion*. On-time delivery has attained a higher degree of importance than ever before, to the extent that some CEOs have given orders not to use the term "store" or "storage" or "inventory" in their presence.

Considerable attention has always been given to *faster delivery*—moving freight from rail to truck, from truck to air—and from ship to air. This is an important feature, but *reliable delivery* is commonly more important, except when the cargo is perishable such as flowers and when a severe need arises from the unexpected, an emergency. The main stream of products flowing through industry are not of this nature. That goods will reliably arrive at a specified interval between ordering and receiving is of paramount importance.

Take the circumstance that a certain warehouse may make delivery any time between next day and 10 days after receiving an order. The customer cannot count on next-day delivery or even in 10 days. The warehouse's delivery times are so irregular the customer does not know what to count on. Probably 10 days is a good number, but since the warehouse does not have a consistent pattern, the customer keeps 15 to 30 days' supply in reserve. This example should bring home the importance of reliable promises and make-good deliveries.

If the customer could count on a 10-day delivery, not 9 and not 11 days, it could consistently order 10 days before needing the new stock and receive it *just in time* before running out of the previous delivery. Then if there were no pricing or freight penalty, or excessive handling costs for ordering in less quantity, the customer could order everyday for what it wants 10 days later and would receive that which was ordered 10 days before. This is really practicing JIT inventory flow—which adds further strength to the claim of the importance of *reliability*.

Reliable delivery performance is much easier to determine than is error-free performance, discussed just before. The warehouse either ships when promised and the carrier gets it there when promised, or a delivery promise is broken. Enough broken promises and the customer has to carry a buffer stock to protect itself, or it looks to a more reliable source.

Carrying a buffer stock increases the customer costs—which is a big negative to the customer. Losing the account to a more reliable competitor is also a big negative for the warehouse company. The right thing is to establish what delivery times the warehouse should provide then stick to them 100 percent. The delivery time standard is 100 percent of what is promised the customer, not 90 percent or 99 percent of these promises.

It is not enough to base the standard on when the warehouse ships except if the customer picks up or if the customer specifies what carrier to use. Then the responsibility of the warehouse ends as the carrier accepts delivery. If the warehouse delivers with its own vehicles or selects the common carrier, the responsibility to fulfill the *delivery* promise remains with the warehouse.

It is true that the legal responsibility for delivery time is taken by the common carrier, but the warehouse has the leverage to enforce these delivery times. Presumably the carrier wants the warehouse freight and can lose the account if the warehouse so decides. This is a good reason why customers should think twice before specifying which common carriers to use for their freight. The customer relieves the warehouse of the monitoring function and the leverage it can exercise with carriers.

The greater importance assigned to reliable delivery in the current squeeze on inventories puts delivery performance high on the critical list. Because of this high priority, it sometimes forces a partnership type of cooperation among customer, carrier, and warehouse. A consistent 100 percent delivery performance requires close coordination of all three. Where the carrier and customer forego the usual counts and inspections that go on prior to accepting responsibility for the shipment, trust is developed out of absolute necessity.

Such partnerships are based on dedicated systems and sharing of costs and cost savings. They do not work unless all benefit from the dedicated system. Special fixtures and other means are employed to make damage and counts obvious, so the chances of error are virtually nonexistent. Adding to this, the warehouse may dedicate certain dock locations and go so far as to install conveyor means for moving the entire load at once into the carrier vehicle that has a companion conveyor to accept the entire load. The customer has another companion conveyor to unload. The entire loading and unloading operations of big rigs can be accomplished within a few minutes. Such dedicated systems are becoming more common to squeeze out the duplicate effort that traditionally exists in material flow between separate responsibilities.

For the main flow of materials, delivery time standards and performance measurement are applicable and needed. Now with electronic communications and information transfer through bar codes and computers, the cost of establishing a good standards and performance system is comparatively low vis-à-vis the benefits that can accrue.

In establishing delivery time standards, the first step is to determine what is necessary to satisfy the company's objectives and what is involved in complying. These will differ between companies and types of business. Sales-oriented companies will legitimately put higher value on quick and reliable delivery service. Production-oriented companies will legitimately put less value on delivery service and more on cost effectiveness.

To adopt standards and performance that reduce the time between order placement and delivery probably means increasing costs. The reason for this is because the warehouse has to overstaff regularly or depend on overtime to assure not falling behind whenever orders peak. Also premium freight must be paid when fewer consolidations, quantity discounts, and other means of freight cost savings are forsaken—to meet the pressing delivery promises.

On the other hand, there are indirect benefits that accompany quick order-cycle time. This type of service becomes the norm in all the warehouse activities; this leads to prompt dispensing with problems as they come up instead of coddling them, which generally makes them only worse as time passes.

The extra costs due to quick order-cycle can be minimized by creative thought. Maybe computer or FAX linkup between customer and warehouse can put the order in the warehouse for action within minutes, thus reducing the order cycle by hours or even days. Perhaps tying into a regular passenger-bus service going to where certain small orders need to go will take more hours or days out of the cycle. Possibly private trucking if adopted will shave more time off the order cycle, provided the cost is not prohibitive. It may cost even less if well managed. The old platitude that "necessity is the mother of invention" turn up ways to reduce the time schedule that otherwise would seem impossible or cost prohibitive. Something as simple as adding a night shift may very well add the time required to send the orders on their way before the roosters crow, saving more hours and possibly even days.

Because missing delivery dates is so often related to inventory outages, there is good reason to include on-time delivery performance with error-free performance and to consider failures of both as errors or missed opportunities.

A way of showing on-time delivery performance is illustrated by Figure 12.3. As described under the graph, the situation represented for on-time

FIGURE 12.3 On-Time Delivery Performance

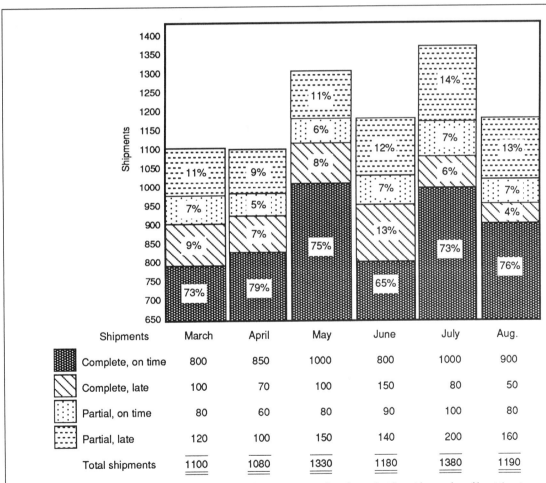

Shipments	March	April	May	June	July	Aug.
Complete, on time	800	850	1000	800	1000	900
Complete, late	100	70	100	150	80	50
Partial, on time	80	60	80	90	100	80
Partial, late	120	100	150	140	200	160
Total shipments	1100	1080	1330	1180	1380	1190

The graph shows a sad performance record and one that is not improving. About 1 out of every 4 shipments is either late or incomplete, which must be stretching customers' tolerance to the limit. Competition has to be virtually nonexistent for customers to take this abuse. The many partial shipments cause excessive work for both the customers and the warehouse. Such performance forces customers to carry a much larger inventory than would be necessary if the warehouse inventory were better managed. If the business is profitable, or can be made profitable, an open invitation is being extended for competition to move in.

delivery is a sad one. The warehouse is definitely in trouble. The graph indicates a horrible warehouse operation whether it is the warehouse management's fault or not. It could be that upper or other management is setting the inventory levels and delivery times—and warehouse management has to work with what others unrealistically commit to which can be the source of all the problems.

The warehouse manager whose operation is represented by the graph is numb from the complaints from customers, the company's sales force, and upper management—or some other group or division that has the responsibilities of inventory management and delivery promises. If the latter is the case, it is bum organization.

SPACE UTILIZATION STANDARDS

Of far greater importance than commonly recognized are space utilization standards. They are often overlooked, perhaps because space costs are regarded by accounting departments as "fixed." Warehouse space should be thought of as variable as is labor, supplies, and utilities, with the same implication that something can and should be done to control it; space should not stand idle any more than workers should.

What Space Utilization Standards Will Do for You

Total cost of a worker with fringe benefits is about equivalent to the cost of leasing 10,000 square feet of space. Of course, this varies but it does highlight the importance of space. You need standards and performance measurement to motivate, utilize, and evaluate worker's effort. Likewise, you need standards and performance measurement to motivate, utilize, and evaluate the best use of space. It is not any easier to lose money in mismanaging workers than it is to lose money by mismanaging space. The big difference is that loss through excess employees is more visible and accountable. Who do you blame when warehouse space is underutilized by, say, 40 percent? You certainly do not order more inventory just to take up the slack.

Valid space utilization standards tell how best to store each SKU, which is called standard storage procedures (SSPs) just as how best to handle materials is called standard operating procedures (SOPs). And how much cubic or square feet of space this will take per unit of inventory is a space utilization standard. For instance, say, SKU 19283 requires 1.37 cubic feet per unit; this then is the space utilization standard, $1.37/ft^3$

If it is easier to deal with square feet instead of cubic feet, the translation is not all that difficult. For example, the same SKU unit requires 0.083 square feet per unit or 8.30 square feet per hundred, or 83.0 square feet per thousand units for a specified means and height of storage.

What is it worth to be able to tell in a moment that a certain new SKU should be stored in a certain way, SSP, at a specific address? And then to determine how much space is available at that location and how much will be left after a certain quantity of this is stored there? The fixed and variable data needed to determine this are as follows—by SKU.

○ Size and weight per unit
○ Strength of packaging

○ Hazard classification

○ Manner it will be received (rail, truck, and so on)

○ Manner it will be shipped (rail, truck, and so on)

○ Unitized or separate handling units

○ Specifications of the unitized load—if unitized

○ Representative quantity of units per inbound receipt

○ Representative quantity of units per customer order

○ Order frequency and what other SKUs are usually shipped with it

○ Whether LIFO or FIFO control applies and if so to what extent

○ Any other data influencing handling and storing

This may seem to be a lot to learn about a new SKU, and it is. Warehouses often have to take on new SKUs without prior knowledge of all this, but this is out of negligence. Complete data like that listed should come with the request for warehousing. This information is a necessary part of the initial SKU design and production. Certainly whoever determines the cost and price of the new SKU has to have it—including the warehouse and total physical distribution costs otherwise the costing and pricing routine have big voids in them.

How to Establish Space Utilization Standards

As there are alternative ways to set handling time standards so there are to set space utilization standards. Which is the best way to store depends on the type of warehousing being performed and the expertise and preference of those who will be most involved in setting, maintaining, and using the standards. The objectives of space utilization standards can be condensed to the following:

○ Logically correct

○ Apply only to that which can be objectively measured, compared, reported, and evaluated

○ Composed of sufficient detailed elements to easily construct new standards

○ Capable of being used for purposes in addition to performance measurement, including methods analyzing, budgeting, costing, scheduling, and planning

○ Easily called forth for CRT viewing or printing in detail and in total

○ Credible to more than just the engineers or whoever else establishes them

CHECKLIST OF STEPS IN SETTING STANDARDS

□ Determine the best way to store every SKU—with next best alternatives when applicable.

This step requires a thorough knowledge of what equipment and space will be available. For instance, there is no need to dwell on cantilever racks for a small amount of storage when you do not have them and there is not enough need to justify acquiring them. Decide how best the product can be stored with present equipment and include a note that cantilever racks would provide a better way when sufficient applicable inventory is acquired to justify them.

The best way to store, standard storage procedure, for each SKU and its inventory and shipping pattern must be determined before space utilization standards can be established. Equally necessary is the knowledge of what equipment will be available and just what it will do. Chapters 9 and 10, about both mobile and fixed equipment, provides an overview of the many different types available in the market.

☐ Determine the optimum storage layout in relation to handling and storing objectives.

> The layout that would permit maximum space utilization is never the same as that which would enable the most efficient material handling. Theoretically, the only time they both could be the absolute best is if there were only one SKU and LIFO (last-in, first-out) inventory control were practiced. Oh yes, another characteristic would be that the SKU could be stacked to maximum storage height without damage. But this is not reality. There is always need to compromise handling and/or space utilization efficiencies to reach the optimum combination, and even this must be within the context of the warehouse objectives.

> Here is a good application for computer simulation of the many alternative storing technique costs in relation to handling costs. This is not an easy exercise, considering the many alternatives that must be considered, but this data must be developed regardless of whether with computer assistance or worked out by hand.

> Probably it is safe to say there will never be a truly optimum handling and storing layout because, even if it were attainable, it would last for but a brief time. Warehousing is constantly in the process of change. This is one of its basic purposes—to absorb supply and demand changes so that the production load can be leveled and customers can be assured of a reliable supply.

☐ Determine the availability, specifications and condition of existing equipment.

> What standard storage procedures can be set depends on the
>   • Available equipment
>   • Product specification
>   • Available space
>   • Efficiency ranking of the material handling alternatives

> Since all must be known (in the context of the objectives) you either go in several directions in search or take them one or two at a time. What equipment the warehouse already has is a good place to start.

> Refer to Chapters 9 and 10 for the many types of equipment used in warehousing.

☐ Determine what additional equipment can be justified and any existing equipment that is excess—to be used elsewhere, sold, traded in, or retired.

> One should not stop with existing equipment regardless of how tight money is for capital expenditures. Even if there were a freeze on such spending, warehouse management should not close their eyes to what is going on in the marketplace. What is learned if not usable now will be when the strings on the moneybag are loosened.

> Then too, there are situations where the payout on equipment acquisition is so quick the company should take advantage regardless of how tight money is. For example, a company is about to take lease on additional, expensive space because the existing space just can take

Assuming a gross weight per case of 20 pounds, the case standard can be converted to 0.0155 square feet per pound (0.31 sq. ft./case ÷ 20.0 lb./case) or 15.5 square feet per 1,000 pounds.

The space-utilization standard used in this example calls for 310 square feet of warehouse space to store each 1,000 cases of this SKU. The standard includes allowances for unusable space, such as aisles and staging areas, and for inventory flexibility.

The flexibility allowance (1.20 in this example) is provided to allow for the fact that all the usable space cannot be fully utilized at any one time, discussed further on.

The example is based on a commodity that is stored on pallets in bulk. Standards can also be developed in the same manner for items stored in racks. The important point is to relate the number of units that can be stored to a specific number of square feet of floor space.

Space utilization standards can be developed using cubic feet instead of square feet. The process of developing cubic space standards is essentially the same as that described in the foregoing example, except for the different unit of measure. Also, standards can be related to the weight of commodities rather than to their sales unit, such as case, gallon, and foot. When there are many different sales units to deal with, it is generally best to convert all of them to pounds. This simplifies the task of working with the standards and reduces the chance of error inherent in using several different units of measure. The validity of standards is not affected by the unit of measure used, if the measure is appropriate and the arithmetic is correct.

Converting all SKUs to their weight has a lot of merit and should not be ruled out without considerable thought. The net and gross weights of each SKU are part of its fixed data and the gross weight is necessary as well for carrier loading and freight costs. For what it is worth, I have always converted space utilization standards to SKU gross weight as the common denominator, because all inventories I have worked with were comprised of several different units of measure: pounds, feet, liters, gallons, cases, and so on. Yes, using weight as the common denominator has a lot to be said for it. You can always convert back to the SKU's most common unit of measure, which is the sales unit of measure, when needed.

The factor of 1.20 used in the example for inventory flexibility is to give recognition to the reality that an active warehouse's total space allocated to storage is never 100 percent full. Always inventories will be reducing by outbound shipments that leave temporary voids. Also when stock is received, the quantity rarely fills exactly the total storage space it is assigned. A continuing attempt should be made to fit the space with the quantity received, but commonly this is futile and not much time should be lost worrying about it. It is an inherent characteristic of warehousing.

An alternative to factoring the standard space to allow for variations in inventory is to not factor for it at all. The space standard results from bare, net measurements of the SKU plus allowances for necessary clearance space around it. That is it—no more. A problem with this, however is that there is no true way to actually reach 100 percent performance, at least in an active warehouse. And psychologically, if for no other reason, standards should be attainable to prevent the attitude taking hold that says: "Don't concern yourself about the standards. I hear there is no way to make 100 percent and maybe not 70 or 80 percent either." There is good use for the bare standards discussed later on, but for performance measurement that the workers will see or learn of, it can cause a severe erosion of credibility.

The amount of the inventory flexibility factor should not be entirely arbitrary. Many things will affect it, and some are measurable, and therefore predictable. For instance, a commodity warehouse with inventory of only a few SKUs will have better actual space utilization than will a general-purpose warehouse carrying many SKUs with many different configurations.

A good way to negate the influence that the number of SKUs has on space utilization performance is to provide a fixed amount of lost space for each SKU. For instance, for bulk-storage standards, one-half of a row is provided for each SKU to allow for the fact that on the average there will be that much storage space lost due to it being a finite different SKU. For pallet rack storage, one-half a pallet position would be allowed for each SKU. This fixed allowance can be added separately like a setup in a machine shop (setup time plus run time), or it can be built into the standard based on its statistical occurrence.

For instance, in a warehouse with random storage (see Chapter 7) and a fast enough inventory turnover that FIFO control is not necessary, the SKUs with the largest quantities will permit the highest actual space utilization. This can be best illustrated by an example. Assume the warehouse is laid out with two different pallet row depths—half with 10 pallets deep and the other 4 deep. Each can be stacked 4 pallets high and the size cases are the same for both. (See Figure 12.4.)

How do you develop the space utilization performance for the two different-quantity SKUs:

- Large-quantity SKU A

  (300 pallets ÷ 4 pallets high) ÷ 10 stacks deep = 7.5 rows

- Small-quantity SKU B

  (40 pallets ÷ 4 pallets high) ÷ 4 stacks deep = 2.5 rows

One-half row of each SKU is empty, but the influence of this on the space utilization for the small quantity SKU is much greater. The percent of space utilization for each SKU is as follows:

Large-Quantity SKU A. Of space for 8 rows of 10 pallets deep, 4 high—a one-half row is not used consisting of (5 stacks × 4 high), or 20 pallet positions. Therefore, of 320 available pallet positions, only 300 are used, resulting in 94 percent utilization (300 ÷ 320).

Small-Quantity SKU B. Of space for 2 rows of 4 pallets deep, 4 high—a one-half row is not used (2 stacks × 4 high), or 8 pallet positions. Therefore, of 32 available pallet positions, only 24 are used, resulting in 75 percent utilization (24 ÷ 32).

This is fairly easy to visualize even though the SKU with the largest quantity and best space utilization has 20 pallet positions not used, and the other with less space utilization has only 8 pallet positions not used.

Although the validity of the inventory flexibility factor is increased if it varies with the quantity and predictability of the different SKUs, this is only significant in determining the specific space that a certain SKU of a specific quantity will take. But for determining the performance for large segments of a warehouse or the total warehouse, one factor such as the 1.2 used in the example, developed by statistical sampling, is adequate and a lot easier to work with.

The factor of 1.54 used previously to provide for aisles, staging, and other nonusable space is calculated from a complete layout of the warehouse storage and work areas. It is determined by the sum of all the space that cannot be used

FIGURE 12.4 Comparison of Space Utilization for Deep and Shallow Bulk Storage, Pallet Loads in this Example

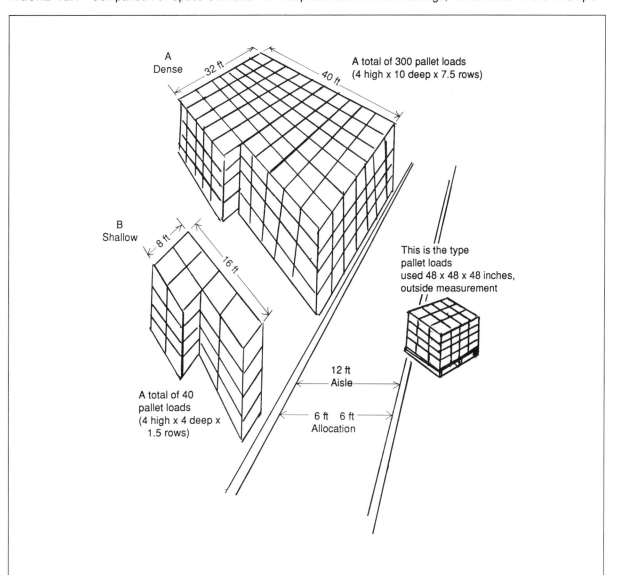

A   **Deep storage.** Of the 320 pallet positions available, one-half row
        consisting of 20 pallet positions is not used. Therefore the net space-
        utilization is 94% (300 ÷ 320).
B   **Shallow storage.** Of the 32 pallet positions available one-half row
        consisting of 8 pallet positions is not used. Therefore the net space-
        utilization is only 75% (24 ÷ 32) compared to 94% for the dense
        storage example.
Allocation of Aisle Space. To allocate the aisle fronting the bulk storage,
        half its width should be assigned to the storage area on the right
        side and the other half should be assigned to the left side.
        Deep storage. 6 feet wide of aisle x 32 feet frontage = 192 sq. ft.
        aisle is assigned to the dense storage area 1,280 sq. ft. (32 feet x
        40 feet). The allocation of aisle would be (1,280 sq. ft. ÷ 192 sq. ft.
        of aisle ÷ 1,280 sq. ft.) = 1.15 factor.
        Shallow Storage. 6 feet wide of aisle x 8 feet frontage = 48 sq. ft.
        aisle is assigned to the shallow storage area 128 sq. ft. (8 feet x
        16 feet). The allocation of aisle would be (128 sq. ft. ÷ 48 sq. ft ÷
        128 sq. ft.) = 1.38 factor. Very poor compared to the 1.15 factor for
        dense storage. Thus, the value of dense storage is illustrated.

for storage divided by the total area concerned. In that example, it is 65 percent. To use this as a factor to convert net standard storage space used, the reciprocal of 65 percent must be determined (1.00 ÷ .65 = 1.54). Therefore, any net standard storage space must be factored by 1.54 to convert to a standard that includes its share of necessary space not usable for storage.

Storage in racks requires a different nonusable space factor than that used for bulk storage and different type racks often require different factors as well. Narrow-aisle equipment permits narrow aisles and the same with turret lift trucks that can turn their forks and load 180 degrees to deposit or retrieve. ASRS installations require totally different space utilization standards. The message is that the nonusable space factor should be tailored to the equipment used.

Figure 12.5 shows a layout utilizing four different types of storage: drive-in racks, pallet racks, cantilever racks, and bulk storage. In layouts like this, it is necessary to prorate the width of the access aisles necessary to service the racks or bulk storage bordering the aisles.

Figure 12.5 and the accompanying explanation exposes the myths that attend rack storage—from the not uncommon warehouse manager's expressions of "I don't have enough room for racks" to "Everything should be in racks." On occasion both these extremes can be true but most often a combination of rack and bulk storage is the best.

There is a dramatic difference in storage density comparing bulk storage and, say, pallet racks. At best, using a narrow-aisle lift truck, the figure shows conversion factors of 1.51 for bulk storage and 2.28 for the pallet racks. Using this same comparison means that if you had a completely pallet-racked warehouse storage area of 228,000 square feet, you could put the same inventory in 151,000 square feet if all the product were stored in bulk. Reality is, however, that many products cannot be bulk stored due to crushing, and more often, not enough inventory of any SKU is kept at one time to justify storing in bulk. You see, bulk storage must be stored deep to effect real economies. One stack of four pallet loads high is not much improvement over four pallet positions in a pallet rack. And the space the stack occupies cannot be used for another SKU until the last pallet has left, while the moment a pallet slot is open in a pallet rack, it can be used for another product.

A more subtle reason to use racks is simply that rack storage looks better than bulk storage, particularly when there are many varying amounts of different SKUs. Racks can bring orderliness to what appears disarray. Although the economies do not justify using racks, they are employed for all the good things an orderly warehouse provides: better housekeeping, higher employee morale, and so on, which are items hard to put a dollar value on, but are very real.

Another thing to recognize about rack storage is that valuable space is lost by the rack itself. Space is taken up by the metal structure and more by clearances to avoid damage in putting away and taking from the racks.

Densities of Different Storage Systems

The conversion factors accompanying Figure 12.5 also provide an insight to density characteristics of different rack systems and corresponding material handling equipment. In brief, the way to increase storage density employs the following three ingredients:

1. Narrower aisles
2. Deeper storage
3. Higher storage

The three limiting ingredients are

1. Personnel safety
2. Accessibility to SKUs
3. Product damage

Accessibility to SKUs directly relates to the quantity inventoried. Small quantities per SKU dictates pallet- or cantilever-type storage racks. Large quantities dictates double-deep pallet racks, drive-in racks, tier racks, and bulk storage in this order of increasing density of storage.

You can have large quantity per SKU, but if the product will not withstand stacking pressure, the support provided by storage racks is necessary to achieve high density. General merchandise warehouses have need for a variety of storage means. Specialized commodity-type warehouses, for instance, those carrying only canned goods, only salt, only flour and such, can limit their means for storing. Perhaps bulk and a few pallet racks to handle very-small-quantity SKUs is as efficient as their storage can ever be.

"If this is all that can be done with such warehousing, what is there to improve?" Two good things are to (1) plan the storage to effect the least travel distance and (2) improve on material handling equipment and procedures. Further, there is the lush area of the amount of inventories to carry and the JIT concept to implement. It is always true that the best way to reduce storage problems and costs is to reduce inventory. Do the job better with less.

Figure 12.5 and the text following explain how you can determine net storage space and the conversion factor for total space.

FIGURE 12.5 How to Determine Net Storage Space and the Conversion Factor for Total Space

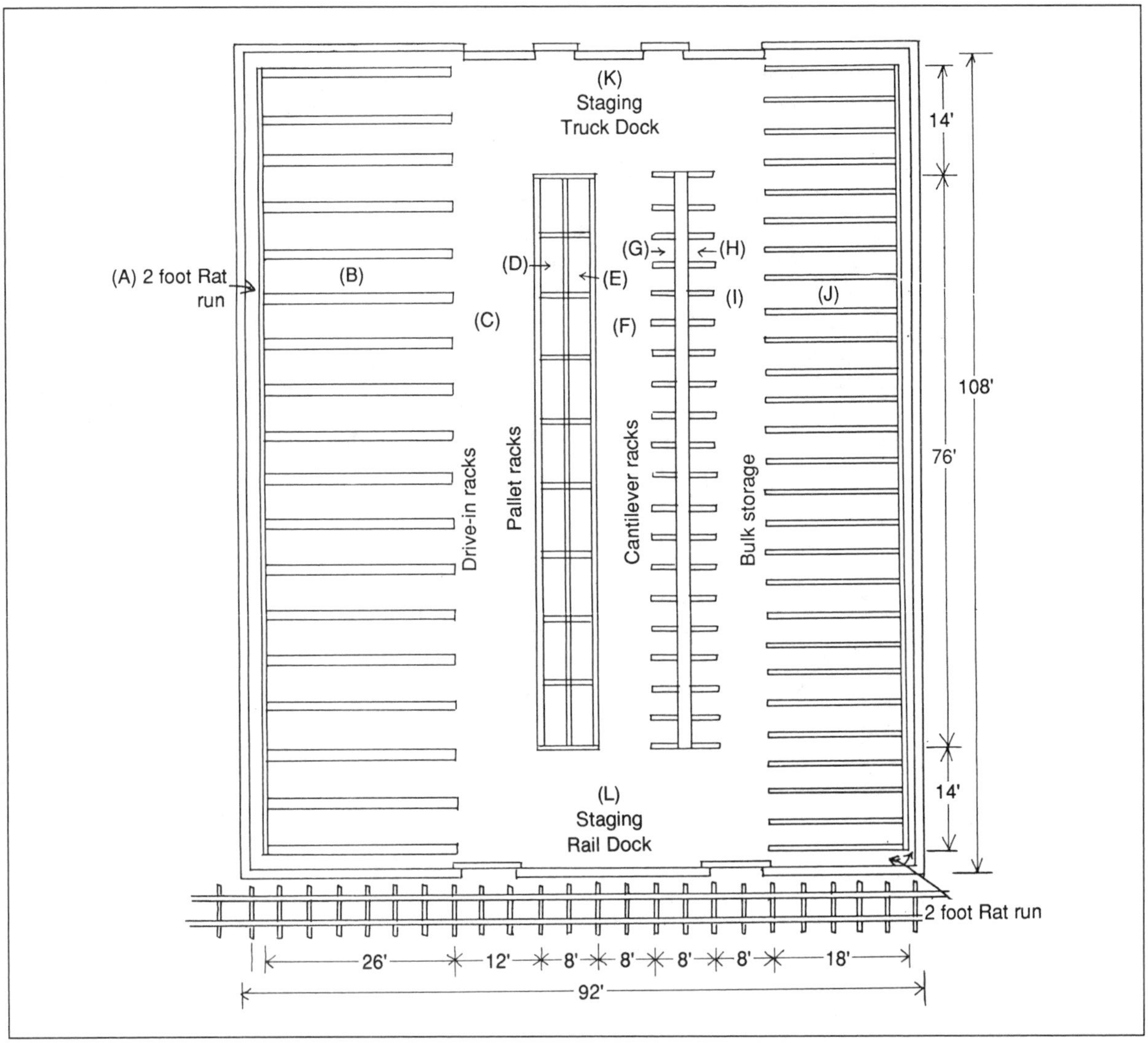

HOW TO DEVELOP THE FACTOR TO CONVERT NET STORAGE SPACE TO TOTAL
WAREHOUSE SPACE

1. Total warehouse space (inside dimensions) 92 ft. × 108 ft. =   9,936 sq. ft.

2. Nonstorage space

    (A) Rat run 2 ft. wide along side walls, *plus*
         front and back walls, less docks:

         2 ft. × (108 ft. + 26 ft. + 18 ft. + 108 ft.
         + 18 ft. + 26 ft.) =   608 sq. ft.

    (K) + (L) staging areas, 2 × 16 ft. × 34 ft.: 50%
         of aisles (C) and (I) that extend into the
         staging areas are assigned to the staging   1,088

    (C) Aisle (12 ft. × 76 ft.) + (2 × 6 ft. × 16 ft.)   1,104

    (F) Aisle 8 ft. × 76 ft.   608

    (I) Aisle (8 ft. × 76 ft.) + (2 × 4 ft. × 16 ft.)   736

    Total nonstorage space =   <u>4,144</u> sq. ft.

3. Net storage space =   <u>5,792</u> sq. ft.

4. Factor to convert net storage space to total warehouse space: $9,936 \div 5,792$ = 1.72

How to Determine Conversion Factor by Storage Section

Nonstorage space that is common to all storage space:

(A) Rat run	608 sq. ft.
(K) + (L) Staging areas	<u>1,024</u>
Total	<u>1,632</u> sq. ft.

1. Drive-in racks (B): 26 ft. × 104 ft.   2,704 sq. ft.
   Two-thirds aisle (C): 12 ft. × 108 ft.   864
   Share of common area $2,704 \div 5,792 \times 1,632$ <u>761</u>
     Total   <u>4,329</u> sq. ft.

   Conversion factor: $4,360 \div 2,704 = \underline{1.61}$

2. Pallet rack (D) 4 ft. × 76 ft.   304 sq. ft.
   One-third aisle (C) × 12 ft. × 76 ft.   304
   Share of common area: $304 \div 5,792 \times 1,632$ <u>86</u>
     Total   694
   Conversion factor: $694 \div 304 = \underline{2.28}$

3. Pallet rack (E): right side only 4 ft. × 76 ft.   304 sq. ft.
   One-half aisle (F) × 8 ft. × 76 ft. =   304
   Share of common area: $304 \div 5,792 \times 1,632$ <u>86</u>
     Total   694
   Conversion factor: $694 \div 304 = \underline{2.28}$

4. Cantilever rack (G) 4 ft. × 76 ft.   304 sq. ft.
   One-half aisle (F) × 8 ft. × 76 ft.   304
   Share of common area: $304 \div 5,792 \times 1,632$ <u>86</u>
     Total   694
   Conversion factor: $694 \div 304 = \underline{2.28}$

5. Cantilever rack (H) 4 ft. × 76 ft.   304 sq. ft.
   One-half aisle (I) × 8 ft. × 76 ft.   304
   Share of common area: $304 \div 5,792 \times 1,632$ <u>86</u>
     Total   694
   Conversion factor: $694 \div 304 = \underline{2.28}$

6. Bulk storage (J): 18 ft. × 104 ft.   1,872 sq. ft.
   One-half aisle (I) × 8 ft. × 108 ft.   432
   Share of common area: $1,872 \div 5,792 \times 1,632$ <u>527</u>
     Total   2,831
   Conversion factor: $2,831 \div 1,872 = \underline{1.51}$

7. Total of all the sections   <u>9,936</u> sq. ft.

This is a very small warehouse, but it serves to illustrate several things about setting space utilization standards particularly where judgment calls are faced. Following is a brief discussion of the less familiar features of the layout.

Rat Run. This is a space of between 18 to 30 inches left next to the wall around the perimeter of the storage for rats and mice. Rodents like to have a solid wall on one side while they stroll, run, and gambol. The space also exposes the dark areas to get at trash that accumulates there. It also serves as an access along the walls inside of the building to spray for insects when this is needed and is not hazardous to the inventories. Further it provides a way of inspecting the backside of storage for whatever problems. Oh yes, it pleases OSHA inspectors too.

Drive-in and Drive-Through Storage Racks. "How are drive-through and drive-in storage racks used?" you ask. The vertical framework in the direction of entry has load supporting flange railings extending into the driveway on both sides. The pallets are supported by the flange railings. It offers a good way to achieve dense storage of pallet loads that cannot be stored one on another due to crushing. If FIFO applies, the *drive-through type* should be used, providing access from each end. A handy accessory is to have roller-skate conveyors on the flanges and a slight decline so the pallet loads can be loaded at one end, flowing via gravity to the other end from which to order pick. Obviously stops are necessary to avoid the load flowing right through.

Wide and Narrow Aisles. Aisle (C) is 12 feet wide, but aisles (F) and (I) are only 8 feet wide. This is intentional to illustrate what is being sacrificed by wide aisles. The width of aisles is dictated by the configuration of the load and the material handling equipment used.

Usually aisles are wide to access cantilever racks because the main purpose of these racks is to store long SKUs. The cantilever racks in the illustration would be just right for an SKU 6 feet long. This is about the longest that can be handled in an 8-foot-wide aisle with a narrow aisle or turret (180 degree load turn). The 12-foot-wide aisle (C) is provided for a conventional, sitdown lift truck. Beyond providing examples of how to relate nonstorage space to the net storage space, Figure 12.5 illustrates the relationship of aisles to space utilization. It comes as no surprise, but it reinforces the contention that it is necessary to increase the depth of storage as well as reduce the width of the aisles to increase space utilization most effectively.

Construction of a Cantilever-Rack Space Utilization Standard

One of the most versatile means of storage is the cantilever rack. See Figure 12.6 for a bird's-eye view of one. Its most common use is for long SKUs, but it can be used in the same manner as a pallet rack or shelving for a great variety of products. All that is needed to use it for many different configurations is to move the uprights closer (than needed for long, rigid commodities) and to put a deck across the arms for a continuous support surface. The singular advantage of these racks is the absence of horizontal obstruction. The singular disadvantage is they generally cost more than pallet racks per cubic foot of storage. This need not be a forever characteristic of cantilever racks, but even if it were, the advantages of cantilevers for many applications can be worth more than their extra cost.

FIGURE 12.6 Cantilever Storage Racks (example used in developing space utilization standards)

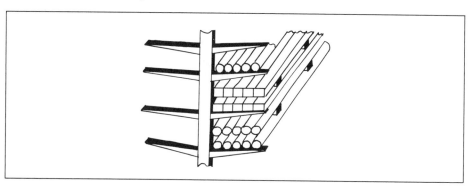

The following are the specific commodity data needed to determine the space utilization standard when stored in the rack depicted in Figure 12.6.

CANTILEVER-RACK SPECIFICATIONS

○ Rack Dimensions

Upright (for arms on both sides)

Height: 20 feet

Arms: 24 inches apart vertically

42 inches apart horizontally

44 inches deep

This arrangement provides 9 storage levels on each side, 18 levels considering both sides. From the top of one arm to the bottom of the next is 24 inches. The arms are all 44 inches long (deep) and tapered from 6 inches to 1½ inches on the end to permit the best utilization of vertical space between arms. This shape also permits conservation of the amount of steel used in relation to where the strength is needed.

The center upright column to which the arms are attached is 8 inches thick. The arms are inclined to make the outer ends 2 inches higher than the end that attaches to center column. The purpose of the incline is to cause round objects to roll toward the column, not off the arms.

COMMODITY SPECIFICATIONS

○ Two types of commodities are to be stored on the arms:

9-inch outside diameter × 10-foot-long steel tubing at 100 pounds each

9-inch outside surface width × 8-inch-high × 10-foot-long steel rectangles at 100 pounds each

Each shape comes in three different alloys, for a total of six different SKUs.

The standard storing procedure is for the units to span over three arms and overhang at each end, 16 inches.

The first layer on each set of arms consists of 5 units, then 3-inch × 3-inch wood spacers support a second layer of 5 units.

The spacers permit the forks of a lift truck to get under the top layer to deposit or retrieve the units.

FIFO, though of minimal concern, is practiced by the computer directing the order pickers to pick by consecutive product lot—which is of concern.

Tags are attached to each unit designating the alloy and the production lot. Should a customer register a complaint, the units involved can be traced back to the warehouse order picker and then back to who produced the items and when.

Standard Operating Procedure   The SKUs are received in filament-taped master packs of two rows of five units each, separated by 3-inch × 3-inch wood spacers. The material is taken from receiving, three master packs at a time, to a temporary position at the end of the racks. A side-moving material handler puts the master packs into the racks.

Standard Computation

Vertical. Nine levels of master packs with ten units per master pack provides 90 units storage per unit length.

Horizontal. Ten lengths with 6-inch clearance between lengths and 6-inch extension beyond the center of the end arms.

Total Units Each Side. Ninety units per length × 10 lengths = 900 units.

Total Units Both Sides. Two sides × 900 units per side = 1,800 units.

Area Occupied
- Total width: 2 sides × 44-inch arms + 8-inch wide center column = 96-inch or 8.0 feet.
- Total length: 10-foot lengths of 120 inches each plus 11 spaces of 6 inches = 1,266 inches or 105.5 feet.
- Total area occupied 8.0-foot width × 105.5-foot length = 844 square feet.

Standard
- Net (bare) standard expressed in units per square foot: 844 square feet ÷ 1,800 units = 0.469 square feet per unit.
- With a 20 percent inventory variation factor: 0.469 square feet per unit × 1.20 factor = 0.563 square feet per unit.
- With nonusable space conversion factor of, say, 1.78. This factor, 1.78 × 0.563 square feet per unit = 1.00 square feet per unit.

These standards can be easily converted to per pound instead of per round or rectangle. Weight provides a common denominator for all SKUs and avoids the all too frequent inventory error of combining in calculations different units of measures such as apples and oranges, bushels and pecks, and the like.

The following are the steps to convert space utilization standards from rounds and rectangles (their most common units of measure) to standard square feet per 100 pounds.

NET STANDARD SPACE
- 0.469 square feet per 9 inches round or 9-inch × 8-inch rectangle × 10 feet long
- Each round and rectangle weights 100 pounds, for sake of simplicity.
- Therefore, the net standard space is 0.469 *square feet per 100 pounds.*

ADDING INVENTORY FLEXIBILITY OF 20 PERCENT
- 0.469 square feet per 100 pounds × 1.20 = *0.563 square feet per 100 pounds.*

ADDING THE PRORATION OF NONSTORABLE SPACE

○ 0.563 square feet per 100 pounds × 1.78 = 1.00 square feet per 100 pounds.

Questions about the use of space has to be faced constantly. Space utilization is basic to warehousing. Answers can be guessed at or figured on the run. Or the answers can be called forth on a CRT terminal that is online with a host computer that provides the best answer and alternatives within seconds.

Take this example. You are advised that production needs you to take an additional 50,000 pounds of the rounds and rectangles because it is shutting down the line for two weeks. Can you take it in? Or must extra space be leased on a short-term basis? Or should you look to a public warehouse to handle it? You know that to separate the inventory will cost a lot more, not just what you pay for the extra space or for a public warehouse to handle it, but it will play havoc with outbound freight consolidations. Freight costs will skyrocket. Worse, customers will not get all the items on their orders together. Nothing seems right except to bring it in to the existing warehouse if at all possible. You know the following two parts of the standard apply:

○ The bare standard of 4.69 square feet per 1,000 pounds.
○ With 20 percent inventory flexibility, 5.63 square feet per 1,000 pounds.

Real-time performance for both are displayed on the CRT. The results are

○ Actual compared to bare standard is 65 percent
○ Actual compared to standard with inventories flexibility is 67 percent

Conclusion: Another 50,000 pounds added to regular inventory will not actually affect the inventory flexibility. It has already been provided for in the existing inventory. The extra 50,000 pounds should be stored completely according to the net standard. Therefore, the 67 percent performance which includes the factor for inventory flexibility can be deducted from the total available.

Of the total capacity for 180,000 pounds, only 67 percent of that is actually being used leaving 33 percent available, which is storage space for about 59,000 pounds (33 percent of 180,000 pounds).

Conclusion: The request to take in another 50,000 pounds can be accommodated with a little to spare.

How Space Standards Should Not Be Used

With all the other type standards covered in this text, there is the clear implication that a low performance rating is bad and a high performance rating is good. This is not so for space utilization standards. The warehouse can have a low rating and that be good, because it shows the inventory can be warehoused in less space than is provided. If inventories are going to stay at this level, an opportunity has surfaced to use the extra space for some other constructive purpose, like leasing it to another company or providing public warehousing for others. You should, of course, start with seeing if some other division of your own company needs more space for production, record files, storekeeping, or whatever.

If the space utilization performance comes in over 100 percent, a problem is indicated. It says that stock is being put in the aisles or in staging areas, or is being stored too high, and crushing can be expected. At a minimum, handling time performance will suffer because some inventory is being stored incorrectly.

Caution should be exercised that warehousing personnel do not get the idea that better than 100 percent performance is good and that this will please headquarters. In situations where warehouses are remote and their management can order in more inventories than policy calls for, an incentive is present to *improve* space utilization performance. More inventory than top management has approved should be a sure way of bringing down the wrath of the gods.

Causes of Poor Space Utilization

Performance of 100 percent should be attainable. In the great warehouse of mythology, performance is always 100 percent. This is where material handling and space utilization meet to form the optimum efficiencies within the constraints of the warehouse's objectives. But, this is not down-to-earth reality.

If a warehouse runs into excessive handling and space difficulties with a space utilization performance of much less than 100 percent, there is definitely something wrong. Any or all of the following could be contributing to this.

Poor Housekeeping. Not keeping the warehouse clean and orderly is a cardinal offense. It is hazardous. It encourages poor handling and storing practices, which result in inventory damage. It is a glaring advertisement that warehouse management does not have its priorities in order. Simply, it does not know what it is doing.

How much better off warehouse management would be to assign good housekeeping top priority. It is my experience that more warehouse managers get axed for bad housekeeping than for any other reason—except for theft in one form or other—but, that is another story. It is no secret that members of top management largely form their opinions about warehouse management from how the warehouse looks. Maybe good customer service is more important at times, but in the long run, good housekeeping contributes to good customer service. It is much easier to improve customer service in a clean and orderly warehouse. It is very difficult in a warehouse where clutter transforms simple routines into stressful projects.

Standard Storing Procedures Not Being Followed. Adhering to how inventories should be stored is often more difficult and time consuming than is just plunking down the loads in the nearest available space. Standard storing procedures (SSPs) are not developed with what is easy being given top priority. Safety, product damage, housekeeping, space utilization, company and warehouse objectives all have higher priority than what is easiest. If all the concerns mentioned are taken care of and this constitutes the easiest way, so much the better. The fact is that by taking care of all these concerns, the cumulative effect results in the easiest way in the long run.

Space Standards Are Wrong. If the standards are established in a professional manner, whether the standards are right is the most unlikely area to look for the source of the problems. Standards are, or should be, the culmination of thorough study, hypothesizing and synthesizing by experts, warehouse management and workers. This process results in valid standards—far better than even the best supervisor's guesses.

Often front-line supervisors can foretell how much space is required and how best to store whatever along with how much time it will take. But this clairvoyance is rooted in past experience and limited experience at that. Establishing standards should take advantage of the supervisor's input and a lot more that supervisors do not have the time or training to pursue. That does not mean standard setters are better, even smarter than operating supervisors. The way the game is played is that each is supposed to be better at their particular profession. The main ingredients that make a good supervisor are that of organizing workers, machines, and any other valid input to do the most effective and efficient job possible. Engineers who set standards are at most one of the operating supervisor's valuable sources of input.

If standards do appear wrong, have them checked. If they are right, have the person doing the checking explain what has to be done to comply—which constitutes a valuable step forward. If they are wrong, have them corrected and move on without looking back. If wrong standards seem chronic, establish a project to correct them.

If the elements of every standard are in computer memory as they should be, the supervisor who is questioning the standard should be able to call forth on the CRT viewer this data and reconcile it with reality without bringing in the standards experts at least in many instances. If the answer sought is not obvious, pass it on to the experts. When a wrong standard is made right, pass this information on to the coordinator of this data to change what is in the computer and to provide a bridge from the wrong performance while operating with the wrong standard to the new standard and the performance that results from it. Any changes made to computer fixed data must be tautly controlled; otherwise, the standards program suffers.

Wrong or Lack of Application. Performance is determined by arithmetically comparing what should be—*standard,* to what is—*actual.* Both parts must be accurate and the right formula followed to produce valid performance measurement. During this country's production heyday, it was not unusual for a company to invest considerable time and money to have industrial engineers set high quality standards. Then, to make little use of them. What seemed worse was that the standards program was thrown out entirely because the standards and resultant performances were improperly used. In retrospect, this was not the worst that could have happened. The very worst was to keep the program going for cosmetic reasons only.

HOW TO CONTROL DEVIATIONS FROM STANDARD OPERATING PROCEDURES AND STANDARD STORING PROCEDURES

An important feature of any procedures manual is that it is religiously followed. This is not to stifle constructive creativeness; just the opposite. One of the main purposes of the manual is to smoothly incorporate better new ways and to have a means of bridging from what is to what will be, so that continuity is not lost. Other important reasons for the manual are for its instructional value and to standardize the best known methods. All procedures of the standard manual should be signed off by the warehouse manager and acknowledged by managers of other departments that are affected.

While standard operating procedures must be followed, occasional deviations from standard are necessary. Perhaps a safety hazard was overlooked or orders must be reshuffled to take care of a customer emergency. A common error of management is to establish standards that have no provision for these deviations. This puts the floor supervisor and the workers in the position of knowingly violating standards. This causes an erosion of the sanctity of the

standards and the authority of management. It is better to acknowledge proce-
durally that there will be exceptions, and to provide for them. This may be as
simple as requiring lift truck operators to get temporary approval from their
immediate supervisor and charging the supervisor with the responsibility of
making certain the off-standard way is justified. This should not be a *rubber
stamp approval.* Often what is requested by the workers should not be approved.
For example, the bulk storage area designated for a certain SKU is full and the
operator requests putting the last three pallet loads from an inbound shipment
in pallet racks nearby. Normally this type of exception would be approved, but
suppose the pallet loads weigh over 2,000 pounds and the load capacity of these
racks is only 1,000 pounds per pallet position. The supervisor should explain to
the operator why this should not be done, and together they determine an acceptable alternative. Also, the supervisor should thank the operator for following procedure by asking first.

The floor supervisor is the person directly responsible for seeing that
SOPs and SSPs are followed; he is also responsible for deviations. If he is not
sure of the consequences of a non-standard procedure, his responsibility is to
involve the warehouse manager in problem solving.

HOW TO BUDGET WAREHOUSE EXPENDITURES AND ITS USES

Warehousing is responsible for its departmental costs as any other department
is. It should budget what it expects to spend and have actual expenditures compared to it to provide performance measurement. See Figure 12.7.

Warehousing's budget should be derived from what is expected from it,
which is derived from the company's formal forecasts of sales, production, and
any other department's that will use warehousing's services. These forecasts
are then translated to work and space requirements and then converted to dollars by its chart of accounts, which is indicated as expense accounts in the form
in Figure 12.7.

Backing up the budget figures should be warehousing's handling time and
space utilization standards factored by expected performance. These are then
converted to the financial budget. Then as expenses are incurred, they are
coded to the appropriate expense account and performance is determined. In
the illustration, performance measurement is showed as over- and undervari-
ances with a section at the bottom of the form to highlight the reasons for
significant variances.

Because the nature of warehousing is to absorb variations of production
and sales, its work load varies and sometimes dramatically. These variations
play havoc with fixed budgets where every interval during the budget period is
the same as far as budgeted amounts are concerned. For this reason "variable"
budgets are often used, which allows for different budgeted amounts by relating
them to the actual work load experienced.

HOW TO GIVE HOUSEKEEPING ITS DUE RECOGNITION

Throughout, this text the subject of good housekeeping is discussed as it relates to other subjects. Here it is dealt with headon. It would not be rash to say
that housekeeping should be more a concern in warehousing than in any other

FIGURE 12.7 Expense and Budget Comparison

EXPENSE AND BUDGET COMPARISON
Warehouse Operations Division
Performance Report

Warehouse _____   Month _____

Manager _____   Year _____

EXPENSE ACCOUNTS	CURRENT MONTH			YEAR-TO-DATE		
	Actual	Budget	Over*	Actual	Budget	Over*
1. Salaries						
2. Wages						
3. Equipment depreciation						
4. Equipment rental						
5. Equipment operation						
6. Equipment repairs						
7. Building depreciation						
8. Building rent						
9. Building repairs						
10. Packing supplies						
11. Office supplies						
12. Travel and lodging						
13. Communications						
14. Utilities						
15. Property taxes						
16. Miscellaneous						
17. Total						

Reasons for significant variances this month: _____

_____

By _____   Date _____

segment of industry. Yes, even more than production or transportation. Every piece of equipment and every operation performed is a generator of debris in one form or another. And every worker's job description, whether in print or not, should include cleaning up after himself or herself. Even when there is a janitorial service the workers must still be responsible for cleaning up the debris they create. Virtually anything that is dropped on the floor, even pieces of string or chips from wood pallets, constitute safety hazards. Even when the workers conscientiously pick up after themselves, there is plenty left for the janitors to do.

Housekeeping considerations are an inseparable part of more than operations—they are involved in facilities design, warehouse layout, and personnel safety.

Guidelines for Good Housekeeping

These following guidelines can be used as a checklist of how things are as well as how they should be.

1. Landscaping is trimmed, watered, and kept free of debris.
2. Any outside storage is neat and orderly.
3. Outside of warehouse is kept attractive and in good repair.
4. Outside paving of truck maneuvering areas, walkways, car parking, steps, and porches are regularly cleaned.
5. Warehouse's rail spur is regularly patrolled to remove debris.
6. Any outside lunch facilities are kept clean and orderly; garbage cans are provided and are regularly serviced.
7. Throwing cigarette butts on the grounds is strictly forbidden. Butt receptacles are provided and serviced.
8. Outside lighting is used and is kept in good repair.
9. Fencing is kept in good repair.
10. Front street and any access roads whether public or warehouse controlled are patrolled regularly to keep free of debris.
11. Outside doors and windows are kept clean and in good repair.
12. Inside walls and ceiling are kept clean, free of spider webs, and painted. (Note that painting is strongly recommended despite the prevailing opinion in many quarters that it is not justified. I believe it has a positive value in housekeeping and employee morale that far outweighs its cost and that a white painted ceiling is esthetically right as well as it reduces lighting costs.)
13. Layout provides for straight parallel aisles avoiding obscure areas.
14. A rat run 18 inches or more wide along all walls is provided and regularly inspected for rodents and insects and kept clear of debris.
15. Storage racks are kept in good repair—no dented or bent parts.
16. Addressing for the stock locator system and capacity figures for storage racks are easy to read and are professional appearing.
17. Pallets and skids are kept in good repair and are orderly stacked in defined areas when not in use.
18. Handling equipment is clean and freshly painted as appropriate.
19. Graffiti is strictly forbidden.
20. Bulletin board and signs are clean, orderly, and with up-to-date materials.
21. Lighting throughout the warehouse is sufficient to permit clear vision. Consult a lighting expert when in doubt.
22. Damaged or any other nonsalable inventories awaiting disposition are given a quality of storage that is equal to salable inventories. This is to avoid further damage or deterioration. Until merchandise is authoritatively declared scrap, it should receive quality care.
23. Salvage or recoup areas are clearly defined and kept clean and orderly, but they still should be in the least conspicuous place in the warehouse.
24. Merchandise that is to be scrapped is to be disposed of regularly, not permitted to become more than a small eye sore.
25. Spills and breakage are cleaned up immediately.

26. Caution is exercised to avoid vermin coming into the warehouse with inbound shipments. Materials from certain areas of the world are more prone to this. When first detected, shut and seal the doors of the van, container, or rail car and have professionally decontaminated before unloading.

27. Restrooms are kept meticulously clean and supplied.

28. Lunchroom is kept meticulously clean and orderly.

29. All inventory storage is kept orderly. Any leaning or otherwise deemed hazardous stacking is to be restacked immediately.

30. Roof is kept in good repair. Any leaks are corrected as soon as weather permits.

31. Aisles and storage areas are clearly identified and marked with paint or a high-quality tape used for this purpose.

32. Aisles are not used for storage except when explicitly authorized by supervision. Even then a red tag shall be attached to it showing when it was authorized and by whom.

33. Smoking in the warehouse is either forbidden or defined areas are provided with regularly maintained butt receptacles.

34. Office areas are to be exemplary for operations, and vice versa.

HOW TO MANAGE FOR SAFETY

Like housekeeping, safety too is mentioned throughout this book as it relates to other subjects. But because of its overwhelming importance this section is exclusively devoted to it.

Guidelines for Safe Warehousing

These guidelines can be used appropriately as a checklist of how things are as well as how things should be.

1. Adherence to the "Guidelines for Good Housekeeping" discussed in the previous section goes a long way toward providing a safe working environment. Rather than repeat them, only those not covered there will be covered here.

2. Only authorized workers will be allowed to use the tools and equipment of warehousing. And only those workers who have been properly trained will be authorized.

3. A standard safe practices manual will be developed by representatives from warehouse management, workers, safety department, and the union if there is one. It will cover standard safe practices for every standard operating procedure and standard storing procedure with cross-referencing capabilities.

4. Any authorized change of standard operating, standard storing or standard safety procedures will be reviewed for its effect on other procedures and changes made as appropriate.

5. Standard safety practices will be established and maintained for each type of the warehouse's equipment.

6. A videocassette file will be maintained of equipment suppliers' tapes of their recommended standard safety practices. Also provided will be the

means to run them conveniently in a quiet room on a good-sized CRT screen. Suppliers who do not have such tapes should be asked to assist in and help pay for preparing the warehouse's own tapes.

7. Following is an example of a standard safety practice for use of pallets and skids:

   a. Pallets and skids shall be of sturdy construction and maintained in good repair.

   b. Capacity limits shall be stenciled on each pallet and skid, and loads shall be held within these limits.

   c. Broken and weakened pallets and skids shall be immediately taken from use and delivered to a designated area for repair or scrap.

   d. Empty pallets and skids shall be stored with the load-bearing surface up in neat, stable stacks in designated areas.

   e. Pallets and skids shall be only of warehouse authorized standard design, size, grade, and construction.

   f. Loaded pallets and skids shall be uniform, with the same pallet pattern for all the same SKUs.

   g. Alternating tier patterns shall be used for each level of carton products. When palletizing perfectly square cartons that cannot have alternating tiers to interlock, authorized twine will be securely tied around the top tier using the standard cinch knot.

   h. Stacking height of pallet loads, one pallet load on another, shall be limited to the top pallet load that will not cause crushing of the bottom pallet load and will not cause the stack to deflect and possibly topple.

13

Bar Codes: Systems and Uses in Warehouse Management

CHAPTER HIGHLIGHTS

Addressed in this chapter are the important ways in which bar coding can be used to improve warehousing in general. This chapter covers the basics of bar coding, applications, fixed data files needed, ongoing systems that use them, then a detailed discussion of the systems and their component functions of bar codes.
Covered are the following:

How bar coding works
Types of available bar codes
Types of printers and readers
Quality considerations
Applications in warehousing

It is interesting to note that the feature of bar coding that has prompted its rapid acceptance throughout commerce is its binary language.

HOW BAR CODES WORK

A bar code is a binary machine language consisting of opaque bars and white spaces. It signals machine action, usually a computer, by pulses of reflective light generated by moving a continuous narrow beam of light across a meaningful set of bars and spaces. A bar-code system consists of the following basic components:

○ A Code	A meaningful arrangement of opaque bars and white spaces.
○ A Printer	A means of printing the code in a manner that can be reliably read.
○ A Reader	A means of reliably reading the code and converting the differences in reflective light intensity to meaningful pulses of electricity.
○ An Electronic Machine	A means to convert the electrical impulses received from the reader to some useful form, memory, or action.

Each of these components has a broad range of alternatives and will have more as the science evolves.

Advantages and Disadvantages of Bar Coding

There are sound and practical reasons why bar coding is developing so rapidly. Basically it is a better way to collect information for the computer—or anything else whose best language is binary.

Main Advantages

ACCURACY: Bar code systems are virtually error free, a prime requisite in an age of specialization and mass production. Errors in modern business are more costly and lethal than ever before.

SPEED: Input to operating systems like computerization is much faster than manual and can be as fast as the speed of light and electricity which is fast beyond real comprehension.

COST: Bar code systems are the lowest-cost input to machines that has ever been devised. Economic payback of appropriate applications is more often measured in months than in years.

RELIABILITY: A well-designed system can be counted on to perform consistently. Consistent, valid information is a prime requisite for good modern business decision making.

SIMPLICITY: What it does and the essentials of how it does it are comparatively simple. In many applications it operates without human attention. Usually only minimal training is required.

OPERATING COSTS: Electrical energy consumption and repair and maintenance are minuscule compared to the human and paperwork alternatives.

SPACE REQUIREMENTS: Readers have negligible space requirements.

ACCEPTANCE: Bar code systems, though highly efficient, usually do not evoke negative reactions from employees and their unions who are concerned about veiled health hazards and losing work to machines. The common reaction is relief from wearisome work.

Main Disadvantages: The disadvantages of bar coding systems are those that accompany any highly specialized function on mass scale. If something does go wrong, it can affect a lot and could be very costly. Fortunately, bar coding is less prone to breakdown than are most other breakthroughs in technology.

BAR CODE STANDARDS

Anyone can develop a new bar code, and in the early stage of the technology many did. But it did not take long to see that this proliferation would result in bar-code chaos. Putting a company's exclusive bar code on all things that should be so coded took a lot of time and effort whose value stayed inside the company. This was all right for applications that were truly internal such as time keeping, addressing of warehouse layouts, and capital equipment identification. But things moving from suppliers to the company and from the company to customers also require a common bar code. To be worthwhile there has to be standardization at least by broad groupings and services so that producers and consumers can use the same code.

On the other hand, there are large segments of business that apply two different types of bar codes for the same type of merchandise. One symbology (language) is, for instance, for their own manufactured products and another is standard when the products are purchased from others. Two different code symbologies can also appear on the same product; one to meet one set of requirements and one to meet another. The codes are preceded by code identifiers so the message in one code is not picked up by the other. Further, the difference in the time to read one code versus two is not all that great in relation to the benefits to be derived from of having or not having a usable bar code system.

It would be best if one type of bar code were used for everything, but this is claimed to be impractical. The common belief in the bar code community is that the range of applications is just too diverse, but this may change in the future.

The essence of the binary language that governs machines today is the "on" and "off" switch. Bar codes are simply a machine-readable expression of on and off. With enough ons and offs the human language can be automatically translated to machine language, and vice versa. A bar code normally expresses "on" with a bar and "off" with a space—but not always. Some codes utilize only bars and the spaces only separate the bars. Wide bars indicate "1" and narrow bars indicate "0." This is called a "discreet" code. A bar code pattern in which the spaces between bars are a part of the code is called a "continuous" code. Combinations of bars and spaces make characters which translate to numbers or letters.

How the Universal Product Code Works

The trick is what pattern of bars and spaces to use to converse with and between machines? Many different bar code variations have been tried, but few have survived. Probably the most common in the United States is the Universal Product code (UPC), used to identify grocery items. Each stock keeping unit (SKU) has a unique bar code pattern which, when read by a scanner at the grocery check out, gives the customer (on a viewer and a paper receipt) how many, a general description of the item, and the price. There are some problems in customer comprehension because of the rapid rate this is done, and the abbreviated descriptions, but the machines, with great efficiency, accuracy, and reliability, do what they are programmed to do.

The UPC includes for each SKU this information:

1. An exclusive SKU code number
2. An abbreviated general description
3. Who manufactured it
4. The quantity, weight, or volume of the package

In the case of a grocery item, the product number is transmitted from the checkout register to the grocery store's host computer, which applies the price and decides whether sales tax is applicable; this data is then transmitted back to the register—all in linear sequence but so fast it seems instantaneous.

The UPC was initially designed specifically for supermarkets in the United States, but since has been incorporated into the World Product Code (WPC) (also known as the EAN and the IAN codes), which permits those having WPC to read UPC—but not the reverse—which indicates more code design work is still needed in this area—even though from another point of view amazing progress has already been made in a relatively short time.

How Logistics Application of Automated Marking and Reading Symbols (Logmars) Works

Another commonly used symbology is called, with extra care, Logistics Application of Automated Marking and Reading Symbols, which fortunately was shortened to Logmars. It was adopted by the federal government as its official bar code symbology, which includes the vast logistical system for the general services administration and the Department of Defense. The specifications of their Logmars is cataloged as MIL-STD-1189. The symbology used is known as Code 39 or Code 3 of 9. Actually both titles are appropriate because there are 39 message characters and 3 of the 9 elements per character are wide. Using the ratio of the number of wide elements to the total elements per character as Code 3 of 9 indicates is a common way to meaningful name the different bar code symbologies.

Code 39 is favored by segments of the private sector as well as government, partly because its use is required for all materials received by the federal government and private suppliers who cater to government find it an advantage to be on the same bar code, naturally and also because it is considered a good code with low error rate and is appropriate for various print surfaces and read capabilities.

How Code 2 of 5 and Code 2 of 5 Interleaved Works

The bar code designed principally for warehouse inventories is called the 2 of 5 Code. It is a discrete code, which means that only the bars carry information.

Because of this the code is easier to print and to achieve a high read rate. It is also self-checking in that each character must have two wide bars and three narrow ones, or it will not read. In binary language the wide bars are 1's and the narrow bars are 0's.

The 2 of 5 code is highly thought of where it applies. Its limitation is that it has low information density because of its simplicity—using only bars to carry information. To include more information it had to be lengthened but was restricted in height because of printer limitations. This resulted in a long code across the scan line to get in all the message but not correspondingly high, which made reads more difficult. The read mechanism and the placement of the bar code had to be held to overly chose tolerances to prevent the scan from drifting off the code preventing a read. This limitation gave birth to a modification to Interleaved 2 of 5.

The Interleaved 2 of 5 Code retains many of the advantages of the 2 of 5 code but makes use of the spaces between the bars as well as the bars. With this modification the capacity for information was substantially increased and Interleaved 2 of 5 became standard for coding corrugated cardboard packages which of course is the most common container in warehousing.

BAR-CODE COMPONENTS

The main components of a bar code system are listed here with discussion following:

1. Bar-code symbology
2. Bar-code printer
3. Bar-code reader

Bar-Code Symbology

The meaning of symbology was discussed earlier in this chapter. The UPC, Logmars Code 39, Code 2 of 5, and Code 2 of 5 Interleaved are but a few of the many different code systems available. A vital concern about coding is to get tied into the code or codes that apply to your business. To develop a new one on your own is no less than bar-code heresy.

Bar-Code Printer

This component of a bar-code system and the science that supports and leads it are more complex. How bar codes are printed and on what surface directly relates to what means will be used to read them. You should pursue these three components together. Generally, the main concern is to provide reliably the best contrast in relation to what reader is being employed. This is not always discernible with the naked eye. For instance use of various colors may be desirable from an esthetics point of view but can result in a low read rate. On the other hand, a code printed with, say, black bars and white spaces may appear ugly and immediately catch the eye in an otherwise highly attractive art scheme. Attractive packaging plays a big part in moving merchandise off the store shelves.

Packaging esthetics does and should influence what the bar code looks like and where it is positioned. This concern has given rise to finding ways to print codes in colors that harmonize rather than conflict with the package esthetics. Improvements are being made in this area as rapidly as any other phase of bar coding which is at a dazzling accelerated rate showing no signs of leveling off. The potential of this ultra-efficient machine language has hardly been tapped.

The main considerations about what will make the optimum match of the printing process and readability follows.

The first concerns the number of units there are to be coded with the identical message. Are there many thousands or only one or a few? Different applications range from one to millions. Generally, when many are to be produced, the bar code is made a part of the package or label. Plastic packaging is normally printed by *converters* (which is the name given to companies who print items such as potato chip bags). Can labels in large quantities are normally printed by commercial printers.

If the bar-code printing requirements are only one or a few at a time, you will find it impractical to have them produced by an outside printer. Probably best for these is to have the codes printed on rolls of pressure-sensitive peal-off labels by a commercial printer. If your needs are for relatively low quantities and many types with little lead time, probably the company should have its own on-site printing facilities.

The reality of bar-code printing is that much of it is printed along with the package. Even when printed independently of the package, commercial printers should be able to print with better quality at lower prices because this is their specialty. The user company's forte is something other than printing; however, provision should be made for small quantities to be printed in house as needed.

Another reason for in-house ability to print relates to cases where management does not know what it needs until it is too late to send out for printing. This has given rise to the need for what is called "on-demand printing." In-house on-demand printing technology has received considerable attention because the need is so great. Now there is something available for almost every need. A common on-demand printer employs dot-matrix impact printing.

Dot-matrix print consists of a series of ink dots arranged so close together the reader accepts the print as being solid. It is a versatile, relatively low-cost in-house type of printing. The printed dots are created by a block of pins being caused to strike an inked ribbon against the bar label stock. This does not produce the highest-quality bar code prints, but apparently it is acceptable in many situations and is being improved over time with sharper edges and more consistent density.

Many other printing processes are used mostly by commercial printers, but in theory if not in practice, all means of printing used by commercial printers can be done by in-house printers as well.

Bar-Code Readers

Bar-code readers, commonly referred to as scanners, come in a wide variety. Each is at its best when used for the specific purposes for which it was designed. Like any other family of business tools that are made by many different suppliers, there are big differences between designs and prices.

Bar-code readers can be classified many different ways. The following is probably as appropriate as any:

1. Hand-held, moving-beam readers
2. Fixed-location, fixed-beam readers

3. Fixed-location, moving-beam readers
4. Photodiode array (PDA) readers

Hand-Held, Moving-Beam Readers   All bar-code readers accomplish their function by illuminating the bar-code symbols and using a light detector to measure the differences in reflective light between bars and spaces. The differences in length of time of scanning between different widths of bars and spaces is detected by a photoreceptor that translates the different time intervals into electronic impulses that provide binary instruction to the host machine, usually a computer but other electronic operational devices as well.

The most common bar-code reader is the hand-held light pen, often referred to as a wand. The reasons for its popularity are its versatility and its low cost. Its versatility comes from it being hand held and can reach any code within arm length and body stretch which takes in the placement of practically all bar codes, but when not, the bar-code materials can be brought within reach. The wand's relatively low cost stems from having no moving parts. The hand provides the power to move the wand over the bar code or to hold the wand in a fixed position as the commodities to be code read pass by.

Fixed-Location, Fixed-Beam Readers   This type reader stays in one spot, for instance, securely attached to a conveyor frame where bar-coded products move past. A limiting feature of this type is that it must read on the first and only pass. For this reason the reader must be close to the bar code as it passes, and the reader beam should extend beyond the height of the bars so the printing voids and bleeds cause less nonreads.

The main advantages of this type reader is that (1) it can operate without human attendance and (2) the initial cost of equipment is less than its compatriot, the fixed-location, moving-beam equipment which of course has movable mechanical parts. Its disadvantage is that it has only one chance to read, and because of this better control must be maintained to assure very close tolerances.

Fixed-Location, Moving Beam Readers   This reader has the unique advantage of automatically moving the beam back and forth over the bar code which provides a greater assurance that a read will result—which is the sole objective of any bar-code reader. The moving beam type is available in both hand-held and fixed-location models. The beam movement across the bar code is automatic and at a constant rate which is important, to get a read. But, it goes further, it moves the beam back and forth to increase its chances even more.

Laser is now being used in some moving-beam readers. The word "laser" is an acronym for light amplification by stimulated emission of radiation. Its beam is made up of only one wave length and one color in contrast to the ordinary light bulb that emits all visible colors and wave lengths. The laser's monochromatic and single wavelength permits better focusing and an independence of distracting lights in its area of operation. Laser has created another new frontier in the vast mostly undeveloped area of bar coding that is so new that the pioneers in the field did not have time to exploit the previous state of light technology before the introduction of laser.

Photodiode Array Readers   The PDA reader employs a different way to tell bars from spaces. It illuminates the entire bar code area at once like a photoflash of a camera; then the pattern of bars and spaces are interpreted in their entirety by a photosensitive semiconductor known as a linear photo-diode array.

It has certain important advantages:

○ Lower cost compared to other types of readers.

○ Ability to read colored print as well as the usual carbon content print.

○ Ready acceptance by users of the hand-held model in particular because the operator feels more control over what is happening by pressing a button to activate it.

○ Ability to average the print coverage and density which tends to negate the problems that the other type readers have with print void and ink bleeds.

High hopes are held for the growth potential of PDA readers with dot-matrix printing. The combination seems to optimize at least for many applications the lower-cost printing and reading with higher human-friendly performance. But suggesting the future for any type combination this early in the evolution of bar coding is risky. It does seem, however, that the marriage of PDA readers and dot-matrix printers at minimum constitute a notable development in bar-code technology.

BAR-CODE QUALITY CONSIDERATIONS

There are two measures of bar-code quality performance: "human friendliness" and "system friendliness." Human friendliness refers to the first- and second-pass read rates. The first-pass read rate (FRR) is the percentage of reads on the first attempt to the total number of attempts. The objective is to get as high a percentage as possible, but anything above 85 percent is generally acceptable except for fixed-location, fixed-beam readers where there is only one chance to read. Here the read rate should be 100 percent, unless there is a loop in the conveyance to keep returning the coded item until a read is effected. The second-read rate (SRR) when there is the opportunity to make a second try should definitely be 100 percent. Actually there is nothing technically wrong with making a second or even several passes to get a read as long as the read is eventually made except that the system is stopped during the brief interval. Worse is that employees become discouraged if it consistently requires several passes to read.

Try to find the problem and fix it. It may be as simple as taking more care in printing the bar code or some extra training so the employee will wand the code better. The salesperson or consultant who is advising on the system may be satisfied with an 85 percent FRR, but whoever in the company is responsible for it should not be. An 85 percent performance any where else in warehouse operations is not acceptable.

The second measure of quality, "system friendliness" refers to errors that result from substituting wrong characters in the code. This and the reasons for it are illustrated and explained in Figure 13.1. Such errors result from print voids and ink bleeds in the symbols, quality defects that are correctable. The substrate, the material on which the symbols are printed, is the problem, or the means of printing or reading the symbols is wrong, or the combination is. If a change in substrate or the means of applying the symbols is necessary to correct the problem of substitutions, so be it. Determine what is necessary, what the alternative solutions are, select the best, and go for it. If this does not do it or the cost is truly unacceptable, try again. You are dealing with a finite number of nature's laws.

FIGURE 13.1 Bar Code: Illustrations of Code 2 of 5, the bar code system for warehouse inventories

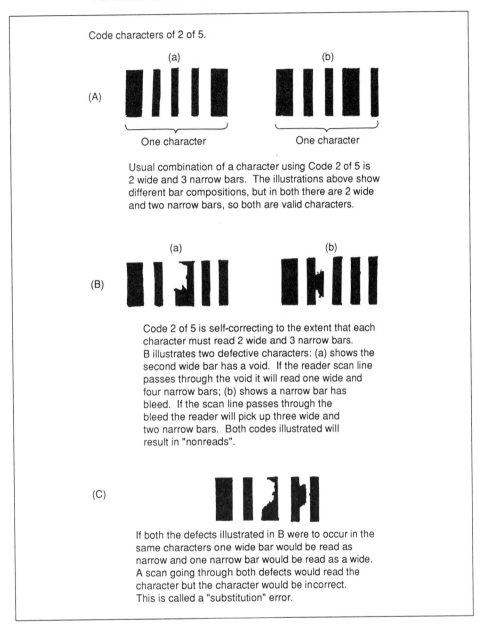

Code characters of 2 of 5.

(a)   (b)

(A)

One character   One character

Usual combination of a character using Code 2 of 5 is 2 wide and 3 narrow bars. The illustrations above show different bar compositions, but in both there are 2 wide and two narrow bars, so both are valid characters.

(a)   (b)

(B)

Code 2 of 5 is self-correcting to the extent that each character must read 2 wide and 3 narrow bars. B illustrates two defective characters: (a) shows the second wide bar has a void. If the reader scan line passes through the void it will read one wide and four narrow bars; (b) shows a narrow bar has bleed. If the scan line passes through the bleed the reader will pick up three wide and two narrow bars. Both codes illustrated will result in "nonreads".

(C)

If both the defects illustrated in B were to occur in the same characters one wide bar would be read as narrow and one narrow bar would be read as a wide. A scan going through both defects would read the character but the character would be incorrect. This is called a "substitution" error.

If the printer leaves voids, bleeds, specks, smearing, or nonuniform density, there are just so many things that can be wrong. The source of the problem has to fall within just a few categories:

PROBLEM Category Evidence	CAUSES
Print voids	Dirty or defective strike hammer
	Dirty or oily substrate
	Defective ribbon
	Improper machine adjustment

Print bleed   Substrate too porous

Substrate not porous enough

Too much ink

Strike pressure too hard

Improper machine adjustment

A similar limited number of reasons apply to any defect causing nonreads and substitutions, which means every problem is solvable. Absolute quality bar coding is one of those things necessary to attain absolute inventory accountability.

The same diligence in eliminating print defects must be applied to eliminating reader defects. The first and main concern is that there must be compatibility of the print and the reader. It is possible to have superb quality printing and absolute quality reading but not have the two work well together. They should be absolutely right for each other as well.

The ultimate objective in print quality is sufficient contrast between bars and background (spaces) to permit the reader to differentiate reliably between the two. Sufficient contrast can be determined only in relation to the reader design and capabilities. The human eye cannot be relied upon. Different readers by design read different print compositions. Some even read etched bar codes on metal. Some bar codes are designed to maintain readability even when exposed to extreme heat and cold.

Once there is the proper match of printed code and reader capabilities, how is print quality defined? It is a measure of reflective light contrast between the bars and the background space. This is expressed as a percentage and is determined as follows: "The light reflected from the background, less the light reflected from the printed bars, divided by light reflected from the background." The result is called the "print contrast ratio," PCR.

There can be another culprit other than those already discussed. It is the environment, which covers many things—from frost and dust on the code to extraneous light causing malfunction. Also, electrical pulses from sources outside the system can trigger unwanted responses. To correct the problem, you must adjust the machine or alter the environment.

BAR-CODE APPLICATIONS IN THE WAREHOUSE

To function well, warehousing has to have certain basic information available for instant recall commonly known as "fixed data"—the sum of which is called the data base. This basic data is called forth as needed and is put back until needed again. Like a customer's "ship to" address, it does not have to be researched every time it is used. Initially it is determined, is double-checked, and remains the same until formally changed. The following are the sets of fixed data files that are maintained by most warehouses or by other departments that feed the data to warehousing as needed.

Outline of Fixed Data Applications

1. CUSTOMER FIXED DATA
   - Proper name
   - Address for correspondence and invoices

- ○ "Ship to" address
- ○ Telephone, telex, and fax numbers for each of the above locations
- ○ Personal contact, title, and name for each of the locations that the warehouse deals with
- ○ Family status
- ○ Credit limitations
- ○ Freight class and rates
- ○ Special quality concerns
- ○ Special loading instructions
- ○ Special delivery instructions
- ○ Freight on Board (F.O.B.) point

Much of this data should be bar coded so that customers or the company salespersons can use bar coding to place orders on the warehouse. This is a good way to reduce order processing time and paperwork.

2. EQUIPMENT FIXED DATA
- ○ Generic name and model number
- ○ Manufacturer's name and date made
- ○ Who it was purchased from date and price
- ○ If leased, leasor, terms of lease, and schedule of payments
- ○ Capacity, capabilities, and other specifications
- ○ Preventive maintenance schedule
- ○ Guarantees
- ○ Depreciation method and schedule
- ○ Insurance coverage

All this data should be in a data base. Exclusive numbers and corresponding bar codes are necessary for each piece of equipment or equipment group as in the case of storage racks and pallets (if permanent type).

3. EMPLOYEE FIXED DATA
- ○ Name (and nickname if appropriate)
- ○ Social security number
- ○ Record of employment: start, vacations, layoffs, recalls, and so on
- ○ Special awards, disciplines, achievements, and so on
- ○ Health status: physical examinations, handicaps, accidents, injuries, and so on
- ○ Education: years, diplomas, degrees, licenses, and so on
- ○ Birthdate
- ○ Family status

All of this information should be in computer memory. Of prime importance is an exclusive number and bar code for each employee name and identification that will be used for payroll and labor distribution and every other computer input that should be identified by employee.

4. STANDARDS OF FOUR TYPES: OPERATING PROCEDURES, OPERATING TIMES, SPACE UTILIZATION, AND SAFE PRACTICES

- Standard operating procedures
    - Identifying name and grouping of each SOP
    - Best engineered way to perform each operating routine, including type of equipment, crew size (most often one), and job classification (if required)
- Standard operating times
    - Identification of each SOT
    - Engineered time to perform each function of warehouse operations
    - Description of elements and elemental times that comprise each SOT, including the allowances built into the elemental times
    - Means to recap all SOT's that comprise each SOP
- Safe Practices
    - Identification of standard safe practices referenced to each type of equipment
    - Cross referenced to each of the three types of standards discussed before
- Space utilization standards
    - Identification of each SUS
    - Reference to the SOP and safe practices of which it is a part—for how to best store each SKU
    - Components of each SUS
        - Bare storage space (1)
        - Bare space factored for inventory flexibility (2)
        - Standard (including flexibility) factored to include unusable space (3) [product of $(1) \times (2) \times (3)$]
- Standard Safe Practices
    A distinct part of each of the other three standards and a separate one for each piece of equipment.

These four types of standards and the elements that comprise each should be stored in computer memory. Each SKU standard should have an exclusive number and bar code.

5. PRODUCT FIXED DATA

- Name and code number of each SKU including manufacturer's name and identification number
- SKU packaging unit (examples: 1 case of 12 10-ounce bottles, 1 case of one 5-gallon container, and so on)
- Net, tare, and gross weights (see Figure 13.2, Component Weights of Unitized Loads, for different types of weights)
- Special environmental requirements (examples: temperature range, humidity, cleanliness, fragility, crushability, and so on)
- Inventory shelf life and rotation requirements (LIFO or FIFO)
- Freight classification
- Hazard considerations

      □ Special handling considerations

      □ Unitized stacking pattern, if any

      □ Skid requirements, if any

All this data should be in the data base and every item bar coded so that complete product fixed data can be called forth for viewing or printing.

6. SUPPLIERS OF INVENTORIES

      □ Proper name and identification number of each supplier cross-referenced to the family of SKUs it supplies so the entire list of this supplier's SKUs can be called forth

      □ Address for placing orders and other correspondence

      □ Telephone, telex, and fax numbers

      □ Personal contact, title, and name

      □ Family status

      □ Carrier preferences

      □ Freight class and rates

         ○ Freight on board point

         ○ Lead time for shipments

         ○ Normal delivery time

         ○ Over, short, and damage concerns

All this data should be in computer memory. Most of it should be bar coded as well to assist in preparation and communication of orders.

7. VENDORS OF WAREHOUSE SUPPLIES

This list is similar to that for suppliers of inventories, described earlier. Rather than repeat it here, please pick and choose what is applicable for this category. You will probably find most of it applicable.

8. LOCATOR ADDRESS SYSTEM

      □ Location address for every storage position

      □ Type of storage at each address: bulk, pallet rack, tier rack, cantilever, and so on

      □ Total bare storage capacity of each position

      □ Exclusive bar code for each address

      □ Ability to change addresses efficiently when stocks are rearranged or addresses are subdivided

Applications of Fixed Data Files

Discussed here are the concepts and concerns about the applications of the fixed data files outlined in the preceding section.

Customer-Related Functions and Systems   In any organized sales and warehousing effort there is need for customer files. Often they are maintained by customer service, which can be a part of sales, but usually and more appropriately a part of warehousing or report to a physical distribution management.

Or it can report independently to the CEO if its importance warrants it—usually in a company heavily oriented to sales such as distributors.

Customer service as an organization unit is largely the beneficiary of data created by others—mainly warehousing, such as the status of inventories, receipts, shipments, deliveries, and so on. They are the go-between of those that are responsible for developing customer sales and those that physically handle the products, warehousing, and/or production.

The few key documents or sets of data that customer service generates are those that cover the actual sale, including returns, claims, credits, and anything else that directly relates to the sales transaction—except issuing the invoice. Most often, the invoice is generated by accounting but can be and probably should be initiated by warehousing as a part of the computer transaction that prepares the shipping documents and relieves inventory. If warehousing issues the invoices, accounting and customer service should have computer tie-in with the invoicing data.

With the fixed data in computer memory along with current inventory status and warehousing's work load, customer service should be able to put together the entire sales order at a computer terminal including a CRT, *without generating any actual paperwork*. If hard copies are needed, "Just cannot get along without them," they can be produced on a computer-linked printer.

An aid to creating the sales order in the computer can be a hard copy listing of all the bar codes to initiate the variable data for a sales transaction. The fixed data, including a sales order form, should be accessible in computer memory. This type of arrangement and accessibility of variable and fixed data can go a long way toward achieving paperless or nearly paperless customer service and warehousing.

The decision whether to opt for a paperless system is an important one.

If not well acquainted with computer and bar-code capabilities, business professionals are genuinely afraid to try it. Here is where those designing the system need to do a good job of selling. It may help to cite that Japanese business is said to conduct business with only 1 percent of the paperwork used by American business.

Equipment-Related Functions and Systems   Most companies keep the equipment file in accounting, not in warehousing. The reasons for this are to apply IRS-approved depreciation and to use this and the related assets in their fiscal functions. Another reason is to hold accountable the operating divisions that actually use it. Still, warehousing has as operational need for the equipment files.

Strong consideration should be given to warehousing maintaining the equipment file because this is where virtually everything that can happen to the equipment happens. The equipment file should be a working file and maintained in a manner to be the most help to those who use it. Every piece of equipment used by warehousing should have an exclusive bar code affixed to it. This means *every* piece of equipment from hand carts to storage racks, to lift trucks, to cranes. Every time a piece of equipment is used by an employee, both the equipment bar code and the employee bar code should be wanded and put into the appropriate computer memory. Further, every time repair and maintenance are performed, the R and M person should wand when the work starts and stops, the employee's identification, the identification of the equipment, and what repair or maintenance is performed. Included should be the time the equipment was taken out and put back into service.

Even an experienced, practical warehouser could be thinking at this point: "I can see doing that for lift trucks, cranes, even racks, but why include inexpensive hand carts and ladders?" Four good reasons follow.

1. Because the work time and space utilization standards are based on using certain types of equipment, and this has to be tied to the standard to determine valid performance.

2. Because knowing that appropriate equipment is available when needed is one of warehousing's primary concerns—which neatly takes care of accountability as well. If less concern is expressed for less costly equipment, this attitude will soon permeate through the work force for all equipment. Taking disciplinary action for the "loss" of even the least expensive will do most to assure not losing the next most expensive and the next, and so on, to the most costly equipment.

3. Because a record of repair and maintenance should be kept for each piece of equipment to monitor the performance of both the R and M workers and the particular piece of equipment involved; further, to make certain that guarantees that come with the equipment are used if applicable.

4. Because the ability to tie a piece of equipment to its R and M history will tell a lot about how well specific operators care for it and how well it is repaired and maintained. It will give objective clues as to whether it is being abused and if more education is needed or, as last resort, that disciplinary action should be taken.

Employee-Related Functions and Systems There are two basic reasons for computerizing and bar-coding functions and systems involving employees: for access to (1) that information commonly kept by the personnel department and (2) that information needed by operating management.

Most of the information is the type the operating management needs, but paradoxically it is most common for the personnel department to keep it. Following the line of reasoning used throughout this text that records should be kept by the group that benefits most from their availability and accuracy, employee fixed data should be maintained by warehousing. Just as inventory records that are needed on a real-time basis should not be maintained by accounting with its particular and at times peculiar priorities, so the same applies to the personnel department and its priorities.

Each employee should have an identification number and corresponding bar code permanently fixed in a plastic or metal card that is kept on his or her person all the time at work. It should be used for checking in and out of the company facilities and to associate with work functions performed. For instance an employee should use the personal bar code to show when he or she enters the facility at the beginning of the shift, leaves at the end of the shift, and may be found any time away during the shift. Then wand the bar code to associate every function performed with equipment used in pursuit of operations. This data should serve all employee time requirements, including payroll, overtime, and labor distribution.

The personal bar code also provides for keeping time by product line, work function, equipment used, and so on, and with greater accuracy than was practical when recorded manually. It also keeps in-process performance on a real-time basis. The poverty of language does not permit adequate praise for the benefits that bar coding provides. It gives supervision finger-tip access to objective, accurate information that it has always wanted but had no practical means of getting.

The question no doubt will surface of whether exempt as well as nonexempt workers should carry personal bar-code cards since they are supposed to be paid more on accomplishment than by time. The answer to this is mainly a matter of company policy. The common practice is to not keep track and certainly not by work projects as the nonexempts are required. However, because this is how it is and has been, it need not be. Certainly in facilities requiring security clearance, it is necessary for everyone to log in and out one way or another. Because of the ease of using a personal bar code, perhaps it should be used more extensively, not to regiment exempt employees but for other reasons which may benefit the company and not take anything away from the exempt employees—such as keeping time on projects that use time as a basis for recharge.

Work-Related Functions and Systems   All standards including operating procedures, work time, and space utilization should be in computer memory and have bar codes to access them. When order picking for example, the employee scans his or her identification bar code, then the location code, then the units of the SKU called for by the order, then counts and inputs the remaining units for an inventory count check. The material picked is then moved to the appropriate staging area according to voice-activated or visually displayed instructions on a CRT. The combination of input of units picked, equipment used, and location activate the applicable work-time standard. The actual time taken is determined by a time-keeping device in the computer. These actual times along with standard times earned are accumulated in computer memory along with data accumulated by shift, by day, by month, and so on for trend performance readings and reports for about any interval or intervals concerned.

The warehouse worker and supervisor should be able to access the SOPs in the computer data base to see how the orders should be received, picked, and staged to earn the standard allotted time. If either disagrees with the computer's description of the SOP, an additional bar-code input should tell the computer to tag it so later the operator and supervisor can call it forth for further discussion. Either they accept the SOP, or another bar-code entry puts it in backlog work for the industrial engineers to check, modify, or convince the worker and supervisor of the rightness of the SOP.

Other uses for operating and storing standards include the important functions of planning, scheduling, forecasting, and analyzing for improvements. Preprinted sheets of bar codes that relate to these functions can provide guidance to access the basic fixed and variable data. Without pencil and paper, only the bar codes with access to the computer data can you do, in a relatively short time the following, otherwise very-time-consuming, projects:

1. Determine work and handling equipment loading to meet sales forecast within the constraints of the stated customer service levels.
2. Determine how much lost work time, if any, is due to lack of equipment and what type of equipment.
3. Objectively justify new equipment or release for disposition excess equipment.
4. Determine space utilization performance at past, current, and future inventory levels by SKU by product type, by storage means, and by storage area.
5. Determine what type and how much space will be required to store properly a new product line being added to the inventory—or how much space will be freed by discontinuing a product line.
6. Determine the most efficient route to sequentially pick a multi-SKU order and alternative routes with their corresponding times.
7. Determine the most efficient storage layout according to receiving and picking lot sizes, volume of shipments, and travel time—within the context of the warehouse service objectives.

8. Schedule work and have access on a real-time basis to progress against schedule.

9. Determine the extra work time, which can be translated to costs, to practice FIFO inventory control faithfully. And determine how much can be saved if the rule were modified to permit the most efficient order picking even when no stock may stay in the warehouse longer than, say, one month.

10. Develop work performance for many different work and location categories on a real-time basis at any desired intervals by
    - Produce line
    - SKU
    - Group of workers
    - Type of handling equipment
    - Shift
    - About any other division of work you may want

11. Develop space utilization performance for the several different categories at any desired point in time by
    - Product line
    - SKU
    - Sections of the facility
    - Type of storage (pallet racks, bulk, and so on)
    - And so on.

Product-Related Functions and Systems Having *valid* product fixed data should receive highest priority because it is used in so many basic warehousing functions. Wrong product data can contaminate and nullify the very foundation of warehouse operations. It would be difficult to find anything warehousing does that wrong product fixed data does not negatively affect—from conveying the wrong message through performance reports to overloading equipment with devastating results.

For example, assume that several different SKUs of different weights are planned for an outbound truck load. The plan calls for a proper distribution of weights inside the truck for safe driving and because the truck will go through a weigh station that checks how the weight is distributed as well as the total weight.

According to the standard weight, the heaviest SKU is loaded in the rear of the truck, but the actual weight is twice that of the erroneous standard. The weigh station cites for too much weight on the back axles and again for being over weight in total. To make matters worse, on the return to the warehouse, the driver, under stress, knowing she will return late and miss an important date, takes a curve too fast, tipping the wrongly loaded truck—all because of an innocuous-appearing error in one SKU weight.

Another, less dramatic example of wrong product data is in the context of a warehouse with an automatic storage and retrieval system (ASRS). The warehouse gets a new SKU whose dimensions are erroneously reported at just one-half actual. The storage analyst determines that the unit load should be put into a certain slot in the high-rise storage racks.

To get all the cases on the pallet, an oversized pallet is used. The employee who built the load suspected something wrong, but recently he had been criticized for not following instructions. So this time—"It will be the way 'they' asked for." When the automatic crane tries to put the oversized load in the too small opening, the result is splinters, broken glass, and vinegar raining from 40 feet above. The crane should have had features that would have prevented this type mishap, but the company went with a cheaper trimmed-back ASRS that left out this particular, rarely needed, costly package.

These are but two examples of wrong product specifications that should highlight what problems can result. Best to do what is necessary to determine the right product fixed data the first time.

Inventory Supplier-Related Functions and Systems   The inventory may be supplied entirely from your own company's production. In this case your only contact would be with the company's production control group, so a computer tie-in should be all that is necessary to communicate effectively and efficiently. Any hard copies needed can be typed automatically by production control's terminal printer. To communicate with outside suppliers or wherever there is not a tie-in with a terminal printer, facsimile transmission is often used.

Facsimile, referred to most often as fax, is a contraction of the Latin words *fac simile,* to "make like." It is a quick, foolproof, and efficient method of transmitting messages, drawings, and so on. It has been around a long time but is experiencing vigorous rebirth in modern business.

Most warehouses receive inventory from several to many different suppliers. If purchase orders (usually of several copies) are prepared from scratch, the extra time for composing, typing, and proofing is costly and fraught with opportunities for error. This is a good application for a computer terminal complete with a CRT viewer and a printer. All the information needed to place an order on a supplier can be conveniently assembled on a CRT. The order can then be transmitted to the supplier via facsimile or a computer link with the customer's computer. The computer should be linked in-house to advise or initiate action for the following:

1. Accounts payable to know what money has been committed and how cash flow is influenced.
2. Warehouse office to update its on order inventory status.
3. Receiving department to update its schedule of what and when materials will come in.
4. Scheduling to determine, by using standards, the work and equipment backlog and storage space requirements,
5. And a lot more depending on how extensive the same common information is harnessed to wring out its utility.

Vendors of Warehouse Supplies   The preparation of purchase orders and communicating them to suppliers can be the same routines as described for inventories, except for different spending and authorization controls.

Of singular importance is that supplies have bar-code identification so that they can be wanded to make certain what is received is what was ordered and to enable this data to be transmitted electronically to close out the purchase order, signal accounts payable the material has been received, clear the backlog of receiving work load, update inventory records, feed the performance measurements standards, and so on. What a marvel these electronic gadgets are when lashed together using the same modest input data to update several vital business functions almost simultaneously and nearly instantaneously. By "nearly instantaneously" is meant at the speed of light about 186,282 miles a second—resulting in an interval considerably less than the time to blink an eye.

You will note that the communication routines for receiving supplies are essentially the same as for receiving product inventories. Definitely it is meant to be. Not uncommon is for a company to exercise tight control on its inventories but just the opposite with its supplies. Stressed here is that supplies be received and returned when necessary with the same attention to accountability as though they were product inventories. Probably a separate receiving door should be used for supplies and exceptions established for purchases out of petty cash, but for certain, all acquisitions made through the purchasing department should come through warehousing with its stringent controls. This includes capital equipment which is authorized entirely different than inventories or supplies but receipts of it should be by warehousing all the same. Companies that treat inventories, supplies, and equipment different are too close to the trees to see they are all part of the same forest.

Location Fixed Data   The prerequisite of having a location fixed-data file is to have an address system. Too bad there is not a magic wand to wave and have an address system instantaneously—because by any means known to date it is a horrendous chore.

A stock locator system provides a way for order pickers to go directly to the specific inventory wanted without wasting time searching for it. There is nothing so wasteful as hunt time. It is not difficult in some warehouses to spend more time searching for stock than picking it. Nearly as bad is that workers have a ready-made excuse for taking extra rest time while filling orders, because when order-picking discipline is lost supervision really cannot tell when the extra time is taken in searching or in dogging it. It does not take long for employees to assume the lack of concern reflected by management that does not put effort into a stock locator system. With a good locator system, pickers can be directed to where to find a particular SKU and the remaining SKUs on the order via the most efficient travel plan.

Until the advent of lower-cost, higher-power computers and bar-coding technology, the worth of maintaining a stock locator system was occasionally debatable. The extra clerical function imposed on warehouse operators when receiving and picking orders plus the increase in clerical effort to maintain current locator records was too big a burden. The related clerical work was formidable. Further, having space utilization performance by any part of the storage area on a real-time basis was not possible because there was no practical means of keeping current with the warehouse workers. Before the advent of bar codes and the ability to wand (read) them at the point and time things were happening, real-time conditions could only be estimated—with all the limitations of guesswork.

The physical inventory check on remaining quantities at the time of picking orders is also dependent on a good locator system. This function is a vital improvement in the accountability of inventories, but it requires that the computer is current with the inventory status. If not, the computer inventory will not reflect current inventory, and to compare current actual inventory on location to a machine inventory that is not current is another exercise in futility.

USE OF COMPUTER AND GRAPHIC PRINTER FOR
ON-DEMAND BAR-CODE PRINTING

Computer software is available and others can be created if need be to print on-demand bar codes. For some applications this way meets the needs better than the separate on-demand printers discussed before. It is certainly worth looking into before setting up other means. A use that seems to be applicable is to print corresponding bar codes with the instructions on the order-picking document. If additional copies are needed, the printer copy can be used to reproduce as many as needed on a copy machine.

The graphic printer will print on paper, such as the picking list, or on continuous self-adhesive label stock. While this application may not sweep the on-demand bar-coding field (or it may), it is an example of how nicely computers and bar codes mesh. Truly, recent computer and bar-coding technologies have opened a new warehousing frontier with remarkable possibilities for improvement.

EXAMPLES OF HOW TO USE COMBINATION BAR CODES AND WEIGH SCALES

One of the fastest-growing segments of bar coding is in combination with weigh scales. When it is more efficient to weigh count than to hand count (the practice since the beginning of commerce), weigh counting should prevail.

There are so many different weigh-count applications in warehousing that the *concept* is the most important thing to get a handle on so that it can be considered for any place where individual units are counted as a repetitive part of a process. No doubt you will find a number of weigh situations that are not good applications, but you will also find a surprising number of good applications. Some of these may be so good they will yield substantial savings and/or improved accountability which translates to more than money, it positively contributes employee morale. No one likes to hear, "You've either erred or someone is ripping us off." This is demoralizing even though the ability to count consistently accurately is a truly unusual talent. Better to let a combination of computer, bar coding, and weigh scales take over boring and error-prone counting tasks wherever applicable—examples follow.

An Automatic Double-Check of Unitized Loads

Generally, how this works is that the unitized load is weighed and its weight has to equal the sum of the standard weights of things that make up the load or something is wrong. What constitutes the wrong something must be determined and corrected before the load is shipped.

The process is simple enough and so efficient every unitized load that can involve wrong counts should be so checked. To minimize the extra effort entailed, a weigh station is made a part of a continuous conveyor and means for automatic producing and affixing bar codes. As the actual weight is determined an automatic comparison is made with what it should weigh using the standard weights. If these weights are within a predetermined, acceptable tolerance, a bar-code label denoting such is automatically printed and affixed to the load which says it has been checked and its right to ship. The load continues on the conveyor unit and passes a bar-code reader that opens a gate which shunts the load to its particular dock for outbound loading.

If the actual weight is out of tolerance, more or less, a bar-code label denoting the standard and actual weight is printed including the variance and affixed to the load. The load continues on the conveyor until it passes the bar-code reader that opens a gate that shunts the load to a make-right station. Here a worker determines what is wrong and fixes it. Another bar-code label is affixed to show the load has been corrected, when, and by whom. It is then directed into the continuous conveyor loop to again go through the weigh routine and on to its particular dock for outbound loading.

Usually the amount of the variance gives a good clue as to what is wrong in the load. For instance, if the entire load were made up of only one SKU with each unit weighing 20 pounds, a variance of a plus 20 pounds would indicate the load has one unit too many. A variance of a minus 60 pounds would indicate that the load has three short. Variances for unitized loads of multiple SKUs are not quite so easy to detect just what is wrong.

Assume the unitized load consist of the following:

Quantity (cases)	SKU Numbers	Weight (pounds)	
		Each	Total
10	654321	10	100
40	123456	20	800
30	456123	30	900
Total 80			1,800

But the automatic weigh station indicates a plus variance of 20 pounds. Any of the following possibilities could apply:

Quantity (cases)	Weight (pounds)	
	Unit	Total
2 more	10	20
1 less	10	
1 more	30	20
2 less	10	
2 more	20	20
2 more	30	
2 less	20	20
5 more	10	
1 less	30	20
. . . and on and on		

This is not as futile as it first appears. Certain combinations are more likely than others.

If such combinations are common, it would pay to have the computer determine the ranking of suspects in descending order. The very worst that can happen is that the unitized load is disassembled to find the culprit or culprits.

Actually if there are many unitized-load errors, even 1 in 1,000, it is better to determine the order-picking problem and correct it than to find more efficient remedies at the weigh station. If the bar-code computer system for ordering described before is religiously followed—or controls mandate it is followed—there should be no variances at the weigh station.

A real concern in the system just discussed about verifying order-picking counts by weighing is that the standard weights used are valid. Some containers have weights printed on the packaging and are so regulated by law. Many do not, and they are of greater concern. Regardless, a good SOP would be to require representative weighings of all new products to the warehouse including changes of existing products. This will serve to verify those weights already printed on the containers and take care of those that are not. A by-product of this will be to establish acceptable tolerances for the weigh-count procedure.

If your SKU unit weights are different from the printed weights on the container, advise the suppliers of your findings after making certain that you are correct. Often the information will be welcomed. When it is not, do not push any harder than is necessary to assure that your warehouse is not incurring a liability.

Sometimes manufacturers intentionally produce a product on the light side. For example, suppose the printed claim for a product is, say, 100 feet by 12 inches wide with a thickness of 0.001 inch. If there is an accepted tolerance of, say, plus or minus 0.0001 inch, a thickness of 0.0009 inch is within tolerance. So production will produce a thinner product that is still within tolerance but makes the material go farther—10 percent farther if production is consistently at 0.0009 inch thickness. Even if only a 0.00095 inch can be held, there is a 5 percent gain. On a mass-produced SKU that can be significant—not far from the profit margin that grocery markets try to get. On a million pounds of production of such a product, a "saving" at 10 percent light is 100,000 pounds—even at 5 percent light 50,000 pounds is not something to turn one's nose up at.

Another caution about the weigh-count system is to make certain tare weights are not ignored. Actually there are eight different types of weights that require consideration for most unitized case loads:

1. Net weight of the material inside of the packages
2. Tare weight of the packages containing material
3. Gross weight of all the material and its packages
4. Tare weight of the case that houses the packages
5. Gross weight of a filled case
6. Gross weight of all cases in the unitized load
7. Tare weight of the unitizing pallet, skid, slip sheet, strapping, corner protectors, plastic wrap, and so on
8. Gross weight of the unitized load

Figure 13.2 illustrates and explains the different weight considerations. Included is a comparison of unitized cased material and unitized metal ingots. It shows for the cased material that the net weight of the product is about 92 percent of the gross unitized load. This compares with about 99.9 percent product weight for the unitized load of metal ingots. The ingots fare so well because two ingots of the product are used for one of the main reasons for pallets and skids—to elevate the load to permit handling with a lift truck—to slip the forks under the load. The elevation also permits slings of a crane to pick up the load.

The breakdown of unit weights as illustrated in Figure 13.2 facilitates finding out what is wrong when a unitized load weighs out of tolerance at the weigh-count station. If, assuming all standard case weights are valid, a minus variance of 36 pounds would indicate a case is missing from the load, the question might well be asked: "Why go through the weigh-count routine when the pallet pattern used makes obvious if a case is missing? You could see the hole where it should be."

This is not necessarily true. A clever thief could substitute an empty case, stuffed tight with paper, inside the load. Another way would be to glue a cut-to-size slip sheet inside the load to support the cases above the void left by removing one two cases. "Who would go to all that trouble for a case or two? The

FIGURE 13.2 Component Weights of Unitized Loads

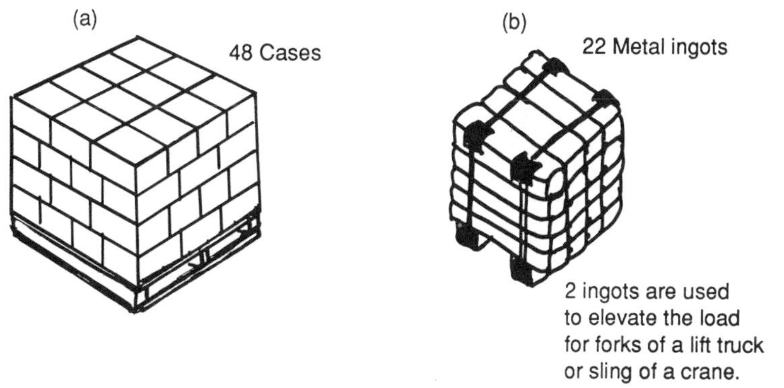

(a) 48 Cases

(b) 22 Metal ingots

2 ingots are used
to elevate the load
for forks of a lift truck
or sling of a crane.

	(a) (pounds)	(b) (pounds)
1. Net weight of each unit of material (inside of package for "a")	2.9 lbs	85 lbs
2. Tare weight of package containing material	0.1	-
3. Gross weight of material and its package	3.0	-
4. Tare weight of the case that houses the packages	1.0	-
5. Gross weight of filled case (ingot). 12 packages/case x 3.0 pounds/package + 1.0 pound/case	37.0	85
6. Gross weight of all unitized cases (ingots): 48 cases x 37 pounds/case (22 ingots x 85 pounds)	1,728.0	1,700
7. Tare weight of unitizing pallet, skid, slip sheet, strapping, corner protectors, plastic wrap, etc.	38.0	2
8. Gross weight of unitized load	1,766.0	1,872

Unitized loads (a) and (b) illustrate the difference in tare weights. There are eight different types of weights that apply to (a) but only three that apply to (b).

customer is going to find out about it for sure. Seems plain stupid to me." First, it may be done for no other reason than its a challenge to see if it can be done. Next, one or two cases of caviar or crab meat is worth doing something about, or it could be a case of wristwatches or calculators. And, finally, let's say it is going to a remote U.S. military outposts that has far bigger problems than missing a couple cases in a shipment. They are happy to get anything and certainly are not going to call attention to themselves for such a small matter as two cases missing out of thousands received. Anyway, "The Joe who ordered them shipped out months ago."

Physical Inventory Using Weight Counting

Another application of bar codes used with weight counting is that of taking physical inventory of many small items. On a hand cart, all necessary apparatus to weigh, print bar codes, and communicate with the computer-stored inventory can be conveniently assembled and manually moved throughout the warehouse. The routine would be like this:

1. Wand your employee identification.
2. Wand the location and the SKU bar codes. With computer agreement so far, weigh the items and automatically transfer the weight to the computer

to convert to the corresponding numerical count and compare with the count in memory.

3. If the count is not the same, double-check the weight. If this is not the problem, instruct computer to accept the new count and put the discrepancy in memory to be later investigated and reconciled.

4. If the count is the same as that in the computer memory, the computer should note agreement, date, time, and the worker's name.

5. Proceed to the next SKU to be inventoried.

This type of physical inventory is particularly applicable to cyclic inventories with the computer randomly selecting which SKUs to weigh count. Whether cyclic inventory taking is used or the routine described in Chapter 14, the remaining quantity of an SKU following the order pick, the chore of physical inventory, and the interruption of business it causes should not be necessary. But the proof in it not being necessary is in the results—which of course should be agreement between the computer's inventory memory and the physical count. If there are discrepancies make certain the system is right first. There will always be variances if parts of the system are in error—such as wrong standard weights, wrong units of measure, and so on. Taking physical inventories is often a waste of time. Correct what is wrong. Do not neglect correcting the system errors by taking physical inventories—no matter how easy they are to take.

14

Inventory Management Techniques and How They Can Improve Warehouse Efficiency

CHAPTER HIGHLIGHTS

This chapter clarifies the role of warehousing in inventory management as well as the techniques and routines that enable warehousing to maximize its contribution to its host company's profits. Warehousing has an inescapable accountability for the inventories in its charge. It also occupies a unique and enviable slot in the company organization to effect higher efficiencies in other divisions as well as its own. Covered are its basic routines of receiving, shipping, and taking physical inventory as well as the basic, time-honored, techniques for improving the composition of the inventory, the objective being that if the inventory is comprised of the "right" product mix to fulfill its objectives (no more, no less) consistently, warehousing makes a major contribution to the greater real efficiency of the company—as well as to its own. Also included in this chapter is theft and how to deal with it, because theft is a distinct part of inventory management.

Warehousing's part in the total inventory game plan is twofold: (1) to handle the product transition from supply to demand effectively and efficiently and (2) to contribute to making better inventory management decisions—keeping in mind that the best way to help is to have one's own operations in exemplary order.

WAREHOUSING'S ROLE IN INVENTORY MANAGEMENT

An absolute undeniable fact of inventory management is that warehousing has the total responsibility for the physical accountability of inventories accepted into its charge. This is so basic to good business practice that it would not be inappropriate to have a large sign over the main portal to each warehouse clearly stating such. This because it is the primary responsibility of warehousing, and it is an essential ingredient of inventory management, which in turn is an essential ingredient of the success of all product-oriented companies.

What type and amount of inventory to carry, and even the service level to provide customers, are not warehousing responsibilities. These are top management concerns. Warehousing's input is essential for making the best decisions of this type, but interdivisional issues are the province of the chief executive officer because commitments of this nature have an impact on the entire company.

TECHNIQUES USED IN THE PHYSICAL MANAGEMENT OF INVENTORY

There are various techniques used to fix warehousing's custodial responsibilities for inventories and to administer them to comply with the company's inventory objectives and plan. The two main techniques are

1. The consistently firm application of the "inventory accountability formula"
2. The formal authorization of what and how much inventory and a way to keep the inventories at the authorized levels

Following are explanations of these two basic techniques for managing inventories.

The Inventory Accountability Formula

The means used to fix warehousing's custodial responsibilities for inventories is the formal and complete documentation of what comes into and goes out of inventory. Within these confines, the basic accountability formula applies:

$$\text{INVENTORY ON HAND} = \text{SHIPMENTS} - \text{RECEIPTS}$$

The use of simple rules of arithmetic makes it possible to rearrange the formula to isolate each of the three elements to determine voids or weaknesses in accountability controls. Following are examples of application, including representative quantities.

> On hand = 1,000 units of an SKU
> Receipts = 1,500 units of an SKU
> Shipments = 500 units of an SKU

ACCOUNTABILITY FORMULAS:

On hand of 1,000 units = receipts of 1,500 – shipments of 500
Receipts of 1,500 units = on hand of 1,000 + shipments of 500
Shipments of 500 units = receipts of 1,500 – on hand of 1,000

These formulas indicate the complete interdependence of the three elements, yet on the other hand, they show how any one element can be isolated from the others. Understanding this and applying it provides the means to reconcile inventories, which can be a scourge when effective controls are not exercised. If one element is deemed "valid," any remaining problems have to be in remaining two elements. If two elements are deemed "valid," the third element has to have any remaining problems. When all three are "valid," the entire inventory is valid.

An example of the application of these formulas follows:

Suppose a physical inventory determines that the warehouse has 1,000 cases of SKU #7321 on hand but the inventory record shows there are only 900 cases on hand—a difference of plus 100.

The first part of the reconciliation should be to check the record inventory thoroughly to see if there is a paperwork error. In this case let's assume that the last receiving report turned in by the night shift, the day before the physical inventory, was not entered into the inventory records. This was the answer. By entering the missed receiving report, the record and physical amounts agree. That took care of that.

Let us assume, however, that the paperwork checks out all right. Then the next step without evidence to the contrary is to double-check the physical inventory. If this discovers the missing 100 units, well and good. That takes care of that. But let us assume that the physical count on recheck is still 900. You have eliminated the possibility of error in the inventory on hand so the culprit has to be in either receiving or shipping. Remember:

Inventory on hand = receipts – shipments

And so the progression goes until the cause of error is found and corrective measures taken. A simple truth that warehouse personnel should keep in mind is that there is "always" an answer as to what causes an inventory error. Sometimes the search for it is long, frustrating and tedious—as though there were no answer. But unless the product vaporized, which is unlikely, it was never received, it was taken away in error, or it is still there.

Before inventories became serious business, it was not uncommon for warehouses to be given a tolerance range of perhaps plus or minus 2 percent. If physical inventories compared to record inventories within 2 percent, the physical count was accepted with the notion that the price of being exact was more than it was worth—and "no one's perfect," "to err is human," and so on. The modern warehousing approach is that no error tolerance is acceptable; that errors are the result of wrong or inadequate procedures; that finding the cause of error justifies the search so that it can be corrected.

Following is a checklist of causes of inventory errors; it is not exhaustive, but it serves to indicate the various types. It is based on manual systems to aid in visualizing the causes. With bar coding and computerization, many of these causes can be eliminated. Greater accuracy is commonly used as a justification for acquisition of these electronic data processing marvels.

CHECKLIST OF INVENTORY ERRORS

Different cutoff times for comparison of physical and record (commonly called "book") inventories

Errors in posting to inventory records

Errors in order picking

Missing receiving and shipping documents

Physically substituting one SKU for another

Confusion in the unit of measure

Wrong SKU number printed on the packages or receiving and shipping forms.

In storage, one SKU is lost behind another SKU

Disposing of damaged merchandise without the proper paperwork

Out and out theft

The Inventory Plan

The inventory plan should be developed by top management and sanctioned by the CEO. It should be based on the company's overall objectives and what each division of the company needs to accomplish its part. All this, however, has to be tempered with what the cost will be to implement and operate the plan. In normal times, the inventory plan should be developed in relation to plans for production and/or for sales. In a seller's market, the production plans should receive priority. In a buyer's market, sales requirements should be given priority. In either type of market, the cost of carrying inventories and warehousing them should be known and evaluated in relation to the company's objectives.

Cost of Carrying Inventories

Following is a list of elements that should be considered in determining the cost of carrying inventories.

A. Interest

B. Freight

C. Work

D. Space

E. Insurance and taxes

F. Loss and damage

G. Obsolescence

An example of the cost computation for carrying inventory appears in the table shown in Figure 14.1.

It is recognized that the interest amount in the table is taken only on the cost of the unit. This is done for sake of simplicity. It should include a proration of costs that are incurred monthly as well. The reader's indulgence will be appreciated. Actually there are many ways to determine cost of inventories. This is only one, but it should serve to indicate that there are a number of elements that go to make up the total cost.

Another important cost relationship in developing the cost of inventory for the inventory plan is the turnover factor.

FIGURE 14.1   Annual Cost of Carrying Inventory for Product "*X*"

Cost Element	Computation	Annual Cost
Interest	$20.00/unit × 10% interest	$2.00 each
Freight, inbound	$1.00/unit	1.00
Labor	$0.50/unit received $0.50	
	$0.04/unit/month upkeep × 12 months 0.48	
	Total	0.98
Space	$0.30/sq. ft./month × 0.25 sq. ft./unit × 12 months	0.90
Insurance	$0.10/year/unit/year	0.10
Taxes	$10.00/$100 assessment @ 25% valuation × $20.00/unit	0.50
Loss and damage	2%/year × $20.00/unit	0.40
Obsolescence	1%/year × $20.00/unit	0.20
Total annual cost of carrying inventory		$6.08 each
Percentage	$6.08 ÷ $20.00	30.4%

The cost of carrying $100,000 of product "X" for one year would be about $30,400 (30.4% × $100,000).

Inventory Turnover

The cost of carrying product "X" for a year is shown to be $6.08 per unit, or 30.4 percent of the product value. This is based on product "X" in the table—being shipped to and received in to the warehouse and remaining there for a full year. But this is not reality for most warehouse products. Units of the same product will be received and shipped many times during a year. How many times is called "turnover."

To compute the inventory carrying cost for one unit of the product, it is necessary to separate the cost elements that are directly related to the activity from the costs that are related to the inventory while it is at rest in storage. Figure 14.2 shows this separation.

FIGURE 14.2   Separation of Activity and Storing Costs, Product "X"

	A Costs Related to Activity per Receipt	B Costs Related to Storing per Year
Interest	—	$2.00
Freight, inbound	$1.00	
Labor		
Receiving	0.50	
Upkeep		0.48
Space	—	0.90
Insurance	—	0.10
Taxes	—	0.50
Loss and damage (split)	0.30	0.10
Obsolence	—	0.20
Total	$1.80/unit/receipt	$4.28/unit/yr

The unit cost of carrying inventory when related to turnover is determined by using the following formula:

$$\text{Unit cost} = A + \frac{B}{\text{turnovers/year}}$$

Examples of how turnover affects inventory costs are shown in Figure 14.3.

FIGURE 14.3 Cost Effects of Inventory Turnover, Product "X"

Turnover per Year	Equation	Inventory Carrying Cost per Unit
1.0	$\$1.80 + \dfrac{\$4.28}{1.0}$	$6.08
2.0	$\$1.80 + \dfrac{\$4.28}{2.0}$	$3.94
4.0	$\$1.80 + \dfrac{\$4.28}{4.0}$	$2.85
100.0	$\$1.80 + \dfrac{\$4.28}{100.0}$	$1.84

As turnover increases, unit costs for carrying inventory decreases. As shown for product "X," the cost decreased from $6.08 per unit (30.4 percent) for one turnover per year to $1.84 per unit (9.2 percent) for 100 turnovers per year. Assuming that all items in a product line are supplied through the warehouse, the turnover rate becomes a very important index of inventory performance. However, under a different distribution plan, turnover may be a completely meaningless or even misleading measure of performance.

Consider a distribution plan that calls for all carload and truckload quantities to be shipped to customers from the manufacturing source and only emergency fill-in orders to be supplied from the warehouse. A high turnover of warehouse inventory for this distribution plan could mean that the distribution system is failing to meet its objective. Probably the manufacturer is falling behind in the shipping schedule; therefore, factory orders have to be placed on the warehouse. This results in a high turnover, but it indicates a costly breakdown in the inventory management.

A Terribly Mistaken Use of Inventory Turnover

The chief industrial engineer shows the CEO how dramatically the cost of carrying inventories can be reduced by increasing the turnover. The CEO grasps the significance right away and sees how she can score a big hit with the board of directors. She has the national sales vice president bring in all the regional sales managers for a special meeting to discuss inventory management. The sales vice president and the regional managers do not know what for but having the CEO the feature speaker indicates something important is afoot. They were not too worried. Their sales were coming in well above target.

The CEO congratulates them on their good sales record, "But," she tells them, "this is not why you are here." Flip charts were used to show how inventory turnover influences unit costs. Illustrated was how warehouse inventories have been turning 3 times a year and how much would be saved if they turned 6 times a year, $1.00 per unit. And how much at 12 times a year, $1.50 per unit.

This, the CEO claimed, would increase the product profitability by 50 percent. The message was concise and clear: "Get your inventory turns up to 6 by the end of this year, 4 months away, and to 8 by May of next year."

The sales managers, back in their regional offices, started cutting warehouse inventories. At the end of two months, the turnover had increased to five turns—but the customers and the company warehouses were screaming about all the stock outages. The national sales vice president became depressed: "It can't be done without losing all of our customers." Then came the revelation about how to do it and keep the CEO, customers, and the warehouse management happy in the process. A direct call to each of the regional sales managers was made. The message: "Put larger orders on the warehouses for them to handle instead of on the production plants" (that had been shipping directly to the customers). "Give the warehouse time to get in stock to handle the increase. Don't make the change all at once though, or all you'll have is outages and back orders."

The scheme worked. By the eighth month, the target was met and exceeded. Inventory turns at the warehouses were pushing nine turns, one better than the CEO had asked. Everyone was happy. The CEO was happy; she was getting more than she had asked for. The production plants were happy; their shipping costs were down because practically all they were shipping were full loads to the warehouses. The warehouse managers were happy; their desire for larger warehouses was materializing. But the industrial engineer who started all this was not happy; in following the progress to see the turnover effect the industrial engineer happened to see how much freight and warehousing costs had soared. Each part of the equation was doing nicely, but the total costs to get materials to customers had nearly doubled. The industrial engineer wondered whether to resign or break the bad news to the CEO and get fired.

Experiences like this have given support for companies to add physical distribution, logistics, or material management departments to their organization. There is a definite need for overall evaluation and control of physical distribution.

Inventory Control and Inventory Control Model

After the company inventory plan has been established, the means to carry it out must be adopted. This is commonly called inventory control. Although there does not seem to be a broad agreement on what elements or terminology make up inventory control, the way it generally works is illustrated in Figure 14.4.

Each SKU has the following elements:

Maximum inventory level

Order point

Order lead time

Order quantity

Minimum inventory level (reserve)

Shipping rate

The terms used in the figure are defined as follows:

Maximum inventory level. The inventory level to order to (700) when actual on hand reaches the order point (200).

Order quantity. The quantity to order (500) is the difference between the order point (200) and the maximum inventory level (700).

FIGURE 14.4 Inventory Control Model

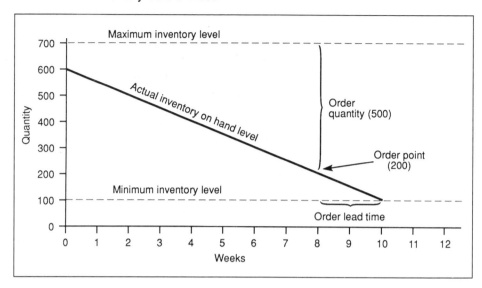

Actual on hand inventory. The quantity of inventory physically on hand (heavy line).

Order point. The quantity on hand (200) that will last (on the average) until a new supply arrives.

Order lead time. The time it takes for the supplier actually to deliver from the time it receives the order.

Minimum inventory level. The amount of inventory kept in "reserve" (also called "buffer," "cushion," or "safety margin") (200) intended to cover customers orders if the supply is delayed or there are more shipments to customers than expected. The amount kept in reserve will be influenced by (1) the delivery reliability of the supplier, (2) the reliability of customer order forecast, and (3) the delivery reliability the warehouse is suppose to provide customers.

Shipping rate. The expected number of units shipped per time interval (50 per week). Figure 14.4 illustrates the following inventory cycle:

○ The starting actual-on-hand inventory is 600. It is being shipped out at a rate of 50 units per week.

○ After eight weeks, the inventory is down to 200 units, which is the order point.

○ An order for 500 units (the order quantity) is placed on the supplier. The order quantity plus the actual amount on hand equals the maximum inventory level.

○ Two weeks after placing the replenishment order, the shipment is received. The actual inventory is now down to the minimum level of 100 units.

○ Receipt of the replenishment order at the point where the actual inventory reaches the minimum level will bring the total-on-hand level back to 600 units (100 plus 500). The inventory cycle then starts again.

Changes should be made in the control levels, quantities, and rates to correspond with seasonal sales fluctuations and other changes in sales patterns.

Also, changes in production and shipping times should be reflected in the order lead time and the order point.

A More Complex Inventory Model

The inventory model used in Figure 14.4 is appropriate for a situation where everything happens as assumed, but for most warehouses this is fiction. Therefore, it is necessary to add a more sophisticated element called "available for planning." It is determined by adding together the quantity on hand at the warehouse and the quantity on order with the supplier to replenish the warehouse inventory (including dates and quantities scheduled for arrival), less the quantity on order with the warehouse to ship to customers (including dates and quantities requested). An example of how "available for planning" (including representative quantities) follows:

A. Quantity on hand at warehouse—800 units (A)

B. Quantity on order with supplier (due in)—600 units (B)

C. Quantity on order with warehouse for customers (due out)—(100) units (C)

D. Quantity available for planning—1,300 units (D)

$$D = A + B - C$$

The available-for-planning factor permits far more precise inventory control. It makes possible *improving the reliability of customer orders being shipped on time with less warehouse inventory,* which is precisely what modern inventory management is all about.

The use of a reserve stock to take care of the difference of what should happen and what actually happens is under fire from companies who are really serious about reducing inventories. Their point is that it is far less costly to eliminate the need for a reserve inventory than to provide for one. Further, improvements do not come about when acceptable allowances for error are made.

FOUR WAYS TO ANALYZE INVENTORIES

Over the years there have been ways to analyze inventories that have stood the test of time. The most common of these are

> ABC analysis
> 20:80 theory/law analysis
> Elapsed time analysis
> Value added analysis

ABC Analysis

Warehousing's primary concerns about inventories is "quantitative" and much less "qualitative" and "financial." How many of what and where are being considered every moment of every workday. The products' grade of excellence—"quality"—and its costs and profitability—"financial"—are the primary concerns of other divisions and the CEO of the company.

As a rule warehousing should care for all its inventories with the very same care unless responsible top management says otherwise and is willing to document it. If it is not viable to ask for it in writing, the warehouse manager should confirm it in writing. Its good to have a "defense" file of any directives that call for giving priority to one product line over another.

ABC analysis is the financial evaluation, ranking, and comparison of inventories, with A's being the most, B's second, and so on. The objective is to find the items that should receive the most attention. "Don't give a dollar item as much attention as you do a hundred-dollar item." And, of course, quantity should be taken into consideration. It may not be true to give most attention to a hundred-dollar item if its potential sales is only, say, 100 units a month and the potential sales of the $1.00 item is 100,000 units, generating ten times as much income.

Of course, the company should be interested in the ABC analysis to evaluate where the company's emphasis should be given. It is just that warehousing should not make decisions of that nature on its own.

20:80 Theory/Law Analysis

This theory of inventories is so important to running a business and most certainly to managing an inventory that it has over time been elevated to and honored as a law, the 20:80 law. It was first discovered or at least give recognition by Vilfredo Pareto who lived roughly a century ago. The theory is referred to as the 20:80 theory or Pareto's law.

Pareto's law so states that the analysis of any warehouse inventory will show that 20 percent of SKUs account for 80 percent of the activity. It also claims that 5 percent of the SKUs will account for 50 percent of the activity. The law is as applicable today as it was the day it was devised. Pareto intended his law to cover quantitative units to be translated into work requirements. This applies wholly and directly to warehousing's current concerns.

The law should not be taken literally. Of course every inventory does not divide neatly into a 20:80 ratio. The inventory you analyze may be that 20 percent of the items account for 75 percent or 84 percent of the volume. This does not take anything away for Pareto's law. What was and is intended is that it provides valuable insights into the nature of inventories.

One of its valuable insights into warehouse inventory management is to suggest where and how different SKUs should be stored to result in the least travel time. And which type of storing and handling equipment to give priority to if there are different best ways to handle different SKUs and there is not enough money to go first class on everything.

Recognition of the law gives credence to the contention that a warehouse laid out according to SKU activity will require many fewer workers than a warehouse laid out at random. Yet in both the workers may appear equally busy. The difference is that laying out inventory according to the 20:80 theory results in being almost surprisingly more productive. Twice as much productivity is attainable in some warehouses, particularly in large ones with many different SKUs.

Elapsed Time Analysis

In most warehousing the elapsed time between when the need to order goods is recognized and when they are delivered is of prime importance in inventory management. It is for this reason the JIT (just-in-time) inventory control has become such a formidable tool in business. Things arrive just in time to be used. But even when JIT is not applicable the elapsed time should be an object of study and refinement.

Often analysis of elapsed time in the order-delivery cycle exposes intervals that can be eliminated or at least shortened. Take the situation where a customer's order for stock is held a couple of days until a salesperson for a warehouse inventory arrives on the weekly circuit of customers. The salesperson holds on to the order for another few days until the circuit ends at the warehouse. Already it has taken, say, two to five days just to get the customers order to the warehouse. At the warehouse, preparing the warehouse release, scheduling, picking, staging, and shipping may take another day or two. Then waiting to consolidate with other orders going to the same area may take another two or three days. Even in transit the order may take an extra day, because it is part of a consolidation that has to be taken to a terminal in the destination area to be segregated, staged, and delivered. In all, the lapsed time from when the customer decides the stock is needed until it is delivered can be five to ten days. Such looseness in the cycle gives rise to the need for large, unproductive, "reserve" inventories.

The elapsed time analysis of this order-delivery cycle is extreme but not uncommon. No doubt there are some that take longer. A lot of time (and money) is wasted in unnecessary elapsed time between occurrences that often should not occur in the first place.

Value Added Analysis

Creating an inventory should be to provide something of value that was not there without it. Analysis can lead to assigning a value to it. For most inventories, this value will be in making goods available sooner than they would be without it. There are, however, many other reasons to create an inventory such as to permit manufacturing to make longer production runs, to protect against rising prices, and so on.

Whatever the reason, the value added by the inventory should be capable of being valued. Sometimes this value can be extreme, such as gaining a regional market that otherwise would be out of the question. Other times it can be proven that the inventory cannot support its costs. Perhaps when the warehouse was initially installed, it made possible capturing a new market for the company. But then things changed and now the reasons for acquiring the warehouse in the first place no longer exist. New roads and better trucking firms make possible delivery times and reliability that are adequate to satisfy customer requirements. A warehouse in the vicinity is not needed for these reasons which were paramount before. But, not having a warehouse there will increase freight costs although not enough to justify the additional inventory and operating costs of the warehouse. A look to the future does not show an increased need for the warehouse. Therefore the warehouse should be closed.

Some countries have value added taxes. The objective of determining value added for this purpose is different from that for determining better inventory management.

RECEIVING PROCEDURE AND ITS IMPORTANCE

The warehousing's accountability for inventories begins as the materials are received into the warehouse. The accountability ends when they are shipped out. Receiving the materials properly is of paramount importance because this is the key element of the accountability formula: receipts = shipments + on hand. If extra care is taken in receiving to be absolutely sure, then when reconciliation is necessary to find errors the task is much easier. You can rule out receiving as a possibility and deal only with shipments and on-hand inventory. If there were errors in receiving, the reconciliations would be much more difficult. The difficulty is not merely an increase of one-third, from two to three elements. It seems at least to double, from two to four times more difficult. Following are the steps and alternatives of a warehouse receiving procedure.

1. The need to have more inventory is recognized.

2. An order for the goods is placed on production either through production control if warehousing and production are in the same company, or through purchasing to an outside supplier.

3. A copy of the order is retained by warehousing to

   a. Plan work and storage.

   b. Include in the on-order and availability-for-planning inventory records.

   c. Use in making certain what is received is what was ordered.

   d. Compare what comes in to what should have come in. That the number of unit loads is correct to release the carrier. Make notes of exceptions (over, short, and damage) on the carrier's delivery receipt before signing it. The carrier is not bound to the correct SKUs being delivered only to the number and condition of separate units (packages, unit loads, pieces) delivered.

4. If received by rail, container, or full truck load, the doors are normally sealed with a special numerically controlled metal looped band. By this means the carrier is responsible for only the car, container, or truckload being delivered—not for its contents unless it is obvious that damage was incurred by the carrier's handling. The important phrase that covers the accountability of sealed shipments is "subject to the shippers load and count." Then if there is anything wrong with the load it is the responsibility of those who loaded and sealed the load, not with the carrier.

5. Whenever there is a difference between warehousing's and the carrier's or supplier's claims of over, short, or damage in a shipment, the warehouse's report prevails. Though this can be argued until the end of time this is how it is. Exceptions to this truly have to be exceptional.

6. After the carrier has been unloaded or with some shipments during the unloading, the warehouse receiver determines the different SKUs and quantities of each. The best way to do this is for the person receiving to determine SKUs and quantities and complete a receiving tally without knowing what is supposed to be there—which is usually found in the packing list. See Figure 14.5 for an example of a receiving tally. It is common to see things as we think they are, not as they really are. Figure 14.6 illustrates this. It is included to help convince you that knowing what *should* be there can influence even the best receiver in determining what *is* there. It will take longer to receive and inspect using a blank tally instead of using the packing list, but this is trivial compared to the trouble caused by receiving errors.

   Figure 14.7 shows the flow of material through a complete receiving operation. It illustrates the alternative routes the material may take depending on

   a. How much of that received is salable and can go directly into salable inventory?

   b. How much is nonsalable and what is wrong with it?

FIGURE 14.5 Receiving Tally

RECEIVING TALLY
Warehouse Operations

Carrier _____ Received by _____ Date _____

Bill of Lading or   Supplier   Vehicle Ident-
Reference No. _____ Company _____ ification No. _____

Product Code No.	Description	Quantity		Condition*
		Tally	Total	

*Explanation

Reconciliation Results   Supplier's
Packing List No. _____

Reconciled by _____ Date _____

FIGURE 14.6 Receiving Procedures

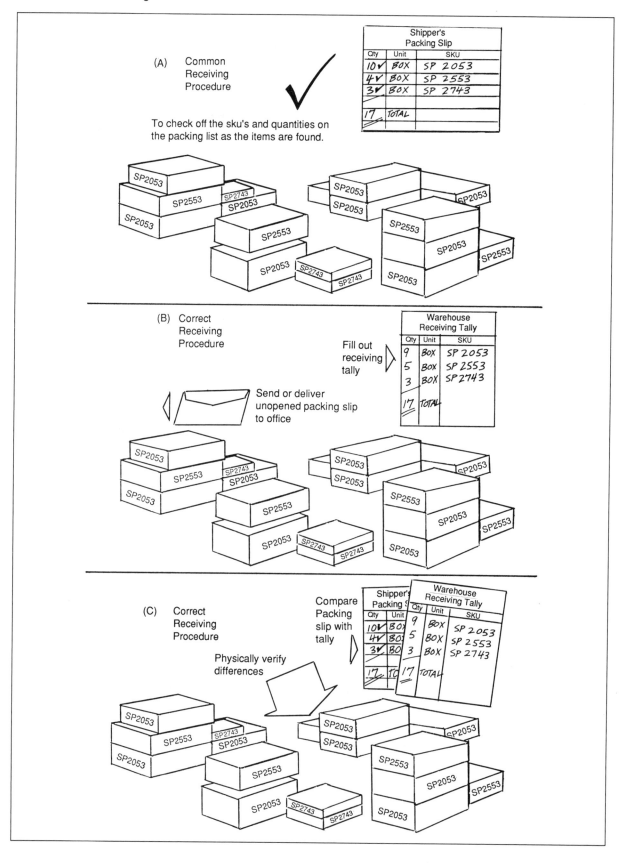

- ○ Notations for each SKU: complete, partial, back-ordered.
- ○ Any special loading and delivery instructions from customer.

The term "transfer" designates that the order is not a sale to an outside customer but is a "transfer" to another location and/or accounting responsibility within the same company. It is only to keep track of inventory within a company. The following are reasons to transfer:

- ○ Move inventory from a production plant to the same company's warehouses.
- ○ Move inventory from one company warehouse to another company warehouse.
- ○ Transfer the inventory ownership responsibility from one division to another within the same company. This may or may not involve physical transfer.

6. The order or orders are loaded on the conveyance and the carrier driver signs for the load, accepting accountability for the load and the number of separate packages or units it comprises. Or if it is a full container or truckload and the doors are sealed, the carrier accepts only the responsibility for the total load unless the seal is already broken when it arrives at destination. If this is so, the carrier is responsible for the "load and count" inside. If the load arrives with the seal intact, it is the shipper's responsibility, the warehouse in this case.

7. Copies of the packing list which is often a part of the warehouse release form are distributed as follows:

- ○ With the bill of lading to the carrier and customer.
- ○ With the bill of lading to accounting to invoice the customer and to match with the carrier's invoice to reconcile and pay the freight invoice.
- ○ To sales to for their records and statistics.
- ○ Filed in warehousing for its records and shipping statistics.

Visualizing all the paperwork involved in the foregoing receiving and shipping procedures should alert concerned minds to the need for bar coding and computerization with terminals that interface with the main frame and ultimately a paperless warehouse.

ALL ABOUT PHYSICAL INVENTORY TAKING

Taking physical inventories is one of the main sources of warehousing woes. Also it is often the source of sizable expenditures. It takes time to prepare for it, time to take it, and time to reconcile and book it. Commonly it requires shutting down operations while taking and reconciling it. That is a lot of unproductive time, stress, and strain for what little it too often provides.

The purposes of taking a physical inventory should not be lost sight of. They are to expose errors and sources of errors so that corrective action may be taken to prevent the errors from happening again. Oh yes, it gives the company controller and other top management, including the CEO and even the board of directors, a sense of security about a big part of the company's assets.

The questions should be asked, does it really do this or is there a better way to achieve the same? Here is explored what is really gained, the alternatives of not doing it, and if there are better ways to accomplishing the same.

It all begins with warehousing and/or accounting maintaining what is called a perpetual inventory. This is a current record of all transactions that influence inventories, including

- ○ Open orders on suppliers of the warehouse inventory
- ○ Open orders on warehouse for specific customers
- ○ Received
- ○ On hand
- ○ Shipped

and miscellaneous transactions such as for damaged and scrapped merchandise and its disposition, returns to inventory, and the like. It is not difficult to think of more things to include, but the big question is what part of it is really worth the time and effort spent.

The record card shown in Figure 14.8 is designed to fit into a Kardex file that provides exposure of the bottom ⅜ inch to show SKU number, product description, and so on. A file cabinet designed for the purpose conveniently holds many inventory record cards. Both sides of the card have the same printed form. An explanation follows for each of the illustrated transactions

7/9	400 is carried over from the backside of the card.
7/10	1,000 is placed on order with the supplier of this SKU to the warehouse increasing the available for planning (AFP) to 1400.
7/15	100 is committed (reserved) for a new AJAX order reducing the AFP to 1300.
7/18	The 100 committed for AJAX is shipped. The 100 was already deducted from the AFP when it was committed so the AFP remains 1300—but the on hand is reduced to 300.
7/21	The order for 1000 placed on the supplier is received. This was already added to the AFP when the order was placed so the AFP remains 1300—but the on hand is increased as well to 1,300.
7/23	400 is committed for a new UGB Company order reducing the AFP to 900.
7/23	100 is committed for a new Acme order reducing the AFP to 800.
7/25	The 400 committed to UGB is shipped. The AFP remains the same but the on hand is reduced to 900.
7/26	The 100 committed to Acme is shipped. The AFP remains the same but the on hand is reduced to 800.

Bar coding interfaced with the computer-held fixed data and perpetual inventory have reduced the time and effort necessary to take and reconcile inventories. It can totally replace taking physical inventory under certain circumstances. This has made possible data and controls that were too costly when manually maintained. But physical inventory taking remains the best way to assure that errors are corrected and to expose foul play.

It is contended that enough checks and balances can be incorporated into bar-code–computer inventory transactions to make an error-free, real-time system. Should something happen that is not intended, programming can be provided to bring attention to it as the transaction is being made instead of waiting to find it with a physical inventory. For example, when an order is picked from a storage slot, the order picker can be required to report back not just how

FIGURE 14.10 Property Loss Procedure

WAREHOUSE OPERATIONS PROCEDURE	DATE _____ ISSUED _____
	SUPERSEDES _____
	APPROVED _____
Subject: PROPERTY LOSS	_____

I. PURPOSE

To establish a uniform procedure for investigating, reporting, and control of unauthorized removal of Company and Employee property.

II. OBJECTIVES

A. To provide the Company with information that will be used to improve the property security program.

B. To improve employee morale and win respect by prudently protecting assets through proper security measures.

III. DEFINITION

A. Property Loss Incident—Any act or physical condition that directly or indirectly indicates unauthorized removal of property belonging to the Company, Employees, or visitors.

IV. PROCEDURE

A. As a matter of policy, at each warehouse the manager has the responsibility for security.

B. The Property Loss Report, Form #1731, should be used for processing the notification, investigation, and action to be taken in each case of identified or suspected property loss.

C. The following steps outline the methods by which notification is made whenever a property loss incident is detected.

1. ALL personnel have a direct responsibility for reporting property loss situations. Failure to report risks being named an accessory to the act.

2. The employee witnessing an apparent theft should obtain the facts and identify participants. If the act is in the process, action should be taken to have the violators apprehended, however, this action should not be by physical force.

There should not be a direct accusation until full investigation has been completed. Accusations and/or physical restraint may provide grounds for false-arrest suits should the investigation provide insufficient proof to support the accusation.

3. The person identifying the situation should contact the warehouse manager immediately.

4. The company's security department should be notified immediately. Advice should be sought about whether the local police should be called in.

5. The warehouse manager should promptly note the information in the first part of the Property Loss Report so that an accurate record of the incident is maintained.

V. INVESTIGATION

A. The warehouse manager should go immediately to the site of the occurrence and develop the facts to complete the Investigation section of the report. (The facts should include the circumstances that made the loss possible and how the act was or was intended to be accomplished.)

B. Warehouse personnel shall avoid making any incriminating statements about the incident during the investigation. The rule that a person is innocent until proven guilty applies 100 percent.

VI. ACTION TO BE TAKEN

A. The warehouse manager should consider all the facts presented to develop proper control measures.

B. Prior to completion of the Action to Be Taken part of the report, the manager is encouraged to discuss with and offer suggestions to the next level up in authority and responsibility.

Legal counsel and labor relations must be consulted before any action is taken to prosecute or terminate any employee for theft. However, if the warehouse labor agreement provides for suspension during investigation this action should be taken immediately if the situation appears to justify such response.

C. In cases of filing charges, police action, and/or dismissal of an employee as a result of dishonesty, the warehouse manager should work jointly with the Company's Safety, Legal, Internal Audit, and Insurance departments.

D. Send copies of the completed Property Loss Report to the Security Department and warehouse administration. In case of theft involving one thousand dollars or more, send additional copies to Insurance and Internal Audit departments.

FIGURE 14.11 Property Loss Report

	Date Report Prepared
PROPERTY LOSS REPORT	**Date or Interval of Loss Occurrence**

NOTIFICATION

Who reported loss (If given freely)	From	Date Reported	Time	☐ A.M. ☐ P.M.

Describe what happened (how do you know of the attempted or actual loss)

Exact location of the occurrence	List items involved and estimate of value (If possible)
Date and time of the occurrence ☐ A.M. ☐ P.M.	Estimate $

INVESTIGATION

Persons interviewed and dates	Witnesses

Circumstances surrounding occurrence: others around, lighting, access to area, how stored

How was loss removed	Route	Date	Time ☐ A.M. ☐ P.M.	Investigator

ACTION TAKEN

If person apprehended, what action was taken

What measures have been taken to prevent recurrence

Describe unrecovered loss, Estimate $	What part of loss was recovered, Estimate $
Signed Title	Date

Form #1731   Distribution of copies: *White* to Security Dept. or equivalent/*Pink* Gen. Acctg Controller/*Canary* Retain

Chapter 15

Public and Contract Warehousing Opportunities

CHAPTER HIGHLIGHTS

Three alternative kinds of warehousing are presented in this chapter: contract, public, and proprietary. The discussion includes their characteristics and how to choose the right one for a given set of circumstances. Both contract and public warehousing are healthy and growing, though contract warehousing is growing faster because the closer cooperation between production, sales, and warehousing results in greater cost savings and lower inventories.

Included in the discussion is how to determine the best type and the best particular warehouse for a particular company's requirements along with what information the prospective user should provide competing warehouses and what the warehouses should provide the prospective users. Also covered is the important inspection by the prospective users of contract or public warehousing and what are the most important things to evaluate, such as government regulations and the warehouses' extent of compliance.

Under certain circumstances, public warehousing is best for users of warehousing; under other circumstances, contract warehousing is best. However, most warehousing is still done by the company that produces the inventory, and is called proprietary warehousing. The decision regarding which to use is not a casual one since warehousing is a vital concern in the health and prosperity of a company.

A characteristic common to public versus contract versus proprietary warehousing is that a once-wise decision does not stay the wisest one forever. Buyouts, mergers, transfers to foreign shores, changing markets, and many more volatile transformations affect inventories and means of physical distribution, which in turn influences where and how companies' products should be warehoused. The effects on warehousing would be even more volatile were it not for the high cost and business disruption incurred by moving inventories. Changing to or from proprietary warehousing involves heavy investment or the write off of heavy investment in employee development, space, and equipment. This chapter covers the types of warehousing available and will help you to decide which is the wisest choice for your firm.

THREE KINDS OF WAREHOUSING

There are three kinds of warehousing:

1. Proprietary
2. Public
3. Contract

Proprietary Warehousing

This is operated as a division of a company whose main business is other than warehousing. For instance, a maker of picture frames has its own warehousing to provide prompt customer delivery and to cushion production from varying customer demands. Sales can sell more because of better delivery service and production can realize lower costs due to longer production runs.

Public Warehousing

This provides the same type service but is owned and operated by a third party, not the producer or consumer of the inventories. By implication, public warehouses offer these services to the public—whoever wants to use and pay for their services. In practice, this is not how it is.

Public warehouses specialize along general, if not specific, product lines. This is out of necessity. There are so many different types of things warehoused, and it is just not viable to provide for all of them. Certainly hazardous materials must not be stored with food, and equipment to handle rod, bar, and wire is altogether different from that to handle spices, and so on.

Public warehouses also specialize according to type of customers served. Probably the most obvious example is that of the grocery trade. Receiving doors and dock space at supermarkets are dedicated to receipts from a certain warehouse. Without this *in* with grocery stores, the normal delay time of minutes will stretch into hours, making the delivery costs totally unacceptable. The same is true with supersized drug, hardware, and other stores that have high throughput.

Public warehouses also specialize by type of transportation—rail, truck, air, barge, and ship—and by environment—cold, cool, and dry storage. Although the basic procedures and philosophy of all public warehouses are the same regardless of the kind of warehousing, there is considerable specialization in each. This does not mean that a public warehouse that carries grocery accounts does not carry other product lines, because in reality many of them do. Mostly what is meant is that the product lines that require similar environment, modes of transportation, and equipment are commonly warehoused together. If, however, there is the least chance of contamination, such as hazardous chemicals and groceries, they should not be warehoused or transported together.

Often a public warehouse company gets its start by handling many different things. Then as one of those product lines takes off, the warehouse company grows with that product line and reduces by attrition those other lines that are not as promising. On the other hand, some public warehousing companies organize to take on about any that comes up. They have the financial and managerial strength to specialize in many different product lines to the extent that they have different specialized facilities in the same cities. They have one address for say industrial solvents and another for hospital supplies.

Characteristically, public warehouses have written agreements, contracts, that spell out their services, charges, and liabilities—and provide for terminating the contract with 30 days' notice. In addition, the backside of the receiving and shipping documents is printed with terms, conditions, and limiting liabilities, including lots of boiler plate in almost unreadable legal jargon.

Some smaller "mom and pop" warehouses do not have written contracts. This does not mean they are at risk for everything that can happen. There is such a thing as implied contract. It works like this. When a man goes to barber and after waiting his turn moves into a barber chair when one is vacant, he is liable for the price of the haircut he gets. The man may claim that he does not owe because there is no contract. "Show me where I signed a contract and I'll gladly pay. I didn't even ask you to cut my hair. I should charge you. I like my hair long." But he does owe. The contract was legally implied.

Another important thing that adds strength to the public warehouses claims is that the warehouse has the storer's (depositor's) inventory in its physical control. The storer had better be reasonable in terms of what the warehouser believes is reasonable, or else. Best that a reasonable and readable contract exist between depositor and warehouser. More about this later in this chapter.

Contract Warehousing

Since most public warehousing is governed by contracts, contract warehousing is, theoretically, no more than public warehousing tailored to a specific company's needs. In practice, however, "contract" warehousing is a fresh new approach to looking at public warehousing and related inventory, services, and transportation.

The essence of contract warehousing is conveyed in the depositor question to the public warehouses: "What can we do to enable you to do this or that for us?" Usually what the depositor wants is better or more services at lower costs. What the warehouser wants is greater assurance that the customer will remain a customer and at charges high enough to make a profit.

Public warehouses have a persistent fear that one or more of its larger customers will decide to do their own warehousing or move it to some other public warehouse. Why public warehouses are generally not into automation and the latest other technologies is mainly due to this phobia. They are understandably reluctant to invest in more efficient, specialized equipment for depositors that can quit them with a contractual 30-day notice.

Adding to these fears is the business climate, in which change is almost the norm. The upheavals caused by mergers, buyouts, bankruptcies, moves to foreign countries, and so on. can wipe out public warehouses or their customers even when they have the lowest-cost and highest-quality service. Thus, with all these uncertainties, the concept implied by contract warehousing was revived with renewed vigor.

BENEFITS OF USING PUBLIC WAREHOUSING

Public warehousing is not a diminishing segment of economic endeavor. Except for not employing advanced technologies as soon as it might, it is healthy as ever and is holding up better than its kin, proprietary warehousing.

The sections that follow concern specific benefits offered by public warehousing.

1. Provides Capability to Expand Market.   For small companies that are growing and large ones that are expanding, public warehousing provides an economical and practical means to reach new markets. To establish one's own warehouses to support this growth is often not prudent, at least until the expansion meets or exceeds expectations. Then the host company can convert to its own warehouses or stay with the public warehouses that were used in the initial expansion. Often, even when a company wants to change over to its own warehouses, its salespeople in the area resist because they believe the service offered by public warehouses exceeds the service they expect from fellow employees.

For small companies wanting to go national with their products, public warehousing can provide for them the same level of service that large companies can provide their customers. It permits small companies to neutralize at least this one advantage that large companies have. The unit cost of warehousing may cost more than for larger volumes, but this is a minor price to pay to enable the Davids of industry to negate the Goliaths—at least for this one important marketing tool.

2. Permits Freight to Move at Lower Rates.   This capability alone could justify perhaps 50 percent of all public warehousing today. But for this, many companies would be out of business. Their product costs can bear consolidated freight rates but not the much higher freight costs that result from shipping small quantities at premium rates.

These lower rates are achieved by the public warehouse serving as a freight consolidator for its customers. The warehouse usually charges extra for the consolidations it effects, but this cost is normally small compared to the freight saving it makes possible. The same consolidation features apply to full container loads shipped by air and by sea. Often the freight savings is enough to offset the total warehousing costs. Conversely, the warehouse benefits by getting income from the warehousing, making the consolidations, and again from the transportation if it has its own carriers.

Sometimes an arrangement can be made with public trucking companies to pay for freight they pickup at the warehouse. They pay this because they incur less time and costs picking up freight at a public warehouse that has several different customers' freight consolidated, all staged and ready to go, than to pick up the same amount of freight separately at different customer locations. Trucking companies are generally anxious to agree to such an arrangement but you should be concerned that you take payment only for that which relates to the work done that directly saves the carriers time and money.

3. Reduces Investment in Warehousing. Public warehousing eliminates the need for the depositor to incur large capital expenditures or lease commitments just getting set up to do one's own warehousing.

4. Provides Means for Profitable Investment in Real Estate. Many warehouse buildings in use today were constructed by warehouse companies primarily motivated by real estate profits. The scheme is to construct all-purpose facilities, use them for public warehousing until the price of the real estate increases to meet the company's objective, then sell, and lease back the facilities or build another warehouse at a less costly site, move the inventories and repeat the process. Either way the real estate developer-warehouser wins. It is not even necessary to sell the facilities. Most of the money can be taken out of them by borrowing to the maximum using the warehouse as collateral.

The success of the plan depends on two things. First that the company provide good warehousing to earn a credible reputation in the field of buyers and sellers of public warehousing. And, second, that the plan is well thought out and well managed. Of prime importance is to locate in areas where real estate has the best chance of appreciation and to have a good all-purpose design that has a broad market of potential buyers when the time comes to sell and move on.

5. Gain Access to Special Features. Many public warehouses have special features that make them unique in the area in which they are located. This can be by design, when a warehouse first sets up for business, or it can evolve into the specialty. Following are examples of special features that cause companies to warehouse with those that have one or more of them instead of setting up to operate their own or go with other warehouses.

- Temperature-controlled, cool and cold storage
- Electric-powered lift trucks versus propane and gas fuel (some customers require the cleaner electric)
- Crane capabilities
- Ultraclean segregated area
- Guard service around the clock
- Especially attractive facilities
- Dedicated dock areas and doors for special customers
- Office space to rent for depositor's sales, customer service, accounting, and so on
- Outside storage capability
- Bin, tank, and special bulk handling and storing means
- Barge and ship dock facilities
- Broken-case order picking
- Special staff functions like customer service, inventory ordering, and so on
- Very-high-capacity lift trucks
- Invoicing for depositors

○ Repackaging service

○ Customer pickup service

○ Rail siding

○ Own trucking operation

○ Delivery priorities with grocery, drug, or other high-volume stores

○ Freight consolidation service

○ Special delivery services to out-of-the-way places like military bases, forestry warehouses, and so on

○ Licenses and bonding for special government privileges

6. *Gain Access to Special Government Privileges.* There are a number of special *privileges,* as they are so dubbed by the government, that are too costly or too much of a nuisance to be worthwhile except in high volume. Many companies need these privileges, but the quantity of their products warehoused is not enough to justify their acquiring and maintaining them economically, for instance, customs inspection where a customs agent must be present or the warehousing of certain hazardous materials where all kinds of paperwork and special physical features of the facility are required. In fact the increasingly stringent controls of the many protective and monitoring government agencies may prove too costly to comply individually. Here a need is filled by public warehousing that could otherwise drive management of small companies out of their minds—if not out of the business.

7. *Part-Time Use of Costly Specialized Equipment.* Some costly material handling equipment is needed but only for a fraction of the time. Rather than acquire and maintain it, the most economical way may be to have the materials requiring it handled by a public warehousing that has the capability and shares the cost with several companies. Cranes and superhigh-capacity lift trucks are examples of this.

The service of the special equipment may be as little as the transfer of extremely heavy objects from an inbound carrier to one making local delivery. But, without the public warehouse that has this capability, it would be necessary to acquire a huge crane or other handling device even though it is used only a few times a month or year.

A crane securely attached to a flat-bed truck is commonly used to deliver heavy pipe or culvert to a job site and position it along trenches where it will be buried. Other uses for this combination equipment is to handle pallet loads of brick, large reels of electrical wire, and other similarly packaged building materials to job sites. When this handling is needed but infrequently, a public warehouse offering it provides a valuable service that cannot generally be performed at reasonable costs. At the same time it will attract other depositors needing the same that would not be interested otherwise.

8. *Availability of Computerization and Bar Coding.* For a public warehouse to have, or be willing to install, compatible computer and bar-code capabilities for customers that want these can be a deciding factor.

Even when the company seeking more space does not have a means of computer tie-in, the public warehouse having a computer and bar-code capabilities has more appeal than does the warehouses that do not, particularly when the warehouse can demonstrate its greater accuracy, speed, and accountability controls. Just the valuable reports that it can provide on a timely basis could be the clincher.

9. *Overflow Warehousing to Level Demand Fluctuations.* Companies having their own warehouses may find it advantageous to use public warehousing for overflow. Carrying enough personnel, space, and equipment to handle peak loads that occur infrequently can cost considerably more than would diverting surge inventories to public warehouses.

Work and inventories selected for the public warehouse should have the least influence on freight costs. Also only customer orders that can be filled complete at the public warehouse should be transferred. Basically, you are saving money by avoiding overload situations at the company warehouse and you do not want to spend this on higher freight costs and unhappy customers.

The public warehouse services and charges including excess freight costs should be monitored just as closely as those incurred by the company warehouse. Further, it should be well understood that the company warehouse's responsibility for service (including errors), costs, and accountability is not reduced when it uses a public warehouse. The company warehouse manager should choose the public warehouse, within the company's rules for this type commitment, and have the same responsibility for its conduct and costs as the company warehouse.

10. *Backup to Assure Inventory Availability.* It is common to provide an auxiliary power source for computers in the event the main electrical power is lost. It is also common to buy futures in commodities to assure they will be available and at a protected price when they are needed. The reasoning behind these actions also applies to backup warehousing: to assure a supply at a known price if the warehouse is put out of business for any reason. Some of these reasons are strike, hurricane, tornado, fire, flood, and earthquake.

Whenever stopping the supply of materials will cause severe hardship, an alternative source should be given serious consideration. To be most effective, the auxiliary supply should be located away from the normal supply. If it is to hedge against strike, the inventory should be a good distance away and of course with a different union. If it is to hedge against earthquake, the auxiliary inventory should be sufficiently away from the suspicious fault. And so it is for each threat. The backup inventory should be located where the threat to the backup supply is minimal and different from the threat related to the primary warehouse.

WHAT TO LOOK FOR IN SELECTING A
PUBLIC WAREHOUSE

The process of selecting a public warehouse should start only after a few vital concerns are satisfied. The first of these is whether warehousing in the community is justified or not. It is not enough that the sales or production management claims it is. Probably from their point of view it is, but there are several other considerations. Is it justified from the physical distribution view point? Then, there is the CEO's viewpoint. Does the warehouse contribute to the company's objectives? Or, for instance, is the company's production capacity for the product line involved already sold out?

1. *Get Competitive Quotations* As every good businessperson knows, it is prudent to get competitive quotations before committing to any substantial purchase. So it is in selecting a public warehouse. Not only are the warehouse and transportation charges substantial, the investment in inventories and the fact that customers will look to the warehouse as an extension of the company combine to cause this to be a very important decision.

It is not easy to change warehouses if the initial decision proves wrong. The cost of moving inventories, disruption of business, and orienting everyone related to it to the new warehouse all gang up to increase the inertia to stay. Usually something drastic has to happen to cause a company to change warehouses. The initial selection process should be good enough to ferret out the potentially drastic things that could materialize—but more than that, it should confirm that what is expected will happen.

For instance, the company could assume that customer orders will be processed and shipped within 24 hours with only weekends and nationally recognized holidays excepted. And the public warehouse will consolidate freight which the manager of the warehouse claims will save an average of 40 percent of freight costs. After moving in, the depositor learns that customer shipments can be made any time up to 72 hours, delay resulting from the warehouse's program to effect freight savings via consolidations. To commit to ship within 24 hours would disrupt the total warehouse freight sequence. "Why didn't you tell us?" "Why didn't you ask? Our other accounts have no problem living with the 72 hour rule."

2. Get Different Quotations Based on the Same Requirements All quotations must be based on the same requirements; otherwise they are largely a waste of time. And yet, though everyone knows better, they are not. The agreed culprit in these circumstances is that the company asking for the quotation does not really know what it wants. It is necessary to learn what is wanted, what can be provided, and at what cost to determine what will fit the company's warehousing and budget requirements.

You must develop requirements that can be used for competitive quotations. This is done in the form of a checklist to sort through to find those things that are applicable for a given set of circumstances.

CHECKLIST FOR TESTING PUBLIC WAREHOUSE'S BUSINESS SOUNDNESS

- □ Length of time company has been practicing public warehousing?
- □ Names of the owners and length of ownership. Are they active in the company? Where do they live?
- □ List of companies now being warehoused for and reference contacts at each.
- □ Financial statements (balance sheet and profit and loss) for the last three years.
- □ Organization of the company by name and title, responsibility, and number of employees.
- □ Bank and credit references.
- □ Copies of liability and fire insurance policies.
- □ List of buildings and main equipment—indicating whether owned or leased. If leased, from whom and expiration dates.
- □ Officers of the company.
- □ Names of board of directors if applicable. If not, names of members of any other group guiding the warehouse company, if any.
- □ If there is a union, which one? If there is more than one union, give names of each and which employees each covers. Include contract expiration dates.

▫ List of any work stoppages during last three years. Include interval stopped and cause, such as strike, lockout, flood, fire, or whatever.

3. *Determine Financial Soundness of Public Warehouses*   The information called for in the checklist is meant to be detailed and complete. When a company puts its inventories and much of its customer service in the hands of a public warehouse, it should pry and root out whatever is pertinent to the warehouse's capabilities for providing the services requested, their intentions and ability to stay in business, and their reputation with companies for which they now warehouse.

"Should the public warehouse get similar information from the companies seeking warehouse services?" Not necessarily. Once a public warehouse has a company's inventories and has been engaged to service customers, a lot of bargaining strength moves to the public warehouse. This power if abused will catch up with the warehouse eventually, but for the present and near future, if all-out war were declared, the public warehouse would have a big advantage. It stems from the expression, "Possession is nine-tenths of the law."

Because of this implied threat, public warehouses have fewer problems with accountants receivable than possibly any other segment of industry. Public warehouses do not have to investigate potential customers financial soundness extensively. They just have to make certain the customer does not deplete its inventories until what is owed is paid in full.

Probably the worst thing that can happen to a customer of public warehousing is for the warehouse to close due to bankruptcy or some other cause. For this reason, the company seeking a warehouse should thoroughly investigate before committing.

4. *Warehouse Management and Ownership*   How the public warehouse company is structured and by whom are good indicators of what performance can be expected. If it is learned that it is a one-person show, a caution flag should be hoisted.

It is important to investigate further. Can others handle the business as well when she or he is not there? Or does the operation flounder at the first mishap when the individual is away? This insight is not easy to come by, but a lot can be learned by listening to the manager explain the warehouse organization and then personally meeting and talking with who would be handling this new business.

The concern about depth in management pertains most to small public warehouses where the absence of one or two can be seriously felt. But large warehouses are not immune from the problem entirely, as some managers carve out territories over which they exert complete control.

Ask if the warehouse has written procedures and then look at them. If they do not have formal written procedures, does the warehouse have written anywhere what services it offers and the communication flow between the depositor and the warehouse. Having written procedures is important but not critically important, because it may only be a sales ploy and what really goes on is something else entirely.

The best way to ferret out the subtleties of the public warehouse company is to give them a formal presentation of the scope and details of what you as the depositor want and go over it thoroughly to eliminate misunderstandings. In the process, both the depositor and the warehouse will learn things about each other that will prove invaluable in calling off further negotiations—or speeding up the agreement and pave the way for smooth operations in the future.

WHAT DEPOSITORS SHOULD GIVE PROSPECTIVE PUBLIC WAREHOUSES

The selection of the best warehouse for a company's physical distribution begins with clearly defining what is to be stored and handled, including sufficient detail for the warehouse to apply its charge rates correctly and to know just what type services are expected. With complete product and service data, the warehouse can avoid guessing. When the warehouse has to guess, it has to quote rates on the high side to cover the unexpected.

Warehousing Requirements

The public warehouse needs first to determine if it is the type of warehousing it can do and if so does it want to do it. Public warehousing is becoming more and more specialized because specialization permits greater efficiencies, reduces chances of errors, and makes the job of managing effectively less stressful. Examples of specialization are the equipment, space, and procedures to handle and store

- Empty cans
- Carpets
- Furniture
- Grocery products
- Pharmaceuticals

Of course temperature-controlled cool and cold storage are prime examples of specialized space. Suppose, for example, the products are metal rod and bar in 20 feet lengths. Handling of this configuration calls for side-moving lift trucks and cantilever storage racks. Learning of this at the outset can save a lot of time and effort if the warehouse is not, or does not want to become, equipped to handle these products.

This does not preclude the warehouse from taking on a different product line. It only lets the warehouse know it requires different type warehousing. Further, it should know if the transportation requirements are different from those used for present warehoused products.

On the other hand, the account may look so good it would be worth becoming equipped to handle it. Either way it can be seen how important is knowing the specifications and requirements before deciding whether even to try for the account.

The following are the types of product information needed by public warehouses to determine if it can or wants to handle an account:

PRODUCT DATA BY PRODUCT LINE
    DESCRIPTION
    NUMBER OF SKUs
    AVERAGE TOTAL INVENTORY
    High side _____, Low side _____, Average _____.
    TERRITORY SERVED
    HOW RECEIVED

Rail _____%, Truck _____%, Other _____%,

Explain _____

Unitized _____%, Floor loaded _____%

If unitized,

    On wood pallets _____, size _____ × _____

    On slip sheets _____, size _____

    For clamp handling _____

    Shrink wrapped _____%

If on pallets or slip sheets, are these to be returned? _____ By what means? _____

Height of unitized load _____

Inbound shipments per day _____, week _____, month _____

HOW SHIPPED

    Rail _____%, Truck _____%, Air _____%,

    Parcel Service _____%, Air express _____%

Typical order consists of

    Number SKUs _____ (line items per order)

    Number of packages

        High side _____, Low side _____,

        Average _____

    Gross weight _____

        High side _____, Low side _____,

        Average _____

Shrink wrap _____%, Banded _____%, Neither _____%

Less-than-package quantities _____. If yes, explain _____.

PRODUCT DATA BY SKU

    Description by SKU or by family of similar SKUs

        Name called

            Package width _____, height _____, length _____

            Cubic feet _____, Gross weight _____

            Number of packages per SKU:

                High side _____, Low side _____,

                Average _____

        Representative product value per cubic foot $_____

        Stackability without crushing. Number of unitized loads? _____

        SKU packages bar coded _____%

            Bar code symbology used, _____

POLICIES AND PROCEDURES

    When out of inventory, yet orders are received to ship

        Back order _____, Cancel _____, Other _____

    Explain receiving overage and shortage policy _____

    Explain physical inventory overages and shortages policy _____

Explain both warehouse caused damage and damage received:

    Policy _____

    Disposition _____

Explain required order processing time from time received by warehouse to time shipped:

Explain physical inventory and reconciliation policies.

Inventory selection by LIFO _____, FIFO _____, No real concern _____ —provided no stock is delayed shipping for over _____ months.

Provide freight consolidation and pool distribution accordingly:

    Only with our company's shipments _____

    With any companies' shipments _____

    Not concerned about _____

    Explain _____

Explain documentation requirements for:

    Receiving

    Shipping

    Inquiries

    Physical inventories

Explain use of computers and bar coding if any _____

WHAT PUBLIC WAREHOUSES SHOULD GIVE PROSPECTIVE CUSTOMERS

Companies seeking public warehousing must provide a clear picture of what types of services it needs or wants. This was addressed in the previous section, "What Depositors Should Give Prospective Public Warehouses." Here is what the public warehouse should provide to the prospective customer company. It is the equivalent of turning up all their cards.

WAREHOUSE COMPANY

    Name _____

    Address _____

    Telex _____

    Fax _____

    Contact name _____

    Telephone _____

1. WAREHOUSE FACILITY DESCRIPTION

    Material construction?

        Tilt wall concrete _____

        Masonry _____

        Metal _____

    Insulation _____, Where _____, Rating _____

    Sprinklered _____, Rating _____

Floor type _____, Capacity _____,

    Condition _____

Age of facilities _____

Single story _____, multiple floors _____

    If multiple floors, how many floors _____

    Number of elevators _____, Size _____, Capacity _____

Yards paved _____, How extensively _____

Neighbors or vacant lots:

    Front _____

    Back _____

    Right side (facing front of warehouse) _____

    Left side _____

Environmental concerns:

    Near residential _____, Distance _____

    Near public buildings (churches, stores, parks, and so on) _____

Truck docks

    Enclosed _____, Sheltered _____, Open _____

    Ground level _____ Elevated _____ Height _____

    Dock levelers, mechanical _____, manual _____

    Number of doors _____

Rail siding _____ Private _____ Shared_____

    Railroad _____

    Reciprocal switching _____

    Switches provided per _____

Rail docks

    Enclosed _____ Sheltered _____ Open _____

    Ground level _____ Elevated _____ Height _____

    Dock levelers, mechanical _____, Manual _____

    Number of doors _____

    Number of car positions for unloading:

        Without moving cars _____, Length of cars _____

2. TYPE STORAGE SPACE

Environmentally controlled:

Type	Range From–to	Storage Height	Square Feet	Cubic Feet
Unheated				
Heated				
Air conditioned				
Cooler				
Freezer				
Humidity				

Outside storage:

    Number of square feet _____

    How secured, explain _____

3. HANDLING EQUIPMENT DESCRIPTION

Lift trucks

Qty	Types*	Powered by Elec., Gas, Propane	Reach		Attachments†
			Capacity	Height	
——	——	——	——	——	——
——	——	——	——	——	——
——	——	——	——	——	——

*Types: conventional sit-down, narrow-aisle stand-up, side moving, order picking, double reach, 180 degree turret, and so on.
†Attachments: Explain types, size, and capacities as applicable.

Cranes (include capacity and attachments): overhead, jib, gantry, and so on.

Conveyors (include application, type, and capacity) belt, roller, skate wheel, ball, monorail, air, carousel, live, gravity, portable, and so on.

Automatic storage and retrieval system ASRS (include application, type, and capacity).

Air float material handlers (include application, type, size, capacity).

Robot floor-based load movers (include application, type, size, and capacity).

4. SECURITY, HEALTH, AND FIRE PREVENTION

On regular police patrol route _____,

Explain _____

Private guard service _____, around the clock _____ nights only _____

Security system _____, Explain _____

Fenced yards _____, type _____, height _____

Watch dog service _____

Eye wash and shower facilities _____

Emergency medical care, explain _____

First-aid supplies on premises _____

First-aid training _____

Sprinkler system _____, rating _____, water pressure _____

Fire extinguishers _____, type _____, location plan _____

Distance to nearest fire station _____

Distance to nearest fire hydrant _____

Distance to nearest professional medical help _____

5. UNION AFFILIATION

Nonunion _____, Union _____

Name _____, contract expiration _____

History of work stoppages for last three years including cause and duration: union _____, lockout _____, natural disaster _____

Describe _____

Durations from _____ to _____

6. WAREHOUSE INSURANCE

Fire amount $_____ Insurer _____

Earthquake $_____ Insurer _____

Flood $_____ Insurer _____

Property $_____ Insurer _____

Accidental damage $_____ Insurer _____

Auto and Truck Collision $_____ Insurer _____

PL & PD $_____ Insurer _____

Umbrella (all else) $_____ Insurer _____

Liability for storer's inventories

7. TAXES

Inventory tax assessment date _____.

Formula used for assessment _____.

Rate as of this date _____.

Note: Special taxes that apply to this warehouse location should be defined as they apply, such as those related to Freeport, storage-in-transit, local income tax, and so on. The public warehouse should give every assistance, but should not take on the responsibilities related to application and interpretation. These should remain with the depositor as they would if the depositor were operating its own warehouse.

8. DATA PROCESSING

Computerizing and bar coding have made far greater penetration into proprietary warehousing than they have into public warehousing. This is mainly because these technologies require stringent disciplines.

VISUAL INSPECTION OF PUBLIC WAREHOUSES

In the quest for the best public warehouse, you should undertake the orientation and questioning suggested in this chapter. But the reality of visual inspection is necessary to further assure the best selection. The retelling of the following experience should convince you. My experience began with my sudden take over of the management of the warehouses of a large building products company. After a few months of visiting and reviewing the operations of all the warehouses, one in particular stood out as having more than its share of problems. The warehouse was clean and orderly, at least the parts I saw. However, a big block of house siding inventory in the center of the main building defied close inspection. I was told this was necessary to make efficient space utilization, and it presented no problem in handling because each SKU could be accessed by the overhead crane. It looked confusing only to me because I was not experienced with the advantages of handling and storing with an overhead crane.

I recall thinking I would like to wander about the warehouse on my own without the manager's talk about the ingenious methods developed and used here to warehouse this gigantic and complex inventory. I never did go it alone, partly because the manager stayed glued to me, but mostly I had the secret concern that I might get lost in the labyrinth of towering bulk storage.

To get some idea of what was going on, I contacted the headquarters audit department, whose annual audits revealed two things: a lot of damage was being incurred, and most of the outbound freight was given to one local carrier that had grown with the warehouse business from a few trucks to a sizable fleet covering a much expanded territory. I asked why nothing had been done about the damaged inventory and was told: "The common unit of measure for production and sale of siding is a 100-foot square but scrap is in pounds. The conversion back and forth is clouded by the production plant's not holding a consistent thickness. As a result, squares can vary in weight easily as much as plus or minus 10 percent." Further, headquarter's accounting records were so full of errors and inconsistencies that it would have been impossible to make a solid case about the excess damage.

On one visit I pointed out that materials in one part of the huge central block of storage were stored so high and in such disorder that it was clearly dangerous. I asked the manager to please have that area restacked safely by the end of two weeks when I would drop in again. "No problem! The reason its that way . . . ." "Don't tell me," I responded. "Don't say you will do it if you won't. Hire more personnel. Rent more equipment, but get it done."

"Don't worry, it'll be done."

Two weeks later I returned. After the usual amenities, I excused myself to go look at our special project. "You stay here, Slick. I see you've got plenty to do." The area had not noticeably changed; there was evidence of but a faint attempt in one corner. I turned on my heels, returned to the office, and said "Slick, you're through." Later that day, I went around the floor introducing myself, shaking hands, and saying I would be taking Slick's place until I brought in another manager. Then I asked the floor supervisor, Mac, to divert a couple of lift truck operators to start dismantling the hazardous side of the block of storage and restack it correctly.

About an hour later Mac came to the office and asked me if I would come with him. "There is something you should see." A few of the towering stacks had been moved revealing the inside of the block—what was not a block at all. It was a blockade, a border of two and three stacks deep hiding an inner core of an almost unbelievably large tangled mess of damaged siding and accessories. There I stood stunned and frothing with anger. I recall wanting to bring Slick back so I could fire him again. Once was just not enough.

This experience is related to emphasize the importance of having someone who knows warehousing conduct the public warehouse inspection. In fact, two should make the inspection: one who has the executive clout and another who has the warehousing expertise. It provides genuine evidence of the commitment of top management.

What to Look for and Document During the Inspection

Record which warehouse is being inspected, when and by whom, including the warehouse name, address, telephone number, and who the contact is. Then provide a brief explanation of the inspection process covering the general things being checked and the means of rating. This explanation should not be so long that it defies reading. It is a summary that provides perspective on how the inspection and evaluation are made.

Provide a comprehensive list of what to look for and offer some insights as to subtleties that should be given closer consideration.

1. Facility Appearance   What impression does the facility give to a passerby? Keep in mind the warehouse will represent the company to its customers who have their orders processed there. Although it is not as important as facilities that have the company name on them, it is important. Suppose it is an eyesore. Bad feelings about it will rub off on the companies that use it, neighbors, and the community in general.

How much an attractive facility is worth depends a lot on the type of company using it.

Things to look for are the landscaping, condition of the building, and paving. Are the yards cluttered with unused equipment? Are the lawn, shrubs, and trees well groomed? Are the docks, driveways, truck maneuvering areas, sidewalks, and rail siding free of debris and in good repair? If it is a metal building, are there dents and torn siding? If it is painted concrete or metal, does it need a fresh coat of paint?

All these esthetic and cosmetic feature point directly at the state of mind of the owners and management. When a warehouse is having trouble inside, commonly the first to be neglected is the outside.

Adding to outside appearances as well as security are night lights. A darkened facility suggests a place to hide and an easier place to rip off. A well-lit place suggests security, pride, and strength. Obviously, given a choice, thieves and vandals will target the darkened facility.

2. Inside Office Appearance   Like the outside, the office appearance has a pronounced effect on the attitude of—and toward—the warehouse company. In turn this spills over to a measurable extent on the companies that are represented there. Above all it should give the impression of being a pleasant place— even if it is not. Visitors are quickly affected by how the staff is housed, and this initiates prejudice in favor or against management which carries over to the entire operation. An attractive, businesslike office indicates that the warehouse company is concerned about its employees and customers.

A private place for conferences with visitors and employees should be provided. In very small warehouses this may be the manager's office; in larger warehouses, it will be a separate conference room. A coffee break and lunchroom with a sink and a microwave should be provided.

3. Operations' Appearance   The first impression is a lasting one, so the wise warehouse manager has the entrance, where visitors are taken into the warehouse proper, open onto the most attractive, if not spectacular, view of storage and material handling. When the workers hear and see the visitors' expressions of Ohs! Ahs! and Wows! they, as well, are so infected.

The first impression by no means is enough. The whole warehouse must be impressive. Some of the things that cause rave reviews of warehouse operations are the following:

- Clean and shining floors.
- Clean, orderly, squared-off storage.
- White painted ceilings.
- Neatly painted yellow-lined aisles.
- Buried roof support columns in bulk storage or between storage racks.
- Fire extinguishers, first-aid kits, eye washes, etcetera, clean and obvious.
- No bent storage racks.

- No leaning stacks.
- No broken pallets.
- Clean orderly bulletin board with current notices and fresh posters.
- Diagonal bulk storage where applicable.
- Clean drinking fountains in working order.
- Clean attractive lunchroom with same facilities as the office lunchroom. Better still, is for both office and warehouse to share the same room when proximity permits.
- Clean roomy restrooms with constant supply of soap and paper including regular emptying of waste baskets and napkin containers. Provide separate rooms for male and female but not for office and warehouse unless distance requires it.
- Clean painted trash disposal containers with lids and emptied regularly.
- Clearly marked and clean rat runs along all storage walls for inspection as well as for rodents to frolic.
- Regular insect and rodent abatement service.
- Designated and clearly identified places for hand tools, powered equipment and accessories when not in use.
- Professional looking stock locator addresses, safety, and other signs.
- Clean uniforms, if only shirts, for all workers.
- Hard hats regularly worn in designated areas including hats for supervision and visitors.

4. Equipment and Automation   Until recently, warehousing was referred to as being labor intensive, having an unusually high ratio of labor compared to other operations. The trend now is toward becoming more equipment intensive. This is the effect of increasing the amount accomplished by workers and with warehouse space. If a good day's work before were for a worker to move 16 tons of something per shift, through improvements in equipment the same can be done, say, in an hour.

Space utilization is following a similar trend. With narrow-aisle handling equipment and high-rise storage, more can be stored per unit of building cost. If the cost of storing a unit of material is $1.00 per unit of time, better space utilization can reduce this cost to, say, $0.50—while systems and procedures analysis may indicate not storing it at all.

5. Computer and Bar-Code Operations   All the great and wonderful things computer and bar coding can achieve (discussed throughout this text) can as well be attained with a public warehouse—with sufficient cooperation. But the subject should be broached early in the investigation of a public warehouse, because if the depositor intends to move toward interfacing all its computer and bar-code operations, it is wise to learn where the public warehousing stands. The warehouse may be quite satisfied with its own stand-alone systems and correctly so.

GOVERNMENT REGULATIONS AND COMPLIANCE

There are over a hundred federal, state, and local regulatory agencies that can legally impose compliance on business, and these are the only the ones have to do with safety, health, and environment. Those with which warehousing has to deal are a formidable but a manageable few. Following are the most common:

ABC	Alcoholic Beverage Commission
PUC	Public Utility Commission (state)
DOT	Department of Transportation
EPA	Environmental Protection Agency
OSHA	Occupational Safety and Health Commission
BATF	Bureau of Alcohol, Tobacco and Firearms
USDA	United States Department of Agriculture
FDA	Food and Drug Administration

One warehouse staff member should have the responsibility of gathering the information on relevant regulations, cataloging it, and keeping it current. This "chief of regulations" should turn the applicable regulations into warehouse language, provide training, effect implementation, and monitor for compliance. Establish a procedures manual and records system for these regulations. Someone must make certain that the warehouse is in compliance. It is said that regulations inspectors who visit operations personally are half won over if they find a current procedures manual and organized records—as they should be. If all this is as it should be, the next steps of implementation and monitoring are relatively easy. If the chief of regulations is having difficulty getting the warehouse employees to go along, the warehouse manager should step in and give assistance as needed.

PUBLIC WAREHOUSING'S LIABILITY TO DEPOSITORS

The issue of liability is an important factor in considering whether or not to use public warehousing. If a company operates its own warehouse, it has within its control the loss of, or damage to, goods due to theft or mishandling. If a company puts its goods in a public warehouse, it loses this direct control. The big question then becomes: What is the liability of a public warehouse to the companies using its services? An attempt is made here to answer this question.

The liability of public warehouses is covered by two laws. In the majority of states, it is the Uniform Commercial Code; in the others, it is the Uniform Warehouse Receipt Act. Although the laws are different, their rules regarding public warehouse liability are quite similar. The one that is most broadly used—the Uniform Commercial Code, Article 7-204(1)—states that:

> A warehouseman is liable for damages for loss of or injury to the goods caused by his failure to exercise such care in regard to them as a reasonably careful man would exercise under like circumstances but unless otherwise agreed his is not liable for damages which could not have been avoided by the exercise of such care.

This law says that a public warehouse is responsible for the care and handling of merchandise in the same manner as a responsible person (or company) would be if he or she were performing his or her own warehousing. The law is reasonable, and it is all that could be expected with regard to liability. A law that was more strict with public warehouses, such as one calling for double indemnity, would only result in increasing the warehouse charges, as well as claims, suits, and legal entanglements.

As a further precaution to clarify the liability of the public warehouse, the American Warehouseman's Association in 1964 adopted for its organization the following "Liability" section in its Terms and Conditions. Section 9a reads:

> The warehouseman assumes no liability for any loss or injury to the goods stored which could not have been avoided by the exercise of reasonable care required by law of a reasonably careful man. Goods are stored at depositor's risk of loss or damage by acts of God, seizure or other acts of civil or military authority, insurrection, riot, strike or enemies of the government, for loss or damage resulting from inadequate packaging or wear and tear, or from any cause not originating in the warehouse or from any cause beyond the warehouseman's control. Warehouseman shall not be responsible for loss or damage resulting from sprinkler leakage, fire, insect or rodent infestation, or any other cause, unless such damage results from his failure to exercise the degree of care required by law.

Both the laws and the terms and conditions attempt to make it clear that a public warehouse is liable for the care of goods only to the extent that a prudent, reasonable, responsible person would care for his or her own goods. This clearly leaves out any liability for those things that may cause loss or damage but are outside the control of the warehouse.

According to these legal and adopted regulations, loss or damage due to the following causes is not the responsibility of the public warehouse, provided that reasonable care is taken to prevent loss or damage during the occurrence.

Hurricane

Tornado

Flood

Earthquake

Fire

Sprinkler leakage

Acts of enemies during war

Strikes

Insurrection

Seizure by the government

Theft by persons not under warehouse controls

Infestation by rodents, insects, germs

Inadequate packaging

The statements of liability cited before seem as reasonable as can be expected. Favoring either the depositor or the public warehouse could inhibit this arrangement for doing business. In practice much of what governs is the desire of both parties to make it all run as smoothly as possible. If either become too difficult to work with, the other has means to give it back in double measure.

Before either decides to quit because of problems with the other every effort should be made to get the problems out on the table and mutually try to effect solutions as business partners not adversaries. If the problems can be solved and the arrangement can continue both will benefit. No public warehousing company prospered long by dumping accounts and no depositor maintained a smooth efficient physical distribution system by bouncing between public warehouses.

BENEFITS OF USING CONTRACT WAREHOUSING

Contract warehousing is a form of public warehousing. Nearly all the coverage of public warehousing also pertains to contract warehousing.

When the buyer and seller come together to find optimum ways to streamline their mutual operations, a fresh perspective can be taken. The principals may include the transportation company or companies if it is determined that the transport of inventories can be best handled by someone other than the storer or the warehouse.

1. Secures the Future A contract is needed that ties both interests together for at least long enough to amortize mutual investments. This so that neither need fear the other's pulling out leaving them holding the bag.

"With the chance that either may have to break the contract due to things beyond their control, how can either count on what will happen?" By contract that specifically addresses this most basic issue. This will require some ingenuity, but it is worth giving it. It is the foundation on which all the good things that can be done by contract warehousing are founded.

CONSIDERATIONS FOR INSURING THE FUTURE

1. Make quitting for any reason a huge financial penalty on the quitter. This penalty payment should be automatic in the event of dissolution. There should be no need to wait for estate settlement or any other delays that can be foreseen.

2. Provide for automatic payment via an insurance policy, a mutually owned asset that automatically reverts to the survivor, or some other legally sure and quick way.

3. If merger or buyout takes place, make agreement binding on the new entity or ensure that the penalty is automatically triggered, just as housing loans become due and payable when sold. The surviving partner in this case should have the option as to initiate the penalty or to continue the arrangement with the new company.

4. Above all else, thoroughly survey how others have handled this vital concern. If a proven good way exists and fits your need, adopt it or adapt to it.

5. Examine what can be achieved by forming a third company to handle this particular warehousing and transportation. Have it owned by both the storer and the warehouse. How this would work need not be delved into here. Enough is to point out that this method of handling thorny authority and responsibilities is a common business practice.

6. Establish means of arbitration. If both the depositor and the warehouse enter a long-term contract even with the best of intentions, some differences are bound to arise. Normally these should be handled with openness. But in the case of deep convictions opposing each other, a procedure should initiate a quick but thorough study to provide, as objectively as possible, a solution that is acceptable to both sides.

   If this fails, there should be provision for arbitration so the two parties do not become deadlocked indefinitely.

2. New Opportunities Arise A long-term contract should encourage both parties to focus on areas beyond those typical of conventional short-term contract. Prepare a flowchart of everything that happens from how and why inventories are ordered for the warehouse to their disposition at the final destination. It should follow the flow of the material but include all communications, documentation, and decision-making issues through the entire cycle. Further, it should include workers' (both clerical and operational) time related to each juncture throughout the chart for both depositor and warehouse. The charts should also include space, equipment, and the time material is moving and at rest.

The flowchart should represent precisely what is done—using the most basic assumptions and documenting even these. The chart should be so portrayed that anyone with even a minimal familiarity with the system can follow it in its entirety.

Next, alternative charts should be prepared showing the effects on service as well so that the total systems are fairly represented. If well prepared, the flowcharts will reveal a wealth of cost-cutting and service improvement possibilities.

Specific areas where contract warehousing should turn up opportunities follow.

1. BETTER WAREHOUSING PLANNING. When the warehouse knows the depositor's plans for inventories and the depositor knows the warehouse's scheduling and planning, a quantum leap in improvements can be effected. These improvements can be greater than those that would result were the company to do its own warehousing. This because attention is focused on what results from the new depositor-warehouse arrangement. Everyone has a tendency to do more and better than if the same things were done between organizational citadels within a company. This is expected ordinary routine, but when separate companies do it, it is extraordinary.

2. INCREASED ACCURACY OF RECEIVING AND SHIPPING. Working together, the means of packaging and unitizing loads can be engineered to assure 100 percent accuracy without the detailed inspection required when the depositor and warehouse are solely looking after their own interests.

3. SPECIALLY DESIGNED LOAD CONTAINERS. Containers that provide for the optimum efficiency of both the warehouse and the consumer can be designed to adapt to the total system of order picking, shipping, receiving, and using. The load containers should take into consideration foolproof ways for making obvious that SKU and quantities are exact.

If the depositor uses the products in certain combinations, attention should be given to providing containers that adapt to all the parts of the assembly as a unitized load. The load can be so designed to be ready to use in the desired quantity and sequence at the depositor's or depositor's customer's workstation.

4. SPECIALIZED MODES OF TRANSPORTATION. The vehicles to transport inventories from the warehouse to the depositors' facilities can be tailored to the specific needs. For example, a compartmentalized van with external access to each compartment can be used to bring the exact combination of products for a complete assembly inside the customer's facility to the specific workstation where the product mix will be used.

If the move is by rail, the same tailoring discussed for trucks can be applied to rail cars. The depositor's spur track should go right to the point inside the facility where the cars' contents will be used. What is accomplished is a complete avoidance of the usual warehousing at the consumer's facility. The delivery is right to the point of usage. This can be thought of as a miniwarehouse at the point the inventory will be used. Companies often call this "material management cells."

5. *IMPROVE LOADING AND UNLOADING TRANSPORT VEHICLES.* Conveyorize loading of the transport vehicles by staging the entire load on a pad of roller or ball conveyor at the edge of the dock that is the exact size of the floor of the truck. Then have the same type conveyor inside the truck so the entire load can be moved at one time into or out of the vehicle as one unit. Then have the same arrangement at the depositor's or customer's facility to remove the entire load as a unit. Similar means can be employed for captive rail cars.

6. *AVOID TRUCK AND RAIL TRANSPORTATION ALTOGETHER.* Have the warehouse locate adjacent to the depositor's facility to avoid the use of trucks and rail cars entirely to transport inventory between the two. Have the inventory move between facilities by pneumatic tubes, conveyors, or robots—or a combination of them.

Variations of these three material movers are monorail, carousels and air float systems. The monorail and carousel have been around for many decades and are well known. The newcomer is the air float to move materials either a pallet load at a time using separate floats, or as a continuous air-float line used in place of a mechanical conveyor.

3. Facilitate Adaptation to Change This important characteristic of contract warehousing can be illustrated by visualizing a host production company that believes its singular forte is production and that auxiliary business functions only dilute its efforts. Concentrating on what it does best and having other companies answer to it for what they do best makes the total more effective and efficient. Further, it divides the inherent headaches caused by rapid expansion or contraction of its business. An example of this follows.

Assume a company initially having 1,000 employees; then there is a sudden opportunity to increase sales income by, say, 30 percent with an increase of only 20 percent in personnel and related costs—making it theoretically a very good business that the company should take on. Following is the division of the 1,000 employees.

	Initial		20% Increase	
Functions	**Personnel**	**%**	**Personnel**	**%**
Production and related	400	40	80	40
Sales and marketing	300	30	60	30
Warehousing and trucking	300	30	60	30
Total	1,000	100%	200	100%

If all the functions are performed within the one company, 200 employees will have to be added. This would constitute a major jolt and disruption of business. Aside from having to interview and select 200 employees, say, 20 percent, 44 employees do not make it past the probation and another 10 percent are replaced within the following few months. Along with the increase in employees the company has to train and provide space and equipment for them. The total effect on the company can be maddening.

Now assume that the company is so organized that it has contracted out sales and marketing, and warehousing and trucking, leaving only production. The same division of personnel would apply as illustrated, but now the host company would be faced with only hiring 80 employees. The other 120 would be divided equally between the sales and marketing—and the warehousing and trucking—companies. Since these contract companies already have accounts other than the subject company, the effects of the expansion would be proportionally less on them. Let's say they already had the equivalent of three times as much business as that of the host company. The effects on the expansion now would be quite different.

Companies	Initial Personnel	Increase	Total	Impact
Production and related	400	80	480	20% (subject company)
Sales and marketing	1,200	60	1,260	5% (another company)
Warehousing and trucking	1,200	60	1,260	5% (another company)
Total	2,800	200	3,000	

Thus, the impact of the expansion is considerably less when the business is divided between companies. It would affect the sales/marketing and warehouse/trucking only 5 percent each. The production company would only have to increase personnel by 80, compared to the 200 if the other functions were also within the company.

The example used deals with the initial company of 1,000 employees, but the same implications would hold for smaller and larger companies. There are other problems in dealing with outside companies when so much of the business is contracted out such as possibly less control, but the fact that it does reduce the impact of expansion and contraction is definitely an advantage of doing business this way.

4. Securing Expertise Otherwise Not Available   Warehousing does require skills different from those used in production and sales, and hiring an outside warehouse expert can benefit a company that tends to give priority to marketing and sales functions and less to warehousing. If this is done, make it abundantly clear that the outside expert is not an employee and never will be. The purpose is to equip warehousing and transportation with the technology, equipment, and training by working with present employees. Then when things are humming, the consultant will drop back to once-a-month monitoring visits to make certain things stay right and smart. Any new and better jobs created in the process should be first offered to veteran employees—provided they will take the necessary training (if any is necessary)—which should be provided by the company.

The expert's priorities are first to set up and equip the warehouse and its transportation to satisfy the CEO's objectives and then to monitor it to see that it continues that way. Other types of warehousing contracts are for outside specialists to manage warehouse inventories to the extent of placing orders for suppliers and to even process customer orders for the warehouse to ship. These contracts are not applicable to all warehouses, but some could and do take good advantage of them.

Suppose, for example a company is an expert in advertising, promotion, and making great deals with suppliers of the inventories needed. But the firm abhors the mechanics of ordering and maintaining inventories, taking customer orders, warehousing, and making certain the customers get what they order in a timely manner. So, everything is contracted out except the fun things like dreaming up what the public wants.

5. Secure Use of Special Government Privileges   There are many government regulations that affect warehousing. Some of these can best be fulfilled by having contracts with public warehouses that already have and maintain the necessary certifications and permits. Those that pertain to free zone privileges constitute a good example. Others are the rights to handle hazardous waste, drugs, bonded wines, etcetera. When a company has need for these special authorizations, it is often more economic to have a contract with a public warehouse that already has the certification handle it.

In situations like this, the company and the warehouse should have longer-term contracts than the usual 30-day notice of public warehousing. This is because more is put at risk. The company needs whatever the government privilege may be, or drastic things will happen. The warehouse is not put at similar risk, but it strongly prefers to be able to count on long-term warehousing commitments, particularly when it is charging enough and there are provisions for raising their rates should costs increase.

OTHER KINDS OF CONTRACT WAREHOUSING

The foregoing covered the vast opportunities made possible when the warehouse and the depositor have a long-term contract to work cooperatively as partners. But there are other types of warehouse contracts that are not motivated by the values of long-range commitment. These do not have the exciting possibilities of the long-term contract warehousing just discussed, but they do provide alternatives that may be the best that can be done at a particular time and circumstance.

Space Lease

To assure that adequate space will be available as needed, a product company will contract for the amount of space it expects to use. This is a lease of space if the warehouse owns its facility or a sublease if it is leasing it. In either case, if the lessee has free access to the space, it should be isolated from the public warehouse space with walls or strong fencing.

An alternative to securing the leased space is for a warehouse to guarantee that the space will be available but not designate where it is except as requested by the lessee. Then the lessee is assured of the space it contracts for, but the company's inventory may be commingled with other customers' inventories.

The advantage of this arrangement is that lease price to the lessee and cost to the owner should be less than for space that is isolated and secured in a specified location. When the warehouse fully honors this agreement, and the product company accepts not being able to pace off its specific area, both benefit because the warehouse has greater flexibility in meeting contractual requirements. The disadvantage is that there is a big temptation for the public warehouse to risk using the space when it is needed to service another customer in the hope that it will be clear when the company with the contract needs it. The warehouse is selling the space twice. Of course, if it gets caught, the chance of losing the customer is almost a certainty, and the chance of getting sued is nearly as certain. At the least, the public warehouse's reputation, its most valuable asset, will suffer.

Workers and Equipment Only as Needed

This alternative can be used with a contract for a given amount of space or the warehouse can charge its usual unit rates for storage and fixed rates per hour for workers and equipment. When storage involves use of storage racks, the most natural way to charge is the normal unit rates. Why? Because how to charge fairly for fixed equipment like this is not as clear as it is by square or cubic feet. Should the racks be amortized over the term of the contract? Should they be amortized over their expected useful life, say 20, 30, or 40 years? Buyers' and sellers' disagreement over this issue could cause more dissension than could any other part of the contract, but the problem can be solved.

When hourly rates are charged for workers and equipment, realistic rates may commonly be much higher than buyers of these services expect. What is overlooked is the high overhead and indirect costs that are incurred when making available the warehouse worker for the time needed. Depending on numerous variables, it is necessary to charge somewhere between three and five times the basic hourly wage rates for the owners to earn a reasonable return on their investment. Even then, many public warehouses could not convert their present unit charge rate to fixed hourly rates in the three to five times range and still stay in business. But if part of their income is derived this way and the remainder via the usual unit charge rates, it may work out. Economies of scale from this added warehousing provide the opportunity to get a better return on investment in total, even if the hourly rate only pays for the worker and space and absorbs part of the overhead. The buyer of time and space should not force too low charges regardless. A good business deal is one that is good for both parties.

Clerical and Customer Service Help

It is not uncommon for a depositor to contract for the clerical service, such as reordering inventories, to back up the physical operations of warehousing. And the same goes for customer service functions normally provided by the depositor. Added to this can be an office for the depositor's sales personnel and a part- or full-time service of a secretary. A great variety of combinations have been tried, and many are probably in operation somewhere. There are good reasons for this.

For salespeople, the warehouse that supplies the customers is where the action is and often the cost of employees, and space is less through warehousing than it would be elsewhere. The economies of scale apply. The warehouse is often accommodating about providing all the sales support it can because having control over the clerical and customer-service functions permits the warehouse to do a better job. It can charge enough to be profitable and still come in less than the cost for the depositor to set up these functions elsewhere.

Index